Reforming Bureaucracy
The Politics of Institutional Choice

Reforming Bureaucracy
The Politics of Institutional Choice

Jack H. Knott
Gary J. Miller

Department of Political Science
Michigan State University

Prentice-Hall, Inc.
Englewood Cliffs, New Jersey 07632

Library of Congress Cataloging-in-Publication Data

Knott, Jack H. (date)
  Reforming bureaucracy.

  Bibliography.
  Includes index.
  1. Bureaucracy—United States.   2. Administrative
agencies—United States—Reorganization.
3. Administrative agencies—United States—Management—
Decision making.   4. Public administration—Decision
making.   I. Miller, Gary J.   II. Title.
JK421.K56   1987   353'.01   86-18711
ISBN 0-13-770090-3

Editorial/production supervision and
   interior design: Linda Zuk, WordCrafters Editorial Services, Inc.
Cover design: Photo Plus Art
Manufacturing buyer: Barbara Kittle

Printed in the United States of America

10   9   8   7   6   5   4   3   2

ISBN 0-13-770090-3 01

Prentice-Hall International, (UK) Limited, *London*
Prentice-Hall of Australia Pty. Limited, *Sydney*
Prentice-Hall Canada, Inc., *Toronto*
Prentice-Hall Hispanoamericana, S.A., *Mexico*
Prentice-Hall of India Private Limited, *New Delhi*
Prentice-Hall of Japan, Inc., *Tokyo*
Prentice-Hall of Southeast Asia Pte. Ltd., *Singapore*
Editora Prentice-Hall do Brasil, Ltda., *Rio de Janeiro*

For our parents
Harold and Alice Knott
and Gerald and Doris Miller

Contents

Preface   ix

1   Introduction   1

Section I   THE ADMINISTRATIVE REFORM MOVEMENT
2   Bureaucracy and Boss Politics   15
3   Progressive Reform: Constituencies, Prescriptions, Tactics   33
4   Scientific Management and Professionalism   55
5   Progressivism to the New Deal:
Reform Principles Become the Administrative Orthodoxy   77

**Section II   ASSESSING THE ORTHODOX MODEL
OF REFORM**
6   Assessing the Reform Model: Is It Efficient?   101
7   Assessing the Reform Model: Is It Really Neutral?   122
8   Assessing the Reform Model: Is It Accountable?   145
9   Explaining Bureaucratic Dysfunctions: Two Models   166

Section III   THE POLITICS OF REFORM
10   The Politics of Administrative Reform:
Individual Rationality vs. Social Irrationality   189
11   The Quest for Technical Efficiency: Budget Reform   208
12   The Quest for Neutral Competence: Personnel Reform   231
13   Institutional Choice: Assessing the Alternatives   254

Index   277

Preface

This book had its origins in the realization by the two authors that, although they came from quite different political science backgrounds, they shared similar instincts about what was important in explaining the behavior of government bureaucracies. We were also convinced, after teaching an undergraduate course in the politics of bureaucracy, that no book captured what we saw as central: Executive-branch politics, like legislative politics, operates under quite distinct "rules of the game." While students of legislative politics have studied the rules of the legislative game extensively, no one had similarly examined the rules of the game in executive-branch politics.

The rules of executive-branch decision making are important for the same reason that the rules of legislative decision making are important: They in large part determine the governmental decisions that are of concern to all of us as citizens. No one doubts that the agricultural policies of Congress would be different if the rules determining the influence and recruitment patterns of the Senate Agriculture Committee were changed. Similarly, we feel, the Department of Agriculture's policy decisions were shaped by the rules determining its internal organization, its staffing, and its budgeting procedures.

In studying police bureaucracies, we realized that the rules of police decision making were no accident—they have been self-consciously chosen by police reformers since shortly after the turn of the century. Since that time, the rules of bureaucratic decision making have been made more hierarchical, more routinized, more insulated from party politics, more subject to the professional norms of a new profession known as police administration. The preferences of party politicians were made to count less; the preferences of professionally trained police administrators were made to count more. Branching out from police to education, medicine, engineering, the military, the foreign service, financial administration, personnel, we kept running across the same kinds of arguments. The reform era after the turn of the century had resulted in the same kinds of institutional choices.

Furthermore, we began to see that the same kinds of institutional choices are being reinforced by contemporary political actors. When the Post Office was reformed into the Postal Service in the Nixon administration, the same institutional model was selected that has informed the creation of countless new bureaucratic agencies since 1900. When the State Department was criticized as being inefficient and stodgy, the orthodox principles of institutional design from the Progressive era were not abandoned, but reinforced. While concern about the size of federal budgets grew, the search for the ideal institutional manifestation of the orthodox principles of rationality and control simply grew more intense.

The reformers repeatedly believed that they could establish a nonpolitical and expert administration. This new rational administration was not supposed to be unduly influenced by parties or congressional politics, but would serve the public interest as the reformers saw it.

While the rhetoric of reform emphasized a nonpolitical administration, this book is an attempt to explain the rules of executive-branch decision making as the result of self-conscious, political choices by legislators, interest group leaders, presidents, and bureaucrats themselves. We argue that these political actors recognize the importance of executive-branch rules, just as they recognize the importance of legislative rules, in determining the policy decisions that they are concerned about. They therefore fight just as hard to reform or maintain executive-branch institutions that shape favorable decisions as they do to reform or maintain a favorable committee structure or election rules for Congress. A move to reorganize the Department of Agriculture will get just as careful a scrutiny from farm groups as would a move to reorganize the subcommittee structure of the House Agriculture Committee. A move to change the personnel procedures for the police department is liable to be just as controversial for local minorities as a move to change the election procedure for the city council.

This book is premised on the belief that rules count and are taken very seriously by political actors. Consequently, the authors made a serious effort to include as many illustrations as possible of emotionally charged political battles in which the rules of bureaucratic structure either determined the outcome of a policy dispute or were themselves the object of political conflict. Due to space limits, we had to leave out as many examples as we put in; however, we hope the reader, especially the student with little background in public administration or political science, will realize that learning about bureaucracy is more than learning about dry procedures and dull people.

Our greatest debt is to Jonathan Bendor, who provided a careful and extensive analysis of our manuscript which changed our thinking and our mode of presentation in more than a few places. Our colleague Thomas Hammond challenged our thinking at an early stage; we hope Tom finds the latest version more to his liking. An anonymous reviewer for Prentice-Hall provided numerous helpful criticisms. The remaining deficiencies are our own responsibility.

We also would like to express our appreciation to the Russell Sage Foundation, which supported Jack Knott for a year in which he was increasingly caught up in the subject matter of this book. We are grateful to Anne Khademian for her help with the index, and to Linda Zuk for an excellent job of getting the manuscript into print. We also owe a large debt of gratitude to David Rohde and the Michigan State University Department of Political Science, who made this book possible both by their warm encouragement and by grants of released time from teaching.

Reforming Bureaucracy
The Politics of Institutional Choice

CHAPTER 1

Introduction

> In politics as in everything else it makes a great difference whose game
> we play. The rules of the game determine the requirements for success.
>
> E. E. Schattschneider, *The Semi-Sovereign People*[1]

The Defense Department's organization and management, according to many critics
from all sides, liberals and conservatives alike, is now in a state of crisis. Weaknesses
in the weapons acquisition process are receiving the most attention in the public
eye, as new accounts indicate that the Defense Department is paying $748 for each
pair of pliers. While spare parts and tools seem to be consistently overpriced, even
larger concerns are voiced about inadequacies in major weapons such as tanks,
airplanes, and even rifles.

It is not only the weapons acquisition process that is under constant fire. The
system of command and control as well as the budget and planning systems within
the Defense Department are criticized by military leaders themselves. In 1982,
General David Jones, retiring chairman of the Joint Chiefs of Staff, told a closed
meeting of the Armed Services Committee that "the U.S. military command system does not work."[2] General Jones was from the Air Force; a recent Army chief of
staff said that "It is surprising that the system works at all in light of its serious
organizational, conceptual, and functional flaws."[3]

Congressional critics of both parties have held hearings and given speeches
arguing that "[the system] is broke, and we need to fix it."[4] The Senate Armed
Services Committee commissioned a several-hundred page Staff Report entitled,
"Defense Organization: The Need for Change."[5] The Staff Report levels severe
criticisms against the weapons acquisition process, the command and control system, and the budgeting and planning procedures. The Report's overall summary
states that the defense organization places far too much emphasis on "technical,
managerial, and bureaucratic skills," to the detriment of "defense mission objectives" and "leadership skills in wartime."

1

One might think that this evidence suggests something "backward" about the Defense Department's organization and management. Yet these severe concerns about defense organization have occurred *after* several generations of reform of the military bureaucracy. Twentieth-century reforms of the military bureaucracy have intended to create a modern, rational organization. Moreover, these bureaucratic reforms have succeeded in their proximal goals. The armed services today are professionally staffed, hierarchically coordinated, technically managed, and "scientifically" budgeted. Anyone who has studied the reforms of the Defense Department from its nineteenth-century roots cannot help but be impressed by the extent to which these reforms have transformed defense operations. And certainly, reforms of this sort were essential to the successful conduct of the two World Wars and to the defense of the U.S. in the modern nuclear age.

Indeed, the Senate Staff Report, while making fundamental criticisms of defense organization, frequently relies on marginal improvements in the current system in its recommendations for change. It suggests, for example, to reduce the number and upgrade the experience of political appointees in the Office of the Secretary of Defense; it also proposes some modifications in the planning and budgeting system.

But the nagging doubt remains: If the transformation of the military bureaucracy can still allow crises in weapons acquisition, budgeting and planning, and the command and control system, *are the underlying principles that motivated the various reforms completely correct?* Are the norms of professionalization, hierarchical control, and technical decision making always good and sufficient bases for bureaucratic reform? Or should we begin to consider broadening and changing our conception of "good" bureaucratic reform?

THE APOTHEOSIS OF RATIONALITY: SIMILARITIES IN ADMINISTRATIVE REFORM[6]

These questions become more compelling when we realize that a similar pattern of reform and crisis has afflicted other bureaucracies. Education, police, highway planners, the Forest Service, the State Department (not to mention business firms), have all undergone similar transformations toward professionalization, hierarchical control, and rationalistic decision making. One of the principal purposes of this book is to argue that a similar conception of reform was self-consciously applied to all of these kinds of public bureaucracies. Reform across all these arenas shared several characteristics.

First, reform was motivated by a desire for greater control of an expanding bureaucracy. In the case of the military, at the turn of the century a successful campaign was waged to free the military from staff agencies that were composed of political hacks, linked closely to Congress. In 1903, the Secretary of War Elihu Root introduced the Progressive ideas (borrowed partly from Germany) of the Army General Staff and the Chief of Staff. Frank Willoughby, the Progressive reformer, proposed in 1921 to unify the various military bureaucracies under one organization, called the Department of National Defense, as a means for gaining more central administrative control."[7] In other cases, city police departments and school districts were the object of similar kinds of centralizing reform. The reformers tended to believe, as Leonard White has pointed out,[8] that clear lines of authority and single chief executives would produce both more efficiency and accountability.

Second, and more importantly, the reforms have assumed that it was possible to create a nonpolitical, essentially technical, government organization and management. That is, the reformers did not attempt to transform the Defense Department by preaching to the officer corps, or psychoanalyzing them, or by changing their political attitudes. They thought they could create a neutral competence in government that would not be overly influenced by the political relations between Congress and the military, or by the clientele relationships between the military and various interest groups such as weapons suppliers. These psychological, social, and political dimensions were defined out of the problem. Instead, administrative reform was approached almost as an engineer would approach the building of a bridge: What organizational structure will best provide the desired goals of efficiency and unified control?

The reformers frequently adopted the private corporation model as the structure that would improve government efficiency, unified control, and public accountability. After World War II, for example, the passage of the National Security Act in 1947 combined the different military services into the single Department of Defense, under command of the Joint Chiefs of Staff and the Secretary of Defense. The Defense Secretary's Office was organized along modern corporation lines, consisting of functional subdivisions headed by Undersecretaries of Defense. Under John F. Kennedy, further bureaucratic reform came in the form of the highly technical Planning-Programming-Budgeting Systems, which was a decision-making system that was supposed to result in the utmost efficiency in resource management and cross-service coordination.

Third, in line with the expectation of a technical solution to the problem of administration, the training of professionals in the field became primarily technical and management-oriented. During the Progressive era, the Army War College was established as a source of technical and professional training for military officers.[9] The service academies at West Point and Annapolis increasingly stressed modern management techniques, resulting in the creation of a cadre of highly trained professional managers for the armed services. Cadets at West Point and Annapolis today, in fact, are being trained almost exclusively as professional managers, with few courses in military history or defense strategy.[10] In the field of education, education administrators now also form an elite group of professionals who command higher salaries and more prestige than teachers. The professional is increasingly evaluated by his ability to manage the organization, rather than by his stock of substantive knowledge.[11]

Fourth, the reformers were convinced of the universality of their prescriptions. While some advances had been made in the understanding of organizations, reformers were quick to adopt standardizations, general rules, and principles for all positions and organizational structures. This created a kind of "false science" of administration in which, for example, personnel "science" was supposed to be able to grade and provide performance tests for all sorts of different government employees.

This "false science" aspect of reform has led many reformers over the decades to advocate naive views about political incentives in organizations and the limits of time and information in decision making. The planning and budgeting system in the Defense Department, for example, requires that plans and budgets be comprehensively reviewed each year, something that participants have no incentive or ability to carry out.[12] Similarly, reform oftentimes has specified technical decision procedures in which goals are supposed to be reasoned out and established prior to and independent of the fiscally constrained political process.

Fifth, the Defense Department reforms were typical of administrative reforms in this century in that they were, by their own predefined standards, less than successful. They did not ensure the kind of smooth efficiency and control that were envisioned ahead of time. Since its creation, the Joint Chiefs of Staff structure has been continually derided by numerous critics, up to and including General Jones, as encouraging inefficiency, immobility, and unresponsiveness. The command problems were apparent in Vietnam, which Jones called an "organizational nightmare," and in the more recent bombing of our Marines in Lebanon. They have been linked with failures in the weapons procurement system in which faulty weapons purchased for one branch of the military often duplicated other faulty weapons systems purchased for other military branches.

Organizational problems are also connected to the inadequate combat-readiness of our military. At the beginning of the Reagan administration, the armed services had enough ammunitions, manpower, and other supplies to fight only a two-week war. After defense spending amounting to almost $1 trillion during Reagan's defense build-up, the armed services now has the ability to fight a four-week war.[13] Not only has the search for the most rational organizational structure not guaranteed accountability or control, critics such as Senator Gary Hart have increasingly identified this structural orientation to reform as the *fundamental* problem: "Bureaucratic behavior thus lies at the core of America's military inadequacies."[14]

Finally, the fact that the reform of the Defense Department has never stopped is typical of American administrative reform. There has been a never-ending struggle on the part of the engineers of Defense Department reforms to tinker with the system in order to find that structure which will finally provide the long-sought goals of control and efficiency. In other words, Defense Department administrative reform has not been a single, isolated event, but an ongoing process by which one can trace the evolution of Defense Department decision making and performance. In addition, by analyzing and criticizing the rationale behind the kinds of structural reforms attempted, one can begin to understand something of the importance of the psychological, social, and political factors which the reformers sometimes choose to ignore.

As stated earlier, the Defense Department is not the only organization which has engaged in ongoing administrative reform. State and local governments have been swept by waves of similar administrative reforms. Indeed, if one looks at the reform movements aimed at police, education, social work, and the regulatory agencies, one is struck by the similarities. As different as the substance of school district administration and Defense Department administration are, in both areas reform has been approached as essentially a technical, administrative problem. Indeed, the rationales for the school district unification movement and the unification of the military services are strikingly similar. Furthermore, both reform movements have relied on the development of a cadre of professional administrators for the implementation of their reforms. In addition, the popular criticisms of school reform sound very much like the criticisms of Defense Department reforms: that they lead to too much bureaucratization and red tape, a lack of public control, and decreasing concern for the original mission of the organization. The same similarities could be noted for other administrative reforms throughout state, local, and federal government.

It is the theme of this book that there is something important to be gained by noticing the similarities in administrative reform across levels of government and functional program areas. That something is the pooled experience of the failures and successes of administrative reform movements in these different settings. Furthermore, if (as we argue) the administrative reforms in these settings have basically similar rationales and similar failures in meeting the self-defined goals of the reformers, then noting those similarities can lead to a larger reevaluation of the basic premises of administrative reform.

DISCONTENT WITH BUREAUCRACY

The military and educational bureaucracies are not the only bureaucracies to suffer through both repeated reform attempts and growing public dissatisfaction. As one famous political scientist has noted, "antibureaucratic sentiment has taken hold like an epidemic."[15]

Voters have supported tax revolts whose organizers have charged bureaucracy with the responsibility for governmental inefficiency and waste. Congressmen have run campaigns charging that bureaucracy is "out of control," either because of ineptitude or avarice, and Congress has invested heavily in congressional staff as a way of improving its own oversight of bureaucracy. Nixon felt that the bureaucracy was subverting his administration's goals, while Carter's presidential campaign was based in large part on his ability to reform bureaucracy, as demonstrated in his performance as governor of Georgia. Most striking of all, perhaps, is the Reagan campaign's assault on bureaucracy as a central element of "big government," and Reagan's interpretation of his election as a mandate to "cut bureaucracy down to size."

Realizing that our contemporary bureaucratic apparatus still faces severe problems despite repeated applications of administrative reform, we may well wonder, what has motivated administrative reform in the United States? Where did our ideas about how to reform bureaucracy come from?

THE ORIGINS OF ADMINISTRATIVE REFORM

The origins of administrative reform in police, in education, in regulation of the economy, and even in defense began in the latter part of the nineteenth century. Moralistic reformers who wanted to end political graft and corruption started to push for a nonpartisan civil service and greater professionalism in government. However, these sporadic reform attempts did not really begin to transform government organization until the Progressive era at the turn of the century. At that time, separate reform movements began in earnest to have a substantial impact on government. In a variety of fields, the Progressive reform movement of the first part of this century marked a watershed period. The Progressives enshrined the notions of control and efficiency in addition to moral judgment about political machines, and, as the means to that end, advanced the notion of a politically neutral bureaucracy, staffed by professional administrative experts. Furthermore, in many city and school district governments and in some state and federal agencies, they were successful in getting their programs of reform adopted.

Often, however, problems of accountability and efficiency persisted even after the Progressive reforms were adopted. This generally did not lead to the abandonment of the Progressive notions of what a good reform was, however. It is our claim that Progressive notions of what makes a good reform were developed further through the New Deal and became the administrative orthodoxy. As Donald Warwick defines it:

> A further prop for bureaucracy lies in the managerial philosophy pervading the federal executive system and for the most part shared by Congress. The basic tenet of this orthodoxy is that efficiency requires a clean line of authority from top to bottom in an organization. The central responsibility of the superior is the faithful implementation of policy directives sent from above and accountability to his own superiors; the key responsibility of the subordinate is obedience.[16]

Harold Seidman, too, discussed the never-ending search for the most rational structure, based on principles of hierarchy, specialization, and expertise, which would realize control and efficiency.[17] Government reforms like those in the Defense Department or virtually any other arena are seen "primarily as a technological problem calling for 'scientific' analysis and the application of fundamental organizational principles."[18] Seidman's experience in government suggested that the main advantage of the administrative orthodoxy is that no one has thought of an alternative. "Flawed and imperfect as they may be, the orthodox 'principles' remain the only simple, readily understood, and comprehensive set of guidelines available to the President and the Congress for resolving problems of executive branch structure. Individual Congressmen can relate them to their own experience within the Congress and in outside organizations."[19]

Terry Moe, in his assessment of the modern presidency, also comments that, "Much of the analysis, evaluation, and reform proposals concerning government organization, even in this age of enlightenment, bears the unmistakable imprint of public administration's formative years, in values as well as theoretical beliefs."[20]

The formative years discussed in this book begin with the precursors and experiments in reform in the nineteenth century, and especially the movement for civil service reform. This is followed by the Golden Age of reform during the Progressive era, with the scientific management and professionalism movements advanced by scholars such as Luther Gulick of the New York Bureau of Municipal Research. The orthodox or classical administrative model, as we will call it, emerged during the Progressive era as the motivator and rationale for administrative reform throughout the rest of the century. The Progressive era was succeeded by the New Deal period, in which reform extended into means for strengthening the chief executive. All three formative periods followed the orthodox institutional prescription for hierarchical control, nonpolitical expertise, and rationalistic decision procedures.

THE VIEWPOINT OF THE BOOK: NEO-INSTITUTIONALISM

The primary focus of this book is on "administrative orthodoxy"—a set of rules about how administrative agencies should be organized and managed. As Seidman argues, these rules were and are fairly cohesive and are well understood by political actors. They were used in the creation of many of the twentieth-century agencies of government, from the city-manager form of government to the federal regulatory agencies, and they continue to be used to this day. For this reason, the first part of this book will deal with the common origins of administrative reform principles as they were manifested in police reform, educational reform, regulatory reform, and elsewhere.

However, we explicitly reject a strict notion of "intellectual determinism." That is, we are not arguing that the orthodox ideas about administrative reforms "caused" all administrative reform in the United States. Rather, we argue that the orthodox "rules" about how to organize a bureaucracy constitute a recognizable "institution" and that this "institution" was chosen at various times and places because a decisive coalition of involved individuals could reach agreement on that particular institution. This approach to explanation is quite consistent with a perspective in modern political science known as "neo-institutionalism," but it requires some clarification and elaboration.

From Behaviorism to Rational Choice

In political science, a school of thought known as "behaviorism" emerged during the late 1950s and 1960s. Behaviorism was a reaction to the institutionalism that had previously dominated political science; institutionalism was seen as legalistic, historical, and dry. Behaviorists felt that the historical study of institutions left out the most vital and fundamental key to politics, which was the behavior of the individual actors: voters, legislators, and bureaucrats. A great deal of research was undertaken to identify what were largely internal determinants of individual behavior. Individual attributes such as party identification were said to determine voter behavior: People voted for Kennedy in 1960 because they felt an identification with the Democratic Party.[21] Individual legislative attitudes were said to determine bureaucratic performance: A legislator voted for an irrigation project for her district because she perceived her role as being that of a delegate.[22] Bureaucratic attitudes were said to determine bureaucratic performance: A bureaucrat refused to bend the rules to help a client because his attitude was that of an "indifferent" or perhaps of a "conserver."[23] The effect of institutions on all of this was downplayed.

In the late 1960s and early 1970s, a new school of thought known as "rational choice" began to challenge early behaviorism. Rational-choice theorists felt that individual behavior could be explained in terms of goal-oriented, purposive behavior. Explanations were based on individual preferences based on individual calculations of gain and loss. Legislators voted for irrigation projects because their goal was reelection, and they perceived a link between the project and their reelection goal.[24] Voters sometimes refused to vote, not because they were inherently apathetic, but because the cost of voting was greater than the probable impact on the outcome.[25] Bureaucrats refused to bend the rules because the probable negative consequences of doing so were greater than the possible rewards.

While the early rational-choice models were still individualistic, the role of institutions became increasingly important. The institutions were seen as being crucial for determining the rules by which individual preferences were aggregated. William Riker gives one example in which four different voting rules would have given four different election winners in a four-candidate race, *even if each individual voter's vote were unchanged*.[26] When the outcome is so sensitive to the election rules, *the rules can be said to determine the outcome as much as the individual attitudes*.

Even worse, the rediscovery of the majority rule paradox, in which every possible alternative can be upset by some majority preferring some other alternative, led to more interest in legislative rules. The reason is that when conditions allow the majority rule paradox, the outcome could be determined by the structuring of the legislative agenda.[27]

The importance of the procedural rules became more obvious in all sorts of rational-choice models of politics. Students of Congress argued that creating subject-area committees in Congress, with a seniority rule for determining committee chairmanship, resulted in quite different outcomes than an alternative set of internal procedural rules based on, for instance, party discipline.[28] Students of local government argued that at-large elections resulted in quite different city council membership and policy outcomes than district-based elections.[29] Rational-choice theorists became fascinated with examples which demonstrated the coercive nature of such institutional rules on group choice. More and more, rational-choice theory fostered the study of institutions which had been ignored since the behavioral revolution; and with the renewed interest in institutions came a renewed interest in history, since institutions (as opposed to individual attitudes and behavior) seemed grounded in historical events.

WHERE DO INSTITUTIONS COME FROM?

From this point, it was a short step to ask, where do the rules that determine group choices come from? How did Congress come to have a committee system? Why do we have independent regulatory agencies setting transportation, energy, and monetary policies? Why do some cities have at-large elections, and others district-based ones? It is only in the past few years that rational-choice theorists have begun to make the observation that if (1) people have different preferences about policy outcomes, and (2) they know that different institutional rules of procedure will produce different policy outcomes, then (3) they will have different preferences over rules. This makes it possible to explain institutions as resulting from the preferences of individuals for institutions.

Although this study is just beginning, several political scientists have begun to examine history to understand how political actors happened to choose the institutions they did. Several examples of this analysis follow.

Choosing the Interstate Commerce Commission

A path-breaking model for this kind of analysis is the study of why Congress has chosen to create the institutions known as independent regulatory agencies. Fiorina[30] and Marshall and Weingast,[31] for instance, studied the creation of the Interstate Commerce Commission in 1887. They demonstrate that the individuals who wanted strict regulation of the railroads and the individuals who wanted minimal enforcement of regulations agreed that regulation through the courts would be stricter than regulation through an independent regulatory board. The strict regulators controlled the House of Representatives and the pro-railroad forces controlled the Senate. The compromise that resulted from this distribution of preferences gave the regulators some of the substance of what they wanted, but created an independent regulatory agency to implement the regulation. The creation of the independent regulatory agency can be viewed as the creation of an institutional rule based on the rational preferences of individuals with different policy goals and a shared understanding of the effects of institutional rules on those policies.[32]

Choosing A New Congress

In 1910, the House of Representatives was split between Democrats, Republican reformers, and Republicans loyal to the heavy-handed Speaker, Joe Cannon. Many of the reformers, like George Norris from Nebraska, had different policy preferences than the pro-business Republican loyalists, but they were unsuccessful in getting their preferred legislation through the House, controlled as it was by Speaker Cannon. In coalition with the Democrats, the Republican reformers unseated Speaker Cannon and changed the rules to allow for less party control of the flow of legislation through the Rules Committee and less party control over assignment and chairing of committees. They brought about an institutional revolution that was expected to, and did, result in different policy outcomes from the House of Representatives.

Choosing At-Large Elections

Steven Maser has analyzed another set of institutional inventions that occurred at about the same time as the congressional revolution, but in local government.[33] Municipalities at this time were undergoing their own revolution consisting of at-large elections, city-manager executives, registration laws, etc. Again, Maser uses a rational-choice, neo-institutional argument, claiming that individuals were concerned with choosing institutions that defended their economic rights and political influence.

CHOOSING ADMINISTRATIVE REFORM

This book addresses the same kind of institutional choice. Beginning at about the same time that Congress unseated Speaker Cannon and at about the same time that cities were choosing at-large council elections, political actors at all levels were choosing to reform the rules of administrative procedure. Like the reforms of the Defense Department and the school systems discussed above, these rules emphasized a straight-line chain of command, task specialization, merit hiring, and the use of written, "scientific" standard operating procedures. This coherent set of procedural rules changed the way in which decisions were made in and about administrative organizations. The rule changes, then, constituted the same kind of institutional transformation that the institution of seniority rule and a strong committee system did for Congress.

We intend to examine this rule change as it occurred in the Progressive era in the same way that Fiorina, Weingast, and McCubbins have analyzed similar institutional transformations of Congress, and the same way that Maser has analyzed institutional transformations of urban elections. That is, we propose to examine what expectations the key political actors had about the effect of those rule changes on the values that were important to them. Why should a decisive coalition of city councilmen, police patrolmen, and other city actors agree to transform police departments along the lines of a bureaucratic, professional hierarchy? Why should this same decision be reached in cities across the country at about the same time? Why should school districts, state health departments, the military, and the State Department all undergo the same kind of transformation at the same time?

We specifically do not argue that the institutional changes that we examine have to be unanimously liked, or liked for the same reasons. Some people were emphatically opposed to the professionalization of police departments or school boards. Those who supported these institutional transformations often supported them for different, even conflicting reasons. Some teachers might have liked the professionalization of school boards because they valued the change in status that was associated with it. Some school board members might have liked it because they thought it would lead to economies in education and lower school taxes. The point is that the people who were necessary for the change found the institutional alternative being advanced by the reformers of the era to be the most attractive one that they could agree on. Like many political changes, the administrative reforms that swept the nation at the time of the Progressive era were achieved not because everyone agreed on ultimate goals, but because a decisive coalition could agree on a common means to different goals.[34]

However this text is not just, or even primarily, a history book. The most important reason to study the institution of professionalized bureaucracy is that it is still being chosen today, just as it was at the beginning of the century. When critics express their dissatisfaction with the Defense Department, they tend to make suggestions for reform that are similar to those that transformed the State Department in the 1920s—more hierarchy, more unity, more professionalization, more rational management techniques. When Nixon rode the crest of public opinion to the first drastic reformation of the Post Office, the institution he chose was in every way compatible with the principles of Progressive reformers three-quarters of a century earlier. When presidents seek to "revitalize the presidency," they tend to seek efficiency and control through structural reform and improved techniques. We want to understand why people choose the same institutional model over and over again.

Rational Choices, Irrational Institutions

The problem of explaining institutional choices as the product of the goal-oriented choices of individuals becomes more difficult and also more interesting in light of the fact that no one seems entirely happy with the result. How can it be that rational people would devise an institution that is so red-tape ridden that it gets nothing done? Why would rational people continue to impose a model of administrative reform that generates high levels of popular discontent with bureaucracy?

Because bureaucracies seem to work so badly, many people would argue that bureaucratic behavior cannot be explained without reference to either individual stupidity or individual malevolence. Lawrence Peter, the author of numerous books on organizations, says, "I am plagued with doubt—I am not quite sure whether the world is run by incompetents who are sincere or by wise guys who are putting us on."[35] Other authors speculate that the public bureaucracies attract less competent students (the better students opting for business administration), or else public bureaucracies provide special attraction to individuals with bizarre traits, such as a power neurosis.

However, this book explicitly rejects the view that bureaucrats are neurotic jokesters or unusually stupid. One of the most profound discoveries of the rational-choice literature is that the *combination* of rational individual decisions can be profoundly inefficient or irrational from a social perspective. The *prisoners' dilemma* summarizes this idea neatly: In certain circumstances, when individuals follow their own rational self-interest, the outcome is one that every individual could agree is inferior to some other outcome;[36] but no one has any individual incentive to change his or her own actions to make the socially preferred outcome happen. The production of public goods, the control of pollution, the exploitation of natural resources, and the overburdening of social services have all been shown to be situations in which rational individual action is exactly wrong for the group.[37] More fundamentally, Kenneth Arrow argued that there is no social-choice mechanism that can be discovered that allows individuals to choose their own actions and guarantees that the social outcome will meet several benign requirements for social rationality.[38] Because of this literature, we do not feel that it is ludicrous to explain bureaucracy as the understandable but inefficient result of reasonable actions by individuals with normal goals.

What This Book Is Not

A neo-institutional approach to public administration reform would be inappropriate if the individuals involved had no real "choice" in the matter. It could be that the historical characters we describe as "choosing" administrative reform were in actuality driven by underlying social and economic forces of which they were individually unconscious. These same forces resulted in the bureaucratization of other societies at similar stages of socioeconomic development. The "choices" of political actors were irrelevant, according to this view, because they had no alternative but to create the city-manager form of government, independent regulatory commissions, independent school boards, autonomous civil service boards, professionalized bureaucracies, etc., that were the American manifestation of this "bureaucratization of the world." We quite freely admit that there were underlying forces, such as industrialization and urbanization, which were necessary conditions for the kinds of institutional reforms that we study in this book, and for the spread of bureaucratic structures. These conditions certainly shaped the choices of administrative reformers by shaping the relative desirability of various organizational and structural forms. However, we insist on the reality of institutional choices for several reasons.

First, we observe that various governmental jurisdictions chose administrative-reform institutions while others did not. Some cities chose to adopt the Progressive package of city-manager administration and nonpartisan, at-large elections; others did not. Furthermore, the hypothesis that urbanization and industrialization "cause" greater bureaucratization cannot be held in simple form, since the larger and more industrialized local jurisdictions were *less* likely to adopt this bureaucratizing reform package than were the smaller, less industrialized localities.[39] School boards overwhelmingly adopted the reform package; counties overwhelmingly did not. Some states underwent an immediate and thorough reform of elections and administrative practices; others were slow to adopt the reforms. Some presidents organized their own management styles around the reform package, and others did not.

Furthermore, the argument that "bureaucratization is inevitable" most often carries with it the Weberian assumption that it is inevitable because it is superior. The mass of twentieth-century social science research disputes this assumption as a blanket generalization. Some elements of bureaucracy are helpful in some ways, but there is no evidence that bureaucratic reform was chosen in just those times and places where it was efficient, and avoided in favor of some alternative structure when it was not. This leaves open the political possibility that administrative reform was chosen by political actors for political reasons that were not necessarily compatible with efficient institutional choices. In fact, in the last chapter of this book, we will present partial evidence that suggests that there exist institutional alternatives to the "administrative orthodoxy" that are at least as viable as the orthodoxy in certain times and places.

OVERVIEW OF THE BOOK

The first five chapters of this book deal with the historical events leading up to the formulation of the orthodox reform institutions, and their selection in the early part of the twentieth century.

Chapters 6 through 8 discuss the current evaluations of the orthodox reform model by psychologists, sociologists, and others. If, as many argue, the kind of bureaucracy that emerged at the beginning of the twentieth century under the Progressives is dysfunctional at the end of the twentieth century, then it is an important problem that the Progressive rationalization for administrative reform persists throughout the twentieth century. The second part of this book addresses the current academic thought on the received organizational wisdom. The best analysis of this received wisdom is that it contains several important omissions. The omissions are analyzed, and the best current organizational wisdom about how organizations actually perform is described.

In Chapter 9, we try to explain the limited successes of the orthodox reform movement, arguing that the institutions of the reform eras created incentives that guided individuals toward just the behaviors that have been regarded as problematic since then. That is, the orthodox reform institutions carried the seeds of their own failure.

Chapter 10 analyzes the continued support for orthodox reform institutions despite their inadequacies. Once again, our explanation is compatible with the growing literature of neo-institutionalism: People continue to choose reformed institutions because they can reach agreement on them as a solution to their own problems. This continued choice of reform institutional structures is found in both budgeting (Chapter 11) and personnel (Chapter 12).

The most fundamental characteristic of the orthodox approach to reform is its view of reform as a nonpolitical, technical problem. The most fundamental criticism of administrative orthodoxy in this book is that administrative reform must be analyzed as a political process. The final chapter of this book deals with the broader implications of dropping the technical, Progressive view of administrative reform. In particular, how does one guarantee accountability of administrative agencies if not by the orthodoxy of more hierarchy and/or greater professionalism? The politics of accountability is basically an open question, one that has yet to be seriously analyzed in American public administration.

NOTES

[1]E. E. SCHATTSCHNEIDER, *The Semi-Sovereign People: A Realist's Guide to Democracy in America* (New York: Holt, Rinehart and Winston, 1960), p. 48.

[2]FRED HIATT, "The War Within the Pentagon," *Washington Post National Weekly Edition*, Aug. 6, 1984. See also David C. Jones, "What's Wrong with the Defense Establishment," in *The Defense Reform Debate*, Asa A. Clark and others, eds. (Baltimore: Johns Hopkins University Press, 1984).

[3]HIATT, "War."

[4]"Defense Organization: The Need for Change," *Armed Forces Journal*, October, 1985, pp. 16–19.

[5]"Defense Organization: The Need for Change," *Staff Report to the Committee on Armed Services United States Senate* (Washington: U.S. Government Printing Office, October 16, 1985).

[6]EUGENE LEWIS, *American Politics in a Bureaucratic Age: Citizens, Constituents, Clients and Victims* (Cambridge: Winthrop, 1977).

[7]"Defense Organization," *Senate Staff Report*, p. 49.

[8]PAUL Y. HAMMOND, *Organizing for Defense: The American Military Establishment in the Twentieth Century* (Westport, Connecticut: Greenwood Press), p. 23.

[9]HAMMOND, *Organizing for Defense*, pp. 18–19.

[10]In response to public criticism, this focus on management as opposed to war is apparently beginning to change at the Army War College. See "War College Turns Again to War," *New York Times*, January 28, 1986, sec. C, p. 1.

[11]GARY HART, "What's Wrong with the Military," *The New York Times Magazine*, February 14, 1982.

[12]"Defense Organization," *Senate Staff Report*, p. 507.

[13]GEORGE C. WILSON and RICK ATKINS, "Defense: Big Bucks, Small Gain," *Washington Post National Weekly Edition*, September 10, 1984, p. 6.

[14]HART, "Military," p. 3.

[15]HERBERT KAUFMAN, "Fear of Bureaucracy: A Raging Pandemic," *Public Administration Review*, 41 (1981), p. 1.

[16]DONALD WARWICK, *A Theory of Public Bureaucracy: Politics, Personality, and Organization in the State Department* (Cambridge: Harvard University Press, 1975), p. 69.

[17]HAROLD SEIDMAN, *Politics, Position, and Power: The Dynamics of Federal Organization*, 2nd ed. (New York: Oxford University Press, 1979).

[18]SEIDMAN, *Politics*, p. 5.

[19]SEIDMAN, *Politics*, p. 8.

[20]TERRY M. MOE, "The Politicized Presidency," in *The New Direction in American Politics*, John E. Chubb and Paul E. Peterson, eds. (Washington, D.C.: Brookings Institute, 1985), p. 265.

[21]ANGUS CAMPBELL, et al., *The American Voter* (New York: John Wiley, 1960).

[22]LEWIS ANTHONY DEXTER, "The Representative and His District," *Human Organization*, 16 (1957).

[23]See ROBERT PRESTHUS, *The Organizational Society: An Analysis and a Theory* (New York: Random House, 1962), pp. 164–286; ANTHONY DOWNS, *Inside Bureaucracy* (Boston: Little, Brown & Co., 1966), p. 96.

[24]DAVID MAYHEW, *Congress: The Electoral Connection* (New Haven: Yale University Press, 1974).

[25]ANTHONY DOWNS, *An Economic Theory of Democracy* (New York: Harper & Row, 1957).

[26]WILLIAM H. RIKER, *Liberalism Against Populism: A Confrontation Between the Theory

of Democracy and the Theory of Social Choice (San Francisco: W. H. Freeman & Co., 1982), pp. 93–94.

[27]RIKER, *Liberalism*, p. 169.

[28]KENNETH SHEPSLE, "Institutional Arrangements and Equilibrium in Multidimensional Voting Models," *American Journal of Political Science*, 23 (1979), pp. 17–59.

[29]ROBERT L. LINEBERRY and EDMUND P. FOWLER, "Reformism and Public Policy in American Cities," *The American Political Science Review*, 61 (1967), pp. 701–716.

[30]MORRIS FIORINA, "Some Thoughts About the Effects of Uncertainty on the Delegation of Legislative Power." Presented to the American Political Science Association convention in Washington, D.C., 1984.

[31]BARRY WEINGAST and WILLIAM MARSHALL. "A Reconsideration of the Railroad Problem: The Economics and Politics of the Interstate Commerce Act." Presented to the American Political Science Association convention in Washington, D.C., 1984.

[32]See also MATHEW D. McCUBBINS, "The Legislative Design of Regulatory Structure," *American Journal of Political Science* 29 (1985), pp. 721–748.

[33]STEPHEN MASER, "Demographic Factors Affecting Constitutional Decisions: The Case of Municipal Charters," *Public Choice* 47 (1985), pp. 149–162.

[34]CHARLES LINDBLOM, "The Science of 'Muddling Through,' " *Public Administration Review* 19 (1959), pp. 79–80.

[35]LAWRENCE J. PETER, *Why Things Go Wrong: Or The Peter Principle Revisited* (New York, 1985), p. 11.

[36]ANATOL RAPOPORT, "Prisoner's Dilemma—Recollections and Observations," in *Rational Man and Irrational Society?*, Brian Barry and Russell Hardin, eds. (Beverly Hills: Sage Publications, 1982), pp. 72–83.

[37]MANCUR OLSON, *The Logic of Collective Action: Public Goods and the Theory of Groups* (Cambridge: Harvard University Press, 1965).

[38]KENNETH J. ARROW, *Social Choice and Individual Values.* 2nd ed. (New Haven: Yale University Press, 1963).

[39]ROBERT L. LINEBERRY and EDMUND P. FOWLER, "Reformism and Public Policy in American Cities," *American Political Science Review* 61 (1967), pp. 701–716.

CHAPTER 2

Bureaucracy and Boss Politics

The Jacksonians may have failed to foresee the damaging consequences of their spoils system, but they perceived, perhaps more clearly than the civil service reformers of a later time, that the implementation of public policy could never be merely "neutral". . . .

Matthew A. Crenson, *The Federal Machine*[1]

When we of the twentieth century think of "bureaucracy," we think of words like "hierarchy," "rules and regulations," and "impersonality." We think of career officials sitting in specialized offices, protecting their jobs. Apart from whatever positive or negative connotations these words carry, the characteristics we tend to think of do largely define the government agencies of the twentieth century: hierarchy, impersonal rules, specialized offices, career bureaucrats. It may be surprising, then, to realize that none of these characteristics were especially applicable to nineteenth-century government agencies.

In the nineteenth century, government agencies were staffed for the most part by amateurs who were likely to be thrown out of office at the next election. The decisions these amateurs made were, for the most part, conditioned by personalities and politics rather than by formal, written rules. Agencies were generally organized geographically, rather than by specialized offices. There were likely to be very few levels of hierarchy between the lowest clerk and the chief executive in a department, and the chief executive might find that his authority in the hierarchy was subject to forces outside of the formal hierarchy, such as the political alliances he did or did not have with party leaders.

These characteristics of nineteenth-century bureaucracy, though they may seem foreign to us today, are the natural result of a rather self-conscious reform movement that first swept state and local governments in the 1830s, and then into the federal government with the administration of Andrew Jackson.

JACKSONIAN REFORM

Up until the presidency of Andrew Jackson, many elective and appointive offices alike had been held by landowning and commercial elites.[2] A number of factors had excluded the masses from politics. The first factor was that in many states they were ineligible to vote. The franchise was limited due to property ownership requirements, which made tenant farmers and the urban lower classes ineligible. Throughout the early nineteenth century, however, requirements were gradually changed to allow universal male suffrage.

Second, landowning and commercial elites often exercised disproportionate influence over other citizens who could vote. The elites used economic influence and the vestiges of colonial traditions of social privilege. Again, this elite advantage increasingly broke down during the early nineteenth century. The individuals who had faced the perils of the frontier and made a place for themselves in the new towns and states established since the American Revolution were not eager to defer to the privileged recipients of inherited wealth and social status. They demanded equal political influence.

Third, the Founding Fathers had written the Constitution precisely because of a fear of mass democracy. Alexander Hamilton, for instance, had exclaimed, "Your people, sir, your people is a great beast." They had hemmed in the influence of the masses in the institutions of the new political system. The Constitution stipulated that the Senate be elected not by the people, but by state legislatures, which the founders thought would represent the elites of the states; and for the presidency, the Constitution established an "electoral college," which the founders felt would insulate the executive from the masses.

The Introduction of the Spoils System

These institutional checks on majoritarian democracy were intolerable to the Americans of the nineteenth century. Between 1815 and 1840, a rash of new state constitutions and municipal charters transformed the institutions of local government. They eliminated the privileged position of elites by requiring long lists of public officials to be elected, an institution known as the "long ballot." The democratization movement reached the national government with the election of the Democratic candidate, Andrew Jackson, to the presidency in 1828. Jackson and his followers believed that the political influence of the masses should dominate American politics, rather than be just one force among many. They used the vehicle of the mass-based political party—another institutional manifestation that the Founding Fathers had not considered—to make sure that the government represented the will of the people. Even the Whigs bowed to the political success of the Democratic party by supporting William Henry Harrison for the presidency in 1840, calling him a "man of the people" and claiming he was born in a log cabin.

One example of the kind of anti-democratic privilege that the Jacksonian Democrats sought to eliminate was the pattern of appointing members of the landowning and commercial elites to federal office—postmasters and customs officials, in large part. Jackson believed that this pattern of appointments had made federal office-holding "a species of property" for the privileged few. The Founding Fathers' belief that office-holding required a special competence and special character was wrong, according to Jackson. This belief made government "an engine for the support of the few at the expense of the many."[3]

Jackson's solution was to make sure that individuals were rotated frequently in their offices to prevent the creation of a protected elite and to make the administrative machinery accountable to the people. The majority party, he believed, should be allowed not only the office of the presidency, but also the privilege of removing officeholders at all levels and replacing them with loyal party members. This practice of replacing incumbent officeholders with supporters of the successful political party became known as the "spoils system" or "patronage system." The offices were viewed as the winnings, or spoils, of the victorious political party. While President Jackson himself increased spoils only moderately during his term in office, his presidency established the rhetoric and the institutions for the rapid development of the spoils system over the next few decades.

The Mutually Reinforcing Nature of Jacksonian Reforms

The institutional changes of the Jacksonian era served to reinforce each other and to create a relatively stable pattern of politics. Because of the extensions of the franchise, it was a large job to get reelected. This large job could only be accomplished by large organizations such as political parties. Political parties were strengthened for this task in part by other institutional changes, such as the spoils system. The spoils system created an army of workers who found it worthwhile to work for the party in exchange for one of the spoils jobs that the successful party had at its disposal. The ward-based elections placed a premium on the kind of neighborhood strength that was the hallmark of party organization. The "long ballot" further strengthened the parties by creating a body of localized offices that could easily be held by party ward leaders.

Politically, the new institutions proved a great success. These institutions organized the vast majority of political activity during the nineteenth century; that is, people found it more beneficial to support the institutions by working within party organizations to achieve their purposes than to oppose the institutions.

At the federal level, the spoils system reached its height under Abraham Lincoln, under whose administration 1,457 out of 1,639 presidentially appointed officials were replaced. Patronage played an important part in Lincoln's attempt to keep the Republican Party and the Union together during the Civil War by being an inducement for loyalty.[4]

At about the same time, the spoils system was being refined to an art at the local level by the party boss of New York, William Marcy Tweed. The party organization in New York was called Tammany Hall, and the contrast between Lincoln and Tweed, both practitioners of spoils politics, demonstrates a common theme in American politics: An effective political technique can be used for either noble or sordid purposes. While Lincoln used patronage to keep the Union together and ended up a hero in American politics, Tweed used it to make himself rich and ended up in prison. A study of Tweed's political organization demonstrates that, while Jackson and his followers supported their institutional reforms to "purify

democracy" and advance public virtue, institutional reforms often have unanticipated consequences. People can find ways of winning under a new set of political
rules that may be objectionable to some of the supporters of the reforms.

THE SPOILS SYSTEM REFINED: TAMMANY HALL

The Society of Saint Tammany was founded in 1789 as a charitable organization,
named after a legendary Delaware Indian chief. By the nineteenth century, however, the Tammany organization began to dominate the Democratic Party in New
York City. The support of the Tammany organization ensured political hopefuls of
the Democratic nomination and, very often, election over rival political parties.
Office in the Tammany club signified influence in the Democratic Party, and
anyone who wanted to rise in the Democratic Party knew that the Tammany
organization was the way to do so. For over eighty years, from 1850 to 1934, the
Tammany organization held a prominent place in New York's politics.

Beginning in 1857, the Tammany organization was dominated as it never had
been before by a single politician named William Marcy Tweed. Tweed was a
political entrepreneur, meaning that he paid out resources in the form of political
favors in order to bring in resources in the form of political support. In doing so, the
balance of resources coming in was enough greater than the resources going out to
make Tweed and his four closest associates (the Tweed Ring) very rich indeed. The
way that he constructed the New York County Courthouse serves as a good illustra-
tion of how the machine worked.[5]

The New York State legislature authorized a new county courthouse in 1858,
specifying that it should not cost more than one quarter of a million dollars, which
was quite sufficient for the job in those days. Work proceeded slowly, however, and
in 1862 Boss Tweed got the legislature to authorize an additional million dollars. In
the subsequent four years, Tweed got authorization for an additional $2.4 million,
totalling $3.6 million, or enough for 14 county courthouses. At that time, Tweed's
opponents demanded an investigation to know why such an excessive amount of
money had been spent and why the courthouse still wasn't finished.

The Board of Supervisors (of which Tweed was president) established a Special Committee to Investigate the Courthouse, and in twelve days the Committee
reported that no graft had taken place in the construction of the courthouse. For this
twelve days work, the Committee submitted a bill of expenses amounting to over
$18,000. The bulk of this bill (over $14,000) was for publishing copies of the report
clearing the Tweed Ring. The firms which received this printing business were, in
fact, owned by Tweed.

With this clean bill of health, the City then spent another $10 million on the
courthouse. A total of $13 million had been spent in 13 years, and by 1871 the
courthouse was still not finished. Over $5.6 million had been spent on furniture,
carpets, and shades. An opponent in the legislature pointed out that more money
was being spent on furnishings for the courthouse than it cost the federal government to run the mail service for a year. The plumber hired by Tammany received
$1.5 million. Another Tweed contractor charged the city $500,000 for plastering
and a million dollars for repairing the same work. Total plastering charges were $2.8
million for a job that should have cost $20,000. As was revealed in later inquiries,
Tweed and his four top henchmen typically got 65% of each contractor's payment.[6]

Payoffs were not just in the form of business contracts, however. To maintain the courthouse heating apparatus, the county hired 32 engineers, firemen, secretaries, clerks, and inspectors. Maneater Cusick, a prizefighter who had spent time in Sing Sing, became the court clerk. William "Pudding" Long became court interpreter, despite the fact that he couldn't read or write. He spent his time looking after Boss Tweed's kennels. But at least these men were alive and well; at one point, five dead men were on the payroll at the courthouse—and they didn't miss a paycheck.

These payoffs and special arrangements occurred during a time of active political competition when there were plenty of people willing to charge Tweed with corruption and to take his place in elective office. Under these conditions, how was it possible for Tweed to be so flagrant for so long? These were the questions that the reformers asked, and by the time they were able to offer a well-developed set of answers, their ideas provided the backbone of the reform movement that swept through the nation in the first part of the twentieth century, leaving us with the origins of our modern political and administrative institutions.

HOW TO KEEP A POLITICAL MACHINE IN POWER

We may examine the Tammany Hall machine as an organization that has an exchange relationship with its environment. Most organizations operating in society need the same general kinds of resources to remain effective. These include political support, manpower, money, and legal authority. Tammany "purchased" each of these kinds of resources with a specific exchange.

Political Support

Tammany Hall was first of all a political organization; to stay in power, it needed political support in the form of votes for its candidates. How did Tammany Hall obtain votes even after its corrupt practices had become well known?

One simple way was to use money. "A political organization has to have money for its business as well as a church," said George Washington Plunkitt, a Tammany leader of the turn of the century.[7] A most important use of this money was to hire what were known as repeater gangs, individuals who would "vote early and often." One Tammany Hall man argued that repeaters should have a full set of whiskers. After voting once they would shave off the beard and vote again, then shave the moustache and vote a third time, then vote a fourth time without the sideburns. Each vote would be in the name of a different registered voter, which would have the additional advantage of keeping a likely opposition voter from voting.

Intimidation was another way of securing votes or, just as effective, preventing the opposition from voting. Gangs of toughs would roam the streets or guard the ballot boxes, threatening violence on those would who vote the "wrong" way. (This was before the days of the secret ballot.) These toughs were sometimes women. In New York, Euchre Katie Burns, the champion heavyweight female brick-hurler of New York, was used to intimidate Republicans. In addition, there was Hell-Cat Maggie, who "filed her front teeth to points and wore long, artificial nails made of brass on her fingers. When she unleashed her battle cry and dashed biting and clawing into a polling place, even the bravest of men lost their poise."[8]

The Tweed Ring also brought about an amazing increase in high-speed naturalization of immigrants. Fake witnesses were brought in, fees were paid by the Tammany Society, and naturalization committees were established in neighborhood offices throughout the city. The results were impressive. Between 1856 and 1867, the annual average naturalization was 9,207; in 1868 alone, the figure jumped to 41,112.

While newspaper publicity was not effective in securing the immigrant votes that Tammany generally relied on, unfavorable news coverage could mobilize the opposition. Therefore, Tammany was careful to keep newspapers under control. Probably no New York City administration enjoyed better newspaper coverage than Tweed did before 1871. He accomplished this feat by distributing ads to 26 daily newspapers and 61 weeklies. In addition, reporters regularly received $200 Christmas gifts from the machine. To no one's surprise, 37 weeklies went out of business when Tweed was sent to jail.[9]

Favors to influential groups were important as well. To guarantee their support in political races, for instance, Tweed gave Catholic church schools and charitable organizations large grants of state money during the years of Tammany influence in the state legislature. Fernando Wood, the New York Mayor who preceded Tweed as head of Tammany Hall, had offered the valuable site on Fifth Avenue for Saint Patrick's Cathedral to the Archdiocese for the nominal sum of $83. Even if active support was not always solicited, passive acceptance by a broad range of influential groups made building an opposition coalition difficult.

By far the most important single source of votes—and the hallmark of the political machine—was precinct work. Precinct work consisted of all those services performed by the rank-and-file political worker in order to deliver votes. The precinct worker's job was to build a network of personal relationships in which as many people as possible felt a personal obligation to vote as he suggested. He would do this by helping immigrants in New York City find relatives, jobs, or housing. He would be the first one on the scene after a fire to help organize emergency relief for the dispossessed; he would organize outings for the kids in the summer; he would be present at all funerals and wakes; he would remember birthdays and be at all times a glad-hander; he would go to court with the parent of a kid in trouble with the law and get the machine's district attorney to let him off with a warning; and in building this entire network of relationships, he would only ask to be paid off on election day. He would then visit every one of these hundreds of friends to make sure that they would vote (and vote correctly), providing transportation to those who needed it.

Manpower

Party workers, then, were essential for securing votes for the political machine. Where did they come from? Why were so many people willing to spend their time organizing a precinct so someone else could be elected to office? The answer is, to get a job. A first step for Tweed in getting to the top of the Tammany Hall organization was an appointment as Deputy Street Commissioner. The position gave him the authority to hire thousands of laborers on the condition that they be loyal party workers. As his biographer said, "It was as if he had been presented with an army. Aldermen, ward leaders, and 'distinguished' city statesmen of all kinds had to apply to him for jobs for their ward supporters. They all had to truck and crawl to Tweed, for without jobs to give, their following would disappear."[10]

George Washington Plunkitt was another very successful ward boss in the Tammany organization who died in 1924 a wealthy and renowned figure. During his later years, however, the Progressive reform movement succeeded in passing a civil service law which required city officials to pass a written examination before being hired. Plunkitt believed that this law was one of the greatest affronts to the political party system. "This civil service law is the biggest fraud of the age. It is the curse of the nation. There can't be no real patriotism while it lasts. How are you going to interest young men in their country if you have no offices to give them when they work for their party?"[11] Plunkitt correctly saw the key link between personal gain and service to the party and the country. Without jobs to offer, the machine would lose its manpower.

While the number of positions that can be granted in reward for faithful service to the party has diminished, they still exist. The mayor of the City of Chicago still has at his disposal six to ten thousand patronage jobs, enough to guarantee an effective party organization. The party leaders also work with union bosses to achieve political discretion in hiring and promoting, which adds several thousand more people who develop some form of loyalty to the administration in power.

Money

If machines get votes partly through manpower, they also get them partly through the use of money—money to hire repeater gangs, to pay for favors, and so forth. Where do machines get their money?

Every public-works project, like the construction of the New York county courthouse, involves the expenditure of large amounts of money. That money can make some people rich—the contractors, the suppliers of materials, the insurers, etc. The contracts for the courthouse were particularly lucrative, and the Tweed Ring didn't just give them away—the kickbacks from the contractors financed the machine.

Tammany politicians also had inside information on future construction sites, including subway lines, new factories, and public buildings. By buying this land cheap in advance, they often turned a very handsome profit once development began. Plunkitt, commenting on his real-estate purchases, confessed, "Somehow I always guessed about right, and shouldn't I enjoy the profit of my foresight? It was rather amusing when the condemnation commissioners came along and found piece after piece of land in the name of George Plunkitt of the Fifth Assembly District, New York City."[12] This information about where city projects were to be built was worth large sums, not only to Plunkitt, who died a millionaire, but to many other land speculators as well.

Another way to get money for the machine was through granting franchises. Companies either went bankrupt or made fortunes depending on whether they got the franchise for a streetcar or for street cleaning or garbage collection. These businesses were (and are) willing to pay for these contracts.

Finally, it has been the practice at various times in history for the party to assess some proportion of the wages earned by individuals who got jobs through party influence. Thus, if you got a job as a judge worth $40,000 a year, you might be asked to contribute a very large proportion of that to the political party that got the job for you. As Plunkitt observed about contributions to the organization in "gratitude" for getting a job, "The sums they pay are accordin' to their salaries and the length of their terms of office, if elected."[13]

Legal Authority

In order to be able to appoint people to bureaucratic positions, to grant franchises, to grant contracts for public work construction, and to grant police protection, the electoral party must have the legal authority to do all these things. In order to get this authority, the local party must not be too powerfully inhibited by the state government. In the United States, the local government is the creature of the state government. The state government can change key local positions from local to appointive; can require audits; can make judges nonpartisan; can take away the authority of local governments to perform certain lucrative functions. For instance, the City of New York had to get state approval before it could even begin to design the county courthouse in 1858.

In order to get the authorization to do these things, local officials need to have influence at the level of the state government, in particular in the state legislature. For instance, Boss Tweed was not mayor of New York City. The position he held, as boss of New York City, was State Senator. He was chairman of the important State Finance Committee, and a leader of the so-called Black Horse Cavalry, a group of legislators who sold their votes for a price.[14] In this way, he guaranteed the legal authorization from the state.

Two of Tweed's most famous exploits were the Tax Levy Bill and the new City Charter. In the former, the City Comptroller was granted the power to raise huge sums for public works through bond issues. Tweed paid more than $100,000 in bribes to legislators to guarantee successful passage, knowing that the money could be made back in the kickbacks from the public-works construction. In the case of the City Charter, the mayor was given the right to appoint the comptroller and the heads of departments, positions which were formerly elective. Tweed, as Commissioner of Public Works in New York City, also gained a seat on the Board of Audit. The bribery cost for this legislation, by Tweed's own admission, was $600,000.[15]

When machines exceed their legal authority, they need legal protection. The ability of the party machine to engage in lucrative graft would be severely limited if they had to worry about being indicted and tried and sent to prison. The best way to avoid indictment is to elect your own district attorney. If you do get indicted, then it is best to have the judges on your side. Once again, the party leaders are best off if the judges are elected on their ticket.

THE PARADOX OF ACCOUNTABILITY

It is worth noting that none of the inducements used by the Tammany machine involved providing effective public services. In order for Tammany Hall to get the necessary legal authority, or financial contributions, or manpower, or even votes, it was not necessary for the party to provide effective police or fire services, clean streets, or good schools. Tammany engaged in explicit exchanges of private goods (money, jobs, contracts) in order to get the resources it needed. Public services, by their nature, cannot be denied to anyone once they are supplied to anyone. For this reason, they would not have fostered a sense of obligation on the part of immigrants to vote for Tammany, or precinct workers to work for Tammany, or contractors to give bribes to Tammany officials.

On the other hand, with a corrupt police department, Tammany could build a sense of obligation and support by "fixing" fines or arrests. Tammany found that it secured more votes by providing emergency support for families burned out of their homes than by providing effective fire code enforcement or fire protection, even though the latter could have kept families from being burned out of their homes in the first place. Like other public goods, fire code enforcement can't be applied in such a way as to discriminate between supporters and non-supporters of Tammany; for that reason, it isn't a very good reward for party loyalty. Tammany specialized in providing services that could be "turned off" by a precinct worker when a citizen proved to be uncooperative. As a result, Tammany workers specialized in building good will by attending wakes, rather than by providing public health services that would keep the infant mortality rate down in immigrant precincts.

Tammany also did not rely on public services in recruiting workers for local government or the political party. Instead, the machine used very direct monetary and power incentives to recruit workers. As Plunkitt expressed so well, patriotism is hard to sustain when no jobs are available. "Before [civil service], when a party won, its workers got everything in sight. That was somethin' to make a man patriotic."[16] Working for a cause other than to win and get the spoils was not the Tammany method, and thus public services suffered.

While Tammany and other big-city political machines relied on lower-class and immigrant votes, they did not supply a set of public services that were attuned to the needs of those groups. The Tammany leaders saw politics as a road to self-advancement, rather than as a means of providing social justice and social reform. In fact, in their public policy decisions, big-city machines seemed to be more in tune with the big corporations which had developed during the last part of the nineteenth century than with the workers who supplied the bulk of their votes.

These corporations needed franchises, utilities, streetcars, and a passive work force, and they were willing to pay somebody to get them. The "boss" was the somebody who could deliver. "Holding the strings of diverse governmental divisions, bureaus, and agencies in his competent hands, the Boss rationalizes the relations between public and private business. He serves as the business community's ambassador in the otherwise alien (and sometimes unfriendly) realm of government. And, in strict businesslike terms, he is well paid for his economic services to his respectable business client."[17] Being able to serve as business's "ambassador" while being reelected with working-class votes was the machine's most fundamental political accomplishment. The hypocrisy of this accomplishment was not hidden to the Progressive reformers, however, and they emphasized this fact in their attack on boss politics.

THE OMNIPRESENT POLITICAL MACHINE

In 1870, the New York Times hired a muckraking editor, who began a campaign against the Tweed Ring. The excesses of the Tweed Ring were made public in 1871, and the Tweed Ring was defeated at the polls in November of that year. Boss Tweed was eventually sent to jail for his crimes. However, getting rid of bossism proved to be more difficult than getting rid of one boss. The Tammany techniques for ensuring the flow of votes, manpower, money, and legal protection were remarkably enduring in New York City. Periodically, the public would be aroused by a newspaper campaign which demonstrated blatant corruption. Reformers, riding the wave of public revulsion, would be swept into public office. However, the regular party organization would bide its time and eventually return to power using the traditional techniques. As Plunkitt observed, "The fact is that a reformer can't last in politics. He can make a show for a while, but he always comes down like a rocket. Politics is as much a regular business as the grocery or the dry-goods or the drug business. You've got to be trained up to it or you're sure to fail."[18]

Other Cities

Because the techniques of party organization were something one could learn and become proficient in, it would have been remarkable if they had not spread to other cities. In fact, they did spread. Under the Jacksonian institutions, with widespread suffrage, large numbers of elective offices, ward-based elections, and party-based appointment of city bureaucrats, the techniques of party-based machine politics were virtually a guaranteed winner. If no one had adopted those techniques in, say, Pittsburgh, then the first politician to use those techniques would be likely to take office.

Thus, the muckraking reporter Lincoln Steffens reports that when the Tweed ring was broken, a man named Christopher L. Magee "spent months in New York looking into Tammany's machine methods and the mistakes which had led to its exposure and disruption."[19] He then returned to Pittsburgh with the conviction that "a ring could be made as safe as a bank." The Pittsburgh structure of government had the same Jacksonian characteristics that made a machine possible in New York, with large, ward-based amateur city councils, and Magee proceeded to build a party organization that was just as successful as Tammany's.

It is true that Pittsburgh had fewer Irish immigrants than New York City, but it turned out that Pittsburgh's Scotch–Irish population was just as amenable to party politics. Similarly, machines were built in Scandinavian Minneapolis and German St. Louis, and native American Philadelphia as well. In San Francisco, the party had close connections with labor unions. In Los Angeles, the machine was basically a tool of the railroads.

State Governments

Party machines were not limited to city politics, however. Southern and midwestern rural counties developed strong machines based on county patronage in the sheriff's office and on road crews. Party machines were led to control state government by necessity, because state governments controlled city governments. Furthermore, state legislatures had the authority to pass bills detrimental to the interests of corporations, so there was a great deal of money to be made in controlling the state legislatures and selling favorable corporate legislation.

In New York state, party leaders could generate money by passing what was known as a "strike bill," which would be so detrimental to a public utility or other corporation that the corporate leaders would be driven to pay large sums of money to "put strike bills to sleep," or kill the legislation. A prominent 1890s boss who emerged as the key link with corporations was Thomas Collier Platt, a New York State senator. Several corporations gave him outright large sums of cash which he would use to support the political campaigns of favored legislators, making those legislators responsive to his leadership in the legislature.

In 1905, the Armstrong Committee of the state legislature undertook an investigation of a scandal that had developed between the legislature, the railroad companies, and two large insurance corporations. A president of one large insurance company stated that the insurance business had suffered from several blackmail attempts in the form of strike legislation. These companies also faced the political tactics of Governor Odell, who "had seen no objection to the introduction of a bill repealing the charter of a company which owed him money."[20] The coordinator of this reciprocal arrangement was Boss Platt, a service for which he and the party were paid handsomely.

The Insurance Department in the State Administration also was implicated. The investigating committee, through its counsel, Charles Evans Hughes, discovered that the department head had not exposed abuses or improper accounting in several firms. The department had also retained the clerk to an insurance company lobbyist as an insurance examiner. Boss Platt had played a role in the appointment, as well as coordinating political appointments in the transportation department, prisons, public works, New York City government, and federal agencies such as the Post Office and the Customs House. Platt was able to put together a variety of influence sources that were characteristic of the state and local bosses of the day:

> The mechanical elements of Platt's autocratic power were: first, control over the nomination and the election machinery through his cooperation with the state committee; second, control over the state legislature through his relations with the oligarchy ruling that body; third, control over the patronage through whatever influence he had with the president, the governor, and the federal, state, and local administrative officers; fourth, his control over the party campaign funds through the relations which he maintained with the directors of certain corporations who were high in financial circles; and lastly, control over the minds of the voters through his intimate relations with party editors and men of influence in the business and political worlds.[21]

Similar machines were constructed in Republican and Democratic states throughout the country. In California, the Southern Pacific lobbyist bought and sold votes on the floor of the California State legislature like a stockbroker. In Wisconsin, a machine relying on influence with the railroads and the lumber companies dominated the state. In the South, there were Democratic party organizations resting on the influence of the agricultural elite.

The Federal Government

Congress was in large part composed of members who owed their election to the party machines in the cities and states where they were elected. This was especially true in the case of the U.S. Senators, since in the nineteenth century they were elected by the state legislature rather than by popular vote. Thus, the party that controlled the state legislature could elect its own Senator, in consultation with the corporations it relied on for financial support. The railroad states were known to control the votes of certain Senators, the mining states other senators, and Standard Oil still others.

Because of this, no single machine elected a majority of the members of Congress, as a single state machine might capture a majority of a state legislature. However, Congress was itself controlled by a strong party organization, and this party organization took on many of the aspects of the party organizations at the local and state level. Exchange relationships between party leadership and others guaranteed a high degree of party discipline.

The dominant congressional party at this time was the Republican party. Joe Cannon, the Republican Speaker of the House of Representatives, through his control of the Rules Committee, other key committees, and the party machinery, ran the House with a dictatorial hand until 1910. As chairman of the Rules Committee, Cannon controlled the appointment of Republican committee members. The members he chose for key committees were invariably senior Republicans who had a long personal and political association with him. Other legislators, who wanted to be appointed to committees dealing with legislation that they were concerned with, would find that Cannon would not make committee appointments until legislation that Cannon was concerned with was passed. Cannon found this an effective means of ensuring the cooperation of the legislators on bills that were important to him.

His Rules Committee could also veto legislation by not allowing it to reach the floor of the House for a vote. This meant that any member of Congress who did not support Cannon could be punished by not having bills necessary for his district passed through the House.[22] He and his coterie had considerable control over a wide range of legislation. This strong party control over legislation, frequently tied to the interests of the corporations that were friendliest to the party machines, convinced reformers that boss politics had penetrated Congress.

BUREAUCRACY AS ADJUNCT TO THE MACHINE

The exchange relationships that supported the machine constituted a set of constraints that shaped the behavior of city agencies. Because the boss needed precinct workers, party loyalty was a requirement of street cleaners and teachers. Because the boss needed money, contracts for city services would go to the highest briber. Because the boss needed legal protection, police and judges had to be "safe." Virtually every aspect of city administration was determined by the political needs of the party machine. We will focus on police, the courts, and education.

Police Administration

In 1892, the Republican Party regained control of the New York State legislature and determined to embarrass the New York City Democrats. They allowed reformers to investigate the city police department and its activities. The resulting investigating commission, called the Lexow Committee, engaged in the first serious legislative examination of corruption in the nation's history. The evidence turned up by the investigation described the way in which the party's political requirements permeated the New York City Police Department. Historians have confirmed this pattern as being typical of police departments of the machine era.

First and foremost, the police supported the electoral requirements of the machine. During the Lexow hearings, Republican ballot clerks and election inspectors "told how the police had threatened Republican voters, ignored Democratic repeaters, tampered with ballot boxes, and committed or permitted, in the committee's words, 'almost every conceivable crime against the elective franchise.' "[23] The police themselves acted as precinct workers, delivering the votes of their families, relatives, neighbors, benevolent associations, and clubs.

It was not only the election-day activities of the police that were constrained by machine requirements. The day-to-day activities were similarly determined. The machine's policy toward vice was tolerant and segregationist—it allowed it in the immigrant districts where it was popular and supported the machine's political ambitions. Furthermore, the typical ward boss made explicit alliances with the underworld of vice. Vice bosses supplied the manpower for repeater gangs and intimidators and financial support for elections. In return, the ward boss promised that the police would overlook the vice operations of the vice chiefs, and harass the vice chief's competitors.

In order to be able to deliver this promise, the party ward boss effectively had to control the police in his ward. The police department was organized to facilitate this control. The police department was geographically decentralized, with police precincts corresponding to the electoral wards by which the political party was organized. The captain of the police precinct was one of the patronage positions that the party ward boss controlled. The ward boss made sure that the police captain of the local precinct was a loyal supporter.

While the police captains were nominally under the authority of the city-wide police chief, in actuality the precinct captains were accountable to the ward party bosses. The police chief had little personnel or operational control at the precinct station. The police captains, on the other hand "ran the checks on applicants to the department, handed out assignments to the recruits, looked into complaints against the patrolmen, and made most of the other decisions that vitally affected the careers of the rank-and-file. Thus it was they, along with the ward leaders, who decided which laws to enforce, whose peace to keep, and which public to service. The authorities further enhanced the captains' influence by treating every precinct like a small department. So long as the captains enjoyed the machine's support, they were virtually invulnerable."[24]

To make sure they enjoyed the machine's support, the precinct captains followed the orders of the party bosses: "They protected their cronies, harassed their enemies, favored their appointees, contributed to their campaigns, and in innumerable ways acknowledged their leadership."[25]

The precinct captains administered personnel policy in a way that was consistent with the goals of the party organization. That is, the party hired and promoted police who performed the political functions needed by the party machine. "Since the police were primarily a political tool rather than a professional law enforcement agency, the composition of the force was all-important. In the absence of any conception of police work as a skilled occupation that demanded special training, political loyalty was the only real qualification for appointment."[26] This was entirely in keeping with the Jacksonian notion that any American could perform any public office adequately, but it also allowed what we would think of as strange behavior in the police departments. Despite regulations requiring that recruits pass physical, medical, and literacy tests and have no criminal record or outstanding debts, the real requirement for a recruit was a political sponsor from the machine. The payment to the machine for a job was either made in political loyalty or money or both. In the 1890s, patrolmen had to pay $300 for their jobs in New York City

and $400 in San Francisco.[27] With the correct political support, all the require-
ments for the recruit would be forthcoming: syphilitics would pass medical exams;
criminals and illiterates joined the force as easily.

As valuable as the patrolman's job was, appointment to higher positions in the
department cost the applicant even more. The going rate in New York City was a
payment to the party machine of $1,600 for a sergeant's job, and upwards of
$12,000 for a captaincy.

How could policemen pay the party organization more for a captain's job than
the job would pay in salary? The answer was that the captain was normally expected
to make more money from graft than the $12,000 he had to pay the ward boss for
the job. Here again, the connection with the local vice operations was all-
important, for "the police did not suppress vice; they licensed it"—for a fee.[28] The
license to operate a den of sin came with a payoff, either directly to the machine or,
more normally, to a low-level police "bag man" who took his share then passed it up
the police hierarchy to the local political boss, each taking a larger share. This
practice applied to burglary rings as well as prostitution or gambling operations.

One of the advantages to the police of this symbiotic relationship with crimi-
nals was that they could be very effective at crime-fighting when they wanted to be.
The most famous detective in the New York City Police Department was Thomas
Byrnes, who "could work miracles of crime detection when needed. If a wealthy
banker lost his watch, or if a particularly valuable piece of property were stolen,
Byrnes could arrange for its return through his contacts in the underworld,"[29]
generally without the conviction of the thief. His book, *Professional Criminals of
America*, made him famous when it came out in 1886.[30] The Lexow commission
in 1894 made it clear that his personal wealth was in the neighborhood of $350,000.
It would be exaggerating very little to say that he ran his own burglary ring; "his"
burglars could steal a piece of property knowing they were protected by their working relationship with Byrnes, and that there would undoubtedly be something in it
for them if Byrnes returned it to the owner for a reward. "In short, Byrnes entered
into a corrupt relationship with professional thieves to cement an equally corrupt
relationship with the financial elite."[31] Byrnes was the first police official fired by
Teddy Roosevelt when he became reform police commissioner of New York City
after the Lexow commission hearings.[32]

Similarly, it was not unheard of for vice detectives to arrest respectable women
for prostitution in order to demand a bribe from their outraged husbands. Pickpock-
ets in New York City established monopolies on geographic areas, and police
helped them maintain their monopolies by arresting interlopers; in exchange, police
got information and money from the pickpocket monopolists.[33]

This picture of tolerance toward vice and cooperation with criminals should
not provide the picture of police as friendly Robin Hoods, stealing from the rich in
league with the poor. The police were, like the rest of the political machine, not
especially humane toward the lower classes that supported them with their votes.
The police were noted for their brutality toward lower-class individuals.[34] The
second policeman fired by Roosevelt was Inspector "Clubber" Williams, who
earned his nickname by breaking skulls in the working-class district of the Lower
East Side.[35] There was normal, routinized violence against criminals and vagrants,
and exceptional violence against workmen on strike. When the machine, in its

capacity as coordinator for the corporate elite, promised to put down strikes, the police were ready and willing to do so.[36]

Thus, the personnel practices, the organization, the crime-regulating routines, and the attitudes toward the public were all determined by the political responsibilities of the police department.

Judicial Administration

Similar constraints operated on other municipal agencies, but the court system was particularly vulnerable. During the nineteenth century, any man could hang out a lawyer's shingle with the approval of the courts. Since the courts were controlled by the machines, then the machines controlled the legal business as well. William Tweed used exactly this route to advance from a partner in a bankrupt chair-manufacturing firm to a partnership in a law firm.

Judges were also appointed not on their legal merits, but on their political loyalties. One of Tweed's most notorious judges, George Barnard, whose brother warned Tweed that "George knows about as much law as a yellow dog," had the habit of spicing his opinions with off-color jokes and obscenities and of whittling pine sticks during lengthy arguments by the counsel.[37] In this manner, machine bosses came to control several key judgeships, making their illegal activities much more difficult to prosecute. This control also fostered the great speed-up in naturalization of immigrants in New York. A judge, like a police patrolman, was first responsible to the political needs of the party machine; that requirement being met, it wasn't necessary to know the law or have good legal judgment.

Educational Administration

The surge of Jacksonian democracy in the early nineteenth century resulted in highly democratized educational administration. School boards of that era were very unlike those of today. They were highly politicized, with large numbers of school board members elected in partisan political fights. For instance, in Philadelphia, there were 42 local school boards of 12 members each; in addition, each local school board sent a representative to a very large city-wide school board. The school districts themselves were small, and generally coincided with the electoral districts of the political party. The superintendents of education were generally amateurs in the Jacksonian tradition, with no advanced technical education.

Because the school board members were elected on party ballots, only loyal party members were nominated and elected. Thus, party leaders were influential in the hiring and firing of teachers, just as they were for policemen, judges, and street cleaners. One school superintendent wrote in 1896, "Nearly all the teachers in our schools get their positions by what is called 'political pull' . . . Politicians wage a war of extermination against all teachers who are not their vassals."[38] In Philadelphia, it was the ward boss who was most influential in hiring the teachers, as was the case with patrolmen; the ward boss kept an eye on the school teachers by means of the janitor, who acted as a spy. The purchasing of school texts and school supplies followed the corrupt practices of the political machines, with purchases going to the highest briber at inflated prices.

Customs Administration

At the federal level, the effectiveness of boss politics on bureaucracy was also visible. One of the clearest examples is the administration of the New York Customs House. The Customs House collected more tariff revenue than the rest of the country put together. The collector of customs at New York was thus one of the most important bureaucrats in the federal government. Although the office was appointed by the President, the President generally deferred to influential members of Congress from New York in his selection. For this reason, the position "was fought over by contending factions in New York politics."[39]

Complaints about corruption in the Customs House were confirmed by a citizens commission in 1877. The men who worked in the Customs House received their appointment as patronage positions; they were "appointed generally at the request of politicians and political associations in this and other States, with little or no examination into the fitness of the appointees beyond the recommendation of their friends."[40] The commission found that, contrary to Jacksonian expectations, this method of selection was insufficient. The appointees were found to be frequently inept, lazy, and greedy. The presidential commission argued that "there can be no adequate protection in the customs service for the honor of the Government, the rights of importers, and the interests of the nation, until the service is freed from the control of party, and organized on a strictly business basis. . . ."[41] President Hayes courageously fired the collector of the port, Chester A. Arthur, a follower of the Senator Roscoe Conkling Republican machine. Three years later, the Conkling machine succeeded in getting Arthur the vice-presidential nomination under Garfield. When Garfield was assassinated by a man who had been unsuccessful in seeking a patronage appointment, Arthur became president.

Corruption at the Customs House seemed to be endemic, however. By the time Teddy Roosevelt was president after the turn of the century, it was still an issue, and Roosevelt instigated a trial of several sugar-refining companies in 1907. The trial testimony revealed that customs officials had underweighed shipments of sugar for years, defrauding the government of millions of dollars of duties on raw sugar. The sugar refineries had such a hold on the patronage appointment of customs officials, through cooperative party leaders in Congress, that uncooperative customs weighers lost their jobs. The Secretary of the Treasury made the following diagnosis: "Unless the customs service can be released from the payment of political debts and exactions and from meeting the supposed exigencies of political organizations, big and little, it will be impossible to have an honest service for any length of time."[42] It was essentially the same prescription that the citizens commission had made three decades earlier: The administration of government must be divorced from the requirements of party politics. This became the primary theme of the Progressive reformers.

CONCLUSION

The Jacksonian democratization reform resulted in the creation of numerous new political and administrative institutions. These institutions, like all institutions, determined which political actors holding which political resources would have influence over political decision making. Ironically, the people who received the most influence under the Jacksonian institutions were not necessarily the most democratic forces. Party bosses and their corporate allies were able to use the Jacksonian institutions of the long ballot, the party caucus, and the spoils system to expand their hold over politics. This unintended consequence of the Jacksonian reform became the basis for the new reform movement which reached a peak after the turn of the century.

NOTES

[1] MATTHEW A. CRENSON, *The Federal Machine: Beginnings of Bureaucracy in Jacksonian America* (Baltimore: Johns Hopkins University Press, 1975), p. 174.

[2] DENNIS R. JUDD, *The Politics of American Cities: Private Power and Public Policy*, 2nd ed. (Boston: Little, Brown, 1984), pp. 18–19.

[3] PAUL P. VAN RIPER, *History of the United States Civil Service* (Evanston: Row, Peterson and Co., 1958), p. 36.

[4] VAN RIPER, *History*, p. 43.

[5] The story of the Tweed Ring and the County Courthouse is told in a lively and informative manner by Alexander Callow, *The Tweed Ring* (London: Oxford University, 1965), pp. 198–206.

[6] CALLOW, *Tweed Ring*, p. 166.

[7] WILLIAM L. RIORDAN, ed., *Plunkitt of Tammany Hall: A Series of Very Plain Talks on Very Practical Politics* (New York: Dutton & Co., 1963), p. 73.

[8] CALLOW, *Tweed Ring*, p. 59.

[9] CALLOW, *Tweed Ring*, pp. 173–177.

[10] CALLOW, *Tweed Ring*, pp. 31–32.

[11] RIORDAN, *Plunkitt*, p. 11.

[12] RIORDAN, *Plunkitt*, p. 4.

[13] RIORDAN, *Plunkitt*, p. 73.

[14] CALLOW, *Tweed Ring*, p. 8.

[15] ALFRED CONNABLE and EDWARD SILVERFARB, *Tigers of Tammany: Nine Men Who Ran New York* (New York: Holt, Rinehart and Winston, 1967).

[16] RIORDAN, *Plunkitt*, p. 14.

[17] ROBERT K. MERTON, *Social Theory and Social Structure* (New York: Free Press, 1957), pp. 77–78.

[18] RIORDAN, *Plunkitt*, p. 19.

[19] LINCOLN STEFFENS, *The Shame of the Cities* (New York: Hill and Wang, 1904), p. 105.

[20] HAROLD F. GOSNELL, *Boss Platt and His New York Machine* (New York: Russell and Russell, 1969), p. 280.

[21] GOSNELL, *Boss Platt*, p. 348.

[22] CHARLES O. JONES, "Joseph G. Cannon and Howard W. Smith: An Essay on the Limits of Leadership in the House of Representatives," *Journal of Politics*, 30 (1968), pp. 617–646.

[23] ROBERT M. FOGELSON, *Big-City Police* (Cambridge: Harvard University Press, 1977), p. 2.

[24] FOGELSON, *Big-City Police*, p. 24.

[25] FOGELSON, *Big-City Police*, p. 25.

[26] SAMUEL WALKER, *A Critical History of Police Reform: The Emergence of Professionalism* (Lexington: D.C. Heath, 1977), p. 11.

[27] FOGELSON, *Big-City Police*, p. 28.

[28] FOGELSON, *Big-City Police*, p. 32; see also WALKER, *Police Reform*, p. 24.

[29] WALKER, *Police Reform*, p. 22.

[30]THOMAS BYRNES, *Professional Criminals of America* (New York: Chelsea House, 1969).

[31]WALKER, *Police Reform*, p. 22.

[32]EDMUND MORRIS, *The Rise of Theodore Roosevelt* (New York: Coward, McCann, and Geoghegan, Inc., 1979), p. 491.

[33]WALKER, *Police Reform*, p. 22.

[34]WALKER, *Police Reform*, p. 15.

[35]MORRIS, *Roosevelt*, p. 491.

[36]WALKER, *Police Reform*, p. 15.

[37]CALLOW, *The Tweed Ring*, p. 136.

[38]DAVID B. TYACK, *The One Best System: A History of American Urban Education* (Cambridge: Harvard University Press, 1974), pp. 97–98.

[39]LEONARD D. WHITE, *The Republican Era: A Study in Administrative History* (New York: The Macmillan Company, 1963), p. 118.

[40]WHITE, *Republican Era*, p. 120.

[41]WHITE, *Republican Era*, p. 120.

[42]GOSNELL, *Boss Platt*, pp. 286–287.

CHAPTER 3

Progressive Reform:
Constituencies, Prescriptions, and Tactics

The heart of Progressivism was the ambition of the new middle class to fulfill its destiny through bureaucratic means.
Robert H. Wiebe, The Search for Order[1]

The party organization of the nineteenth century was a finely honed machine for meeting the needs of a variety of constituencies: corporations seeking franchises, tariffs, or other favors; immigrants seeking housing, information, or a sense of ethnic identity in a new world; local newspapers seeking support through public advertisements; the municipal work force seeking jobs through political patronage. Together, these constituencies were an effective political force protecting the patronage system and other linkages between bureaucracies and the party organization.

For the most part, new constituencies found it more advantageous during most of the nineteenth century to work within the institutional framework of parties, amateur legislatures, and spoils bureaucracies than to fight it. What group or coalition of groups had any reason to stand up to the political machine? What were the constituencies for reform?

THE CONSTITUENCIES FOR REFORM

It would have taken a farsighted political scientist indeed to picture the loose coalition of groups that were to support what was to be known as the Progressive movement in the beginning of the twentieth century. He might surmise that the groups who supported the few experiments in reform in the nineteenth century might serve as potential allies of the Progressives. There were two nineteenth-century groups in particular—the populists and the civil service reformers—that had promoted a moralistic attack on the undemocratic and special-interest character of the corrupt political parties. During the intense party competition of the 1880s and 1890s, both of these groups had acted as pivotal constituencies for achieving thin margins of victory for the Democrats and the Republicans. While after 1900 neither of these groups sustained the kind of political activism that characterized their heyday, the civil service and populist constituencies did serve as important allies to the core groups in the Progressive movement.

By the turn of the century, a new political administrative reform movement had emerged that wasn't satisfied with an isolated reformist victory; they saw the opportunity to transform the operation of government. The Progressive coalitions, in addition to the moralistic civil service reformers and the populists, included the growing power of middle-class taxpayers, small businessmen, and professionals of various sorts. The preferences of these groups were often sharply different, but there was enough overlap that they were able to work together to bring about a surprisingly effective transformation of public administration in the United States.

Populists

Populism was the name given to the agrarian political revolt of the South and West in the 1890s. The movement had been composed of farmers and small merchants who felt themselves the victims of railroads, bankers, and other large economic forces which often dominated the economies and governments of the western states.[2]

Responding to the Populist pressure, Congress created the first regulatory commission in 1887, known as the Interstate Commerce Commission (ICC). The bill that established the ICC was passed by midwestern and southern legislators in response to a two-decade crescendo of rural demands for effective railroad regulation.[3] Originally housed in the Department of the Interior, the election of Benjamin Harrison, a railroad lawyer, to the Presidency in 1888 led Congress to remove it from the Department and presumably from Harrison's influence. The first ICC chairman, Thomas Cooley, set the ICC off to an energetic, but false, start. Hard times in the 1890s, lack of support from Congress, and especially opposition by a Supreme Court dedicated to laissez faire, contributed to the decline of the ICC into a state of self-confessed powerlessness.

The Populists gathered to the banner of William Jennings Bryan, the Democratic candidate of 1896, but his defeat by the regular Republican William McKinley was regarded as the death knell of the Populist movement. After 1900, however, when Progressives began to call for effective regulation of the railroads, the Populists were an important part of their successful coalition in California, Wisconsin, Nebraska, and other western states.

Civil Service Reformers

Beginning after the Civil War, there was a small but growing number of people who saw the problem of patronage primarily in moralistic terms. They were often people like Senator Charles Sumner or George William Curtis, who had been emancipationists before the war and saw the patronage system as a source of villainy equivalent to the slavery system.

The nineteenth-century "gentlemen reformers," or Mugwumps, had little in common with the nineteenth-century Populists. The populists were rural and small-town Southerners and Westerners, often with little education and less money, whereas the "civil service" reformers defined their goal as putting the "best men" (generally upper-class or professional men) back in office in place of the party hacks. Historian Richard Hofstadter mentions that a few of these aristocratic reformers noticed "with bemused irony" a certain kinship of goals with the populist "masses"—both groups were opposed to the special influence of railroads, banks, and others in a corrupt political alliance with party bosses.[4] However, this theoretical kinship had no political significance until both groups were able to rally behind the banner of Progressivism after it was clearly defined at the beginning of the twentieth century.

Unlike the gentlemen reformers, Progressives thought it was insufficient simply to "throw the rascals out" and vote the "best men" back into office. Instead, they felt the institutions of government should be studied "scientifically" and the rules changed to make it possible for public officials to govern more effectively.[5] However, this modification in the reform program was one that the gentlemen reformers could easily live with, making it possible to enlist their support for the Progressive reform cause.

Similarly, in the western states, the Populists liked the fact that the Progressives were attempting to eliminate the special influence of railroad officials and other corporation leaders. A contemporary wrote that the reform movement was based on "the insistence by the best men in all political parties that special, minority, and corrupt influence in government—national, state, and city—be removed; . . . (and) the demand that the structure or machinery of government, which has hitherto been admirably adapted to control by the few, be so changed and modified, that it will be difficult for the few, and easier for the many, to control."[6]

Thus, two groups that had had nothing in common in the nineteenth century now were united behind the new coalitional banner of the Progressives. This coalition was possible only because the leadership of Progressivism altered both the goals of reform and its social acceptability. Hofstadter notes, "As the demand for reform spread from the farmers to the middle class and from the Populist Party into the major parties, it became more powerful and more highly regarded. . . . Above all, Progressivism differed from Populism in the fact that the middle classes of the cities not only joined the trend toward protest but took over its leadership."[7]

Middle-Class Taxpayers

Picture a middle-class professional or small businessman at the turn of the century. He is educated and has ideas about democracy that clash sharply with government run by party machine. He wants to believe that every vote has equal weight and that an intelligent person like himself has a chance to voice his opinion. Being a family man, he strongly supports clean, safe streets in the cities and wants his children to receive a good, sound education in the public schools. If he runs a small business, a further concern is fair and open competition with large corporations. Since he has high expenses and a moderate income, however, he does not want the burden of heavy taxes. For him, elections should be democratic and government administration should work efficiently to get the job done, much the way he handles his own business or profession.

But this turn-of-the-century, middle-class citizen is not very content. He sees that elections are fixed in advance, that a citizen might get beaten or killed by voting for the "wrong" party, that the streets are dirty and crime-ridden while his property is taxed to support idle street cleaners and corrupt police. To make matters worse, with the approval of the city government, the transportation company has just raised the price of riding to work, and other large corporations seem intent on using political influence to drive him out of business.

Not surprisingly, many middle-class citizens wholeheartedly agreed with Woodrow Wilson's 1887 description of what was wrong with government:

> The poisonous atmosphere of city government, the crooked secrets of state administration, the confusion, sinecurism, and corruption ever and again discovered in the bureaux at Washington forbid us to believe that any clear conceptions of what constitutes good administration are as yet very widely current in the United States. [8]

The middle class, however, saw these administrative inadequacies as one manifestation of a more fundamental political problem: Upright, solid citizens who know how to read and write and who may own a little property had been pushed out of politics. Government was dominated instead by certain wealthy individuals and corporations who used political bosses to manipulate the illiterate poor, a group that was continually expanding through immigration. "Nearly all the problems which vex society," wrote Wilson, "have their sources above or below the middle-class man. From above come the problems of predatory wealth . . . from below come the problems of poverty and pigheaded and brutish criminality." The political lightning rod of middle-class wrath was the party machines, which had harnessed the voting power of the masses to the wealth of the corporations, running roughshod over the democratic ideals of free elections and accountable administration.

The Urban Merchant Class

The urban merchant class had considerable economic incentive to support reform. While the party bosses were effectively supplying what the large corporations needed in the way of streetcar franchises from the city council, or tax breaks for the railroads from a state legislature, or a tariff from Congress, they were doing a less effective job of supplying the urban services that were essential to urban merchants. The merchants wanted clean streets, police protection, and fire protection so that their customers could shop downtown without worrying about mud or a pickpocket. Not that the bosses were immune to bribes from the merchant class; however, it was harder to arrange bribes from large numbers of small merchants than it was for a single corporate officer to arrange for a streetcar franchise.

What the merchants wanted, and what the Progressive reformers promised, was a system of public administration in which public amenities would be provided automatically, without bribes, by an efficient, routinized bureaucracy. The merchant class responded very favorably to the idea of public agencies programmed by hierarchy and rules and professional training to perform the functions they needed to conduct business profitably.

It was this merchant class that fought for reform of the New York customs office. They were infuriated by the constant need to pay bribes to get service from Roscoe Conkling's political hacks who were staffing the customs house from top to bottom. They were also infuriated by the fact that the political hacks were basic incompetents who spent a great deal of their time in blatantly political activity. The delays and confusion caused by the patronage staffing of the Customs House meant business losses to the urban merchants, and they were willing to support the reformers who challenged Boss Conkling and his corporate allies.[9]

The Post Office was another federal service that was of vital importance to the urban merchants. The postmaster's job was, of course, the classic patronage post, to be allocated by means of congressional sponsorship. When businessmen compared notes and found out that other people had experienced the delays and inadequacies that frustrated them, they funded reform investigations. These investigations noted that there were post offices "where bags of undelivered mail lay forgotten in locked rooms," and they found out that the reformed Prussian and British postal services were several times more cost effective.[10] While the corporate leaders were cool to post office reform, the urban merchants regarded it as essential.

When Teddy Roosevelt came from his South Dakota ranch to work for the Civil Service Commission in 1889, he won the hearts of many urban merchants by engaging in a running battle with the Postmaster General over reform of the Post Office. Roosevelt exposed cases of blatant partisan campaign work by postal employees in Baltimore and blatant inefficiencies and corruption by postal employees in Milwaukee, and blasted the Postmaster General for his continued attempts to cover up the problem. However, the Postmaster General had been the first Republican fund-raiser to raise significant amounts of the new corporate wealth for the 1888 Republican campaign, and therefore had the support of both the president and the Republican party leaders in Congress. Roosevelt therefore scored few successes as civil service commissioner, but he did begin to develop the urban merchant class support that was so important to him as President when he put the Post Office under civil service staffing.[11]

As important as the Post Office and Customs House were to the urban merchant groups, even more important were the urban bureaucracies. They were frequently very expensive and generally inadequate. When Democratic Boss William Marcy Tweed spend over $5 million on furnishings for the New York County courthouse, Republican Boss Conkling complained that "more money was spent for furnishings than it cost the Grant Administration to run the United States mail service, as much as the yearly cost of collecting the customs revenue."[12] So the urban merchants became primary supporters (although rarely leaders) of the Progressive reform of city administration.

Urban Social Reformers

A fifth element of the Progressive coalition was social reformers. This group, once again, had quite distinct goals from the other four elements of the coalition, but they could agree with the other elements on a reform agenda.

The social reformers sought a more effective way of guaranteeing a minimally decent life for the urban poor. Various upper-class altruists had made it their business during the nineteenth century to "visit" the poor, to pay for orphanages and "settlement houses," to fund relief for the "truly needy." However, there was an increasing perception by the end of the century that industrialization and urbanization were creating poor people systematically, and that traditional efforts could only modify the worst effects. There was also an increasing perception that urban political machines were a means of exploiting the poor rather than helping them.

This discontent with traditional social reform efforts led directly to new social reform movements that attempted to change city government. For instance, just before the turn of the century, a new organization called the Association for Improving the Condition of the Poor (AICP) was created. It believed that government reform was necessary; it demonstrated that the Tammany machine was mismanaging city money that was supposed to be used to operate public bathhouses for the poor. It also found that sickness was widespread because of the city's ineffective milk inspection. Leaders of the AICP included Dr. William Allen, who was influential in pointing out that urban merchants, the middle-class taxpayers, and the civil service gentlemen reformers could all benefit, as well as the poor, from more effective municipal administration.[13]

The Progressive Coalition

The question became, what should a reformed municipal agency or federal customs house look like? What kind of structure would facilitate prompt delivery of the mail, or neutral enforcement of the law, or efficient cleaning of the streets? The reformers pictured a government agency that would be very nearly the opposite of the Jacksonian standard: Where Jacksonian bureaucracy had been composed of amateurs, they would hire professional experts; where the Jacksonian bureaucracy had been informal and political, they would impose administration by formal, written rules; where the Jacksonian bureaucracy had been decentralized to geographic wards, they would require a centralized hierarchy.

The urban merchants, the professional middle-class, the rural Populists, and the northeastern gentlemen may seem to be a disparate and unlikely coalition. What is important is that, for their own reasons, they were able to unite behind a fairly consistent prescription for administrative reform.[14] This prescription, which seemed to promise the hope of effective urban services for the merchant class, reduction of taxes for the middle class, social services for the poor, and regulation of the railroads for the populists, is sketched below.

THE REFORM PRESCRIPTION: SEPARATING POLITICS FROM ADMINISTRATION

The most important aspect of the Progressive movement, as far as this book is concerned, was its prescription for administrative reform. While the article on the "Study of Administration" by Woodrow Wilson did not have much actual historical impact on the Progressive movement, looking back from our vantage point we realize that it represents the most articulate exposition of the Progressive prescription for reform.

Wilson and the Science of Administration

Wilson believed that democratic countries such as the United States had neglected the science of administration in contrast to the more authoritarian regimes of the European continent, which seemed to be much further advanced in their administrative theories and practices. Compared with the continent, American administration appeared amateurish and riddled with politics and influence peddling. While Wilson opposed the authoritarian character of continental regimes, he strongly believed that the administrative science of the continent could be profitably combined with the democratic ideals of America. Unlike many of his contemporaries, Wilson saw no obstacle to this marriage between democracy and scientific administration. "A free man," he once wrote, "has the same bodily organs, the same executive parts, as the slave, however different may be his motives, his services, his energies. Monarchies and democracies, radically different as they are in other respects, have in reality much the same business to look to."[15]

The reason democratic countries such as the United States had not developed a science of administration was the pervasive intrusion of politics into all areas of government, including the administration of policy. The use of administrative science to implement democratic political objectives thus depends on a careful differentiation, or separation, between politics and administration. While elections and legislatures must, of necessity, use politics to set societal objectives, the execution of these objectives must be accomplished by an administrative apparatus that maintains a strict political neutrality. Administration, therefore, must accept democratic political objectives as given and work only to elaborate their details in faithful implementation. "(A)dministration lies outside the proper sphere of politics," wrote Wilson. "Administrative questions are not political questions. Although politics sets the tasks for administration, it should not be suffered to manipulate its offices."[16]

Since administrators are supposed to be politically neutral, accountability is the first great goal of administrative science. Accountability requires administrative devotion to the goals set by the democratic polity. Administrators must be responsible to the elected political leaders by faithfully implementing their programs; administrators are not to be involved in deciding upon or imposing policies of their own. "Neutral competence" is the term used by Herbert Kaufman to best describe this role that administrators are supposed to play.[17] "Steady, hearty allegiance to the policy of the government they serve will constitute good behavior," Wilson maintained. "That policy will have no taint of officialism about it. It will not be the creation of permanent officials but of statesmen whose responsibility to public opinion will be direct and inevitable."[18]

Efficiency is the closely related second goal. By making administration politically neutral, the reformers believed it would be possible to copy the efficient continental mode of administration. Again, according to Wilson, it is the distinction between politics and administration that "makes the comparative method so safe in the field of administration." If a monarchist managed a bureau well, Wilson thought he could learn the monarchist's business methods without abandoning his own democratic principles. "He may serve his king; I will continue to serve the people; but I should like to serve my sovereign as well as he serves his."[19]

Thus, the purpose of the study of administration is greater efficiency—to carry out in the least costly manner the goals set by the political leaders. As Wilson states it, the purpose is "to rescue executive methods from the confusion and costliness of empirical experiment and set them upon foundations laid deep in stable principle."[20]

The New York Municipal Research Bureau

What separated Wilson from his contemporaries in 1887 was the idea that administration could and should be a science. Other reformers in 1887 were primarily moralists who thought it would be sufficient to "throw the rascals out" and replace them with moral men. Wilson's article was not very influential at the time; it wasn't until 1900 that Frank Goodnow, often called the "Father of Public Administration," wrote a major book which expanded on Wilson's themes.[21] Goodnow, like Wilson, stressed the goal of efficiency more than morality and claimed that efficiency could only be achieved by "scientific" observation and analysis. He attributed the failures of the party machines not to moral corruption so much as to a misunderstanding: "The adoption of the 'spoils system,' as it was called, was possible because of the failure to distinguish administration from politics."[22] Once the technical nature of administration was admitted and recognized, then someone could and should go to work developing "scientific" principles of efficient administration.

Goodnow's book, unlike Wilson's article, had a tremendous, immediate impact. Its impact was aided by the fact that the gentlemen reformers of New York City had succeeded in throwing the Tammany rascals out in 1900, only to see their mayor (Seth Low, president of Columbia) reform less than they had hoped. The reason for Low's inadequacies, according to Goodnow's followers, was the absence of a theory of administration to guide the actions of a mayor with the best of intentions. Three men, Dr. William H. Allen, Henry Bruere, and Dr. Frederick Cleveland, set out to remedy this failure by doing what Goodnow and Wilson had just talked about: scientifically observing and developing the correct principles of administration.[23]

These three men, known as "The ABC's," created the New York Municipal Research Bureau and helped develop what they firmly believed to be a science of administration. They did so by scrupulously detailed observations of the actual workings of government agencies, first in New York City, then by invitation to other cities, counties, and state governments around the country. They carefully detailed the inadequacies of party-based administration, showing how millions of dollars were wasted by corruption, by faulty purchasing plans, by unsound personnel practices, by haphazard accounting techniques. They created the idea of a municipal "budget" or plan for spending the revenues available to governments, and developed techniques of municipal accounting to determine if funds were spent according to the plan. As later reform mayors were elected in New York City and elsewhere, they had an opportunity to implement their ideas and demonstrate the improvements that were possible.

"A Strong Structural Likeness": Efficiency Through Structural Reform

Allen, Bruere, and Cleveland's early proposals were quite specific and concrete, suggesting to the City of Los Angeles in their 1913 study of that city's administrative methods that the Water Works should make purchases through the city's centralized purchasing agent and that the city treasurer should keep the city's revenues in banks where it could earn interest instead of sitting idle in a vault.[24] Increasingly, however, they came to see more clearly that there were fundamental principles of administration that were the foundation of their specific proposals. These principles had been hinted at by Wilson and Goodnow: creation of specialized offices, standardization and simplification of procedures, centralization of administrative authority under a single executive. As Wilson had written, "So far as administrative functions are concerned, all governments have a strong structural likeness; more than that, if they are to be uniformly useful and efficient, they *must* have a strong structural likeness."[25] Their attempts to clearly define and refine the ideal "structural likeness" continued for several decades, but a summary of the primary structural principles that they relied on throughout the period follows.

Trained "meritocracy." The people selected to staff government agencies should be hired on the basis of merit rather than by the spoils system used by the machine. The merit system relies on a system of tests to document the ability of the applicant and is institutionalized in a "civil service" system which designs and administers the tests. Wilson was an ardent supporter of the civil service and a president of the National Civil Service League, which advocated the broadening of the merit principle within the government. In 1887, just four years after the passage of the Pendleton Act which established a civil service system for parts of the federal government, Wilson argued that this act was the first step toward better administration:

> We must regard civil-service reform in its present stages as but a prelude to a fuller administrative reform. We are now rectifying methods of appointment; we must go on to adjust executive functions more fitly and to prescribe better methods of executive organization and action. Civil-service reform is thus but a moral preparation for what is to follow. It is clearing the moral atmosphere of official life by establishing the sanctity of public office as a public trust, and, by making the service unpartisan, it is opening the way for making it businesslike.[26]

Hierarchy. Wilson described the ideal organization as a blend of trained personnel and hierarchy: "a corps of civil servants prepared by special schooling and drilled, after appointment, into a perfected organization, with appropriate hierarchy and characteristic discipline."[27] A hierarchical organization, with those below subject to the authority of those above, is necessary to maintain the accountability of the public organization.

This principle of hierarchy, it was noted, meant that individuals must have hierarchical authority commensurate with their responsibility. As the New York Bureau of Municipal Research noted in its 1913 study of Los Angeles, "The head of the Bureau of Streets has the responsibility for the Bureau's results, but has not been granted adequate administrative powers."[28] That is, his position in the hierarchy did not let him direct the actions of individuals whose decisions would affect the conditions of the streets.

Increasingly, Progressive reformers came to believe that any fractionalization of administrative authority in a government would result in bureaucrats working at cross-purposes to each other. Consequently, they increasingly came to recommend that all lines of authority lead ultimately to a single administrative executive. As we will discuss later, the New York Bureau and other Progressives increasingly came to support budgeting, personnel, and other reforms that would increase the unity of the executive branch under a single chief executive—another major departure from Jacksonian administration.

Administration by rules. Once in office, officials are not given carte blanche to carry out policy as they see best; on the contrary, they are expected to administer within and through a system of rules which clearly guide official behavior. Wilson seemed confident of the ability of science to create a system of rules by which the routines of government could be administered, and this became the principal article of faith of the empiricists working at the New York Bureau of Municipal Research.

Organizational specialization.   Another element that led to efficiency, it was increasingly believed, was specialization among officials. The American civil service, which was so ardently supported by Wilson, worked toward this end from the start. While the British civil service system had created a body of generalists, who took "merit" exams on the classics, the Pendleton Act in the United States required that the exams be "practical in character" and oriented toward special skills that would be required of the officeholder. "A technically schooled civil service," wrote Wilson, "will presently have become indispensable."[29]

Not only were the individuals in an agency to be specialists, but the organization itself should embody a division of labor through a structure of sub-offices for different tasks. Progressive reformers, for example, focused a great deal of attention on the need for organizational specialization within the police departments. It was argued that special squads for investigation, vice, narcotics, and other purposes, each attached to the central department hierarchy rather than to the district station houses, would be able to perform these vital functions more effectively and efficiently. At the same time, reformers did not think that the police should have to spend most of their time censoring movies, operating ambulances, inspecting boilers, monitoring markets, or supervising elections. The reformers believed that these non-police functions were more efficiently carried out by other agencies.[30]

The promise of efficiency through a reorganization of functions into specialized offices became a hallmark of the reform movement, and one that politicians were quick to put to the electoral test. As early as 1900, a foremost Progressive politician, Robert La Follette, promised Wisconsin a more economical administration through reorganization. "I believe it will be possible to effect a material saving to the State, without any injury to the public service, through a reduction in the number and a reorganization of the force of employees in the public service."[31] Reformers believed that a reorganization of functions would reveal unnecessary, redundant personnel, which the correct organizational structure could eliminate.

Simplicity and clear-cut responsibility.   Two other battle cries of the Progressive reformers were simplicity and clear responsibility. The haphazard and often overlapping jurisdictions that characterized public administration were anathema. For administration to be efficient, wrote Wilson, "it must discover the simplest arrangements by which responsibility can be unmistakably fixed upon officials."[32] One way of achieving clear lines of responsibility is centralization. Administrative authority should not be divided or obscured, for then it becomes irresponsible. Heads of departments and divisions must have single authority over their operations, and in this manner, the public may more easily watch and call them to account if necessary.

Again and again throughout the Progressive period and afterward, organizational reform based on hierarchy, a merit system, neutral rules, specialization, simplicity, and clear-cut responsibility was fought for as part of the reform program, especially by the Progressives who sought to transform local government and administration. "They envisioned the emergence of a professional public bureaucracy composed of socially conscious officials."[33] Progressive mayors elected in Cincinnati, Los Angeles, Cleveland, and elsewhere established an administrative pattern that included replacement of party hacks with professional experts in engineering, education, and public health; centralization of police and fire departments under a strengthened hierarchy; routinization of fiscal policy and accounting procedures through a system of written forms and memoranda; and a reorganization of governmental agencies on a more rational division of labor. The hallmarks of bureaucracy became the platform of Progressive reform.

TACTICS OF REFORM

While the Progressive prescription for a reformed agency was not completely rigorous or perfectly well defined, it is striking to look back from a vantage point nearly a century later to see how consistent the reformers were in their portrayal of a bureaucratic agency that was so different from the nineteenth-century standard. However, while the existence of a fairly precise reform prescription was a necessary condition for reform, it was hardly sufficient. The problem remained: how to get sufficient political power to implement their reform prescription.

The tactics used by the Progressives were many and varied. Sometimes they worked through the party system; sometimes they subverted the party system. Sometimes they concentrated on electoral victory; sometimes they sought to implement administrative reform from within the agencies. When they gained victory at one level of government (say, the cities), they would attempt to consolidate their power with victory at another (the states). Always they sought to change the rules when they could, so that they would have a better chance of getting power in future contests. The following array of tactics is perhaps the most striking example in American history of a political coalition self-consciously changing the rules of the game in mid-stream, knowing that changing the rules would change the outcomes of government.

Using Party Competition

The coalition of reformers that we identified above had not "gelled" before 1900, so there was little chance of a direct assault on the strong two-party system and its control of bureaucracy. However, the relatively few civil service reformers of the period were clever at turning the two-party competition to their own advantage by turning the parties against each other.

A fascinating example of this technique is offered by the original civil service act, the Pendleton Act of 1883. This act preceded the period of Progressive reform strength by two decades, and in fact was passed because of the dynamics of the two-party system rather than the strength of reformers. It was introduced in 1881 by the Democrats, who were hoping to get it passed in a form that would limit the patronage of the Republicans who had swept the election of 1880. The Democrats were especially interested in an anti-assessment clause that would have prohibited Republicans from assessing public employees a fraction of their salaries for future Republican campaigns.

The 1881 assassination of President Garfield by a disgruntled office seeker did little to change the shape of the party competition between the regular Democrats

and the regular Republicans. What it did do was provide the reformers an opportunity to exploit their position in the balance of power in numerous state and local
campaigns around the country. They campaigned against the Republicans for not
taking action on civil service reform. The margins of victory for the Republicans
had been razor thin in 1880 before the assassination, and the small reform opposition was sufficient to defeat Republicans in precisely those states where the reformers were most able to play the pivotal role: New York, New Jersey, Pennsylvania,
and Ohio.[34] Republicans lost control of the House, and the Senate was in a virtual
tie. The Democrats were correctly believed to be on the verge of taking power in the
White House in 1884.

Under these different conditions, civil service reform looked more attractive to
the Republicans. By passing a civil service reform act before the next election, they
could, in effect, give President Arthur (who was the successor to Garfield and an old
Customs House Republican) the right to tenure current Republican officeholders
before the Democrats could elect Cleveland into office. Democratic support for
civil service reform could still be guaranteed by including the anti-assessment
clause, prohibiting money raising among Republican spoilsmen. The Pendleton
Act was passed in 1883 on the basis of this mutually advantageous logroll between
the parties.

The original Pendleton Act was very limited in scope, covering only ten
percent of the federal employees, but granting the president some discretion in
expanding the scope of civil service. The party in control of the White House
changed in 1884, 1888, 1892, and 1896. In each of these transitions, the lame-duck
president would extend the scope of the civil service act, protecting his appointees
against the incoming president's appointment power. By 1900, almost half of the
federal employees were covered by civil service.[35] Reformers had leashed the power
of party competition to subvert the primary resource of party organization: the
patronage system.

Fighting the Party System with Party Tactics: Wisconsin

While Plunkitt believed that Progressives lacked the political know-how and
endurance to succeed themselves in office, Wisconsin is the most dramatic instance
proving this expectation wrong. Wisconsin state politics had been dominated by two
giant railroads, the Chicago and North Western and the Chicago, Milwaukee, and
St. Paul. Together with the lumber barons, these corporations successfully defended monied interests in the state through an alliance with the regular Republican
machine.

Robert La Follette had earned the enmity of these interests throughout the
1890s by "an unceasing attack on the party bosses, bitter, personal, violent, and
unavailing."[36] He seemed to be the model of the kind of reformer that Plunkitt
scorned: unwilling to compromise and too proud to search for votes through the
traditional techniques of the machine. However, by 1900 he had a strong following
in Wisconsin among farmers, university alumni, public officials, and Scandinavians. In that year, he put himself forward as a moderate gubernatorial candidate
capable of uniting the Republican party. Despite the fact that some of the state's
party regulars regarded his party-harmony campaign as a trick, he was able to
conciliate enough local Republican party officials to get the party's nomination and
win the election with the help of the party machine. Once in office, however, he

returned to his 1890s reform platform, fighting hard for two reform issues, one aimed directly at the corporations, the other at the party bosses.

The first issue was an ad valorem property taxation of the railroads to make them pay their share of the state's taxes; the second was a primary election law to replace the boss-dominated caucus-and-convention system. Here, the problems of reformers around the country were made evident: Despite the fact that La Follette had secured election, the legislature was still controlled by professional politicians who owed their political lives to the corporations and to the political machines. These groups fought the reform measures, confident that the reform movement would burn itself out with the election of a reform governor. La Follette himself was quite aware of the difference between electing a reform governor and passing reform legislation, and he was most aware of the difficulty of sustaining the reform effort. He confided to one of his supporters, regarding the primary election bill, "Give us this law and we can hold the state forever." He hoped that the passage of significant reform legislation would change the rules of the game sufficiently to make it possible for a reform movement to last rather than wilt on the vine.

During his first two-year term (1900–1902), La Follette was completely unsuccessful; neither of the reform bills he backed was passed. In 1902, he made the failure of these bills a major campaign issue. Unlike many Progressive reformers, he was able to dominate the Republican convention of 1902, get reelected, and see his program of electoral and economic reform passed during his second term and succeeding terms of office.

La Follette accomplished this seemingly impossible feat by beating the party regulars at their own game—he built his own political machine. La Follette's machine was based on many of the traditional elements of the regular machine: patronage, ethnic appeals, money from wealthy backers, favorable newspaper coverage, support from the court system, a thorough voter-mobilizing organization, and even strong-arm tactics. The Scandinavians formed a solid voting bloc for La Follette, and the Germans were assiduously courted with some success. Much of the financial backing came from Isaac Stephenson, a millionaire lumber baron of the sort that typically supported the regular party organization but who was disgruntled with the bosses for failing to reward his past support with a nomination to the U.S. Senate. His backing was secured in exchange for La Follette's promise to nominate him for a Senate seat, which he won in 1907. Stephenson was also instrumental in establishing the *Milwaukee Free Press*, which became an essential outlet for Progressive propaganda, battling the boss-dominated *Sentinel* of the same city.

While Progressives in other states felt a great deal of ambivalence and distrust of unions, the pragmatic La Follette was very friendly toward the Wisconsin unions, which supported him enthusiastically. As a result, the Progressive cause in Wisconsin was much more thoroughly committed to social programs such as safety legislation, workmen's compensation, and employer liability laws.

The "soldier" who walks the streets and gets out the vote became a third element in La Follette's success. The La Follette machine relied on patronage to recruit the soldiers, and the state government became the employer of Progressives during the La Follette administration. The most striking case of Progressive patronage was the state game wardens. "At election time the deputy wardens distributed pamphlets, posters, and sample ballots. In districts where close contests were expected, several of them would work as a team, calling on party members, getting out the vote, and even providing vehicles to take voters to the polls."[37]

Professors, students, and alumni of the University of Wisconsin formed another center of support. The reform emphasis on "expertise" instead of "patronage" as a basis for hiring attracted a number of university people. Ironically, patronage motivated the desire for jobs by the "experts": "The number of university graduates in state positions steadily increased [under La Follette], and the opportunity for college-trained young men to enter public service tended to become identified with the progressive cause."[38]

The university link became especially crucial as the election of 1904 neared. La Follette had just succeeded in forcing his reforms through the legislature, but there was a great deal of fear that if the elections went the wrong way, what had been done would be quickly undone by a new legislature and governor. As the Republican convention approached, the control of the convention would be determined by rulings regarding disputed county delegations. In order to keep the crucial decisions from being determined by bands of stalwart rowdies on the floor of the convention, the Progressives used their own "intimidators" to control the floor: "former university football players, professional athletes, and other husky characters."[39] These guards were successful in keeping all the machine backers except committee-approved delegates off the floor of the convention. This allowed the Progressives to so dominate the convention's proceedings that the machine Republicans bolted the convention to form their own rump convention. This event marked the final defeat of the machine politicians and the victory of Progressivism for the decade to come.

The case of Wisconsin proved that reformers did not have to be "morning glories"; they could succeed themselves in office. However, it posed a more fundamental dilemma to Progressives: They could beat the political machines at their own game, but in doing so, were they denying the principles for which they were fighting?

One answer to this question was that "the ends justify the means." Lincoln Steffens, the reforming muckraker of *McClure's Magazine*, wrote just prior to the crucial 1904 election that La Follette was using his power in the public interest rather than in the interest of the giant corporations.

Furthermore, although La Follette amassed a large amount of personal power as the head of a political machine, he did, in fact, risk that power in the interest of institutional reform. Having developed a state-wide patronage system, he then abolished much of it by instituting a civil service system; having amassed a great deal of executive power, he then divided it by creating nonpartisan, independent commissions to regulate railroads, industrial conditions, taxes, and forests. He also appointed strong, able individuals to staff these commissions, and to a large extent let them forge their own policy. Most striking of all, after achieving complete control of the party convention machinery, he continued to endorse electoral reform based on primary elections. Other bosses before and after La Follette had exploited the reform issue to consolidate personal power. Had he followed this course, La Follette might well be remembered as just another political boss rather than as a successful reformer.

It can be argued that La Follette's institutional reforms were not great sacrifices on his part. Even though state game wardens became civil service rather than patronage appointees, they still supported La Follette all the more strongly because their positions were more secure under civil service than the spoils system. The appointment of intellectuals to state commissions merely consolidated his support among the academic community. Since La Follette was not likely to lose an election under the primary law, his support for electoral reform, even after he had gained control over the state's political machinery, was no great sacrifice. Whether or not La Follette's institutionalization of reform was a sacrifice or a smart political move, the fact remains that his administration is a prime example of an attack on bossism through the boss's own tactics.

Attacking the Party System: Changing the Rules

Stephen Skowronek makes a convincing argument that after 1900 the reform coalition was, for the first time, strong enough to make a frontal attack on the party system. In his words, "At the dawn of the twentieth century, opposition to party bosses and imperious judges was being voiced by a number of reform movements that otherwise had little in common. . . . After 1900, the doors of power opened to those who saw a national administrative apparatus as the centerpiece of a new governmental order."[40] This resulted in a systematic attempt to change the rules of the electoral game to the advantage of their own coalition.

Of greatest importance was direct democracy, in which people voted and expressed their opinions without the intervention of political parties or big corporation lobbies. The creation of a modern version of town democracy, the reformers reasoned, required the destruction of these intermediate political organizations that stood between the people and their government. The political party and the corporate lobby, buying votes and perpetrating fraud, distorted the democratic process by elevating party, corporate, and private gain above the public interest. Average citizens saw their needs and preferences ignored, while the special interests profited handsomely.

The Progressives supported several measures designed to weaken the party-based political machine. At the polling booth, they advocated nonpartisan ballots, and in many cities party identification was left off altogether. They also demanded secret ballots in order to minimize the influence of party ward heelers on susceptible voters. As for the electoral system, the Progressives promoted the party primary as a means to democratize the nomination process and eliminate the influence of the party bosses. Another measure to circumvent partisan influence was the referendum or direct-voter initiative that merely required concerned citizens to collect a specified number of signatures for their proposals to be placed on the ballot. A related procedure was the recall initiative, which in principle could be used by citizens to remove corrupt politicians from office during their term. Furthermore, reformers advocated at-large elections for cities rather than ward elections where the influence of the party machine was strongest.

Not all of these reforms, however, had the desired democratizing effect that the Progressives supported with their rhetoric. A good example was the requirement that citizens permanently register before they receive the right to vote. These registration laws, advocated for the purpose of minimizing the possibility of corruption, also had the effect of disenfranchising a large number of immigrants and other lower-class individuals who could not satisfy the residency requirements. Some reformers even went to far as to directly advocate disenfranchisement for blacks, the poor, and the illiterate.[41] While mouthing the slogans of "direct democracy" and "rule by the many rather than the few," the consequences of many of these reforms worked to the benefit of a newly emergent and powerful special interest: the middle class.

Starting with the Grassroots: The City Manager Movement

Another political tactic of the reformers was to change the rules of the game most thoroughly at the level of government in which they were strongest: the local government. While it was often not possible to enact a wholesale transformation of a state government like Ohio or Texas, it was possible to systematically transform the rules in individual cities of a modest size, especially where the political machine was vulnerable because of an emergency or because of a growing middle-class population. When the opportunity arose, reformers would transform both the electoral system and the administrative system, generally to one of the model reformed institutions known as the commission or city manager form of government.

One of the early attempts to reform urban institutions was the commission form of government. A hurricane flooding the city of Galveston, Texas, in 1900 left 6,000 people dead, and the machine city government was totally incapable of handling the situation. The state legislature passed an emergency government plan for Galveston that created a five-person commission with combined legislative and executive powers. The governor appointed three members of the commission, while the citizens elected two members.[42] The plan met with such success that the commission plan spread rapidly among reform-minded, middle-sized cities.

The emphasis in each of these cities was on simplification as a means for achieving greater accountability. While citizens in noncommission cities often had to elect dozens of minor municipal offices (there were 334 names on the Chicago ballot in 1906), the citizens in commission cities elected and held accountable only five commission members. The commission members, as a group, made city-wide policy; individually, each commissioner was responsible for one of the five consolidated executive departments.

One reformer felt that this commission form of government, although an improvement over boss politics, had not gone far enough. Richard S. Childs, a leading Progressive reformer, was general manager of the Bon Ami Corporation. As organizer of the National Short Ballot Organization (the president of which was Woodrow Wilson), Childs campaigned against the long ballot with its numerous, minor elective offices, calling it the "politicians' ballot" because it played into the hands of party machines. While the commission form of government was consistent with the short ballot, the commission violated the Progressive principle of separation of politics from administration—the same commissioners both created and administered policy. Childs' response was the "commission-manager" plan, which constituted legislative authority in a commission or council and constituted executive authority in an appointed, not elected, city manager. Like the board of directors of a corporation, the commission would be responsible for policy definition and accountable to the voters, just as corporation directors are accountable to stockholders. The city manager would be responsible to the council for the efficient execution of its policy, much like the executive officer of a corporation. Said one supporter: The chief improvement of the plan "over previous commission plans is the creation of this city manager, thus completing the resemblance of the plan to the private business corporation with its well-demonstrated capacity for efficiency."[43]

Childs publicized this plan through the officers and staff of the National Short Ballot Organization, with several small cities in North and South Carolina adopting it early in 1913. The first large city to adopt the plan was Dayton, Ohio. Dayton had been a highly partisan city with administrative departments that were notoriously inefficient. When a flood in 1913 demonstrated the total incapacity of the city administration to deal with an emergency, John Patterson, the head of the National Cash Register Company in Dayton, took charge of emergency relief administration and was shortly thereafter elected to a reformed city council with the mandate to create a council-manager system. The city manager selected in Dayton, Henry M. Waite, set a pattern that was to endure for decades in that he was politically neutral, an outsider, and a civil engineer.[44] Waite announced, "I insist that when I employ men for work in my department that they be selected for their efficiency and not because of any political affiliation or in payment of any political debt."[45] He introduced centralized purchasing and centralized bookkeeping to decrease corruption and increase efficiency, and even administered a new public welfare program which the previous machine government had completely failed to do. The welfare program consisted of milk inspection, medical examinations for children, a municipal employment agency, and other services.

Waite became a public figure and did much to gain national publicity for the council-manager plan. By 1915, dozens of cities were switching to this form of government every year. Adoptions of this Progressive invention continued throughout the decade of the 1920s, and by 1928 a total of 364 cities were council-manager cities.[46] It is clear that much of its popular appeal was due to the congruity of the institution with Progressive ideals. The city council's complete authority over the tenure of the city manager seemed to ensure accountability. The fact that the city council members had no administrative responsibilities, while the manager had no political standing, seemed to ensure neutrality, and the manager's professional status was required to promote efficiency.

Reform through Executive Leadership: Teddy Roosevelt

While the typical nineteenth-century city government gave the mayor only weak powers, the federal government was only somewhat different. After the Civil War, the radical Republicans had instituted a system of congressional domination of the federal government which almost resulted in the removal from office of President Johnson. The theory, as stated by Senator John Sherman, was that "The executive department of a republic like ours should be subordinate to the legislative department. The President should obey and enforce the laws, leaving to the people the duty of correcting any errors committed by their representatives in Congress."[47] President Grant excepted the position as clerk and administrator to Congress, and, although succeeding presidents struggled against this view to various extents, it wasn't until Teddy Roosevelt, the Progressive successor to William McKinley, that something like a constitutional balance between president and Congress was restored.

Theodore Roosevelt was an ambitious reformer who found it useful to use the party organization when it was to his advantage and to turn on party leadership when that was more useful. In 1880, Roosevelt joined the Twenty-first District Republican Association in New York City and came under the tutelage of Jacob Hess, a New York politician identified with the machine. He was elected to a seat in the lower house of the New York State legislature. Although the youngest man in the legislature at the time, Roosevelt gained considerable publicity and reputation as a fearless attacker of the spoils system and other forms of corruption, and proposed several reforms for the government of New York City.[48] "Biting the hand that feeds you" became a Roosevelt strategy. How, then, could he survive through a long and successful political career?

Roosevelt followed a dual political strategy that both placated the party organization and generated popular support for his views among a wide range of groups. His policies were generally progressive, but he never failed to consult party organization men about appointments, legislative strategies, and other matters. In fact, when he was considered for nomination as Governor of New York, State Senator Thomas C. Platt, the chairman of the State Republican Committee, referred to Roosevelt as a party "regular." Roosevelt's main liability, of course, was his earlier effort to extend civil service reform when he was head of the Civil Service Commission; but, publicly declaring his support for the organization, Roosevelt became an "available" candidate.

In many respects, Roosevelt presented the organization leadership with a problem and an opportunity in 1898. The Republicans faced an uphill battle with the Democrats in the approaching election for New York Governor. Tammany had just won a sweeping electoral victory in New York City the year before, and the anti-machine Republicans had blamed Boss Platt for the debacle. The Republican machine had been hurt by discoveries of corruption in the regulation of the insurance industry. In addition, there was a growing independent movement in the cities. In New York City, the Citizen's Union, founded in 1897, served as a Progressive political organization for professionals and businessmen. These independent groups even put up candidates for office, and at times received middle-class and working-class support. Wooing these groups to the Republican cause became a dangerous game for the party machine, but one that Platt and other machine leaders reluctantly played for fear of political defeat. They had to support Roosevelt because his popularity with independents spelled the margin of victory in a close election.

Roosevelt's tactics in the gubernatorial campaign of 1898 both worried and pleased the Republican leadership. The candidate insisted on "stumping" the state, using hoopla and pomp to rouse popular support. He also grandly attacked the Tammany machine for its corruption and called Richard Croker, the Tammany boss, a crook. Roosevelt won with a 17,000 vote plurality out of 1,300,000 total votes cast. Ironically, Roosevelt's tactics, being extremely expensive, had to be paid through additional levies upon officials and officeholders in the Republican party. Since Roosevelt's plurality was thin, Platt boasted that he had "saved Roosevelt."

Once in office, Roosevelt used the resources of the power of the news media and the executive powers of the governorship to press his policies of reform. One early clash came over the Franchise Tax Bill, which required the taxation of public utilities, including franchises of street, railway, gas, electric light, and telephone companies. Roosevelt vigorously pursued this bill and got it passed over the opposition of the organization. He also used his veto powers and annual governor's message to gain support for his policies.

The consequence of these tactics was a further strengthening of the executive power over and against the legislature. This trend had already begun with the two governors prior to Roosevelt. Former Governors Morton and Black, for example, had sent special messages and supported successfully such measures as the Civil Service Bill, the Election Law, and the Supplemental Supply Bill. The difference with Roosevelt was more in style and confrontation politics. By working behind the scenes and keeping organization men in power, Platt and the machine had not felt overly threatened by these earlier reforms, even though they opposed them. Roosevelt's departure from past practice, however, was to make flamboyant appeals to the public and the press and to openly oppose machine preferences for spoils positions, thus popularizing reform ideas and discrediting the tactics and power of the organization. However, even these developments might not have mortally wounded the Platt organization, had Roosevelt not succeeded to the presidency.

After Roosevelt's first term as governor, Platt was determined to prevent a second term, but Roosevelt's enormous popularity made any frontal assault on his candidacy a foolhardy move. An alternative strategy was chosen which was designed to turn Roosevelt's attention from New York to national politics. Platt decided that the safest place for Roosevelt would be as vice president on the ticket with McKinley. Since vice presidents generally had little to do and only a minor influence on national policy, Roosevelt would be placed "in the wings" for the foreseeable future. The death of President McKinley one year later, however, brought Roosevelt "out of the wings" and onto center stage as the most powerful political figure in the country.

As president, Roosevelt continued to mobilize public support in order to counter the political influence of the bosses. A striking example of this came in 1903, when he concentrated public attention on a bill to regulate corporations. Public support forced Congress to pass the bill, when otherwise it would have given in to corporate lobbyists and party bosses who opposed the bill. Roosevelt used similar tactics to extend the civil service system, reform the New York Custom House, regulate the meat-packing industry, and resurrect the virtually defunct Interstate Commerce Commission. Roosevelt personified the belief that substantive reform went hand in hand with a strengthened executive branch.

"Eliminating" Politics: The Independent Commissions

One of the most effective political tactics of reformers was to remove certain aspects of policy making from arenas where they could not compete effectively with political parties to arenas where they had a competitive advantage. The "politically independent" regulatory commission was a structural form that could be created in moments when public support was high, and then would remain as an island of nonpartisan influence even when public support waned.

Although the Progressives did not invent the idea of an "independent regulatory commission," they did provide an ideology that justified the existence of an administrative agency outside the cabinet-level departments, and therefore presumptively "independent" of partisan political control. The Interstate Commerce Commission, which had become virtually an empty shell after McKinley's election to the presidency in 1896, changed radically with the coming of the Progressives, and especially the reform-minded Theodore Roosevelt. One of his first acts after taking office in 1904 was to ask Congress to strengthen the emasculated ICC. Throughout 1905, Roosevelt campaigned in the West and South for rate regulation; this campaign successfully culminated in the passage of the Hepburn Act of 1906, which "made the ICC, not the courts, the dominant government agency regulating railroads."[49] The increased responsibilities of the ICC were reflected in increased staff, which jumped from 178 persons to 527 in 1909. The first dramatic test of the ICC's ability to carry out its new regulatory burden was the Eastern Rate case of 1910–1911. The railroads had requested higher rates to reflect their higher costs after ten years of inflation. Western farmers, eastern manufacturers, and the public in general opposed the request, making the ICC hearings front-page news. The publicity surrounding this case engendered even more support for the Progressive cause, and further strengthened the ICC throughout the period up to World War I.

The Republican Party split in 1912 when the Progressive Republicans bolted the convention in Chicago and nominated Roosevelt as a third-party candidate. The Democrats nominated their own Progressive, Woodrow Wilson. Wilson took a strong position against the Progressive bugaboo: corporate monopoly. "I take my stand absolutely, where every progressive ought to take his stand, on the proposition that private monopoly is indefensible and intolerable."[50] Wilson's election led to the creation of the second independent regulatory commission as the preferred solution for the new reform administration.

Believing that the Sherman Act of 1890 had not resulted in sufficiently effective antitrust action, Wilson proposed a trade commission as "an indispensable instrument of information, as a clearing house for the facts by which both the public and the managers of great business undertakings shall be guided, and as an instrumentality for doing justice to business where the processes of the courts . . . are inadequate."[51] The Federal Trade Commission Act of 1914 met Wilson's demands for an independent regulatory body. Although the FTC had a vague mandate and moved slowly in its early years, it did undertake a major investigation of the food industry during World War I. The Commission discovered evidence of collusion among the five largest meatpackers, which led to a major political controversy and, ultimately, in 1921, to the transferral of the regulation of the meatpacking industry to the Secretary of Agriculture.

Government by independent commissions became a Progressive institutional reform at the state level as well as at the federal level. The state of Wisconsin was the first to demonstrate the usefulness of this form of government under the leadership of La Follette. La Follette's number-one administrative reform was the creation of a Railroad Commission to monitor a railroad industry that had dominated the state's politics as well as its economy for many years. It took La Follette five years to overcome the powerful political opposition of the railroads, but the three-person, nonpartisan Commission was established in 1905. It was given a wide degree of control over railroad rates and also over schedules, construction, maintenance, and service. La Follette appointed three experts to the board, who by all accounts did a highly successful, innovative job with a very difficult assignment. La Follette and the Progressives also set up a civil service commission, a state board of forestry, a state capitol commission, an industrial commission to monitor industrial safety, and so many other commissions that opponents claimed the government was run by commissions instead of by the legislature. The commissions performed much, if not most, of the work that transformed Wisconsin into a model for other states.

CONCLUSION

The theme of this chapter is that the Progressive reform movement constituted a purposeful coalition of constituencies who felt they could do better than they were doing with the nineteenth century style of party-dominated public administration. They were able to agree on a set of rule changes that they thought would better advance their interests, and pursued a disparate set of tactics to implement those rule changes.

While this chapter examined the "core" of the Progressive political coalition, the next chapter will examine two groups which were, in fact, close allies of the Progressives. These are the business advocates of scientific management, and the professional associations. While these groups did not generally identify themselves as fighting for the Progressive platform of electoral and administrative reforms, their goals were harmonious with those of the Progressives as regards the bureaucratization of government agencies. Indeed, one important explanation for the successful spread of the structural reform features of the Progressives was that their allies, often operating internally to particular government agencies, were able to institute those reforms *regardless* of the electoral successes of Progressive candidates.

NOTES

[1]ROBERT WIEBE, *The Search for Order: 1877–1920* (New York: Hill and Wang, a division of Farrar, Straus & Giroux, Inc., 1967), p. 166.

[2]NORMAN POLLACK, *The Populist Response to Industrial America* (New York: W. W. Norton & Co., 1962).

[3]ARI HOOGENBOOM, and OLIVE HOOGENBOOM, A *History of the ICC: From Panacea to Palliative* (New York: W. W. Norton & Co., 1976), p. 13.

[4]RICHARD HOFSTADTER, *The Age of Reform: From Bryan to F.D.R.* (New York: Alfred A. Knopf, 1955), p. 91.

[5]JANE S. DAHLBERG, *The New York Bureau of Municipal Research: Pioneer in Government Administration* (New York: New York University Press, 1966), p. 19.

[6]BENJAMIN PARKE DE WITT, *The Progressive Movement: A Non-Partisan, Comprehensive Discussion of Current Tendencies in American Politics* (New York: The Macmillan Company, 1915), p. 5.

[7]HOFSTADTER, *Age of Reform*, p. 131.

[8]WOODROW WILSON, "The Study of Administration," *Political Science Quarterly*, 2 (1887). Reprinted in *Classics of Public Administration*, Jay M. Shafritz and Albert C. Hyde, eds. (Oak Park: Moore Publishing Co., 1911), p. 5.

[9]STEPHEN SKOWRONEK, *Building a New American State: The Expansion of National Administrative Capacities, 1877–1920* (Cambridge: Cambridge University Press, 1982), pp. 68–82.

[10]SKOWRONEK, *Building a New American State*, p. 51.

[11]EDMUND MORRIS, *The Rise of Theodore Roosevelt* (New York: Coward, McCann, and Geoghegan, Inc., 1979), pp. 395–427.

[12]ALEXANDER B. CALLOW, JR., *The Tweed Ring* (London: Oxford University Press, 1966), p. 202.

[13]DAHLBERG, *The New York Bureau*, p. 11.

[14]WIEBE, *Search for Order*, pp. 160–169.

[15]WILSON, "The Study of Administration," p. 15.

[16]WILSON, "The Study of Administration," p. 10.
[17]HERBERT KAUFMAN, "Emerging Conflicts in the Doctrines of Public Administration," *American Political Science Review*, 50 (1956), 1057–1073; pagination is from reprint in *The Politics of the Federal Bureaucracy*, Alan A. Altshuler, ed. (New York: Dodd, Mead and Co., 1972), pp. 72–87.
[18]WILSON, "The Study of Administration," p. 14.
[19]WILSON, "The Study of Administration," p. 16.
[20]WILSON, "The Study of Administration," p. 11.
[21]FRANK J. GOODNOW, *Politics and Administration: A Study in Government* (New York: Russell & Russell, 1900).
[22]GOODNOW, *Politics and Administration, p. 111.*
[23]DAHLBERG, *The New York Bureau*, pp. 10–17.
[24]NEW YORK BUREAU OF MUNICIPAL RESEARCH, *Administrative Methods of the City Government of Los Angeles, California: Report of a Preliminary Survey of Certain City Departments Made for the Municipal League of Los Angeles* (Los Angeles: The Municipal League of Los Angeles, 1913), pp. 8–19.
[25]WILSON, "The Study of Administration," p. 15.
[26]WILSON, "The Study of Administration," p. 10.
[27]WILSON, "The Study of Administration," pp. 13–14.
[28]NEW YORK BUREAU OF MUNICIPAL RESEARCH, *Los Angeles, p. 8.*
[29]WILSON, "The Study of Administration," p. 13.
[30]ROBERT M. FOGELSON, *Big-City Police* (Cambridge: Harvard University Press, 1977), p. 52.
[31]ROBERT S. MAXWELL, *La Follette and the Rise of the Progressives in Wisconsin*, p. 90.
[32]WILSON, "The Study of Administration," p. 12.
[33]MARTIN J. SCHIESL, *The Politics of Efficiency: Municipal Administration and Reform in America, 1880–1920* (Berkeley: University of California Press, 1977), p. 151.
[34]SKOWRONEK, *Building a New American State*, pp. 65–68.
[35]SKOWRONEK, *Building a New American State*, p. 69.
[36]MAXWELL, *La Follette*, p. 13.
[37]MAXWELL, *La Follette*, p. 64.
[38]MAXWELL, *La Follette*, p. 59.
[39]MAXWELL, *La Follette*, p. 68.
[40]SKOWRONEK, *Building a New American State*, p. 165.
[41]MORGAN KOUSSER, *The Shaping of Southern Politics: Suffrage Restriction and the Establishment of the One-Party South, 1880–1910* (New Haven: Yale University Press, 1974), p. 229.
[42]BRADLEY ROBERT RICE, *Progressive Cities: The Commission Government Movement in America, 1901–1920* (Austin: University of Texas Press, 1977), pp. 1–18.
[43]SCHIESL, *Politics of Efficiency*, p. 174.
[44]LEONARD D. WHITE, *The City Manager*, (Chicago: University of Chicago Press, 1927), pp. 72–73.
[45]SCHIESL, *Politics of Efficiency*, p. 179.
[46]WHITE, *City Manager*, p. 126.
[47]LEONARD D. WHITE, *The Republican Era: 1869–1901, A Study in Administrative History* (New York: The Macmillan Co., 1963), p. 21.
[48]MORRIS, *Theodore Roosevelt*, pp. 159–182.
[49]HOOGENBOOM and HOOGENBOOM, *A History of the ICC*, p. 53.
[50]WOODROW WILSON, *The New Freedom: A Call for the Emancipation of the Generous Energies of a People* (Englewood Cliffs: Prentice-Hall, Inc., 1961), p. 105.
[51]LOUIS M. KOHLMEIER, JR., *The Regulators: Watchdog Agencies and the Public Interest* (New York: Harper & Row, 1969), p. 253.

CHAPTER 4

Scientific Management and Professionalism

The cultural triumph of Progressivism, which proved more lasting than its political victories, was inseparable from the rise in status and power of professionals in new occupations and organizational hierarchies.

Paul Starr, *The Social Transformation of American Medicine*[1]

The core coalition identified in the previous chapter fought for and won lasting political victories in a variety of local governments. The Progressive coalition's victories were just as complete in some western states, including California, Nebraska, and Wisconsin. In other cities and states, however, their political victories often remained incomplete or only transitory. In New York, for instance, reformers won a hard-fought victory when the voters became aroused over particularly blatant, machine-style corruption, only to lose power to party regulars in subsequent elections. Tammany Hall regulars said that the reformers were "mornin' glories"; they "looked lovely in the mornin' and withered up in a short time, while the regular machines went on flourishin' forever, like fine old oaks."[2]

Yet even in jurisdictions where reform never triumphed politically, administrative agencies often became more hierarchical, more staffed by trained experts, more immune to the influence of party regulars. How can this be accounted for? In large part, administrative reforms were often helped along by administrators themselves, who increasingly abandoned party machines in order to fight for job tenure, professional autonomy, and the status of the technical expert. In that regard, they were greatly helped by two movements that were distinct yet overlapped in time and membership with the Progressives: the scientific management movement and the movement for greater autonomy within the professions.

SCIENTIFIC MANAGEMENT

Woodrow Wilson had written that "The field of administration is a field of business."[3] Most Progressives agreed that government would be much improved if it could administer its affairs with businesslike efficiency. It is somewhat ironic, then, that one of the allies of the Progressives was a man who became famous for his claim that contemporary businesses were themselves not being run with businesslike efficiency.

Increasing firm size and technical specialization during the nineteenth century led to a need for greater coordination within the firm. The people who felt this need most sharply were those charged with the day-to-day problems of running the engines of industry: the mechanical engineers.

> With mechanization of production, the mechanical engineers came to acquire a strategic position in the social structure of enterprise. The foundation in 1880 of the American Society of Mechanical Engineers was an indication of the growing importance of this profession . . . many early publications and papers read in the ASME were dealing with ways of applying engineering principles . . . in the administration and organization of the workshop.[4]

The most serious, methodical, and influential movement to come from ASME was "scientific management." The movement was associated with one of the early presidents of ASME, Frederick Winslow Taylor, who, like many writers of his time, pictured the industrial organization as a great machine. Taylor carried this conception forward to a compulsive concern with the mechanical efficiency of each of the organization's component parts. One early research interest of his, for example, was the efficiency of iron work. He did experiments that demonstrated the superiority of a round-nose cutting tool to a diamond-point tool, showing that the most efficient cutting speed was precisely the speed of the round-nose tool. He also discovered that the right chemical composition of steel for the cutting tool could increase cutting speed by 700 percent. He thus became preoccupied with "the one best way" for doing each aspect of a task; this preoccupation led to 40,000 experiments in metal cutting over a period of 26 years.

But Taylor was concerned with more than just mechanical engineering. He wanted to improve the efficiency of the organization at its most fundamental level: the arrangement of individuals in the workshop, their supervisor, their materials, their incentive system. He became convinced that there was "one best way" of organizing the shop, if it could only be discovered. His basic technique for discovering the "one best way" of organizing was the time-and-motion study. He would break each task down into its "elementary operations" and then experiment with alternative ways of performing each operation. He would then use a stopwatch to find the most efficient method, applying the results to establish a standard for other workers.

His chart for observing handwork on machine tools included places for notes on the depth and length of each cut, how the tool was used, and with what effect. It included five categories for describing how the individual got ready to do the job, 15 categories for how he set the work, 7 categories for how he set the tool, 7 for extra handwork, and 14 for how he removed the work. Each element of every step was timed with a stopwatch and compared with the ideal time. All unnecessary movements were eliminated, and the time required for each element was reduced by proper positioning of materials. The total time standard was created by adding the ideal time for each element, plus any necessary resting time. (Studies were also done to see whether several short rests or few long rests were more efficient.) He effectively demonstrated that the same individual, working with the same tools and the same technology, could drastically reduce costs just by proper organization.

Taylor's study of hand-carrying pig iron from yard pile to freight car is one of his most famous time-and-motion studies. His guinea pig was a man named Schmidt, who was carrying about twelve and a half tons of pig iron a day, and getting paid $1.14 for it, at a labor cost per ton of 9.1 cents. Taylor did a series of tests on the effect of working pace, rest periods, method of handling the load, and method of compensation. One of his findings was that a man carrying 92 pounds of pig iron should be under load 45 percent of the day for greatest efficiency. By using the most efficient combination of such factors, plus a wage incentive, Schmidt began to carry forty seven and a half tons of pig iron a day, earning $1.85, while the labor cost per ton dropped to 3.9 cents.[5]

Taylor argued that both laborers and management could be made better off by the use of his scientific management techniques. Schmidt was earning more money on an incentive basis, and management was paying reduced costs. Taylor felt that the improvement of efficiency was the primary responsibility of management, which had in the past adopted no systematic approach whatsoever to the selection and training of employees. The training of a new employee often consisted of handing him a shovel and showing him where a group of men were shoveling coal into a furnace. Taylor also criticized management's traditional "rule-of-thumb" methods for supervising employees in the chain of command. Although the famous robber barons of the last century had amassed huge fortunes despite their unsystematic techniques, in the future he believed the competitive edge in business would be given to firms with scientific management skills. By showing how both sides could be made better off through increased organizational productivity, he foresaw an increasingly large role for trained, scientific managers, even in the area of labor–management disputes. In fact, as scientific management revealed the most valid pay methods, there would be no occasion for labor–management disputes: you can't argue with scientific facts.

Nevertheless, Taylorism made enemies in both camps. Employers often hated Taylor because he wasn't very diplomatic in pointing out that they had been poor managers at best, and stupid fools more often than not. They resisted his clear evidence that showed how they could improve profits by changing work conditions and incentives. They felt that their authority and discretion as entrepreneurs and owners of capital were threatened by this pushy engineer, who was, after all, nothing but a technician with no property or fortune of his own. His advocacy of careful, studious management seemed to them to be the opposite of the intuitive risk-taking that had so recently made millionaires out of J. P. Morgan, John Rockefeller, Andrew Carnegie, and others. Indeed, Taylor *was* advocating that the authority of capital be replaced by the expertise of the scientist, incorporated into general rules for management. This led him to quite explicit comparisons of "financier" as greedy villain versus engineer as hero, which did nothing to promote amity between the two.[6] Indeed, it was Taylor's interference with customary authority patterns that led to his being fired from Bethlehem Steel, where his system of scientific management had had its first trial.

An even more extreme degree of distrust existed between labor unions and Taylorites. The moral of Taylor's story about Schmidt, the pig iron carrier, was quite different as told by labor unions: Taylor was manipulating and exploiting workers, forcing them to work much harder for only a few pennies more a day. Even more importantly, Taylor was attacking the basis of the labor movement by saying that individual workers would be better off without union organization.

Taylor had no interest in trying to win unions over to his side. He was convinced that the worst problem facing management was loafing or "soldiering" among employees, and every one of his public statements on scientific management developed the advantages of his system as a way of eliminating this problem: "Incentives were important because man was naturally lazy and the worker had learned under most previous systems of management that it was not in his interest to work hard." Hard work, thought Taylor, was good for the worker as well as for the employer because it built the character of the worker. Taylor wrote, "Too great liberty results in a large number of people going wrong who would be right if they had been forced into good habits." Unions, according to Taylor, were instruments by which workers intended to organize opposition to hard work. "If Unions will compel their members to do a full day's work and compel every man in the union to learn his trade, then we will be with them."[7]

Although opposition from unions and industry was strong, Taylor did have one natural set of allies: the Progressives. The vehicle for the alliance between proponents of scientific management and Progressive reformers was the Interstate Commerce Commission. In the ICC's Eastern Rate case of 1910, railroad management sought rate increases and were supported by railroad unions; but eastern shippers hired a famous Progressive lawyer named Louis Brandeis, who used novel methods to oppose the increases. He claimed that the railroads would not need the extra revenue generated by rate increases if they would only use the new science of management being developed by Taylor and others. In fact, Brandeis promised to save the railroads a million dollars a day, giving his arguments front-page coverage in the daily newspapers.[8] Brandeis brought in engineer after engineer (naming them "efficiency experts") to describe how scientific management had profited other industries.

Scientific Management and the "Efficiency Craze"

Scientific management became a popular craze, and "efficiency" a cult. Efficiency societies were formed in all the large cities; popular books on efficiency appeared in stores. Harrington Emerson, the railroad expert, "offered a twenty-four-lesson home-study course in efficiency, which was to provide 'the short-cut to business success.' "[9] Even churches and universities formed efficiency committees, and the "principles of domestic engineering" were distributed to improve the efficiency of housewives. Melville Dewey invented the Dewey Decimal system for the sake of efficiency, and began to spell his name "Melvil Dui" for the same reason.

Progressive reformers were ardent supporters of the efficiency craze and of scientific management, and immediately began to propose that scientific management be used in government. Taylor's book, *Scientific Management*, was required reading at the New York Municipal Research Bureau's training school.[10] Government arsenals became an early governmental testing ground for Taylorism. However, the arsenals were also one of the early strongholds of unionism, and unions fought Taylorism by striking and by lobbying Congress, hoping to outlaw the use of the stopwatch and Taylorist incentive systems. The controversy surrounding scientific management from both the Eastern Rate case and then the arsenals led to a Congressional investigation into scientific management in 1911.

Taylor's testimony before the House of Representatives during this investigation came at a time when the Progressive movement was at its peak, and the similarities between Progressivism and Taylorism were immediately obvious. Both felt the opposition from the capitalists on the one hand, and from working-class organizations on the other. Both Taylor and Wilsonian Progressives believed in a science of management, based on the expertise of specialists; both emphasized structural reform of the organization as the means to greater efficiency. Taylor was in agreement with regard to the principle of hierarchy. Workers must "do what they are told promptly and without asking questions or making suggestions . . . it is absolutely necessary for every man in an organization to become one of a train of gear wheels." The value of such rules was that they created in potentially lazy employees "the habit of doing what is right."[11] Structurally, the Progressives and Taylor favored the same kind of organization.

Taylor proceeded to make the linkages stronger by speaking to the same "public interest" that Progressives counted on for support. Contrasting the public interest with the narrower interests of labor and capital, Taylor made it clear that the interests of the public would gain the most from scientific management: "It is inconceivable that a man should devote his time and life to this sort of thing for the sake of making money for a whole lot of manufacturers."[12] Says one observer:

> The role of the consulting scientific management engineer, upholding "science" in the factory against the narrow vision and vested interests of worker and employer, bore some resemblance to that of the middle-class reformer in society upholding the public interest against the pressure of both capital and labor. When Taylor invoked the public interest, scientific management was drawn toward that growing company of progressives who set the tone for the era.[13]

Scientific Management and Education

After the popularization of scientific management by the Eastern Rate case and the congressional investigations, scientific management played a dramatic role in aiding the Progressives and their fight for restructuring of public administration. An example of the impact of scientific management is the field of education.

Before the reform period, as noted in Chapter 2, administration of the schools was in the hands of large, politicized school boards. Party officials were influential in the hiring and firing of teachers, and the purchasing of school texts and school supplies followed the corrupt practices of the political machine.

In reaction against these corrupt political practices, a group of educational reformers sought to transform the American educational system. The members of the movement were mostly "business and professional elites, including university people and the new school managers."[14] The foremost goal of the movement was to "take the schools out of politics." The strategy adopted by the reformers was to centralize the school boards and thus to take power away from the local ward bosses. Once power was concentrated, then a process could begin that would delegate responsibility to professional "experts."

Centralization was the first order of business. School boards were reduced in size and individual board members were elected in at-large, city-wide elections rather than from political wards. This form of election kept control from the ward bosses and generally resulted in the election of business and professional people who had the resources and reputation to win the more expensive city-wide elections.[15] This result was seen as favorable to the reformers because businessmen were seen as being disinterested (having made their fortunes already) and capable of running the school district in a businesslike (and presumably efficient) manner.

When the scientific management craze hit the country in 1910, a wave of pro-reform criticism of schools filled periodicals and dominated educational meetings. The *Ladies Home Journal*, for instance, carried a series of articles in 1912 which argued that the country should be getting better results from the $400 million spent on education every year.[16] The severe attack threatened American educators, but also posed an opportunity. If educators could argue to business-oriented school boards that they were (or were in the process of becoming) the "efficiency experts" of education, then they could make the transition from low-status servants of the political machine to high-status professionals, administrators, and experts. As a result, "educational efficiency experts" began to appear in 1912, advocating "student efficiency tests" and asking students if they had "a regular schedule of study," took part in wholesome exercises, and took joy in school work. Experts, who were often professors of education, were called in to conduct hundreds of "school surveys" at hundreds of school districts. These "experts" asked two very limited questions: "What return is the community getting from its investment in the schools? How can the investment be made to yield greater returns?"[17] Although a few thoughtful scholars denied that these questions captured the sum total of educational experience, the school boards approved and justified this rather simplistic extension of scientific management from the factories to the schools.

In the name of educational efficiency, these experts advocated reforms that were based on nothing more than the manufacturing analogy. Students were called "raw materials," schools were called "factories," school officials became school "administrators." The platoon system, in which different squads of students held classes at different times during the day, was advocated on the grounds that businessmen would never conceive of using a manufacturing plant for only one shift a day.

Efficiency experts also developed and advocated the use of extensive record-keeping systems to demonstrate efficiency. These systems kept track of student attendance, teacher hours, and teacher salaries, and led to recommendations such as the abolition of Greek as a course of study, since the small number of teachers per pupil led to a very high cost for this language as opposed to other subjects. Lacking any real measures of productivity, efficiency experts were left with crude accounting measures as the basis for their "time-and-motion" studies. Similar considerations led to recommendations of larger classes, more classes and fewer free hours for teachers, and uniform treatment of students (no matter what their differences in needs).

Despite the dubious nature of their recommendations, efficiency experts had an enormous impact on the field. One of the most lasting effects was on the establishment of a profession of educational administration. With the claim (however weak) that educational efficiency was the legitimate basis of a "science of educational administration," the individuals who practiced that science suddenly could claim the same kind of professional status and autonomy that was being claimed by medicine and the law. Educational administration became a recognized area of study at universities between 1910 and 1920. The substance of educational study became much less philosophical and more technical at the same time. The imposition of a large body of routine record keeping led to the development of large school bureaucracies, and administering these large bureaucracies became itself a requirement of the educational administrator, a development which made educational administration simultaneously more demanding and more prestigious.

The ideology of administration taught at schools of administration was clearly in touch with that of the Progressives. The administrators were taught that accountability was one of the major goals of educational administration. Frank Spaulding, one of the giants of the new profession, taught that the "great lesson" which every school administrator must learn is that "the American school is a creation of the people; that the people control, and will continue to control, the administration of it. He will do well to resign himself to this situation; he will do still better to accept it with hearty approval."[18]

At the same time, however, that the ideology of accountability was being taught, the claim to "professional expertness" was providing the new educational administrators with reasons to demand some autonomy and discretion from the school boards. Administrators "used the business–industrial analogy to strengthen their position and defend themselves by arguing that to operate the schools efficiently, they, the experts, needed to have authority comparable to that of a manager of a corporation." Despite the weakness of the analogy, editorials in professional magazines argued that "the school board should delegate authority to its 'expert agents' because the educational problems were 'too complicated for untrained hands' and because 'conditions in school administration are similar to the management of a large business.' A man at the head of a big commercial enterprise is given a free hand."[19] This was a theme that was often repeated.

> By 1918 the idea of a separate profession of school administration was firmly established. To be sure, a decade later administrators were still engaged in the effort to convince themselves and the American people that they deserved a distinct professional status, but these efforts were made to reinforce and extend a domain, not to establish it in the first place. They had already convinced themselves and doubtless many others that they were experts and they had an increasing number of professional schools, programs, courses, and graduates to prove it.[20]

The development of this new profession depended on the centralization of the school boards and the corporate model of delegation and accountability.

> With centralization and the corporate model in the large cities came the growth of vast and layered bureaucracies of specialized offices, differentiation of patterns of schooling to the specifications of the new "science" of education, Byzantine organization charts, tens of thousands of incumbents protected by tenure, and many people within the city bewildered about how to influence the behemoth that had promised accountability.[21]

By basing their claim for professional autonomy and status on the analogy of the industrial executive, the fate and status of the new education profession came to depend on the existence of large, modern school bureaucracies. Indeed, the record keeping, the cost accounting, the coordination of the platoon system, more complete supervision of employees, the development of "tracking," and upgraded standards for teachers all lent themselves to larger bureaucracies. In education, as in other areas, the reform movement constituted a force for bureaucracy headed by a professional elite whose claim to legitimacy increasingly was based on its ability to manage bureaucracy. In 1900, the school official would have called himself a scholar or an educational philosopher. After the Progressive era, he would learn to call himself a "school administrator" or "school executive."[22] Thus, (as Paul Starr says of the medical profession) the emergence of a new educational profession at the head of a new educational bureaucracy helped establish the "cultural triumph" of Progressivism, lasting longer than its political triumph.[23]

PROFESSIONALS AND AUTONOMY

The development of the profession of educational administration shows how one profession benefited from the scientific management ideology of expertness. It also suggests that the profession benefited from the Progressive support for administrative neutrality and a commission-manager form of governing. Moreover, what was true for education was true for most of the professions. Professions both prospered under the Progressive reforms and furthered Progressive structural reform within the bureaucracies that they came to dominate.

The Jacksonian era had been hard on the professions. The Jacksonian attack on "privilege" of all sorts had meant that state legislatures in this era had not been responsive to professional demands for licensing. After all, requiring a state-issued license to practice medicine or the law was equivalent to granting a monopoly franchise to a business; "public hostility gradually took its toll, and as the adherents of Andrew Jackson were moving into positions of authority, the bar associations were being ousted from authority."[24] The same thing could be said for the medical profession.

As the century progressed, another threat to the professions emerged in the form of the giant corporation. The corporate lawyers who appeared in the latter part of the nineteenth century were salaried business employees and not independent professionals.

> Many attorneys feared that they would become merely clerks, identified more closely with the businesses that employed them than with their fellow professionals. Perhaps some day all attorneys would be employees. Those who did not become employees . . . were worried that the corporations would take away clients or patients, or alter the conditions of practice so that they would no longer be able to maintain the traditional fiduciary relationship with the people who came to them for help.[25]

Engineers, seeking professional autonomy at the same time, felt a threat from the same source. "Realistically, the chief threat to professional independence lay with the great railroad corporations."[26] Some professional organizations sought to set membership standards in such a way that they would not be dominated by employees of the railroads.

Doctors also felt threatened. The morale of the medical profession had declined during the Jacksonian era, an era in which specialization was discouraged, education was unstandardized, and entrance to the profession was relatively open.[27] In the latter part of the nineteenth century, statistics show that physician earnings barely exceeded those of other skilled tradesmen, such as mechanics or plumbers. A doctor in 1888 lamented that ". . . a physician in this country can never possibly acquire by his toil the incomes readily made in other occupations now recognized as professions." As Paul Starr observes, "This would put most doctors at the lower end of the middle class."[28] The low fees for life examinations forced on doctors by the life insurance companies also challenged their professional autonomy. Even more threatening was the corporate interest in prepaid, fixed medical plans. "By the 1890s some corporations began to install medical-care plans for their employees, and mutual benefit societies sought to provide medical care for their members at a fixed price. The medical societies objected vehemently."[29]

At the same time, the professions felt a loss of control over their own membership. The numbers of physicians increased rapidly, growing faster than the population in the second half of the nineteenth century. Medical schools also proliferated, expanding from 52 in 1850 to 160 in 1900, while the population of the U.S. increased by only 138 percent.[30] As a result of conflict and rivalry between medical schools, state medical associations found themselves with decreased control over appointments to boards of medical examiners.

> The professionals wanted, in effect, more control over their own work. They felt that their status and power depended on their ability to control the quality and number of persons admitted to the profession and to maintain discipline. The professional wanted to create an abstract standard, enforced by his peers or by the state if necessary, that would guide and hence stand between the individual professional and those who might otherwise have arbitrary power over him.[31]

To further professional interests meant, as it turned out, abandoning laissez faire, the dominant philosophy of the courts and the corporations, and advocating with the Progressives a more active interventionist role for the state. The unity between the professional interests and the Progressive political goals meant to one famous observer that the Progressive movement took on the nature of a "status revolution" of professionals seeking to rise out of the obscurity of the working class.[32]

This change in direction required the professionals to strengthen and reorganize their national and state associations. In 1900, the American Medical Association covered only part of the nation and had only 8,000 members. It became a national organization in 1901, and by 1910 could boast 70,000 members, half the physicians in the country. By 1920, it contained 60 percent of the physicians. The American Dental Association became a national organization in 1913. The American Bar Association also embarked on a series of reforms to establish a mass national membership and a unified national policy.

At the same time, professional associations began to appeal more vigorously for state action that would guarantee professional autonomy: "One of the primary aims of professional reorganization was to help create a licensing board where none existed or—where one already did—to tighten the profession's liaison with the board and to bolster its effectiveness. The greatest single spurt in the creation of new licensing boards in states across the country came between 1911 and 1915."[33] This period was, of course, the high-water mark for Progressive reform. Licensing boards, while creatures of the state, were generally controlled by the professions themselves, guaranteeing professional control of entrance and discipline.

As Paul Starr argues for the medical profession, the authority of professionalism became institutionalized "in a system of standardized education and licensing." Previously, a few individual doctors had wide authority and respect due to their intelligence and personality, but authority did not belong to the physicians as a group. Once professional authority became institutionalized, however, "authority no longer depended on individual character and lay attitudes; instead, it was increasingly built into the structure of institutions."[34]

For the physicians, institutionalization meant that medical societies controlled the standards and admission practices of medical schools and the medical examination for licensure; they made malpractice insurance and legal defense a direct service of membership; they fostered laws requiring that prescription drugs be approved by a physician; and they could threaten professional ostracism, which involved denial of hospital privileges and of referrals for specialists.[35]

One student of the professions explicitly links the professional demand for autonomy and the Progressive movement:

> The new attitude of professional associations toward the uses of public government was not only a reaction to the maturing of the industrial revolution but also both a cause and a symptom of structural changes in public government itself. In the last quarter of the nineteenth century, in many areas, certain business interests (particularly railroad interests) had gained almost monopoly power over political parties and hence over legislatures, the executive branch, and the judiciary. In that same period a pluralism of power was building up in the socioeconomic sphere. . . . The pressure of these many new groups wanting access undoubtedly played a major role in the 1910 revolt in Congress against the power of the Speaker and his controlling clique, a revolt that resulted in a diffusion of power and of access points in Congress.[36]

There is something of a paradox in private, professional associations demanding autonomy but using the power of the state through licensing boards to achieve it. However, this paradox of private power controlling agencies of the state is not rare.[37] The medical and legal professions found their control over the licensing boards to be the perfect solution to their problem, and the Progressive premises of expertise and separation of politics from administration were the political means to enforce that solution.

This congruence between the Progressive prescription for administrative reform and the political goals of professionals can be found over and over again, not just in educational administration, law, and medicine, but in a variety of other established or emerging professions. The rest of this chapter illustrates that in the area of social work, law enforcement, and the military, the Progressive imposition of a politics/administration dichotomy, combined with the Progressive equation of efficiency with expertise, allowed the development of new "public professions" where none had existed before. Time and again, the definition of professional expertise often consisted of the ability to manage bureaucracies; that is, professionalism in social work, law enforcement, and the military meant professional management of large, hierarchical, specialized organizations. Thus, the interests of the new public professionals required them to fight from within the agencies for the expansion and consolidation of the Progressive reform model of administration. With the establishment of public professions in social work, law enforcement, and the military, the professionals themselves carried out the work of administrative reform, regardless of the electoral victories of Progressive politicians.

Professional Social Work and Bureaucracy

During the nineteenth century, poverty was seen as being caused by intemperance or indolence, and the professional social worker was seen as an inappropriate person to rectify the moral lapse. Rather, the voluntary visitor from the middle class, giving advice and counsel in a friendly, guiding fashion, was thought to be the best cure for poverty.

> The paid worker, it was true, offered her skill, experience, and technical know-how to the poor, but the volunteer offered herself—and this offer of oneself was the only foundation upon which to build the friendship between classes which would avert the worst consequences of an urban-industrial society.[38]

Thus, as in so many other areas, nineteenth-century America showed a distinct bias toward the volunteer over the professional expert, and toward personalistic interaction over hierarchy and rules; and once again, it was the Progressive era that was to replace the former with the latter.

By the early part of the twentieth century, leadership in social service agencies already was shifting from volunteers with high social status to professionals with status based on their claim to expertise. As with education, professionalism was accompanied by the structural reform of the organization in such a way as to ensure hierarchical control of the organization by professionals.

> An occupational group, aspiring to professional status, had arisen with a future closely linked to that of the agencies. . . . To carve out a niche, the social worker had to attain hegemony within the agency; that task was facilitated by bureaucratic pressures nurturing professionalism at the expense of voluntarism.[39]

Social workers found the Progressive model of professional autonomy within a bureaucratic structure the ideal political vehicle for reversing the nineteenth-century pattern of volunteer domination over paid employees.

As in education, the first step was acceptance of the Progressive doctrine of a separation between policy and administration. This doctrine played a crucial role in the redefinition of the relationship between the professional and the amateur. In education, the politicized school board member had run all aspects of the educational process until the Progressive reforms provided support for administrative discretion by a trained professional. Similarly, in social work, the high-status volunteers had dominated social work through the board of directors of the various charities and settlement houses. The board members had participated actively in the administration and social work of the organization, and no sharp distinction had existed in the functions of the board members and their paid employees (although a distinction in status existed to the advantage of the volunteers).

In the Progressive era, however, professional social workers increasingly took the stance that high social standing and good intentions were no substitute for expert training and skills. According to Roy Lubove in *The Professional Altruist*, "The acceptance to this point of view was essential to the paid worker's professional aspirations. To some degree, her unrelenting emphasis upon efficiency represented an effort to win board support for her claims to technical competence and leadership prerogatives. No board member, as a trustee of other people's money, could dispute the desirability of efficiency as an agency goal, and the word served as a potent weapon in defense of professionalization."[40] This drive for professional autonomy coincided with the height of the Progressive reform movement.

In both education and social work, the administrative professional equated efficiency with professional autonomy (whether or not this was justified by the state of development of professional learning). "This bureaucratic imperative of efficiency linked with the professional subculture to limit and control voluntarism; in the eyes of the social worker seeking professional recognition, the agency goal of efficiency and her monopoly of treatment and administrative responsibilities were inseparable."[41] Despite the differences between party-controlled school districts and private charities controlled by upper-class society women, both succumbed to the ideology of bureaucratic efficiency and professional dominance during the Progressive years.

The important point for our purposes is that professionals saw the structural, bureaucratic reforms of the Progressives as conducive to their professional interests rather than inimical to them. In social work, the "quest for efficiency and administrative technique in social agency operations paralleled the caseworker's efforts to reduce the range of intuition, subjectivity, and unpredictability in her own work. In both cases the volunteer introduced an element of uncertainty. . . . Volunteer service conflicted with the administrator's desire for rational, efficient organization and the social worker's identification with the agency as a vehicle for professional achievement." The management of volunteers and the "triumph of bureaucracy was complete by the 1920s."[42]

As in education reform, the sustained success of the Progressives at the polls was not absolutely necessary for the success of much of their package of structural reforms. The structural features of bureaucracy had another proponent, and in the long run a more important one: the paid professional, who worked continuously for the features of bureaucratic organization because that form of organization was regarded as essential for professional autonomy and control.

Police Professionalism and Bureaucratic Reform

Although police departments were created in the middle of the nineteenth century in response to a series of ethnic and other kinds of riots, there is very little evidence that they were effective in controlling those riots. As Samuel Walker notes in his study of police professionalism, "The police did little to end mob violence. Violence continued to be a prominent feature of American life. Racial violence, industrial strife, and other forms of disorder continued with little interference from the police. A profound irony lies at the heart of American police history: the police had little effect on the very social problem that ostensibly brought them into being." What the police did do was become a source of patronage, muscle, and income for political machines. Because of this, police reform played an important part in the Progressive movement. Walker states, "In many respects, reform was an attempt by elite groups—especially business and professional interests—to break the power of the working-class based political machines that dominated the police."[43]

The Progressive reform of the police, like the reform of other institutions, centered around the simultaneous professionalization and bureaucratization of the police agencies. "Reform ideas that had enjoyed a fugitive existence at best over the previous thirty years suddenly coalesced around the idea of professionalization." For structural reformers, "professionalization meant streamlining the administrative procedures of the police department itself. . . . Many police reformers believed that the managerial style of the modern corporation, with its emphasis on efficiency and the ability to demonstrate results, was the proper model for the police. To this end they believed that administrative control should be centralized within the department and that police executives should exercise more direct control over the work of the patrolmen." Professionalism in police became identified with hierarchical control over subordinates. The professionals in policing, for all practical purposes, were the police administrators, not the patrolmen. Professionalism in policing, as in medicine, education, and social work, became identified with a bureaucratic structure of professionals over nonprofessionals. As Walker notes, "The dilemma of whether the police should be genuine professionals or simply bureaucrats also runs throughout police history in this century. . . . In the end, it was the police chiefs who became professionalized, not the patrolmen."[44]

The first leaders of the administrative reform movement within policing were the experts at the New York Bureau of Municipal Research. This agency introduced a style of police investigations that it called "nonpartisan" and "scientific."[45] The Bureau investigated at least seventeen major police departments around the country, finding identically deplorable conditions in all but Milwaukee and making identical Progressive recommendations. As the Bureau wrote for Reading, Pennsylvania:

> The police department has been a part of the political system, controlled by partisan affiliations, its appointments and policies influenced, its progress and efficiency impaired by political sentiment under the theory 'to the victor belongs the spoils.'[46]

Police professionalism required autonomy from this style of politics, and bureaucratic neutrality was offered as the safest haven for professionalism. Thus, in Reading and in the other cities which it visited, the Municipal Research Bureau recommended hierarchical centralization under a police chief, more sergeants for better supervision of patrolmen, "scientific" planning of patrol procedures, civil service, better training, clearer rules and regulations, and other bureaucratic features.

These reforms were initiated in city after city as reform mayors were elected. The structural changes that ensued were often overwhelming. However, the structural changes were not impervious to distortion by machine politicians. In 1913, for instance, Frank Hague ran as a reformer in the five-person city-commission form of government in Jersey City. Under the city-commission form, itself a product of Progressive reform, each commissioner was responsible for administering one area of city government, and Hague became the director of public safety. Walker says that, "Hague began to build his political machine by 'reforming' the police department." He centralized power under himself and gained complete control over civil service procedures for the police. He increased the number of police officers until, by the year of his departure as mayor (1940), the $3.55 million annual budget was almost three times that of comparable Rochester, New York. Jersey City had one of the highest property tax rates and lowest rates of patrolmen on duty of any city in the country: "Hague's use of the Jersey City police exposed one of the major limitations of "efficiency"-oriented police professionalization. In the wrong hands, the instruments of reform could become the basis of despotism."[47]

The pattern of structural reform followed by exposure of the durability and flexibility of the political machine was repeated elsewhere. When Judge Samuel Seabury investigated the New York City magistrates' courts in the early 1930s, it was obvious that the performance of the police department in the previous decade of Tammany Rule was not so different from earlier periods of Tammany rule, despite the Progressive success in shaping public opinion about the ideal modes of administration. Seabury's investigation "almost immediately uncovered a racket in which innocent women were framed as prostitutes by an alliance of police officers, bondsmen, lawyers, assorted court clerks and fixers, magistrates, and inevitably, the politicians in power who were responsible for political appointments around the lowest criminal courts in New York City."[48]

The same thing was true around the nation. The reform movement, according to Robert Fogelson, "fell short of its main objectives. Although the reformers weakened the connection between politics and policing, and ward leaders still had more to say than anybody else about departmental policies and practices. . . . The machine politicians proved to be formidable opponents. When they dominated city hall, which was most of the time, they could usually prevail on the authorities to sidetrack, postpone, or vote down the reform schemes. Even when the reformers took over, the politicians could generally count on their cronies in the police forces, prosecutor's offices, local courts, and other agencies to undo any inopportune changes."[49]

While the machine politicians had learned to make various kinds of accommodations with the structural reform of police, this does not mean that the reform movement had had no effect. The 1920s had seen the fulfillment of many of the structural reforms proposed by the Progressives: the emergence of "scientific policing" with crime labs, fingerprinting, and radio-controlled automobile patrolmen. Civil service had become nearly universal by the 1930s. It was possible to make a career in police work without worrying too much about political influence stopping a career or retirement benefits. According to Walker, in the 1870s and 1880s there were no policemen who had left the force because of retirement. Over 37 percent had resigned voluntarily, while the rest had been fired for one reason or another. By the 1940s, however, almost 78 percent of the police were leaving the force due to death or retirement. Most police recruits received some training before being put on the street; in-service training was even standard practice at some forward-looking departments. "The areas of progress . . . more accurately represented the bureaucratization of the police rather than professionalization. That is to say, police organizations became more complex, more elaborate, and more governed by impersonal rules of procedure."[50] The true professionals in the police force were the professional administrators.

The principal effect of the Progressive-era police reform movement was in changing the norms by which police departments were judged by the public.

> Although the reformers had not made much progress in their crusade to save urban America since the Lexow Committee investigation, they had profoundly influenced the development of the big-city police in at least one important though easily overlooked way. By the late 1920s and early 1930s they had transformed the quintessential principles of the Progressive movement into the conventional wisdom of the American people.[51]

The disclosures of continuing corrupt practices within the police department served merely to strengthen the public consensus regarding the applicability of the Progressive model of administrative reform as it applied to the police.

> But the consensus did generate a set of norms to evaluate the policies and practices of the big-city police and, by implication, to judge the integrity and competence of the policemen and politicians responsible for them. It also undermined the traditional assumptions about policing, discredited the policies and practices that derived from them, and in the process placed the ward leaders and their friends in the police departments on the defensive. In other words, this consensus laid the groundwork on which a later generation of reformers would attempt to transform the big-city police. More than the patrol cars, call boxes, and signal systems, and even more than the civil service, special squads and service pensions, this consensus was the enduring legacy of the first wave of police reform.[52]

This legacy became the foundation of later, more successful periods of police reform during the 1930s and 1940s.

The second wave of reformers, which appeared in the 1930s, was different in one important respect: They had worked their way up from the ranks, rather than by operating outside the police department in the style of Teddy Roosevelt, Reverend Charles Parkhurst, and other Progressive-era police reformers. The second wave of reformers were those who wanted to professionalize the police department because they themselves wanted to be police professionals. The progressive model of administrative reform served as a useful weapon for the professional reformers because the public had been educated to it, and because it was so consistent with their own professional aims. When a national uproar over crime arose in the early 1930s, the police professionals were able to use that issue, combined with the public's Progressive norms regarding the desirability of neutral professional police, to consolidate the bureaucratic autonomy and professional independence of police agencies.

According to Walker, "The sense of national emergency with respect to crime derived largely from a few spectacular and well-publicized crimes in the early 1930s."[53] These included the kidnapping of the infant son of Charles Lindbergh, and the crime sprees of the Chicago-style gangsters, including Pretty Boy Floyd and Baby Face Nelson. The police reformers were able to capitalize on this fear, as well as on the expectation of political change during the New Deal era, to push for further structural changes that consolidated the autonomy of police agencies from municipal machines.

In the 1930s, Fogelson says, the San Francisco voters approved an amendment to the city charter "that increased the chief's power at the expense of the police board." Similar changes followed in Atlanta, Los Angeles, and elsewhere. The police chiefs in those cities had always been subjected to intense pressures from politicians, pressures that had occasionally made them irrelevant in the ward-based scheme of politics and administration. Fogelson remarks, "But as a result of the reform movement they were fairly well insulated, and as the years passed, increasingly so, from the day-to-day meddling in departmental affairs that had been commonplace a generation before."[54]

However, it was just this day-to-day meddling that the politicians relied on as the basis for their influence with patrolmen and the public alike. The insulation which police agencies were increasingly getting decreased the ability of machine politicians to deliver on their promises of jobs and influence, further weakening their political influence in a downward spiral. Despite the erratic performance of reforming politicians at the polls, the Progressive reform ideology provided the basis for the increasing insulation of bureaucratic agencies from the influence of the political machines. The bureaucracies took on a bureaucratic life of their own, and reformers within the bureaucracies were increasingly able to proceed with their agenda of professionalization without worrying about the electoral success of any specific candidate at the polls.

Military Professionalism and the Bureaucracy

Although the Civil War produced a mass conscription army of over one million men, the postwar period saw the dismantling of the regular army down to the small size it had held after the founding of the republic. When the Germans under Bismarck handed the French a humiliating defeat in 1870, the American army consisted of only around 30,000 men and officers; by 1875, just prior to an era of violent industrial labor strife inaugurated by the railroad strike of 1877, the regular U.S. Army had shrunk to 25,000 enlisted men and 2,161 officers. Demilitarization dominated defense policy during this period up to the Spanish–American War.

The small regular army depended for its welfare on the operation of political patronage in the Congress: "The political significance of the tiny bank of regulars supported in peacetime rested largely on the pork barrel contracts and development projects its Washington staff would contribute to congressional constituencies."[55] The dependence of the army on the political machine meant that local interests, rather than national defense policies, dominated resource allocation. This situation angered many "military officers who had been catapulted to positions of power and prestige during the Civil War [and who] found that their total dependence on party strategy and electoral circumstances had placed them in a precarious position with dismal career prospects in the postwar era."[56] Many of these officers left the military and followed Ulysses S. Grant into politics.

Congressmen exercised influence through the bureaus of the War Department in Washington. Political patronage positions made up most of the bureau staffs. These staffs, under the leadership of the Adjutant General, held the power over line divisions where all of the regular army officers, including commanding generals, worked. The generals resented this political-civilian dominance of the national military organization, especially since the generals often found themselves relegated to rural and frontier army posts away from the urban centers in the East.

The degenerate state of the U.S. regular army and its officers led several intellectuals in the military to begin advocating dramatic reforms in military organization and policy. The reform-minded group, says Skowronek, sought "to establish the autonomy and integrity of the military profession and to institutionalize a place for it at the center of a new American state." These men saw the government's demilitarization policy as a "war on the army" brought about by amateurs who were ignorant of vital national defense issues. They argued that a standing army could not possibly threaten the viability of the democratic republic and proposed "thorough administrative reforms carried out in the name of professionalism."[57]

A prominent member of this group, Emory Upton, wrote two books arguing for the adoption of the Prussian model in the United States.[58] These books argued that the army needed to "bring the new professional elements into the center power." Since these books, and the discussions of them, framed the early debate over army reform, it is worth examining their proposals in detail.

Upton favored the creation of a General Staff that would have authority over line and staff functions and concern itself with long-range planning, coordination, and intelligence. He preferred that the president ignore the Secretary of War and go directly to the General Staff for military advice. The Commanding General of the regular army would preside over the General Staff and report directly to the president. Upton wanted legislation over organization and resources for the army to be prepared by planning experts at the General Staff and merely be submitted to Congress for approval. Professionals should maintain the authority over initiating budget requests and formulating legislation.[59] Further, Upton prescribed a professional education and merit examinations for military officers and upgraded training for enlisted men. He wanted to establish postgraduate schools in technical training and strategic and theoretical analysis.

But the regular army confronted a domestic competitor. The state militias, composed of citizen-soldiers who served part time, consumed the bulk of military resources in the settled parts of the country. Urban areas, in particular, depended on local militias to keep the peace and defend against attack; the regular, line army found itself posted to remote parts in troublesome frontier and Indian territories. Efforts to professionalize and centralize control over the regular army, and possibly even extend professional standards and control to the militia, confronted strong political opposition from state governors and other interests attached to the militia organizations.

Upton proposed, therefore, to concentrate power and penetrate central controls and standards throughout the country. He wanted to relegate the state militias to riot control and local issues. He did not want them to engage in front-line defense of any U.S. territory. In their place, he recommended an "expansible" national regular army of skeleton design that could be greatly expanded to full size and strength in case of emergency. Regular units would not come under the local supervision of militia commanders, as commonly occurred during this period. Prior to reform, the national army actually operated as a supplement to amateur, local militias. Upton wanted "all the units necessary for wartime [to be] organized by professional officers of the regular army and filled by regular enlisted men."[60]

Upton maintained that his program would not cost more than current arrangements nor involve a larger-sized army. He felt that the greater professionalism and efficiency of a national army could greatly increase defense capability without adding significantly to costs. His reforms would "internally integrate and externally insulate the army hierarchy; inhibit the establishment of long-term ties between politicians and officers; establish a multi-faceted and dynamic military career; and constantly ensure the highest-caliber talent for army leadership."[61]

The success of such a radical reform proposal remained politically impossible for the rest of the nineteenth century. The formation of the militias into a National

Guard represented the most formidable political opponent to army professionalism. Some elements within the Guard favored a national army reform program, but the impetus for joining forces with the army never got very far, due to local and state politics: "The party machines had packed the states' Adjutant Generals' offices with patronage appointees, leaving the militia top-heavy with political generals, disorganized at the line, and vulnerable to federal meddling."[62]

At the national level, the Secretary of War controlled the "distribution of war department patronage and had some access to troops on the line."[63] His office and the top bureau staff, therefore, constituted a second political opponent of army reform. In addition, the administrative branches developed close ties with the party machines in Congress, and in peacetime, "even the President's authority over the armed forces took second place to these horizontal relationships."[64] The General Staff idea threatened to dismantle these close ties between the military bureaus and the Congress.

Other army intellectuals, while supporting Upton's reforms in principle, argued that the structure of American democracy made it "impossible to organize and discipline an effective army from the point of view of military experts." Lieutenant Colonel James Pettit maintained that "our entire system of government, from the township to the White House, [is] based on partisan politics." He added that "one man power, the strong commander" could not be sustained under our system of partisan politics. Skowronek concludes that "From a turn-of-the-century professional's point of view, the most basic operating standards of the early American states—patronage appointment, pork barrel politics, and a radical devolution of authority—posed insuperable obstacles to national administrative organization."[65]

In spite of this political opposition, some limited advances occurred in the professionalism of the army prior to 1900. In 1878, army intellectuals founded a national military professional association called "The Military Service Institution of the U.S." The association also published its own journal entitled *United Service*. The army succeeded in setting up a specialized school at Fort Leavenworth in 1881 called the School of Application for Cavalry and Infantry. The army even established officer lyceums at every field outpost and in 1890 instituted examinations for promotion to ranks below lieutenant. One further success occurred with the building of new coastal gun batteries in collaboration with the growing U.S. steel industry. For the first time in peacetime, an alliance emerged between urban commercial interests, big industry, and the regular army.

With the successes of the Spanish–American War and the ascension to the White House of Theodore Roosevelt, the prospects for army reform grew brighter. In 1901, an executive order established the Army War College. The Secretary of War, Elihu Root, set out to restructure the entire system of military education leading up to the new college. In conjunction with these educational changes, Root sought to centralize administrative control over the War Department. He created new positions of assistant war secretary, a general staff, and a chief of the general staff directly responsible to the secretary himself. Finally, Root attempted to gain more national control over the state militias and raise their standards and responsiveness to the central headquarters of the regular army.

The Secretary of War followed a practical course to accomplish these objectives. He offered greater federal financial assistance and prestige to the local units in return for stricter federal enforcement of standards and control. His strategy for the

General Staff left its relations with the administrative bureaus ambiguous. In his arguments for the staff, he stressed the purposes of planning, coordination, and preparedness rather than management and control. Finally, Root informed Congress that appointments and promotions would be based on merit examination, not on the advice of Congress.

Some of these reforms did not survive after Root and Roosevelt left office. Congress had opposed the professionalization of the military all along. It joined forces with ousted or resentful officers in the War Department's bureaus to reinstate the position of Adjutant General and to reject the plan for a new National Guard under professional control. Still, the basic reforms remained intact, such that by 1920, "The institution that late-century military professionals scorned as a debased appendage of local interests and an all-consuming democratic politics had, in the intervening years, undergone an organizational, procedural, and intellectual transformation. . . . The army had become a powerful bureaucratic institution in its own right. . . ."[66]

In Paul Hammond's definitive work on the history of defense organization, he maintains that "it was only the professional part of the [German] system which its British and American supporters sought to borrow."[67] He suggests that the reformers had a blind spot for the politics of the new professionalism because they paid no attention to the relationship among the German general staff, the war minister, and the Emperor. What was the reason for this oversight of the relationship between the generals and the politicians?

> The answer seems to lie not, as it is often supposed, in the German background of the Army reforms, but in what was, though implicit, the most potent influence upon Root's own approach to reorganization in the Army: the American experience with large-scale business organization and the Progressive adaptation of it to government.

Hammond also believes that Root's reports of army reform "remain today the most definitive exposition on the theory of Army departmental organization available."[68]

The new-found strength of the professional-bureaucratic reformers in the army thus did not signal an end to politics. The transformation merely shifted partisan politics to a politics of interest groups and congressional committees in the orbit of the new bureaucracy. Skowronek concludes that "A tangle of authority arrayed around bureaucratic power defined the new institutional politics. . . ."[69]

INTEGRATION: THE PUBLIC PROFESSIONS

In all of the public professions examined in this chapter, similar histories of reform are in evidence. The foremost thrust of reform in each field was to remove the political influence of the machines, which was seen as the major obstacle to the development of professional expertise and professional autonomy. The success of professional autonomy was linked very early on with the model of bureaucracy, which was based on professional expertise and neutrality.

In each case, it was the administrators who were clearly "in control" of the profession, with teachers, patrolmen, and soldiers seen as subordinate to educational administrators, police administrators, and military officers, respectively. In the medical profession, doctors sought control of hospitals and clearly came to represent the basic authority in those institutions, despite the presence of other professionals, in particular the nurses and medical assistants. The system seemed geared toward obeying the doctor as the boss, with the other professionals as his employees.[70] Public professions, likewise, succeeded in establishing status and authority hierarchies in public agencies. Elite professional subgroups within the public professions controlled the top bureaucratic positions in the organizations, while the lesser professional subgroups occupied the employee roles. Professional success became identified with professional dominance of organizational hierarchies by members of a profession. As Starr documents in the case of medicine, it was this professional dominance of twentieth-century bureaucracies that ensured the "cultural triumph of Progressivism," more lasting than Progressivism's political triumph.

In summary, we have seen that the nineteenth-century civil service and depoliticization experiments had, by the turn of the century, joined forces with a progressive middle class of businessmen and professionals to push for broad, new concepts of expertise, accountability, and efficiency in government. This political movement benefited greatly from related societal developments in the professions and in scientific management. However, the leading progressive theorists also had envisioned a greater role for central management and planning through executive leadership, but this last component of reform did not take hold until the New Deal under Franklin Roosevelt and afterwards. In the following chapter, we examine the changing political conditions that made this next, major reform possible, and the consequences of the reform for administration. Together, these three reform milestones—the late nineteenth-century reform experiments, the Progressive reform triumph, and the New Deal consolidation—provide us with the essential dimensions of what we refer to today as the orthodox or classical model of administration.

NOTES

[1]PAUL STARR, *The Social Transformation of American Medicine: The Rise of a Sovereign Profession and the Making of a Vast Industry* (New York: Basic Books, 1982), p. 19. Copyright © 1981 by Paul Starr. Reprinted by permission of Basic Books, Inc., Publishers.

[2]WILLIAM L. RIORDAN, ed., *Plunkitt of Tammany Hall: A Series of Very Plain Talks on Very Practical Politics* (New York: E.P. Dutton & Co., Inc., 1963), p. 17.

[3]WOODROW WILSON, "The Study of Administration," *Political Science Quarterly*, 2 (1887). Reprinted in *Classics of Public Administration*, Jay M. Shafritz and Albert C. Hyde, eds. (Oak Park: Moore Publishing Co., 1978), p. 10.

[4]NICOS P. MOUZELIS, *Organization and Bureaucracy: An Analysis of Modern Theories* (Chicago: Aldine Publishing, 1967), p. 80.

[5]FREDERICK W. TAYLOR, *The Principles of Scientific Management* (New York: W. W. Norton & Co., 1911), pp. 42–47.

[6]SAMUEL HABER, *Efficiency and Uplift* (Chicago, 1964), p. 28.

[7]HABER, *Efficiency and Uplift*, pp. 20, 23, and 33.

[8]HABER, *Efficiency and Uplift*, p. 53.

[9]HABER, *Efficiency and Uplift*, p. 56.

[10]JANE S. DAHLBERG, *The New York Bureau of Municipal Research: Pioneer in Government Administration* (New York: New York University Press, 1966), p. 42.

[11]HABER, *Efficiency and Uplift*, pp. 20 and 24.

[12]HABER, *Efficiency and Uplift*, p. 29.
[13]HABER, *Efficiency and Uplift*, p. 28.
[14]DAVID B. TYACK, *The One Best System: A History of American Urban Education* (Cambridge: Harvard University Press, 1974), p. 126.
[15]TYACK, *One Best System*, pp. 127 and 128.
[16]RAYMOND E. CALLAHAN, *Education and the Cult of Efficiency: A Study of the Social Forces that Have Shaped the Administration of the Public Schools* (Chicago: University of Chicago Press, 1962), p. 51.
[17]CALLAHAN, *Education*, pp. 109 and 113.
[18]CALLAHAN, *Education*, p. 192.
[19]CALLAHAN, *Education*, p. 209.
[20]CALLAHAN, *Education*, p. 219.
[21]TYACK, *One Best System*, p. 176.
[22]CALLAHAN, *Education*, preface.
[23]STARR, *Social Transformation*, p. 19.
[24]MATTHEW CRENSON, *The Federal Machine: Beginnings of Bureaucracy in Jacksonian America* (Baltimore: Johns Hopkins University Press, 1975), p. 35.
[25]CORINNE LATHROP GIBB, *Hidden Hierarchies: The Professions and Government* (New York: Harper & Row, 1966), p. 36.
[26]EDWIN T. LAYTON, JR., *The Revolt of the Engineers: Social Responsibility and the American Engineering Profession* (Baltimore: Johns Hopkins University Press, 1986), p. 30.
[27]ROSEMARY STEVENS, *American Medicine and the Public Interest* (New Haven: Yale University Press, 1971), pp. 30–33.
[28]STARR, *Social Transformation*, pp. 84 and 86.
[29]GIBB, *Hidden Hierarchies*, p. 36; see also STARR, *Social Transformation*, p. 22.
[30]STARR, *Social Transformation*, p. 110.
[31]GIBB, *Hidden Hierarchies*, p. 37.
[32]RICHARD HOFSTADTER, *The Age of Reform: From Bryan to F.D.R.* (New York: Alfred A. Knopf, 1955), pp. 148–164.
[33]GIBB, *Hidden Hierarchies*, p. 42.
[34]STARR, *Social Transformation*, pp. 19 and 20.
[35]STARR, *Social Transformation*, p. 111.
[36]GIBB, *Hidden Hierarchies*, p. 45.
[37]GRANT McCONNELL, *Private Power and American Democracy* (New York: Vintage Books, 1966).
[38]ROY LUBOVE, *The Professional Altruist: The Emergence of Social Work as a Career 1880–1930* (Cambridge: Harvard University Press, 1966), p. 14.
[39]LUBOVE, *Professional Altruist*, p. 159.
[40]LUBOVE, *Professional Altruist*, pp. 164–165.
[41]LUBOVE, *Professional Altruist*, p. 160.
[42]LUBOVE, *Professional Altruist*, pp. 161–162.
[43]SAMUEL WALKER, *A Critical History of Police Reform: The Emergence of Professionalism* (Lexington: D.C. Heath & Co., 1977), p. 5.
[44]WALKER, *Police Reform*, pp. 53 and 56.
[45]WALKER, *Police Reform*, p. 59.
[46]WALKER, *Police Reform*, pp. 60–61.
[47]WALKER, *Police Reform*, pp. 69 and 70.
[48]HERBERT MITGANG, *The Man Who Rode the Tiger* (New York: Norton, 1979), p. 181.
[49]ROBERT M. FOGELSON, *Big-City Police* (Cambridge: Harvard University Press, 1977), p. 110.
[50]WALKER, *Police Reform*, pp. 9 and 135.
[51]FOGELSON, *Big-City Police*, p. 136.

[52]FOGELSON, *Big-City Police*, pp. 139–140.
[53]WALKER, *Police Reform*, p. 152.
[54]FOGELSON, *Big-City Police*, p. 176.
[55]STEPHEN SKOWRONEK, *Building a New American State: The Expansion of National Administrative Capacities 1877–1920* (Cambridge: Cambridge University Press, 1982), p. 86. Reprinted by permission of Cambridge University Press.
[56]SKOWRONEK, *New American State*, p. 89.
[57]SKOWRONEK, *New American State*, p. 89.
[58]EMORY UPTON, *The Armies of Asia and Europe* (New York: Appleton, 1878); and *The Military Policy of the United States* (Washington Government Printing Office, 1904).
[59]SKOWRONEK, *New American State*, p. 90.
[60]SKOWRONEK, *New American State*, p. 91.
[61]SKOWRONEK, *New American State*, p. 90.
[62]SKOWRONEK, *New American State*, p. 96.
[63]SKOWRONEK, *New American State*, p. 96.
[64]SKOWRONEK, *New American State*, p. 97.
[65]SKOWRONEK, *New American State*, pp. 118–119.
[66]SKOWRONEK, *New American State*, p. 246.
[67]PAUL Y. HAMMOND, *Organizing for Defense: The American Military Establishment in the Twentieth Century* (Westport, Connecticut: Greenwood Press, 1961), p. 16.
[68]HAMMOND, *Organizing for Defense*, pp. 17 and 23.
[69]SKOWRONEK, *New American State*, p. 247.
[70]STARR, *Social Transformation*, pp. 131–140.

CHAPTER 5

Progressivism to the New Deal:
Reform Principles Become
the Administrative Orthodoxy

> The foundations of effective management in public affairs, no less than
> in private, are well known. . . . They have been written into
> constitutions, charters, and articles of incorporation. . . . What we
> need is not a new principle, but a modernizing of our managerial
> equipment.
>
> The Brownlow Committee, 1937[1]

Faltering electoral success for Progressive candidates after 1915 did not sound the death knell of Progressive Reform in American government. On the contrary, reform ideas and practices proved very resilient and capable of growth in spite of the continued electoral presence of traditional political machines. Even during the "rush to normalcy" of the 1920s, when political reform of every kind was suspect, much of the administrative machinery of Progressivism not only held its ground, but grew in importance. It was during the 1920s that the city-manager movement consolidated its hold on the middle-sized cities in the country, and the budgetary reforms of the New York Bureau of Municipal Research were most rapidly extended. The bureaucratization of the nation's school systems also continued at a furious pace. In 1921, the Budget and Accounting Act attempted to rationalize and routinize the federal budgeting procedure.

Congress, reversing its position of the nineteenth century, greatly extended the civil service under Hoover's administration to a new high of 80 percent of federal employment. In addition, the 1920s brought the transformation of the U.S. State Department. As late as Wilson's administration, the Secretary of State, William Jennings Bryan, had remained a firm believer in the patronage system. But the Rogers Act of 1924, which established a merit system for the State Department, and in fact created the new profession of Foreign Service Officer, changed these old practices.

Fundamentally, the reason why reform principles were extended and institutionalized after World War I was that *they served a political purpose for political actors faced with certain kinds of decisions.* Congress, interest groups, and administrators themselves found it politically useful to mold government agencies according to reform principles. By the time of the New Deal, even a president whose personal administrative style was fundamentally opposed to that of the Progressives found it politically useful to pay lip service to the established principles of what was by then called "administrative orthodoxy."

CONGRESSIONAL SUPPORT FOR PROFESSIONAL, NONPARTISAN AGENCIES

The most striking instance of a change in attitudes toward the Progressive reform model of bureaucratic structure occurred in Congress. In the nineteenth century, Congress had been an intransigent foe of civil service, and a strong force for personalism and party influence in the administration of the Post Office, the Customs Office, the military, and other federal agencies. Individual members of Congress relied on patronage as a reelection resource, and the party organizations represented in Congress wanted to keep the administration of federal agencies open to their partisan requirements. However, after the Progressive era, Congress' attitude toward public administration was completely different. It would have been hard to find a member of Congress who would have gone on record supporting patronage and partisan influence in administrative agencies.

Congressional support for reform was not just for speeches and public image—it was real. Members of Congress voted by large margins for extension of the civil service. They voted to extend the merit principle to the State Department in 1924 with the Rogers Act. They voted to give the President the organizational means to produce a comprehensive executive budget proposal in the Budget and Accounting Act of 1921. They further promoted the neutralization and bureaucratization of the bureaucracy by creating the General Accounting Office, the most effective watchdog for bureaucratic inefficiency, corruption, and partisanship. They passed budgets that allowed the hiring of professional experts in agriculture, commerce, labor, and a variety of other areas. The Hatch Act, passed in 1939, specifically prohibited federal employees from participating in the electoral activities in which postal employees and other federal agents had participated with such gusto in the nineteenth century. These were measures that indicated more than a cosmetic congressional interest in the bureaucratization of the federal government.

One might ask, however, what advantage did this bureaucratization hold for members of Congress that would replace the lost advantage of patronage? Civil servants could no longer work for the reelection of members of Congress or for the party in power. What could the professionalized civil servants of the twentieth century do for Congress that would take the place of direct electioneering by the patronage workers of the nineteenth century?

Serving Organized Interests

The new role for bureaucrats in the twentieth century was to provide efficient, particularized services to the emerging organized interest groups. There had been few organized interest groups engaging in electioneering in the nineteenth century. Farm groups would engage in social protest during hard times, then disappear. Professional groups had been weak or nonexistent since the Jacksonian era. Labor unions had also been weak, and relatively uninvolved in politics. A few of the most powerful corporation leaders had influence in politics, but their influence was primarily the influence of individuals of wealth and power, not as leaders of interest groups. The one exception to this pattern was the Grand Army of the Republic, the organization of Civil War veterans, which exercised enormous influence as the only large-scale, enduring organized interest group of the latter part of the nineteenth century.

This all changed drastically during the Progressive era. Each profession organized or strengthened its own professional association during this time. Corporations organized into trade associations that became actively involved in politics. Labor unions exercised more influence in politics. Women's groups were highly organized and active during the Progressive era.

Each of these groups articulated demands that involved the services of a federal agency. The veterans demanded the efficient delivery of service from the Veterans Bureau. The automotive industry and drivers demanded better roads. Women's groups supported the Children's Bureau.

The emergence of these organized interest-group demands implied that members of Congress could hope to get reelected by meeting those demands. However, meeting those demands, in turn, implied a professionalized, efficient bureaucracy; and, at least in the minds of most of the public since the scientific management craze, an efficient bureaucracy meant one that was organized according to "scientific" rules and staffed by professionals with civil service tenure who were given the opportunity to structure their organization in tidy, hierarchical, specialized offices. As a result, members of Congress found it more politically advantageous to fight for and support professionalized, "neutral" bureaucracies than to fight for control of patronage jobs in partisan bureaucracies.

This pattern spread throughout the government. The roads lobby, consisting of the emerging auto industry, contractors, and the American Automobile Association (formed in 1902) fought for federal aid to states for highway construction. The result was the first set of massive cash grants from the federal government to the states. This pattern-setting form of federal aid came with a congressional requirement: A professional bureaucracy of highway planners must be created in each state which received the federal aid. In response, specialized highway departments were created in each of the states at virtually the same time. Independent federal financing made these state highway departments largely autonomous from the rest of state government. Authority in the state highway departments came to rest with a professional elite of civil engineers who designed the roads. The benefits—to both legislators and bureaucrats—of creating a professionalized, neutral bureaucracy to meet the demand for good roads were clear and immediate.

Interest Groups Organized by Bureaucracies

The smart bureaucrat was the one who rode the crest of this wave—the bureaucrat who was able to convince Congress that there were political gains to be achieved by serving organized interest groups. Of course, the bureaucrat who could not point to an organized interest group constituency demanding his professional services was at a disadvantage compared to the bureaucrat who could. Several bureaucracies, therefore, went out of their way to organize constituencies when those constituencies were slow to organize themselves.

In 1912, for instance, when the furor over scientific management was still very much in the air, the Secretary of Commerce and Labor, Charles Nagel, organized a meeting at the Department offices of a large number of local business groups. The businessmen favored the establishment of a national conference of local business groups, so the Secretary obligingly sent out 2,000 invitations to commercial organizations for a Washington conference that Nagel called to order. The conference created the Chamber of Commerce of the United States, the leading national business lobbyist, and one of the leading supporters of the pro-business activities of the Department of Commerce.[2]

A similar history lies behind the formation of the Rivers and Harbors Congress (now called the Water Resources Congress), which is the primary national lobbyist for the Army Corps of Engineers. It consists of contractors, barge companies, and others who have a reason to gain by the projects of the Corps, along with individual officers of the Corps and members of Congress. The Corps officers themselves organized the Congress in 1901.

The government played an even more nurturing role in the creation of the Farm Bureau.

> The Farm Bureau, which is now the largest of the farm organizations, and the only one with a nationwide membership, was from the very beginning completely different from other farm organizations. For the Farm Bureau was created by the government. The Smith–Lever Act of 1914 provided that the federal government would share, with the states, the cost of programs for providing what have come to be called 'county agents,' who furnish farmers information on improved methods of husbandry developed by the agricultural colleges and the agricultural experiment stations.[3]

States often mandated that only counties which organized farmers into "Farm Bureaus" would get a county agent and other state aid. State organizations of farm bureaus created the national organization in 1919, called the American Farm Bureau Federation.

Interest Groups vs. Parties

Thus, one of the significant developments of the Progressive era was that national business, professional, and other interest groups began to exercise autonomous political influence in Congress for the professional services of government agencies. These interest groups, whether consciously or not, seemed to be in a competition with political parties for influence on governmental decision making. To the extent that Congress was led by party leaders, the individual interest groups had to get in line along with other interest groups to lobby those party leaders for the particular concerns of their organized constituencies.

It is not surprising, then, that new middle-class, professional, and business interests supported the overturning of party influence in Congress at this time. Concerned groups came to understand that they could win political power through organized action outside of the two traditional parties. Farmers, unions, professional associations of all kinds, mercantile interests, and other groups came to be identified not solely with one party, but rather with particular sets of policies that fostered their respective interests. What these groups wanted, according to Richard McCormick, "was governmental help in its own endeavors and restraints upon—instead of special favors for—its rivals."[4] By replacing centralized party influence, they could hope to increase the influence of decentralized interest groups.

The Progressive electoral reforms increasingly allowed a variety of middle-class and professional interests to be represented *outside of the party system*. The Progressives created a rationale for opposing the political party organization of the machine and encouraged new patterns of voting behavior. Voter turnout declined for the presidential election from 78 percent in 1880 to 56 percent in 1916. Comparable figures for the gubernatorial election were 62 percent to 48 percent. Ticket splitting also greatly increased. The number of counties in which the trailing Republican fell at least 5 percent behind the ticket leader increased from just over 4 percent in 1894 to just over 40 percent in 1910. Both of these changes have remained a permanent feature of American voting behavior to this day.

One of the effects of the attack on parties was to weaken the hold of party bosses on legislators, including members of Congress.[5] Individual legislators were also less beholden to party leaders in Congress because they had, by this time, less patronage to dispense as a reelection resource. Being a strong party member in Congress must have looked increasingly unattractive as the reform era progressed. Party-based voting in the House, which had been at 50 percent in 1897 after McKinley's resounding Republican victory, decreased during the reform era to 35 percent in 1905 and to 23 percent in 1911.[6] Legislators found it necessary to vote with their interest group constituencies rather than with party leaders.

The turning point came in early 1910. Joseph Cannon, since 1903 the dictatorial Speaker, had run the House through the absolute power to appoint committees and their chairmen and to determine what legislation got to the floor of the House. Individuals had to follow his leadership or lose the ability to serve their newly organized constituencies through service on the right committees and the passage of the right legislation. Representative Nelson of Wisconsin pointed out in 1910 that Republicans who had chosen their constituencies over loyalty to Cannon had been punished and "humiliated." "We are fighting for the right of free, fair, and full representation in this body for our respective constituencies. . . . We are fighting with our Democratic brethren for the common right of equal representation in this House, and for the right of way of progressive legislation in this Congress."[7]

The Progressive Republicans, voting with the Democrats, succeeded in passing a set of rules that kept the Speaker from controlling the flow of legislation through the chairman of the Rules Committee, and deprived the Speaker of the unilateral right to appoint House standing committees and their chairmen.[8] This significant rule change allowed for the development of the seniority system, by which members could hope to make a career in the House by serving on (and possibly becoming chairman of) committees of vital importance to their respective constituencies. Moreover, by stopping the party-controlled flow of legislation through the Rules Committee, the new system allowed for the development of the norm of reciprocity, by which members of each committee mutually deferred to other committees in their own policy arenas. All of these changes were crucial for the development of interest-group representation in Congress outside of the party system. As David Rohde and Kenneth Shepsle summarize it:

> Policy diversity grew within the Republican party with the rise of the Progressives, and the members also found that centralized power interfered with their individual goal seeking. This produced the revolt against Cannon and the redistribution of power within the House. Policy goals were not widely shared within the parties, so arrangements were designed over time to maximize the ability of members to satisfy their constituents and thus tighten their hold on their seats.[9]

Congress and Independent Regulatory Commissions

In the nineteenth century, reelection chances rose and fell with one's party. In the twentieth century, individual members of Congress increasingly felt that their reelection chances resulted from their individual success at pleasing interest groups in their own districts. The rise of modern interest groups thus presented an electoral opportunity to members of Congress; but they also presented a threat—what if different interest groups in one's congressional district demand quite opposite policies?

The Progressive institution of independent regulatory commissions provided an answer to the problem of cross-pressuring interest groups, which was a major problem for members of Congress during this era. Anti-business feeling reached a new height during the early Progressive years. By the time Wilson was elected in 1912, the time seemed right for another attempt at government regulation of unfair business practices. On the other hand, elements of the business community were strongly opposed to certain kinds of antitrust regulation. How might members of Congress deal with these cross-cutting pressures? The Progressives supplied one answer: *Let Congress delegate the problem to an independent regulatory authority composed of professional experts who would create policy according to scientific principles to maximize efficiency and effectiveness*; and, incidentally, it would get individual members of Congress off the hook.

The result was the delegation by Congress of regulatory authority to an independent commission, this time the Federal Trade Commission (FTC), with vague powers to investigate the operation of corporations and to regulate unfair trade practices. Unable to reach agreement between its anti-business and pro-business elements, Congress failed to specify exactly what the goals and procedures of the new commission should be. This meant that the FTC had to define for itself what its job was.[10] One of its few major investigations in the early years was of the food industry during World War I. It uncovered evidence of collusion among the five largest meatpackers. This led to a political struggle which, in effect, the meatpackers won. They succeeded in getting Congress to take regulation of meatpacking away from the FTC and transfer it to the more hospitable political environment of the Department of Agriculture. This confirmed the political wisdom of Congress's actions. Congress earned political benefits by creating the FTC to "do something" about business, but it also got benefits from meatpackers by protecting the industry from any serious regulation by the FTC. The delegation of regulatory powers from Congress to the independent agency allowed Congress to have it both ways, and the Progressive concepts of political neutrality and technical efficiency legitimized the entire process.

According to recent political scientists, this option of delegating difficult decisions to independent commissions has become a generalized pattern of Congressional behavior. Morris Fiorina argues that Congress normally chooses to legislate directly when the benefits are not mixed with costs, but that regulation allows Congress to escape the costs of cross-pressured decision-making.[11] As Matthew McCubbins argues, "Under circumstances of high conflict of interest, congressmen will prefer to pass the hot potato to the administering agency by delegating to the agency a large scope over the policies to be pursued."[12] However, it is worth pointing out that this delegation became standard practice only after the Progressives established the political popularity of government by professional experts.

EXECUTIVE SUPPORT FOR ADMINISTRATIVE REFORM

The period just before the Progressive era was the one in which the strength of the presidency was at its weakest in American history. President Grant had largely acceded to the view of the Republican Congress that the president should be primarily the chief clerk serving the congressional will. Most symptomatic of this condition was the fact that one of the chief constitutional rights of the president, the right to appoint federal employees, had been systematically handed over to members of Congress. Through senatorial courtesy and other extra-constitutional norms, the president was expected to hand out federal appointments as patronage positions to supporters of members of Congress. While presidents after Grant had struggled to reassert presidential prerogatives in this and other areas, their successes were quite limited. [13]

Several elements of the Progressive recipe for reform must have looked ideally suited to chief executives like Teddy Roosevelt, who were looking for a means to reinvigorate the presidency, the governor's office, and local executives. Roosevelt, long a supporter of civil service, had greatly extended it as president; but he struggled to keep presidential control over the Civil Service Commission. Furthermore, without completely denying the right of congressional party supporters to nominate their own supporters for the remaining patronage positions, he had insisted that the ultimate right of appointment was the president's.

It wasn't just civil service that was attractive to chief executives. Increasingly throughout the Progressive era, reformers at the New York Municipal Research Bureau, at state capitals across the country, and at the White House were agreeing that the structural principles of hierarchy and administrative vigor necessarily meant that the executive must be strengthened. This was welcome news to state governors, who had long been bound by Jacksonian-era constitutions that made them only the most obvious of many elected state administrators on the long ballot, and which had denied them effective control over budgets or state organizations. However, the ideas supporting more effective executive management confronted sharp opposition in Congress and among those Progressives primarily interested in economy and efficiency. Not until the New Deal did these ideas really take hold at the federal level.

The Early Executive Management Movement

The 1905 Keep Commission was significant primarily because it was the first reorganization commission to be created by a president without congressional sanction, although its recommendations and methods of operation reflected congressional interest in economy and efficiency through the elimination of duplication and overlap.

The Taft Presidential Commission of 1911, however, altered course and made "good administration" a prime concern of the president, not just the Congress. The Commission produced one of the first published reports in support of the idea that the executive departments should be grouped by function in an hierarchical arrangement, with the president as the natural head of the administration. It stated: "Only by grouping services according to their character can substantial progress be made in eliminating duplication of work. . . . Until the Head of a department is called upon to deal exclusively with matters falling in one or a very few distinct fields, effective supervision and control is impossible." Frederick Cleveland and the other notable commission members, W. F. Willoughby and Frank Goodnow, were "breaking new ground with notions of functional departmentalization in 1911." In a paper delivered in 1913, Cleveland wrote, "At this time what the country needs . . . is a real executive using the powers already conferred; leadership that will demand for itself a competent staff that may be used to keep the executive informed about what is going on. . . ."[14] Cleveland developed these ideas while serving as head of the New York Bureau of Municipal Research.

The analogy that served the reformers best was the large business corporation. The president would play the role of chief executive officer, while the Congress would be relegated to the role of the Board of Directors, with influence only over broad policy directives. According to Peri Arnold, the Commission took a "markedly strong and modern-sounding position on presidential power and authority over administration."[15]

Executive Management Continued in the Twenties

The banner of executive management was raised again in 1920, when Congress established the Joint Committee on Reorganization. Although the Committee was a congressional creation, it opted to ask the president to propose a reorganization plan rather than make its own proposals. The intellectual thrust of the committee came from Herbert Hoover, the Secretary of Commerce in the Harding Cabinet. Hoover had also heavily influenced the ideas in Leonard White's influential public administration text, where White describes reorganization based on "major purpose under single-headed responsibility."[16]

Similar to the earlier President's Commission of 1911, the Joint Committee went far beyond the older concerns of economy and efficiency. W. F. Willoughby testified on January 10, 1924, that the "goal of economy was minor compared to the necessity of government to be able to plan its future expenditures and competently recommend policy to Congress." Hoover also reiterated these views by placing the focus on "better comprehension" of expenditures and "long-view policies."[17] Their arguments centered on management and executive leadership, not on the economy focus of the Congress.

The recommendations of the Harding and Taft Presidential Commissions never had much impact on the operation of the executive branch. Congress was dead set against shifting responsibility for administrative oversight to the President, and also opposed an increase in the size of the presidential office. Even when Hoover eventually became President, the Congress defeated his proposals for reorganization. Hoover complained that "vested officials, vested habits, organized propaganda groups . . . surround Congress with a confusing fog of opposition."[18] He then argued for "much larger powers of independent action" for the president to bring about a real reorganization of the executive branch.

The proposals and work of the Presidential Commissions served as a foundation for a substantial public-administration literature in the 1920s. The people most identified with this literature are Frederick Cleveland, Leonard White, and W. F. Willoughby, all professors of government at eastern universities. Cleveland argued that, "The subject before us is that of organization—organization for efficient group action. Organization-for-group action is essentially an arrangement of the personnel of an associate body or society for leadership."[19] Cleveland also argued for institutionalizing executive leadership and reducing the influence of Congress over administration.

Willoughby and White reiterated Cleveland's call for a strengthened executive to serve as the focal point for managing the executive branch. Willoughby stated that, "within the administrative branch responsibility and power must be more strongly centralized and a more integrated system of administration services be built up."[20] He no longer believed that the doctrine of "separation of powers" was necessary; the problem was not oppressive power but weak and ineffective administration, which could only be improved through rationalization of the executive.

THE NEW DEAL: CONGRESS AND THE PRESIDENT REACH A NEW ACCOMMODATION

In many ways, the reasons that made reform models an institutional success during the 1920s were even stronger during the crisis of the New Deal. Those reformers who politically supported the New Deal's social ideology especially perceived the need for strong central planning and executive leadership, and this perspective emerged for the first time as a powerful political force at the federal level of government. In contrast, the New Deal also saw the Progressive reform ideology used by those concerned with government ineptitude to justify an extension of the powers of independent regulatory agencies, the final victory of civil service, and a renewed search for the ideal of scientific management. The inherent contradiction in reform ideology between independent and expert commissions versus strong executive leadership did not present reformers from aggressively pursuing advances in both areas. These administrative principles provided a way for the president and Congress to reach a new accommodation, a new constitutional balance in an era in which the rapid growth of administration threatened both branches of government.

The Executive Management Movement in the New Deal

The first three years of the depression under Hoover led to a crescendo of voices in favor of dramatically reorganizing the federal government to make it work more effectively. Just prior to Franklin Roosevelt's ascension to power, Herbert Hoover had proposed a significant reorganization of the executive branch along Progressive lines, but had been rebuffed in Congress largely because members thought Roosevelt should have a free hand to propose his own reorganization schemes. When Roosevelt took office, he had no staff assistants, and the Bureau of the Budget, which was the primary presidential administrative support unit, had only 45 full-time employees.[21] Many people, therefore, thought that Roosevelt would take up reorganization as his first priority of business.

Instead, Roosevelt initially ignored reorganization and management, at least as perceived by the orthodox tradition. During Roosevelt's presidency, the size and scope of the federal government grew dramatically. The New Deal administration created many new agencies, bureaus, and commissions, which became known by their acronyms and were referred to collectively as the ABC agencies. Nonetheless, Roosevelt seemed to prefer an unorthodox, almost chaotic approach to the executive branch. He created agencies that overlapped with other agencies' jurisdictions and fostered conflict among them. During his first term he hired over 250,000 people, only one-fifth of whom came under civil service. Roosevelt deliberately bypassed the civil service because "New Deal agencies needed to be organized swiftly and manned by sympathetic, specialized personnel."[22]

By 1936, however, it became much more politically attractive for Roosevelt finally to turn toward consolidating power in this growing bureaucratic sprawl. The growth in new agencies, plus the earlier proliferation of independent commissions, led many critics to complain of the crazy-quilt character of the federal government. They began to paint an undesirable picture of the president's management capabilities.[23] Roosevelt's response was the establishment of the President's Committee on Administrative Management.

The three members of the Committee were all veterans of the Progressive-era structural reform movement. Charles Merriam had been a Progressive candidate for Mayor of Chicago in 1911. Luther Gulick had been trained at the New York Municipal Research Bureau, and was a disciple of Frederick Cleveland during the period in which the New York Municipal Research Bureau was developing the principles of management; in 1921 Gulick had been appointed director of the Municipal Research Bureau's successor, the New York Institute of Public Administration. Louis Brownlow, the chairman, had been one of the country's first city managers and leading proponents of Progressive-style reform.

The Brownlow Committee, as it was known, produced a highly influential report on the administration of the executive branch. The Committee recommended six formal executive assistants for Roosevelt plus additional staff. It intended to create an Executive Office of the White House to enable a transfer of the Budget Bureau from Treasury to the White House and an expansion of budget planning. The Executive Office also would house the National Resources Planning Board to coordinate water and other national resources activities. The proposal would have abolished the Comptroller General, who provided Congress with pre-audits of agency expenditures. Instead, the budget clearinghouse function would reside solely with the Budget Bureau, allowing Congress only a post-audit of expenditures.

The Committee also recommended a major reorganization of executive departments and agencies that entailed grouping agencies by function under twelve major executive departments. The reorganization would incorporate such independent-minded bureaus as the Forest Service, the Army Corps of Engineers, and the Public Health Service. In addition, the Committee proposed to incorporate the independent regulatory commissions and public corporations into the main executive departments as regular divisional units.[24] The consolidations would have produced entirely new departments, such as the Department of Conservation and the Department of Welfare.

Finally, the Committee report recommended the creation of a single civil service administrator to replace the Civil Service Commission. It favored an expansion of the merit system and significantly higher salaries for civil servants. It recommended a revamping of the accounting system of the federal government and a streamlining of the rules for civil service.

The Committee's report, however, which came out on January 20, 1937, only four weeks prior to Roosevelt's "court-packing" scheme, was greeted by Congress with "shock and stupor."[25] Congress took the position that, "Since the location of a bureau often influenced its policy, the decisions involved something more than efficient administration."[26] The reorganization proposal thus intensified the institutional conflict between the Congress and the presidency for control of policy. Groups concerned about executive powers protested the strengthening of the presidency and compared Roosevelt to the European dictators, forcing him to publicly deny that he sought dictatorial powers.

Almost immediately upon its submission to Congress, interest groups sought exemption from consolidation for their favored agencies. Timber, farming, and range interests objected to moving the Forest Service into a new Department of Conservation; the American Medical Association rejected the proposal to move the Public Health Service into a new Department of Welfare; the veterans' organizations opposed moving the Veterans Administration into a cabinet department; labor unions opposed the appointment of a single civil service administrator in place of the Civil Service Commission; the Rivers and Harbors Congress rejected subjecting the Army Corp of Engineers to a National Resources Planning Board; and the "special interests surrounding the commission" fought the transfer of the Interstate Commerce Commission, as well as other regulatory commissions, into cabinet departments.

The interest groups "attacked the plan because it threatened their influence over government bureaus."[27] Most of them had "welded tight bonds with the federal agencies serving them"; yet for the most part, "these groups sympathized with the broader aims of reorganization; they merely wanted exemption for the particular function of special interest to them."[28] For example, by opposing the transfer of the Forest Service into the new Department of Conservation, these groups denied themselves the possible long-term benefit of an active Conservation Department.

More conservative opponents of the New Deal opposed any creation of a Welfare Department because they thought it would institutionalize welfare spending. These critics, including many Democrats, wanted economy to be a primary goal of the reorganization plan. They perceived the reorganization proposals primarily in policy terms, believing that the proposals would enhance presidential power and thus the social programs of big spending which characterized the New Deal. Richard Polenberg states that the members of the Brownlow Committee wanted "to remove the administrative obstacles that hindered Roosevelt's efforts to implement the New Deal."[29]

Given the strong political opposition to the initial report, the first reorganization bill went down to defeat, marking one of the lowest tides in Roosevelt's presidential popularity. Part of the reason for the defeat rests with Brownlow's tactics. He resolutely refused to bring any members of Congress into the planning of the proposal and instead presented it to the Congress as a finished package. He also insisted on complete secrecy and no changes in the report, raising unnecessary fears over the report's purpose and scope. At one point, Luther Gulick refused to discuss the details of the plans for reorganization, arguing that "We are not going into those details. . . . We are engaged as efficiency engineers."[30]

Two years later, however, Roosevelt's star was on the rise again, and he submitted renewed reorganization proposals, albeit ones that were markedly watered down from the 1937 version. The bill that passed went through quickly. It basically granted the president the right to submit reorganization proposals to Congress subject to majority veto in both houses. Through this procedure, the president secured the new Executive Office of the President, six presidential assistants, and the transfer of the Budget Bureau into the new White House Office. The bill also placed the National Resources Planning Board in the Executive Office, but its powers were curtailed compared with earlier proposals.

The modernization of the civil service system, higher salaries, new accounting procedures, and the creation of entirely new departments were dropped. Nonetheless, the Reorganization Act of 1939 began to implement the theories of the Brownlow Report and over the succeeding years other recommendations were passed. The Committee continued to make itself felt for a long time, despite an initial poor reception to its work.

The Brownlow Committee did not create a wholly new conception of administration, but rather forcefully argued for implementing the established doctrine of administration at the federal level of government. The members of the Committee proposed several concrete changes that accurately reflected the administrative orthodoxy of the time. Polenberg states that, "The program accurately represented the administrative theories of the Committee members; students of government had urged similar reforms for many years."[31] A student of the New York Municipal Research Bureau claims that the President's Committee "suggested to President Roosevelt certain administrative reorganizations following the principles evolved by the Bureau. . . . The Office of the Presidency became an embodiment of the philosophy of government which had evolved from the ideals and methods of municipal research."[32] Even the 1937 Report of the President's Committee states, "The foundations of effective management in public affairs, no less than in private, are well known. . . . They have been written into constitutions, charters, and articles of incorporation. . . ." The Report adds that, "What we need is not a new principle (of administration) but a modernizing of our managerial equipment."[33]

Although the Report concentrated on the problem of better management, it did not ignore the Progressive concern for accountability. The Report maintains that a stronger executive, supported by an adequate staff and modern budget, is the best way "of making good the popular will in a people's government."[34] The Committee wanted to make the national government "an effective instrument for carrying out the will of the Nation."[35] The positions reflected the propositions of Cleveland's paper delivered in 1913 which called for leadership to keep the chief executive accountable to the people. They also parallel the Progressive notion of direct democracy as first stated by Woodrow Wilson in the 1880s. The parallels are not surprising in light of the fact that some of the leading authors of the Report were, in fact, old Progressives.

Neither did the Brownlow Committee abandon neutral competence as the proper role for officials, but rather it made the extension of civil service a major tenet of its reform proposals. In many ways, therefore, the Report achieves for the federal government what the budget and city-manager movements had already accomplished in the 1920s for the nation's cities. By 1930, nearly 400 cities had adopted a city-manager form of government and this form had completely superseded the earlier, short-lived commission structure. In addition, the manager form was accompanied by arguments that a single manager better served "direct democracy" and the manager's expertise likewise served to improve efficiency.[36]

One member of the Brownlow Committee, Luther Gulick, joined with a colleague, Lyndall Urwick, to publish a series of articles on administration.[37] These papers, including in particular Gulick's "Notes on the Theory of Organization," became widely recognized as the fullest statement yet of the reform administrative model. The articles argue in favor of single-headed accountability, a single chain of command, simplicity, comprehensiveness, narrow span of control, and specialization by area, function, or process. The articles conclude with advice on organizing the chief executive's office in an integrated and comprehensive fashion, based on the kinds of activities which constitute management. Gulick used the now-famous acronym POSDCORB to stand for this integrated management structure; it stands for planning, organizing, staffing, directing, coordinating, reporting, and budgeting. These ideas were directly related to the principles developed by the New York Municipal Research Bureau during the early days of the Progressive era.[38]

The Brownlow Report culminated three decades of reforms, the various strands of which finally came together in the reform of the federal government's structure and procedures. Reform was never a monolithic movement; some strands of reform placed more emphasis on the executive, others on efficiency, and still others on accountability.[39] Nevertheless, these strands of reform are found in the earliest Progressive recommendations, both on the local and national levels of government.

These contradictory strands came out in the political debate over the 1937 reorganization bill. The most prominent professional opponent of the Brownlow Report was the Brookings Institution. In its criticism of the Report, Brookings emphasized the practical side of administration: "It denied that a 'single controlling principle' existed; reorganization must be pragmatic."[40] Brookings proposed to study individual agencies and their needs rather than impose a standard, top-down structure on the whole government. The Institution also preserved a greater role for the legislature and worried about the usurpation of executive power by the president. Despite these disagreements, Brookings did support a strengthening of the presidential office, especially in budgeting.

The reform model of administration was strongly identified with the Roosevelt administration and a partisan, New Deal philosophy of government. One significant step toward bipartisan acceptance of the reforms was taken during the Truman administration. The Commission of the Organization of the Executive Branch of the Government (known as the Hoover Commission due to the dominant role of its chairman, Herbert Hoover) was set up by a Republican Congress to "straighten out" the executive branch. But as Peri Arnold convincingly argues, the Commission's final recommendations produced a very different result.[41]

Chairman Hoover initially saw the Hoover Commission as a partisan instrument and even invited aides of the Republican presidential hopeful, Governor Thomas Dewey, to attend the meetings and sent copies of the Report to the Dewey Campaign Headquarters. With President Truman's surprise victory, however, the tone of the Commission changed. Truman decided to support the Hoover Commission because he perceived correctly that its recommendations were directed at strengthening the chief executive's power. For Hoover's part, he stayed with his views, expressed years earlier in the 1920s, in favor of a strengthened managerial presidency. Harold Seidman writes, for instance, that the Commission's report supported its presidential recommendations with "the hard core of the fundamentalist dogma" and clearly relied on orthodox or reform administrative theory to bolster its concept of a strengthened chief executive.[42] Chairman Hoover, in the introduction to the Commission's Report, states:

> The President, and under him his chief lieutenants, the department heads, must be held responsible and accountable to the people and the Congress for the conduct of the executive branch. Responsibility and accountability are impossible without authority—the power to direct. The exercise of authority is impossible without clear lines of command from the top to the bottom, and a return line of responsibility and accountability from the bottom to the top.[43]

Peri Arnold concludes that Hoover "envisioned a solution to the problems of the Presidency in his own orthodox, hierarchical model of organization." Hoover organized his study of the presidency "on what he (Hoover) would call an expert rather than a political basis."[44] Donald K. Price, a member of the Commission, also believed that the Commission contributed to "something approaching a workable theory on the fundamental nature of the Presidency." As a consequence, "the whole Republican Party came to share the assumptions and grant the legitimacy of the expansive, institutional Presidency."

Regulation in the New Deal

After World War I, there was a long period of economic prosperity and urban growth, leading to renewed public confidence in business institutions. The stock market crash of 1929 and the resulting Depression reversed all this. By 1932, dissatisfaction with American business leaders was widespread as revelation of stock-market shenanigans led to the public perception that business was responsible for the current mess.

As public demand for regulation of business rose again, the institutional mechanism chosen was, once again, the independent regulatory commission. Rather than having Congress write explicit laws that could be enforced through the courts, numerous new agencies were created and Congress delegated effective decision-making authority to the agencies. Once again, the Progressive ideals of a politics/administration dichotomy and administrative expertise were much used to legitimize this course of action, but the political advantages were also quite apparent.

The Supreme Court wrote in 1934 that the independent regulatory agencies were "created with the avowed purpose of lodging functions in a body specifically competent to deal with them by reason of information, experience, and careful study of the business and economic conditions of the industry affected."[45] For Congress, they also served the purpose of being easy objects of blame if the New Deal experiments should fail; indeed, many of the New Deal agencies were under threat of congressional dissolution. Nevertheless, Congress was not averse to taking credit for the agencies if they succeeded. At the same time, Roosevelt favored creating new agencies for his own political reasons. It was easier for Roosevelt to create new agencies, independent of the old cabinet-level departments and staffed with technocrats who were loyal to the New Deal vision of remaking society.

Thus, over and over again Congress chose to delegate broad grants of authority to regulatory agencies. The wording of the legislation was generally ambiguous, reflecting Congress's unwillingness or inability to make hard policy choices in certain areas. Instead, the typical statutes for a regulatory agency would require the agency to regulate in the "public interest, convenience, and necessity." Congress continued to "buy" the reform ideology of neutral competence by expert administrators because it was politically convenient to do so.

The Hatch Act and the Civil Service

As regards personnel administration, the New Deal began with a move away from the merit principle. In the staffing of the newly created New Deal agencies, FDR did not want to rely on bureaucrats hired under previous Republican administrations, who were generally felt to be hostile to New Deal ideas. He therefore arranged for the staffing of these new agencies to be largely outside of the civil service. After two years in office, sixty new agencies had been created with 100,000 new jobs, all exempted from civil service procedures.[46] As a result, the proportion of federal employees covered by civil service dropped to 60 percent, the lowest since Teddy Roosevelt's first term. Roosevelt simply hired these experts outside of the merit system. James Farley, FDR's Postmaster General, openly used patronage as a source of political support during the first term.[47]

This does not mean that the staffing of these agencies was opposed to the Progressive ideals of specialized expertise. The personnel officers of the New Deal agencies, especially the Tennessee Valley Authority, were often highly trained industrial personnel officers whose personnel work set new standards in federal agencies. Even more importantly, FDR relied more than any previous president on economists, agricultural scientists, and technicians of a variety of sorts. Said one presidential assistant, "For the first time, short of war, the government had tapped the moral and intellectual energies of the college-bred middle classes."[48] However, Roosevelt relied on partisan expertise rather than neutral competence as a principle of hiring.

Franklin Roosevelt also recognized the political attractiveness of the merit system, and continued to pledge his loyalty to that principle to the public and to the National Civil Service Reform League. Fraud and corruption were "surprisingly negligible."[49]

A variety of political pressures combined to reverse the trend after 1936. First of all, a variety of good government groups were publicizing the patronage patterns of FDR's first term, and receiving a good public response. In March of 1936, the Gallup Poll asked whether government jobs should be given to "those who help put their political party in office or those who receive the highest marks in Civil Service examinations?" and 88 percent of those responding supported the merit system.[50]

Furthermore, the Republican candidate for president in 1936, Alf Landon of Kansas, made a flat commitment to civil service principles. Roosevelt, worrying about losing votes on this issue, made several executive orders in the summer of 1936 that strengthened the use of the civil service registers in the appointment of postmasters and other positions.

After the 1936 election, Congressman Robert Ramspeck of Georgia, a strong supporter of civil service, rose to the chairmanship of the House Civil Service

Committee. From this position, Ramspeck was able to secure several key pieces of legislation that Roosevelt and the rest of Congress were willing to support.

The crucial event occurred with the midterm election of 1938. On this occasion, President Roosevelt decided to use his patronage powers to try to defeat Democrats in Congress who were not supporting his legislation. As news of this got out, it became clear to members of Congress that control of patronage was no longer in their hands; centralization of personnel administration in the executive branch meant that patronage was no longer a resource for congressional reelection *unless the president went along*. As personnel administration had become increasingly under presidential control, it had finally become a means for the president to control Congress, very nearly the reverse of the condition during the era of weak presidents and strong Congresses at the end of the nineteenth century.

With this lesson in mind, Congress had little to lose—and everything to gain—by a complete fulfillment of the reform principles of merit hiring, tenure, and neutrality. In 1939, Congress passed the Hatch Act outlawing partisan political activity by federal employees, whether or not they were covered by civil service regulations, and by many state and local bureaucrats as well. In the same year, Congress amended the Social Security Act to require that all state and local employees working for programs subsidized by federal Social Security and other welfare funds be covered by state merit systems. These two pieces of legislation greatly extended the civil service, but in 1940 they were surpassed by the Ramspeck Act, which authorized extended coverage of the civil service system to virtually every nonpolitical appointee in the federal service. President Roosevelt, by then in his third term, quickly took full advantage of this authority to bring the employees who had been hired in his first two terms of office into the civil service system, thus institutionally protecting his New Deal programs for decades to come. By 1943, the civil service system was nearly complete in the federal government.

> The implicit promise of the Pendleton Act appeared to have been largely fulfilled. The basic criteria of the merit system—(1) selection by examination, (2) tenure for good behavior, and (3) political neutrality—had been met for most of the federal service.[51]

FDR and the New Deal

The reliance on "experts," the spread of "independent" regulatory agencies, the ultimate success of the civil service merit system, the search for "scientific management" in the departments and the agencies, all are features of the New Deal that demonstrate the continued acceptance of the logic of the Progressive structural reforms. However, we also argue that the continued acceptance of this logic was ultimately a political phenomenon: Key political actors in Congress, the interest groups, and the agencies themselves all found that accepting the logic protected their own political interests. The most striking case of this, though, has to do with the president who led the country through the New Deal. He helped create the independent regulatory agencies, he sparked the management movement, he furthered the reliance on expertise, despite the fact that his own personal style of administration demonstrates *a completely different logic from that of the reform model he seemed to be supporting*.

While this logic will be more completely discussed in the final chapter of this book, it is worth mentioning some of its essential characteristics. FDR believed in competition and redundancy within the bureaucracy rather than the neatness and specialized coordination advanced by his own Brownlow Committee. He was, first and foremost, a partisan politico, who extended the work of the civil service reformers to its fulfillment primarily for the political benefits to be derived. His was a very personalistic style of administration, rather than one characterized by rigid rules and regulations, as in the formal model of bureaucracy. Furthermore, unlike the classical reformers, he rejected efficiency as the primary goal of government.

Nevertheless, FDR's unique, personalistic administrative style did not (and perhaps could not) survive him in the federal government. The end result of the administrative reforms of the New Deal was a strengthening of the classical structure of hierarchy, specialization, rules, and merit staffing. For better or worse, these structural ideas of the Progressives were now melded with the New Deal reforms of the Brownlow Committee and others to become the *administrative orthodoxy*. Despite the brief glimpse of an alternative administrative structure seen in FDR's personal administrative style, federal, state, and local officials were to return to the administrative orthodoxy time and again as they structured and restructured their agencies.

THE INSTITUTIONALIZED REFORM AGENCY

Frederick Mosher describes the era from 1906–1937 as the era of "government by the efficient." Combining the Progressive movement and the New Deal, he sees a period in which "a science of work and management" were elaborated, along with the "proliferation of specializations, accompanied by the development of the career idea within each."[52] In other words, by the end of World War II, the "typical" government agency had seen the impact of several bouts with the reform idea, and gradually institutionalized various reform concepts such as the separation of politics and administration, professional dominance of agency administration, and the use of hierarchy and rules to enforce the hegemony of professional ideals on nonprofessionals within the agency. No agency so clearly demonstrates this as the Forest Service. Since good, detailed administrative studies of federal agencies are rare, we will turn to the classic study of the Forest Service done by Herbert Kaufman, which is an excellent inside account of the achievement of administrative control through hierarchical specialization, rules and regulations, and professionalism.[53]

The Forest Service was born during the heyday of Progressive reform.[54] Prior to 1905, the jurisdiction over national forests was lodged in the Interior Department, while the development of forestry was the responsibility of the Bureau of Forestry in the Department of Agriculture. In 1905, these functions were merged into the Agricultural Department under the leadership of Gifford Pinchot, the first chief of the Forest Service. By the late 1950s the forest preserves under the jurisdiction of the Forest Service had grown to over 181 million acres in 42 states and one U.S. territory. But, even then, this land constituted only a small fraction of the total forest land used for commercial purpose in the United States. Hence, the Forest Service retained interests and activities in research, forest legislation, information and education, and cooperative public/private forest planning in addition to public lands management.

This vast array of lands and multiple functions creates numerous centrifugal and divisive forces that work on the forest rangers in each area. Recall our earlier reference to the patrolman who was required to use a call box periodically to inform the police station of his activities. The forest ranger is much more remote from headquarters, but, like the patrolman, he has tasks that require his individual discretion and judgment. Also like the patrolman, the forest ranger may be easily enticed into adopting the preferences, interests, and outlook of citizens with whom he has dealings to the denial of the more general goals of the organization. Finally, patrolmen, forest rangers, and others who are "out in the field" away from central headquarters often develop philosophies of self-help and independence which further tend to magnify individual preferences over organizational goals. Thus, forest rangers do not automatically operate as part of one unified organization; quite to the contrary, the pressures and forces surrounding them work toward disunity and a multiplicity of behaviors and attitudes.

Hierarchy and rules. How, then, has the Forest Service produced a single, unified entity in which "field behavior (is) consistent with headquarters directives and suggestions?"[55] The answer, according to Kaufman, is found in the elaborate hierarchy of controls, standard operating procedures, and rules that make up the formal structure and operating code of the organization. For the most part, this hierarchy and mode of operation are based on the orthodox model of organization.

To begin with, the layers of hierarchy in the organization derive from the principle of narrow span of control. "The Chief constitutes the apex of a traditional administrative pyramid—or, perhaps more accurately, what amounts to two pyramids. One is organized for the administration of the national forests . . . the other is organized for research." Under the Chief are six Assistant Chiefs, who together constitute a single administrative unit, often referred to as the "staff." In theory, says Kaufman, the Assistant Chiefs are "merely arms of the Chief, extensions of his official will and personality. . . ." Each Assistant Chief, in turn, is head of a highly specialized staff: "The Assistant Chief for Research has eight divisions under him; the one for National Forest Resource Management has seven; administration, five; state and private forestry, four; Programming Planning and Legislation, two; and lands, two."[56]

Below the Washington level, the organization is divided into regional foresters and experiment stations (to simplify, we will drop the research pyramid at this point). Each regional forester (there are ten of them) is responsible for all the functions of the Forest Service, except research: "Each of the functions is under an Assistant regional forester (there are eleven of these), but several may be combined under one if the workload of the region in those activities is light; no region actually has eleven assistant regional foresters . . . but most have eight or nine. Like the Assistant Chiefs, they are said to act for their bosses in whatever they do, and each has a staff."[57]

Each of the forest regions is divided into national forests "headed by forest supervisors, whose responsibilities encompass all the foregoing functions but state and private forestry."[58] These supervisors have two kinds of assistants: the line officials who oversee specific functions, and pure staff, who have a more advisory capacity. Again, the number of line officials and their functions depends on the character of the workload, but the numbers range from two to five.

At the bottom of this pyramid are the ranger districts, which usually number from two to eleven, and constitute the smallest geographic subdivision in national forest administration. The districts are headed by rangers, the lowest ranking professional officers with responsibilities for administrative units. Below rangers are technicians, seasonal laborers, and some assistants; the ranger is involved in most of the functions of the Service that are applicable to his district.

The pyramid is based on the principle of narrow span of control (five to ten people) at each level, specialization, single chain of command (one chief with functional assistants), and administrative units divided by functional activity and geographic region. The structure of the pyramid is reinforced by an elaborate system of rules, regulations, written reports, and inspections. The pyramid produces over 100 different statistical summaries, plus special reports on certain kinds of important transactions (such as timber sales and special-use permits) as well as peculiar or unusual situations. The ranger is required to keep a daily diary of his activities that is detailed down to an hour-by-hour account and which, besides being sent to headquarters periodically, also will be read by inspectors at various intervals. Finally, the ranger is subject to two kinds of inspections, one for an overall assessment of performance, called the General Integrating Inspection, and another for particular activity areas, termed the Functional Inspection.

Professional unity. While the formal rules and procedures are quite formidable, perhaps the main way that the Forest Service achieves control is through a process of professionalization that internalizes organizational goals in rangers' actions and attitudes. In the 1950s, 90 percent of the Forest Service's professional positions were staffed by foresters, and the Service required a particular kind of forestry training at colleges and universities. As a consequence, with very few exceptions, the people who ran the agency were foresters who had spent their entire careers working for the agency.

This professional training and agency socialization were bolstered by the Service's practice of moving personnel from one location to another so that few local ties and loyalties could be developed apart from the Forest Service itself. This procedure also offered a check on ranger performance, since someone else takes over the ranger's job when he leaves. The Service, in addition, promoted an organizational ideology of professionalism, esprit de corps, and loyalty, with symbols of badge, uniform, and rank. All these procedures helped to build an identity with the organization and voluntary conformity to its goals. Kaufman writes:

> Much that happens to a professional forester in the Forest Service thus tends to tighten the links binding him to the organization. His experiences and his environment gradually infuse into him a view of the world and a hierarchy of preferences coinciding with those of his colleagues. They tie him to his fellow, to the agency . . . They practically merge the individual identity with the identity of the organization; the organization is as much a part of the members as they are of it.[59]

Hierarchical specialization contributes to the unity of command. At each level, "a single, determinate individual (is) formally empowered to issue decisions with respect to all functions." Second, tendencies toward fragmentation have been thwarted by "the elaboration of the body of preformed decisions and the refinement of methods of detecting and discouraging deviation from them." As forest management became more complex and diverse, "the central controls were multiplied" from a single-book manual that could be carried in a forester's back pocket to a virtual library of rules and regulations. In addition, "Increases in the number and specificity of preformed decisions at all levels" helped reduce the deviance from "the ambiguities of instructions framed in general terms. . . ." Third, the concentration on one profession, forestry, homogenized ideas and responses to problems: "establishing the predominance of a single profession throughout the organization does not end the troubles entirely. But it certainly reduces them materially."[60]

The product of these efforts, according to Kaufman, is a professional, bureaucratic agency that has not been susceptible to scandal, including graft, collusion with special interests, local favoritism, or other forms of corruption (even though the opportunities are there in the commercial and recreational uses of the forests); nor has the agency been plagued by protests, sabotage, revolts, or strikes among employees. In addition, the Service appears to have achieved a high degree of efficiency and effectiveness. Kaufman says that there has been a "responsiveness of production to changes in leadership objectives; and the steady march of performance records towards goals of the leaders. . . ."[61] The Service has been able to shift men to new locations with little disruption and expect a high esprit de corps, even with hard work for modest pay.

CONTROLLING THE REFORMED ADMINISTRATIVE AGENCY: THE NEW ACCOMMODATION

The portrait that Kaufman paints of the Forest Service is of an ideal reform agency. It is an agency composed of professionals who have a high degree of fiscal integrity and substantive expertise; an organization that relies on hierarchy, specialization, and standard operating procedures to produce integrated decisions and actions; and an organization whose goals are quantified as much as feasible through performance measures and detailed records of targets and actions to achieve them, making the organization accountable to the top leadership and the public. Throughout the first half of the century, the Progressives were able to make their expectations about the functioning of such a bureaucracy the expectations of Congress, interest groups, and the general public. They had established the administrative orthodoxy of the twentieth century.

The institutions of administrative orthodoxy did not just define the internal operations of reformed agencies. They also helped define the balance of power external to the agency, for control of the twentieth-century bureaucracy was just as much an issue between Congress and the president as had been control of the nineteenth-century bureaucracy. While the battle in the nineteenth century had been fought over appointment power and patronage, that issue had been largely settled by the universalization of federal civil service. At issue in the twentieth century were the budgetary funds, the organization, and the legislative directives shaping the actions of the bureaucracy. And here the principles of executive budgeting and executive management, developed by the Progressives, had provided the basis for a new accommodation.

The accommodation was, for the most part, that the president should propose while the Congress maintain its formal powers to legislate, budget, and organize. The president's budgetary powers gave him the right to set the budgetary agenda, an agenda that Congress could, however, change as it felt the political need to do so.

Similarly, the reorganization powers of the president gave him to the right to set the reorganization agenda, again subject to Congress's veto powers, which it could use when reelection requirements dictated. In addition, the president's greatly improved Executive Office gave him the opportunity to make legislative and policy proposals.

Formally, then, the president gained little. There was very little the president could do about legislation, budgets, or reorganization when the reelection requirements of Congress dictated certain courses of action. This accommodation gives the members of Congress the opportunity to reap the electoral benefits described at the beginning of this chapter—claiming credit for the favorable actions of professionally managed bureaucracies and avoiding blame for the unfavorable decisions of "independent" commissions. Both these possibilities have been illustrated with the case of the Forest Service.

For instance, it has been frequently proposed (by presidents Nixon and Carter, among others) that the Forest Service be shifted from the Agriculture to Interior Department. Members of Congress with environmental constituencies have been able to earn credit with environmentalists who are suspicious of the Interior Department's conservation record by repeatedly vetoing this proposal.[62] On the other hand, when environmentalists felt during the 1960s that the lumber industries had "captured" the Forest Service and members of Congress were cross-pressured by the lumber industry and environmentalists, Congress was able to take refuge in the much-vaunted "professional independence" of the Forest Service, so as not to take too much political damage from either side. Congress passed a law in 1960 requiring that the national forests be administered for "outdoor recreation, range, timber, watershed, and wildlife and fish purposes," and requiring the Forest Service to do its professional best to meet all these quite conflicting purposes at the same time. "The act has frequently been criticized as an abdication of congressional responsibility over the national forests because it is fairly vague and allows the service to make discretionary judgments among competing uses."[63] Of course, that is just the political benefit of being able to delegate responsibility to independent, professional agencies.

While the formal powers and political requirements of Congress are protected sufficiently by the new accommodation of president and Congress, informally the office of the president gained a great deal by the executive management and executive budgetary movements as they were initially developed in the Progressive era and modified and instituted during the New Deal. The president was given the tools to bargain with an uncertain or divided Congress, and to take the lead in the implementation of legislative policy.

FURTHER QUESTIONS

Ironically, by the 1970s, the Forest Service was under attack as inefficient, politicized, and unaccountable. Environmentalists charged that it was politically a tool of the large lumber companies. They used as evidence the clear-cutting policies of the Forest Service, which conservationists charged were a wasteful and destructive policy designed to guarantee large profits for the lumber companies who were allowed access to national forest lands. Congressional supporters of the environmentalists charged that the Forest Service was out of congressional control, making forestry policy themselves instead of neutrally implementing congressional decisions.[64]

These critiques of the Forest Service were repeated during the 1960s and 1970s with regard to other institutional manifestations of the reform era: the professionalized police departments, highway departments, and school districts; city managers; the State Department; the paragon of professional law enforcement, the FBI; the reorganized and reformed Defense Department; the independent regulatory agencies. Virtually every bureaucratic manifestation of the orthodox reform movement was attacked as inefficient, or politicized, or unaccountable, or all three.

Increasingly, social scientists from various disciplines also began to have doubts about the organization theory which linked bureaucracy with these desired values. As one critic of police reform noted, the unanticipated consequences of the reform movement are the problems we face today: "Professionalization had led to the growth of complex bureaucratic structures; a new generation of reformers faced the problem of taming and humanizing the new animal."[65]

One might well be led to ask, what if agencies had institutionalized an alternative model of reform? As an example, what if the Forest Service had incorporated FDR's leadership style, with control through competition rather than heavy-handed hierarchy, innovation through pluralism of ideas rather than professional planning, and an emphasis on individual responsibility rather than individual rule-following? Is it possible that some of the problems facing government agencies in the 1960s and 1970s would have been less severe, rather than more severe, if the orthodox model of reform had been ameliorated by some of FDR's ideas?

The purpose of the next few chapters is to analyze these complaints against the reform models. To the extent that they are justified, we hope to analyze why the reformed bureaucracies failed to live up to the expectations of their creators, and at the same time to understand why the institutional prescriptions of orthodox administration theory continue to be adopted today.

NOTES

[1]*Report of the President's Committee on Administrative Management* (Washington, D.C., 1937), pp. 16–17.

[2]GRANT McCONNELL, *Private Power and American Democracy* (New York: Vintage Books, 1966), p. 59.

[3]MANCUR OLSON, JR., *The Logic of Collective Action: Public Goods and the Theory of Groups* (New York: Schocken Books, 1965), p. 149.

[4]RICHARD L. McCORMICK, *From Realignment to Reform: Political Change in New York State, 1892–1910* (Ithaca: Cornell University Press, 1979), p. 264.

[5]PETER SWENSON, "The Influence of Recruitment on the Structure of Power in the House, 1870–1940," *Legislative Studies Quarterly*, 7 (1982), p. 22.

[6]DAVID W. ROHDE and KENNETH A. SHEPSLE, "The Ambiguous Role of Leadership in Woodrow Wilson's Congress." Delivered at the 1985 annual meeting of the American Political Science Association, New Orleans, August 29–September 1, 1985.

[7]GEORGE GALLOWAY, *History of the House of Representatives* (New York: Thomas Y. Crowell Co., 1976), p. 58.

[8]For an interesting firsthand account by the Progressive leader of the revolt, see George W. Norris, *Fighting Liberal* (New York: The Macmillan Co., 1946), pp. 107–119.

[9]ROHDE and SHEPSLE, "Wilson's Congress," pp. 15–16.

[10]GABRIEL KOLKO, *The Triumph of Conservatism: A Reinterpretation of American History, 1900–1916* (Chicago: Quadrangle Books, 1963), p. 270.

[11]MORRIS FIORINA, "Group Concentration and the Delegation of Legislative Authority" (mimeo) (Pasadena: California Institute of Technology, 1982).

[12]MATTHEW D. McCUBBINS, "The Legislative Design of Regulatory Structure," *American Journal of Political Science,* 29 (1985), p. 741.

[13]LEONARD D. WHITE, *The Republican Era: A Study in Administrative History* (New York: The Macmillan Company, 1963).

[14]PERI E. ARNOLD, "Executive Reorganization and Administrative Theory: The Origin of the Managerial Presidency." Delivered to the Annual Meeting of the American Political Science Association, Chicago, September 2–5. 1976.

[15]ARNOLD, "Executive Reorganization," p. 10.

[16]ARNOLD, "Executive Reorganization," p. 13.

[17]ARNOLD, "Executive Reorganization," p. 15.

[18]ARNOLD, "Executive Reorganization," p. 20.

[19]ARNOLD, "Executive Reorganization," p. 22.

[20]ARNOLD, "Executive Reorganization," p. 23.

[21]LARRY BERMAN, *The Office of Management and Budget and the Presidency, 1921–1979* (Princeton: Princeton University Press, 1979)

[22]RICHARD POLENBERG, *Reorganizing Roosevelt's Government: The Controversy Over Executive Reorganization, 1936–1939* (Cambridge: Harvard University Press, 1966), p. 22.

[23]POLENBERG, *Roosevelt's Government,* p. 25.

[24]*Report of the President's Committee,* p. 17.

[25]*New York Times,* Jan. 17, 1937, sec. IV, p. 7.

[26]POLENBERG, *Roosevelt's Government,* p. 192.

[27]POLENBERG, *Roosevelt's Government,* p. 193.

[28]POLENBERG, *Roosevelt's Government,* p. 79.

[29]POLENBERG, *Roosevelt's Government,* p. 191.

[30]POLENBERG, *Roosevelt's Government,* p. 46.

[31]POLENBERG, *Roosevelt's Government,* p. 21.

[32]JANE S. DAHLBERG, *The New York Bureau of Municipal Research: Pioneer in Government Administration* (New York: New York University Press, 1966), pp. 241–242.

[33]*Report of the President's Committee,* pp. 16–17.

[34]*Report of the President's Committee,* p. 17.

[35]*Report of the President's Committee,* p. 18.

[36]BRADLEY RICE, *Progressive Cities* (Austin: University of Texas Press, 1977), pp. 106–107.

[37]LUTHER GULICK, and LYNDALL URWICK, *Papers on the Science of Administration* (New York: Institute of Public Administration, 1937).

[38]DAHLBERG, *New York Bureau,* p. 56, fn. 4.

[39]HERBERT KAUFMAN, "Emerging Conflicts in the Doctrines of Public Administration," *American Political Science Review,* 50 (1956), pp. 1057–1073.

[40]POLENBERG, *Roosevelt's Government,* p. 40.

[41]PERI E. ARNOLD, "Herbert Hoover and the Continuity of American Public Policy," *Public Policy,* 20 (1972), pp. 525–544.

[42]HAROLD SEIDMAN, *Politics, Position, and Power: The Dynamics of Federal Organization,* 2nd ed. (New York: Oxford University Press, 1975), p. 4.

[43]The Commission on Organization of the Executive Branch of the Government, *General Management of the Executive Branch, A Report to the Congress,* February 1949, p. 1.

[44]PERI E. ARNOLD, "The First Hoover Commission and the Managerial Presidency," *Journal of Politics,* 38 (1976), pp. 64, 70.

[45]LOUIS M. KOHLMEIER, JR., *The Regulators: Watchdog Agencies and the Public Interest* (New York: Harper & Row Publishers, 1969), p. 29.

[46]PAUL P. VAN RIPER, *History of the United States Civil Service* (Evanston: Row, Peterson and Co., 1958), p. 320.

[47]VAN RIPER, *Civil Service*, p. 318.

[48]VAN RIPER, *Civil Service*, pp. 322 and 325.

[49]VAN RIPER, *Civil Service*, p. 321.

[50]VAN RIPER, *Civil Service*, p. 332.

[51]VAN RIPER, *Civil Service*, p. 360.

[52]FREDERICK C. MOSHER, *Democracy and the Public Service*, 2nd ed. (New York: Oxford University Press, 1982), p. 81.

[53]HERBERT KAUFMAN, *The Forest Ranger: A Study in Administrative Behavior* (Baltimore: Johns Hopkins University Press, 1960).

[54]SAMUEL P. HAYS, *Conservation and the Gospel of Efficiency: The Progressive Conservation Movement 1890–1920* (New York: Atheneum, 1975).

[55]KAUFMAN, *Forest Ranger*, p. x.

[56]KAUFMAN, *Forest Ranger*, pp. 40–43.

[57]KAUFMAN, *Forest Ranger*, p. 45.

[58]KAUFMAN, *Forest Ranger*, p. 45.

[59]KAUFMAN, *Forest Ranger*, p. 197.

[60]KAUFMAN, *Forest Ranger*, pp. 197, 211, 213, and 214–215.

[61]KAUFMAN, *Forest Ranger*, p. 204.

[62]PAUL J. CULHANE, *Public Lands Politics: Interest Group Influence on the Forest Service and the Bureau of Land Management* (Baltimore: Johns Hopkins Press, 1981), p. 50.

[63]CULHANE, *Public Lands*, p. 53.

[64]CULHANE, *Public Lands*, p. 338.

[65]SAMUEL WALKER, *A Critical History of Police Reform: The Emergence of Professionalism* (Lexington: D.C. Heath, 1977), p. 173.

CHAPTER 6

Assessing the Reform Model:
Is It Efficient?

When the time-study man came around, I set the speed at 180. I knew damn well he would ask me to push it up, so I started low enough. He finally pushed me up to 445, and I ran the job later at 610. If I'd started at 445, they'd have timed it at 610. . . . It's up to you to figure out how to fool them more than they allow for.

Industrial worker, quoted in
William Foote Whyte, *Money and Motivation*[1]

For half of a century, the orthodox reform ideas originating in the Progressive era determined the way we thought administration should be organized in this country. By the end of that time, however, a growing number of people in schools of social science and public administration no longer believed that the professional bureaucracy spawned by the reform movements would guarantee efficiency, accountability, and neutrality. In fact, for many of these critics, bureaucracy came to embody the very inefficiency and unaccountable political power that the reformers had sought to eradicate. What caused this change in expectations about orthodox administrative reforms?

The overall theme of the literature discussed in this chapter is that the bureaucratic model proposed by Progressives and institutionalized as the "classical" or "orthodox" model of management by the end of the New Deal does not guarantee efficiency, contrary to reformers' claims. It is not the purpose of this paper to argue that organizations with the characteristics of the reform model—hierarchy, specialization, written rules, and expertise—are necessarily inefficient. We argue, rather, that managers came to discover built-in tensions between hierarchy and specialization, between written rules and reliance on expertise. These tensions were not anticipated by the original thinkers of the reform tradition. Managers who relied solely on the accepted orthodoxies of the reform movement increasingly discovered "unanticipated consequences" that were often as unpleasant as they were unexpected.

This suggests that the classical model was not so much wrong as limited in explanatory value. It focuses on factors that do not go very far to explain or determine the performance of real-world organizations. Therefore, to the extent that the classical model continues to inform real-world reform attempts, it continues to distract those reformers from the factors which can have a greater impact on the success of their reform efforts.

THE HUMAN RELATIONS CRITIQUE

Outside of Chicago, in a town called Cicero, the Bell System's manufacturing subsidiary, Western Electric, makes switchboards and other electrical equipment for the various Bell Telephone companies. In the 1930s and 1940s, Western Electric was in the forefront of the scientific management movement, and the company's professional managers were anxious to implement Frederick Taylor's ideas. In an effort to improve productivity, the company initiated a series of experiments at the Hawthorne Plant in Cicero. Their expectation was that changes in the work environment, the rate of work, and the formal incentive systems in the plant would lead to increased output. These hypotheses, and the procedures to test them, were clearly inspired by the writings of Taylor.[2]

Lighting was one of the factors in the work environment that concerned them. To test the effects of lighting on worker performance, they placed one group of workers in a special room where the lighting was periodically altered. As a control, another group of workers was placed in a different room where the lighting was kept constant. They first increased the lighting in the room of the experimental group; the result was an increase in the workers' productivity, as might be expected. They then decreased the lighting of the experimental group, but the workers' output continued to go up, quite contrary to expectations. Unconvinced by these initial results, the experimenters decreased the lighting further and further, but the output of the workers continued to go up until the room was so dark that it was literally like working under a full moon. Only then did productivity begin to fall off. Meanwhile, back at the control group, the experimenters became further confused because the productivity of the workers continued to go up for no apparent reason, since the lighting was constant.[3]

After several years of study, the experimenters came to the conclusion that factors affecting the behavior of the workers at the Hawthorne Plant had not been present in Frederick Taylor's study of Schmidt, the pig-iron carrier. First and foremost, it became apparent that the Hawthorne plant's workers were responding to the attention being given to them by management, and this special attention applied to both the experimental and the control group. This increase in morale as a response to special attention was called the "Hawthorne effect," and while this effect had appeared unexpectedly to confound the Hawthorne studies, the significance of it was not lost on the experimenters. Perhaps the morale of the work group was more important as a determinant of productivity, the experimenters reasoned, than all those physical factors that Taylor had manipulated in his time-and-motion experiments.

To pursue this discovery, they initiated another series of experiments on group morale. The results seemed to indicate that the "informal work group" was a key factor in explaining productivity. The informal work group consisted of a worker's friends and associates in the work situation. Over time, the worker comes to identify with this group and may socialize with them during coffee breaks or after work. The experimenters learned that the group tended to reinforce certain kinds of behavior and to ostracize those members who did not conform.

One norm of behavior, for example, was to limit "slacking." If the members of the group did not feel that one member was working as hard as he or she could, making work difficult for the rest of the group, then the group might try to force the "slacker" to work harder, first by gentle ribbing, then by more severe sanctions such as ostracism. On the other hand, if someone in the work group performed work at rates that far exceeded the output of the other members, then the group would condemn this behavior as "rate-busting." Rate-busting was just as bad a violation of informal work group norms, because it made other workers look lazy and could get them in trouble with the boss.

Notice how different these kinds of concerns are than those we have discussed in earlier chapters. The unit of analysis is now the group rather than the individual, and the central determinant is the abstract psychological concept of "group norm" instead of concrete, structural concepts such as hierarchy and merit hiring that can be observed in the official documents of an organization. A whole new approach to organizations was developing out of the Hawthorne studies that used groups and group social psychology to explain behavior, rather than the formal institution coercing individual compliance with formal rules and regulations.

According to this new approach, the way to improve productivity in the organization was to manipulate groups and their norms. This approach was believed to be more efficacious than the mechanical reshuffling of the organization chart or the equally mechanical writing of rules and regulations detailing the required behavior of individuals. As F.J. Roethlisberger wrote in his influential description of the Hawthorne studies, "output is a form of social behavior."[4] Furthermore, the social norms of the small group were regarded as more powerful than the formal rules and hierarchy of an organization. If the informal work group had established norms about group productivity, then these norms would determine group behavior, despite any number of written rules and the commands of higher-ups in the hierarchy.

While Taylor's individual-oriented "incentive wages" could influence certain people, this limited view missed the big picture. "Most of us want the satisfaction that comes from being accepted and recognized as people of worth by our friends and work associates," wrote Roethlisberger. "Money is only a small part of this social recognition."[5]

A Hierarchy of Needs

If this approach to organizational analysis was to be fruitful, it obviously required a different set of assumptions about human needs than that which informed Frederick Taylor. The person who, more than any other, supplied this different set of assumptions was a psychologist named Abraham Maslow, who wrote a paper in 1943 called "A Theory of Human Motivation."[6] Maslow said that there was a hierarchy of human needs, and that the simpler needs required fulfillment before the complex needs could be dealt with. Human beings first attend to physiological needs, making sure that hunger and thirst are satisfied. They then turn to safety needs, looking for a place where they can be secure from danger and the elements. Only then do they become concerned about the need for love from other individuals. Once a person has been accepted as part of a group, according to Maslow, he will then attempt to earn the esteem or respect of others. Fifth and last in his hierarchy of needs is the need for self-actualization: "A musician must make music, an artist must paint, a poet must write, if he is to be ultimately happy. What a man can be, he must be. This need we may call self-actualization."

The socio-psychologists who were impressed by Maslow's ideas argued that the formal structure of the bureaucratic organization had not responded to any of these needs, except perhaps the physiological ones. Hence, employees created an informal organization within the formal organization to satisfy their other needs. Co-workers became friends; within the friendship group they gave and received acceptance and esteem. They related to each other as multidimensional people with talents and hobbies that were not required on the job but which made their lives meaningful. For these reasons, the informal work groups were treasured and protected by the employees.

Theory Y

The socio-psychologists who embraced Maslow's theories criticized the Progressive/scientific management approach to organizations and proposed an alternative approach they called the "human relations" approach. The human relations approach to organizations provides a radically different set of expectations regarding the efficacy of hierarchy, specialization, rules and regulations, and expertise. This change in perspective is nowhere more apparent than in the work of Douglas McGregor.

McGregor contrasts what he calls Theory X and Theory Y.[7] McGregor identifies Theory X as the "conventional conception" of management, derived from Frederick Taylor and the Progressives, which is based on the assumption that "most people must be coerced, controlled, directed, threatened with punishment to get them to put forth adequate effort toward the achievement of organizational objectives."[8] Theory X, therefore, controls employees' behavior through hierarchy and formal rules, pay incentives, and threats of dismissal. This is quite wrong, according to McGregor. It creates a situation in which the psychological health of the individual is in conflict with the formal structure of the organization, and neither the individual nor the organization will prosper in the resulting tension.

In contrast, McGregor proposed Theory Y, which is a departure from the conventional approach of "scientific management." Theory Y is based on the assumption that "The average human being learns under proper conditions, not only to accept but to seek responsibility."[9] Such individuals may appear lazy in other organizations because Theory X has taught them that that is what is expected of them. "If employees are lazy, indifferent, unwilling to take responsibility, intransigent, uncreative, uncooperative, Theory Y implies that the causes lie in management's methods of organization and control."[10] Explicitly relying on Maslow's hierarchy of needs, McGregor claims that it is management's job to arrange organizational roles so that individuals can realize their higher needs in the performance of their jobs.

The furtherance of this new mode of management radically alters much of the conventional, bureaucratic structure and attacks most of the fundamental characteristics of the Progressive model of efficient, accountable bureaucracy. McGregor suggests that decentralization and delegation are a "step in the right direction" toward Theory Y. Decentralization is carried out by means of decreasing hierarchy, rather than increasing it. A flat organization with few levels of hierarchy and a large span of control (i.e., a large number of people reporting to each manager) makes it impossible for the managers to use Theory X. This absence of hierarchy is good, according to McGregor, because it allows the individual greater freedom and autonomy, which is psychologically healthy for the individual and good for the organization because it encourages initiative and imagination.

Similarly, another step in the right direction is job enlargement, which consists of reducing the degree of specialization in the organization. Individuals should not have highly specialized tasks, because it results in boredom and loss of self-esteem. A large number of generalists, each of whom does a great variety of tasks that often overlap with the assignment of other generalists, is more healthy, according to McGregor. It encourages a greater sense of self-worth and higher morale, helping the informal work group to support organizational goals rather than work against them.

McGregor is also opposed to excessive rules and regulations in an organization. Instead, McGregor would institute a performance appraisal in which individuals are given a great deal of autonomy to perform their jobs as they see fit, with the evaluation of the individual's role determined by final outcomes rather than adherence to rules.

One could hardly imagine, then, a more drastic and fundamental challenge to the classical model of bureaucracy. McGregor is arguing that hierarchy, specialization, and written rules and regulations all contribute to organizational *inefficiency* rather than efficiency. This idea has had a great deal of impact, not only in academic circles, but among consultants to businesses and governments.

Human Relations Consultants

The consultants who are sympathetic to McGregor's ideas have developed an entirely different method of helping organizations than that used by the "efficiency experts" who followed in the footsteps of Frederick Taylor. The organizational consultants of the human relations school do not use stopwatches; instead, they rely on changing the informal organization, the patterns of leadership and supervision, and communication patterns. One means they use to attempt to bring about these changes is sensitivity training groups, also known as T groups.

The T group consists of ten to sixteen people, including one or two trainers. The group may meet for a whole weekend or for one or two hours a day for several weeks. The trainers encourage better communication among participants by trying to help each member of the group better understand the thoughts and feelings of others, as well as his or her own thoughts. They encourage free and frank interaction to help each other achieve "authenticity," and may begin with various exercises to break down inhibitions and defenses. As one advocate wrote, "A person is most free to learn when he establishes authentic relationships with other people and thereby increases his sense of self-esteem and decreases his defensiveness. In authentic relationships persons can be open, honest, and direct with one another so that they are communicating what they are actually feeling rather than masking their feelings."[11]

Evaluation of Human Relations

Evaluations of sensitivity training and the human relations approach have been mixed. Some critics claim that, while improved communication in a weekend sensitivity training session may "feel good," it does little to change the realities of the work situation on Monday morning. If this is true, participants may regret the frank remarks exchanged during the training session. Charles Perrow argues that there is little empirical evidence that sensitivity training "works," or that the propositions of the human relations approach improve our understanding of organizational behavior.[12] Perrow especially doubts that human relations theorists account for the real conflicts of interest over power and resources in the organization.

Perhaps the most thorough criticism of the human relations approach was by Victor Vroom. Vroom criticized the logic of the human relations approach, which claims that satisfied workers will be more productive workers. Vroom points out that this assertion divorces effort from incentive.[13] Why should people who are already satisfied work any harder? In a thorough review of the psychological and sociological literature, Vroom claims to demonstrate that the efforts of human relations advocates to promote job satisfaction are successful, but that there is no evidence that job satisfaction directly promotes performance.[14]

This criticism strikes at the heart of the human relations approach, and provides the basis for much of the rest of the analysis of organizations and organizational structure. For the human relations approach, in reacting against the cold-hearted manipulation of Theory X, denied or avoided the incentives operating on individuals. They were correct in pointing out that individuals have more complicated goals than simply earning wages, but they were probably incorrect to abandon the need for management to concern itself with manipulating incentives in order to affect organizational behavior. Every structure will define a set of incentives for individuals to follow, and we will argue in this book that individuals respond quite closely to the incentive structure that is built into the rule system of an organization.

In the 1930s, for example, the Western Electric Hawthorne plant was laying off workers because of the business slump. Some observers have maintained that workers responded by restricting output in an attempt to save their jobs. Economic analysis, in addition, attributes performance to structural factors of economic scale more than to human satisfaction. The introduction of Ford Motor's assembly line, for instance, reduced the amount of time required to manufacture an automobile from 121 hours to 93 minutes. This may well have decreased worker job satisfaction in the process, as human relations advocates claim; nevertheless, the economic gain realized from that change makes it impossible to reverse. In a highly structured work situation such as the Ford assembly line or the State Department, critics maintain that the connection between attitudes and performance is tenuous. The determinant of performance is whether the rules and hierarchical organization define and structure the job in such a way as to provide an incentive for individuals to perform the specialized tasks that are asked of them.

The sociologists discussed in the next section discuss exactly this question. Like the human relations school, they assume that individuals have complex social goals in addition to simply short-term maximization of wages. However, unlike the human relations school, they do not believe that satisfaction of these complex goals is sufficient for job performance; rather, their explanations are consistent with the behavioral assumption that individuals will perform their assigned tasks if the performance of those tasks furthers their individual goals more than the nonperformance of their tasks would. On this ground, too, these sociologists find reason to criticize the classical managerial orthodoxy.

THE SOCIOLOGICAL CRITIQUE

In the early 1950s, a sociologist named Alvin Gouldner studied a factory in northern Indiana, one that was organized on a bureaucratic model. Gouldner found that the use of general and impersonal rules in a hierarchical setting tended to increase the visibility of power relations within the bureaucracy; that is, everyone was always conscious of who was superior to whom in the organization. These highly visible power relations, in turn, caused a high level of interpersonal tension, since subordinates were often dissatisfied with a situation in which they were always made to feel inferior in authority and status.[15]

The subordinates became unhappy and unwilling to do more than the minimum that was demanded of them. The bureaucratic structure aided them in this desire, because the written rules of procedure that are a hallmark of managerial orthodoxy clearly stated the minimal level of cooperative behavior expected of the subordinates. The result was that subordinates could refuse to innovate or work any harder than the minimal definition of cooperation given by the written rules of procedure. Thus, the use of hierarchy created a motivation for subordinates to be uncooperative.

This would have been satisfactory if it were possible to write the rules of procedure in such a way that the minimal levels of effort defined in those rules were sufficient for the needs of the firm. However, managers were always finding that they needed subordinates to do something that was not clearly stated in the rules as the subordinates' responsibility. For instance, the person charged with repairing one aspect of the machinery could save the firm a lot of money if he would, on his own, correct malfunctioning machinery that was outside of his jurisdiction. If the repairman is feeling disgruntled with the organization, however, he might well ignore the faulty machinery simply because it is out of his jurisdiction. If the people on the assembly line were to call attention to shoddy work that comes down the line to them, that would help keep product quality up. However, someone who is feeling unhappy with the organization might well decide that he doesn't want to "tell tales" on his coworkers up the line—and besides, he is just supposed to turn this one bolt; he's not paid to be a quality-control officer. A supply clerk might save the firm money by rushing spare parts to keep the assembly line going; but a rebellious supply clerk might well decide to stick with an inappropriate standard operating procedure which requires filling requisitions in the order that they are received, despite the fact that the next six requisitions are clearly less important than the seventh, crucial requisition.

What can the management do to get the repairman, the assembly line worker, and the supply clerk to deviate from standard operating procedure when it is clearly in the company's interest to do so? As Gouldner points out, the managerial orthodoxy inherited from the Progressives and the scientific management school leaves only two options—*more* hierarchy and *more* rules.

By hiring more foremen for the line, they can have the production manager tell the foremen to order the line workers to report faulty products going by; and if the foremen see something that the lineworkers should have reported but didn't, they will have the lineworkers' pay docked. Similar measures to incorporate orders into the rules would get repairmen to report machinery that is out of order, or supply clerks to change the standard operating procedure to establish some priority of need in filling requisitions.

While these changes in the hierarchy and rules may have the short-term effects that are needed for the firm, they also exacerbate the factors that caused the problem in the first place: The extra foremen giving more orders make the subordinates even more resentful of the more obvious power relations in the firm, so that they become even more unwilling to go beyond the necessary level of cooperation given in the now more stringent rules. This leads them to be even more uncooperative in the future, which leads in turn to even greater reliance on hierarchy and rules by managers, which leads to more hostility by subordinates, and on and on. Gouldner saw the managerial orthodoxy leading to a vicious cycle of deteriorating efficiency.

Anthony Downs, in his classic *Inside Bureaucracy*, called this the "rigidity cycle," since the end result is an organization that is unable to escape the increasingly rigid behaviors that are fixed in their increasingly specified hierarchy and rules.[16] Like Gouldner, he saw the basic cause being that "top officials constantly search for more effective means of control," and in this search they turn to an increased reliance on rules and hierarchy, which leads to more rigidity, less satisfactory performance, and an even greater need for control, which starts the cycle of hierarchy and rules over again.[17]

The Rigidity Cycle: A Bureaucratic Dysfunction

The rigidity cycle is an example of a "bureaucratic dysfunction" in which the essential elements of professionalized bureaucracy (hierarchy, rules, specialization, expert staffing) lead to inefficiency rather than efficiency.[18] In this case, the efficient operation of virtually any organization requires employees to be willing to be a trifle flexible or innovative in response to certain situations where the normal operating procedures are inadequate for organizational purposes. Not only factory workers but also (and especially) policemen, teachers, public health nurses, and virtually any official who interacts with the public must be willing to respond flexibly with the organizational well-being in mind, or the organization will suffer. No organization can program or predefine in the rules *all* the individual behaviors that are necessary for organizational success. Any teacher that simply follows a set of written rules will fail miserably, at least with children with exceptional emotional problems or intellectual abilities. Similarly, no set of rules can clearly define when a policemen should or should not shoot in situations where he and innocent bystanders are endangered either way (although police departments have worked hard to come up with rules that cover as many cases as possible).

While every organization needs flexible subordinates, the kind of impersonal, standardized, authoritarian management advocated by Taylor and implicit in the administrative reform model is, according to Gouldner, exactly the wrong kind of supervisory style to get that desired result. According to Gouldner, this managerial orthodoxy promotes the kind of careful, cautious, "red-tape" behavior that has made the word "bureaucrat" an epithet rather than a synonym for efficiency.

Position Classification and Rigidity

A specific example of how the rule structure of a bureaucracy plays a part in defining minimal standards for subordinate behavior is provided by Frederick Mosher, an expert in personnel administration. Mosher focuses on "position classification," which is "the thesis that the content of a given position or class of positions be the hub around which other personnel actions and indeed management generally should revolve."[19] Position classification is a means of defining individual job roles by a set of written rules and organizing the management of the organization around those written rules. Position classification emerged with the scientific management approach to personnel, and is a natural extension of the bureaucratic tenet that organizations consist of offices, not personalities, that are defined by rules in a hierarchy. "Thirty years ago classification had become the jumping-off point for most activities in the field of personnel: pay, recruitment and selection, placement, promotions, transfers, efficiency ratings, even training. It provided the blocks for what some have called the building-block theory of organization—an essentially static and mechanistic concept."[20]

Of course, position classification is not necessarily dysfunctional, any more than hierarchy or rules are necessarily dysfunctional. Mosher writes, "Indeed, it is hard to imagine a sizeable organization operating without at least a skeleton of a classification plan even if it is unwritten."[21] The problem is, however, that these building blocks have defined organizational behavior so well that they have formed a wall inhibiting bureaucratic initiative and flexibility. To quote Mosher:

> To the extent that it is coercive and binding, detailed and specific, and difficult to change, classification has the effects of: retarding organizational change and adaptation; inhibiting special, ad hoc assignments or otherwise working 'out of class'; discouraging recognition of unusual contributions and competence through rapid advancement.[22]

In other words, position classification defines minimum standards of individual performance that becomes not only increasingly unacceptable, but increasingly constraining as superiors make them more and more specific. It rewards bureaucrats who shrug their shoulders and say, "that's not my job" when a new and difficult situation arises. The incentive and indeed the opportunity to break out of these minimalist, mechanistic job definitions diminishes with time as the rigidity cycle tightens.

Rigidity in Street-Level Bureaucracy

Once again, it is worth emphasizing that increasing organizational rigidity might not be a problem in some organizational settings. It may work well in some assembly-line organizations where individual behavior should be machinelike and programmed and individual job dissatisfaction doesn't have too large an impact on job performance.

Organizational rigidity must be more or less dysfunctional for public agencies. This is made clear in Michael Lipsky's classic book about street-level public professions, including teaching, police, and social work.[23] In these cases, a rigidity cycle may be triggered by a slightly different mechanism than that mentioned by

Gouldner. These street-level bureaucrats often do not have superiors breathing down their necks making them feel their status inferiority. They may necessarily have some job autonomy in the field. However, they often do feel, according to Lipsky, inadequate resources for the job they are charged with, along with idealized job expectations, and they often feel either physically threatened or a psychological threat to their authority, or both.

In such conditions, Lipsky argues, bureaucrats often perceive the bureaucratic routines given by the written rules and procedures of the organization as being the only way of protecting their authority and dealing with inadequate resources. The routines then become "ends in themselves." "To attack the routine is to appear to attack the structure. Clients who challenge the bureaucratic routines are taught this lesson. . . ."[24]

Similarly, in response to threats, rules and regulations become "avoidance strategies," ways of disengaging personally from a client and his or her problems. In addition, the ambiguous or idealized job description can best be made concrete and manageable by defining the job through a set of rules and regulations which, once again, become ends in themselves, blocking more flexible or more innovative approaches to the organizational goal.

Through this process, the efficient bureaucratic machine becomes slower, more inflexible, more unresponsive to the needs of the client. The student in the classroom discovers that the teacher is more concerned with keeping order through a set of standard operating procedures than with listening to students' thoughts about the day's lesson. The social-work client finds that rules and regulations prevent the social worker from doing anything about his or her special problem. The street gang knows that the police officer is "just there to do a job," which to them means following an established routine of patrol with as little hassle as possible.

Bureaucratic Dysfunction: Goal Displacement

The rigidity cycle, in which employees are caught up in an ever-tightening web of control, is related to another bureaucratic dysfunction known as goal displacement. When the rigidity cycle starts to give greater and greater emphasis to the rules rather than the purposes of the organization, goal displacement occurs. In effect, goal displacement means that employees substitute a concern for organizational procedures in the place of original organizational goals. Thus, the procedures become ends in themselves and their connection to any more constructive purpose is lost.

Because classical bureaucracy relies heavily on formal rules, structure, and procedures to achieve organizational performance, critics maintain that it is particularly susceptible to goal displacement. In public bureaucracies, this problem is especially acute because of the difficulty of defining and measuring objectives or purposes. This difficulty makes the concreteness of rules attractive. Since crime rates in big cities, for example, are caused by several factors beyond the control of police forces, the police department may resort to setting the number of police officers per precinct as the organizational goal. Likewise, welfare agencies may concentrate on the number of cases processed rather than on the effects of their activities on clients. Filling out forms properly and meeting quotas on time eventually displaces citizen welfare as the ultimate purpose of the organization.

Other Bureaucratic Dysfunctions: Trained Incapacity

Gouldner was not the only sociologist to discover "bureaucratic dysfunctions." Robert Merton, for instance, suggested that the bureaucratic model leads to something called "trained incapacity."[25]

Modern bureaucrats are certainly skilled, trained personnel, unlike the political hacks of the nineteenth century. But are these skilled, trained personnel always the most responsive, most accountable, and most efficient? Perhaps not. Because bureaucracy trains its employees in very specialized, narrow areas, bureaucrats may be unable to see beyond the special requirements of their own jobs to get the "big picture" of what is best for the organization as a whole.[26]

A striking example of this occurred during the Cuban missile crisis. The major decision made by the Kennedy administration during this crisis was whether to respond with an air strike or with a naval blockade. Both options had their supporters. Representatives of the Navy were among the supporters of the blockade, and Curtis LeMay, the Air Force Chief of Staff, was a supporter of the air strike. The naval blockade of Cuba was the option chosen, with the possibility of an air strike held in reserve as a threat to the Russians.

For several days, the world held its breath to see whether a nuclear confrontation would result. The Russians finally agreed to withdraw their missiles. This did not satisfy LeMay, however; seeing the opportunity for an air strike slipping away, he suggested to Kennedy that "we attack Monday in any case."[27] LeMay's training as an Air Force strategic planner had led him to see the advantages of the use of air power but had blinded him to the *big picture* and its dangers. Kennedy's conception of the usefulness of force led him to consider not only the military strategy, but also the political and diplomatic aspects of the choice of response.

Bureaucratic Dysfunction: Dual System of Authority

The classical reformers argued for a style of administration that was both hierarchical and specialized. A superior at any level of an organization is likely to oversee the efforts of a variety of trained specialists. A few superiors may be brilliant enough to monitor the activities of many, varied specialists. For example, Admiral Hyman Rickover, the creator of the nuclear navy, seemed to know as much about engineering and seamanship as all of his subordinates combined. Robert Moses, the construction coordinator of the City of New York, seemed to know as much about law as his legal assistants and as much about bridge-building as his architects. These remarkable men cannot serve as the bureaucratic norm, however. At most levels in a bureaucracy, a professional doctor, lawyer, engineer, or scientist is supervised by someone who has no specialized knowledge of medicine, law, engineering, or science. The head of the Bureau of Standards is normally a famous physicist; he reports to the Secretary of Commerce, who normally has no knowledge of physics. The Chief of the Forest Service is a professional forester who reports to the Secretary of Agriculture.

What occurs in these situations is very often a conflict between the hierarchical authority of the superior and the expert authority of the subordinate. The professional subordinate resents taking orders from someone who does not share his or her professional training and point of view, while the superior is likely to feel defensive about this lack of training, yet reluctant to give up his rights and responsibilities as boss.

Again, the Cuban missile crisis offers a striking example of this bureaucratic dysfunction. After Kennedy decided on the blockade as the best way of averting a nuclear showdown with Russia, the job of carrying out the blockade was handed to the Chief of Naval Operations, Admiral George Anderson. However, Kennedy was particular that the purpose of this blockade was not a conventional one, and therefore the blockade should not be carried out in conventional ways. Secretary of Defense Robert McNamara explained that

> The object of the operation was not to shoot Russians but to communicate a political message from President Kennedy to Chairman Khrushchev. . . . By the conventional rules, blockade was an act of war and the first Soviet ship that refused to submit to boarding and search risked being sent to the bottom. But this was a military action with a political objective. Khrushchev must somehow be persuaded to pull back, rather than goaded into retaliation.[28]

Kennedy sent McNamara to make sure that Admiral Anderson understood that the purpose of the blockade was a political rather than military one, and would run the blockade with this in mind.

Here was a situation where, if ever, McNamara had all the authority that hierarchy could give a person. He was speaking for the President of the United States and Commander in Chief in a situation in which all concerned felt that the survival of civilization was dependent on the behavior of subordinates in his hierarchy. He was issuing directives to an immediate subordinate in a bureaucracy that was famous for its emphasis on recognizing hierarchical authority.

Nevertheless, McNamara found resistance to the president's wishes from Anderson, resistance that was based on Anderson's claim to the authority of trained expertise. Anderson did not snap his heels and say, "Yes, sir!" when McNamara explained his mission, so McNamara felt compelled to use logic, to explain the President's feelings at length, to question the details of the operation.

> At one point McNamara asked Anderson what he would do if a Soviet ship's captain refused to answer questions about his cargo. At that point the Navy man picked up the *Manual of Naval Regulations* and, waving it in McNamara's face, shouted, "It's all in there." To which McNamara replied, "I don't give a damn what John Paul Jones would have done, I want to know what you are going to do, now." The encounter ended on Anderson's remark: "Now, Mr. Secretary, if you and your Deputy will go back to your offices, the Navy will run the blockade."[29]

At a critical moment in world history, Anderson used his authority as an expert and keeper of the "rules" to challenge the hierarchical authority of the president.

BUREAUCRATIC DYSFUNCTIONS AND THE PROFESSIONS

One might suppose that professionals in a bureaucracy would have an ameliorating influence on these dysfunctional problems. After all, the Progressives were not simply advocating a bureaucracy, they were advocating a professionalized bureaucracy, composed of trained experts who are committed to a point of view. Presumably, these professionals would not be as uncooperative as the subordinates in

Gouldner's factory. Surely a bureaucracy composed of professionals could not be as rigid and inefficient as one composed of clerks or untrained workers.

Gouldner, in his discussion of bureaucratic dysfunctions, suggested that organizations should de-emphasize the hierarchical element of bureaucracy as much as possible, while emphasizing the professional training of its members. This has been seconded by others,[30] including Peter Blau.[31] Blau feels that professionalism promotes the internalization of organizational goals, so that employees do not displace goals by treating techniques and red tape as ends in themselves. Says Blau, "A professional orientation makes officials concerned with impediments to efficient operations and directs them to attempt adjustments."[32] In fact, one student of professionalism, Eliott Friedson, has observed, "By virtually all writers, expertise and professions are equated with a flexible, creative and equalitarian way of organizing work, while bureaucracy is associated with rigidity, and with mechanical and authoritarian ways."[33]

However, Friedson also notes that the evidence for the flexibility, equalitarian outlook, and efficiency of professionalism stems from analyses of professionals *as they interact with other professionals*. In other words, they look at the interaction of the partners in a law firm, or the physicians in a medical practice, or the academics within a university department. In most public organizations, however, professionals are necessarily placed in a work environment that consists of nonprofessionals or members of other professions. In this case, Friedson argues, professionals tend to use bureaucratic hierarchy to consolidate their authority over others in the organization. The reason is that simply relying on their expertise is too cumbersome a way of controlling members outside the profession.

The sociologist Charles Perrow is in agreement. He argues that large professional organizations must involve status differences that amount to hierarchy. Furthermore, as individual professionals rise in this hierarchy, they must develop and depend on their expertise as managers more than their expertise as professionals.[34]

Friedson further argues that the structural similarities in professional bureaucracies may result in consequences similar to those disparaged in nonprofessional bureaucracies:

> The authority of expertise is in fact problematic, requiring in its functional form the time-consuming and not always successful effort of persuading others that its "orders" are at once true and appropriate. As a special kind of occupation, professions have attempted to solve the problem of persuasion [or control] by obtaining institutional powers and prerogatives which on occasion even coerce their clients into compliance. The expertise of the professional is institutionalized into something similar to bureaucratic office. Indeed, a division of labor ordered by professional rather than by administrative authority contains within it mechanisms and consequences similar to those described as the pathologies of bureaucracy.[35]

If this is accurate, then the problem of bureaucratic dysfunctions is more fundamental than we might have guessed. If professionals use the managerial orthodoxy to assert their own control over bureaucracies, and if this process recreates bureaucratic dysfunctions, then these problems cannot be eliminated by professionalizing the work force.

Professional Capture of Bureaucracy

We noted in Chapter 4 that professionals certainly were among the main supporters and beneficiaries of the Progressive reform movement. The politics/administration dichotomy provided a natural defense for professional autonomy from political interference and professional self-management of licensing and client relationships. The Progressive deification of expertise further promoted professional status goals, and bureaucratic specialization could easily be interpreted to mean specialization on the basis of professional expertise rather than clientele or geography. Furthermore, the emphasis on a written body of rules was compatible with the professional emphasis on a written body of ideas.

Friedson argues, however, that the compatibility of professionals and the Progressive model of administration further extend to encompass the notion of hierarchy. Professionals, Friedson notes, not only want autonomy from political outsiders and the public, they also want control of their work environment. Capturing control of a hierarchy guaranteed this professional goal. He cites the example of medicine, of which he says:

> It has the authority to direct and evaluate the work of others without in turn being subject to formal direction and evaluation by them. Paradoxically, its autonomy is sustained by the dominance of its expertise in the division of labor.[36]

While physicians and nurses both claim to be professionals, physicians are clearly the dominant profession in medicine because they control the hierarchy of medical bureaucracies. This form of professional dominance within individual bureaucracies has been repeated so frequently in twentieth-century public agencies that Mosher has given it a name: professional capture.

Professional Capture of Public Agencies

The major work on professionals in public bureaucracies has been done by Frederick Mosher, who notes that professionals in public agencies have made it a point to seek both autonomy from political "outsiders" and dominance over nonprofessional subordinates in an agency. Combining autonomy and dominance, Mosher arrives at the notion of professional capture, which has these features:

> 1. the given profession has staked its territory within the appropriate governmental agency or agencies, usually with the boundaries coterminous with those of the organization itself;
> 2. within its organization it has formed an elite corps with substantial control over the operations of the agency, significant influence on agency policies, and high internal prestige;
> 3. to the extent possible, it has assumed control over employment policies and individual personnel actions for its own members in the agency and also over the employment of employees not in the elite profession;
> 4. it has provided its members the opportunities, assurances, and protections of a career system of employment.[37]

Among the professions that have followed this pattern are civil engineers within state and local transportation and public works bureaucracies, lawyers within the Department of Justice, doctors within medical hospitals and research institutes (public and private), foresters within the Forest Service, Foreign Service diplomats within the State Department, and the officer corps within the military. In all of these cases, the professions have used the Progressive notion of the politics/administration dichotomy to insulate themselves from the influence of political nonprofessionals, while using the Progressive managerial orthodoxy to establish a system of hierarchy and rules by which to dominate the bureaucracy.

Professional Careerism and Bureaucratic Dysfunctions

The payoff for all of this is the career system of employment for professional members, Mosher's item four. This career system is defined as:

> the expectation that individuals will be recruited soon after completion of their education; that they will spend the bulk of their working lives in the same organization; that they will be advanced periodically as they gain experience and seniority, such advancement made on the basis of competition with their peers; and that they will be protected in such advancement against competition with outsiders.[38]

According to Mosher, the professional goal of careerism in public agencies has not worked out ideally. Careerism has led to the same kinds of bureaucratic dysfunctions in professionally dominated bureaucracies that were noted by sociologists who studied the bureaucratization of private industry. For instance, careerism discourages lateral entry, which is the hiring of "new blood" at the middle levels of bureaucracy. Lateral entry can be the means for breaking up a pattern of rigidity and inflexibility in a bureaucracy, but it is eliminated in professionalized bureaucracies because it also diminishes the chances of advancement for members of the profession already in the bureaucracy.

Careerism also "provides built-in, though usually unwritten, incentives for individuals to pursue orthodox careers within the agency and to avoid unusual assignments which might sidetrack or delay advancements."[39] Mosher argues that this discourages creativity, innovation, and risk-taking because of the fear by younger professionals that they will be regarded as unprofessional or unorthodox (which is often considered the same thing) by older colleagues in the profession. Mosher concludes that professional careerism "is probably the principal ingredient of the cement which binds an agency into a strong, autonomous, and perhaps impervious entity against outsiders—whether above in the Executive Branch or outside in the legislature or the public. It is apparent that many aspects of careerism run counter to effective government responsiveness to the needs of the temporary society."[40]

Professionalism and Dysfunctions

Besides supporting careerism, professionalism itself is seen as a source of bureaucratic dysfunctions. Friedson points to patient dissatisfaction with doctor-dominated hospitals as the clearest example of how professional domination may lead to bureaucratic pathologies that negatively affect the client.[41] Patients in the medical system often exhibit frustration at their inability to get information from employees in the system, at the insensitivity to patient feelings, and at their feeling of being simply an inhuman cog in the medical machine. These problems are well documented in the medical profession, and are clearly the exact analogies to problems clients experience in dealing with nonprofessionalized bureaucracies: "The professionally organized division of labor has pathologies similar to those said to stem from bureaucracy."[42]

Mosher agrees, pointing to such pathologies as the rigidity cycle, goal displacement, and trained incapacity in professionally captured public bureaucracies. He points out that professional capture of a bureaucracy guarantees only one hegemonic point of view when confronting a new problem. For this reason, professionals frequently find solutions to problems that address only the part of the problem they are concerned with.

As examples, highway engineers historically ignored environmental considerations in designing their highways; this fact was one of the principal motivators for environmentalists who supported legislation which mandated highway agencies to write environmental impact statements before construction. Public health agencies are dominated by a profession which has regarded its principal challenge as communicable disease; this helps explain the inability or unwillingness of state and local public health bureaucracies to respond to the new challenge posed by the Love Canal incident. The Army and Navy professionals between the world wars were convinced of the importance of the infantry and of the indestructibility of the battleship; they ended up court-martialing General Billy Mitchell when he kept arguing that air power would be the key to future military success. Thus, the dominance of a single profession in a bureaucracy means the dominance of a single idea, which looks very much like the notion of "trained incapacity" mentioned earlier.

Frank Levy and his colleagues provide several examples of the impact of professionals on policy outcomes.[43] They find, for example, that the engineers in a local department of transportation used a professional model of traffic flow to determine where funds should be allocated in the street system of Oakland, California. The more heavily traveled a street was, the more money the engineers wanted to spend to widen, straighten, and resurface it. Hence, main arteries had funding priority over less well-traveled neighborhood streets.

The problem with this approach to street planning, as the authors point out, is the negative consequences for the residents both along the arteries and in the neighborhoods. The allocation of resources encouraged the further concentration of traffic, which meant that residents along the arteries had their front lawns chopped off for additional lanes. Noise levels and congestion increased. The principal beneficiaries were not the city's residents, but the wealthier suburbanites who used the arteries to get in and out of town quickly. The poorer residents tended to be the ones most affected by the increased noise and pollution. Had the street engineers included variables other than traffic circulation in their analysis (variables such as neighborhood preservation, air pollution, and low-income ridership) their budget allocations might have looked quite different, resulting in more money for maintenance of low-income residential streets off the main arteries.

Whether traffic circulation, neighborhood preservation, or some other value should compromise the dominant value for street planning is a difficult political issue; in this case, the conflict was solved simply by professionals imposing their standards on bureaucratic decision making. What is clear is that the professional engineers had ignored for several years the concerns of a certain group of residents. They were able to do so because the professional reform model had legitimized their hierarchical dominance within the department of transportation, and insulated that agency from city politics. Any attempt to challenge the professional control over allocation of funds in the department would have been met by a cry of "partisan politics interfering with professional expertise," a cry that has been the first line of defense for professional bureraucrats ever since the Progressive era.

The Oakland library was also dominated by professionals for several years, during which time the cost of circulating a book jumped ahead of other comparable libraries and the rate of circulation fell to an embarrassingly low level. While most libraries have three nonprofessional staff members for every two professionals, in the Oakland library over half of the staff were professional librarians. The large professional staff, who are paid more than nonprofessionals, meant that 85 percent of the library budget went to salaries, compared to 68 percent for most other public libraries in California. The large sums for salaries, in turn, squeezed out spending on books. The Oakland library spent less on books than twelve comparable cities, and a small fraction of the three leading cities. "Books are a residual category" in the budget.[44]

Levy and colleagues discovered that the professional librarians defined the purpose of the library as a repository for fine books rather than as a service institution for the Oakland residents. This conformed with the status ranking within the profession, where professionals in such repositories have more prestige than professionals who guarantee a flow of mass literature to the general public. Whether the Oakland public library was an appropriate setting for a repository of fine books was not settled outside of the library system. The professionals who ran the library simply purchased expensive books that were in little demand by citizens who preferred easier reading, trade books, and other, less prestigious materials. This was the reason for the decline in circulation rates.

In organization structure, the library was also affected by professional concerns. The central library, because of its greater prestige, was given more money and attention than the branch libraries. This, too, hurt circulation. Many professionals at the central library were doing work that could be handled by less educated clerks or secretarial staff. Little money was placed in the budget for repairing the branch buildings or locating them in convenient sites for clientele that could not travel far. In sum, the library was centralized, with far too many professionals at the top of the hierarchy. Younger professionals at the branch libraries were afraid to "rock the boat" for fear of being passed over for promotion to the more prestigious jobs at the central library. The result of professional dominance was inefficiency: low circulation and high cost with little regard for the preferences of the varied Oakland clientele.

In response to these problems, the authors recommended a shift in budget priorities away from professional personnel and toward the needs and demands of lower- and middle-income users, who were the bulk of the population in Oakland. This new orientation would entail spending more money on books, especially those suited for trades and popular reading, renovation of run-down branches, and making the library more accessible and attractive to a variety of people.

The Oakland City Task Force, however, took "an essentially administrative view of the problem. Its emphasis is on building seven new library structures equidistant from current users, who are expected to drive to them."[45] Levy and his colleagues express skepticism that the city can afford these new expenditures or that the new libraries will reach the poorer and less mobile sections of the population. Nonetheless, each new library will have its own "complement of professionals" and will thus further the career goals of the professionals in the system.

CONCLUSION: WHY DO BUREAUCRACIES DIFFER?

The purpose of this chapter has not been to argue that every professionalized hierarchy is subject to bureaucratic dysfunctions, nor that the bureaucratic reforms of the Progressive Era and the New Deal made public agencies perform less efficiently. Few would deny that these reforms resulted in vast improvements over the nineteenth century standard of administrative performance. The programs sponsored by Progressives and New Dealers—including regulation of food quality, management of forest resources, improvement of agricultural techniques, rural electrification, Social Security, and others—were largely successes. Without the administrative improvements sponsored by the same reformers, they would have been impossible to attempt.

The successes of the administrative reform movement are supported by other bits of evidence. Most clients who have to interact with the Social Security Administration, the Post Office, or local bureaucracies such as police and fire come away satisfied that the bureaucrats they deal with are competent, fair, and helpful. Furthermore, this contrasts sharply with citizen evaluations of bureaucracies in other countries. In one study, done in 1963, 83 percent of Americans felt their bureaucrats try to give equal treatment, compared to 65% in West Germany, 53% in Italy, and 42% in Mexico.[46] By all accounts, administration in most developing countries does involve the kind of endemic, systematic corruption that was described in Jacksonian America, but that seems to have largely disappeared in such American institutions as the post office, the General Land Office, and the customs offices.

In light of this evidence, it is all the more striking that bureaucrats and bureaucracy have received increasingly negative public attention in recent decades. Congressional and presidential candidates get elected by promising to go to Washington to control it, or to cut it down to size.

One reason for this attack on bureaucracy may be the very success of the administrative reform movement in raising expectations about the performance of bureaucracy. As discussed in previous chapters, one of the most lasting effects of the Progressive reform movement was the new expectation that bureaucrats could and would be efficient, neutral, and accountable. Yet the problems that public bureaucracies are set to work on are by nature the ones that private businesses cannot hope to handle effectively: enduring poverty, long-term management of complex ecological effects like solid-waste pollution, development of effective national security strategies in an era of potential nuclear holocaust. And on top of that, bureaucracy is expected to be an agent of social change: as Charles Goodsell notes, "Bureaucracy is expected not only to be perfect, but to perfect society."[47]

Another defense of public bureaucracies is that they clearly should not all be tarred with the same brush. When the New York Police Department uncovers corruption in its vice squad, that does not mean that all police officials are suspect. When Congress discovers abuses by federal intelligence agencies, that does not mean that all bureaucrats are powercrazed. When investigations reveal that the Defense Department is paying over $1000 each for nylon spool caps that should cost 26 cents apiece, that does not mean that all bureaucrats are inefficient dolts.

Indeed, the literature reviewed in this chapter has provided substantial evidence of the possibilities for bureaucratic inefficiency, without explaining when or where we should expect particular bureaucratic dysfunctions to appear. Some bureaucrats evince "trained incapacity," but not all do. Some organizations seem to be on a downward spiral of increasing rigidity, but not all do. In a study by James D. Thompson of two Air Force wings with identical hierarchical chains of command, identical regulations, identical staffing patterns, and similar internal organizations, he found their performances to be quite different.[48] One seemed to evince a more striking pattern of bureaucratic rigidity than the other.

However, *unexplained variations in bureaucratic performance are the primary challenge to the adequacy of administrative orthodoxy.* If the administrative orthodoxy "works," why shouldn't every similarly structured bureaucracy (with hierarchy, rules, trained experts) be similarly effective? Yet other carefully paired studies of state wildlife commissions,[49] state liquor agencies,[50] and other organizations show that two organizations identically structured following the reform prescription of hierarchy, specialization, rules, and staffing can perform quite differently with regard to efficiency. This implies that the reform orthodoxy is inadequate because the variables that determine bureaucractic efficiency are *not* those structural variables that the orthodoxy specifies as being crucial.

In Chapter 9 we will seek an explanation for why bureaucractic dysfunctions strike some professionalized bureaucracies and not others. In the meantime, however, we want to continue the assessment of the performance of reformed bureaucracies. Are they neutral? Are they accountable?

FIGURE 6-1 Hypothetical Links Between Bureaucratic Charcteristics and Bureaucratic Dysfunctions

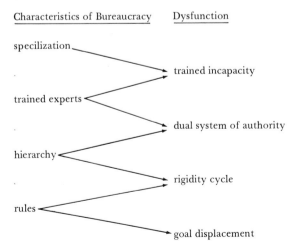

Characteristics of Bureaucracy   Dysfunction

specilization

trained incapacity

trained experts

dual system of authority

hierarchy

rigidity cycle

rules

goal displacement

NOTES

[1] WILLIAM FOOTE WHYTE, _Money and Motivation: An Analysis of Incentives in Industry_ (New York: Harper and Row, 1955), pp. 15-16. Reprinted by permission of Harper & Row, Publishers.

[2] FREDERICK WINSLOW TAYLOR, _Scientific Management_ (New York: Harper & Row Publishers, 1911).

[3] F. J. ROETHLISBERGER, _Management and Morale_ (Cambridge: Harvard University Press, 1965), pp. 9–11.

[4] ROETHLISBERGER, _Management_, p. 22.

[5] ROETHLISBERGER, _Management_, p. 24.

[6] ABRAHAM MASLOW, "A Theory of Human Motivation," _Psychological Review_, 50 (1943), pp. 370–396.

[7] DOUGLAS MCGREGOR, _The Human Side of Enterprise_ (New York: McGraw-Hill, 1960).

[8] McGREGOR, _Enterprise_, p. 34.

[9] McGREGOR, _Enterprise_, p. 48.

[10] McGREGOR, _Enterprise_, p. 48.

[11] CHARLES SEASHORE, "What is Sensitivity Training?," _Management Forum_, 2 (1968).

[12] CHARLES PERROW, _Complex Organizations: A Critical Essay_ (Glenview: Scott, Foresman, 1972), pp. 115–118.

[13] VICTOR H. VROOM, _Work and Motivation_ (New York: John Wiley & Sons, Inc., 1964), p. 181.

[14] VROOM, _Work_, pp. 186–187.

[15] ALVIN GOULDNER, _Patterns of Industrial Bureaucracy_ (New York: The Free Press, 1954).

[16] ANTHONY DOWNS, _Inside Bureaucracy_ (Boston: Little, Brown, 1967), pp. 158–166.

[17] DOWNS, _Inside Bureaucracy_, p. 160.

[18] These dysfunctions are summarized in James March and Herbert Simon, _Organizations_ (New York: John Wiley and Sons, Inc., 1958), pp. 36–47.

[19] FREDERICK C. MOSHER, "The Public Service in the Temporary Society," _Public Administration Review_, 31 (1971), p. 58.

[20] MOSHER, "The Public Service," p. 58.

[21] MOSHER, "The Public Service," p. 58.

[22] MOSHER, "The Public Service," p. 59.

[23] MICHAEL LIPSKY, _Street-Level Bureaucracy: Dilemmas of the Individual in Public Services_ (New York: Russell Sage Foundation, 1980).

[24] LIPSKY, _Street-Level Bureaucracy_, p. 140.

[25] ROBERT K. MERTON, "Bureaucratic Structure and Personality," _Social Forces_, 17 (1940), pp. 560–568; reprinted in _Reader in Bureaucracy_, Robert Merton, et al., eds. (New York: Free Press, 1952), pp. 361–371.

[26] LIPSKY, _Street-Level Bureaucracy_, p. 147.

[27] GRAHAM ALLISON, _Essence of Decision: Explaining the Cuban Missile Crisis_ (Boston: Little, Brown & Co., 1971), p. 266.

[28] ELIE ABEL, _The Missile Crisis_ (Philadelphia, 1966), p. 155.

[29] ALLISON, _Essence_, pp. 131–132.

[30] VICTOR A. THOMPSON, _Bureaucracy and Innovation_ (University, Alabama: University of Alabama Press, 1969).

[31] PETER M. BLAU, _The Dynamics of Bureaucracy_, 2nd ed. (Chicago: University of Chicago Press, 1963)

[32] BLAU, _Dynamics_, p. 258.

[33]ELIOTT FRIEDSON, "Dominant Professions, Bureaucracy, and Client Services," in *Organizations and Clients: Essays in the Sociology of Service*, William R. Rosengren and Mark Lefton, eds. (Columbus: Charles E. Merrill Publishing Co., 1970), p. 72.

[34]PERROW, *Complex Organizations*, pp. 35, 58.

[35]FRIEDSON, "Dominant Professions," pp. 73–74.

[36]FRIEDSON, "Dominant Professions," p. 77.

[37]FREDERICK MOSHER, *Democracy and the Public Service*, 2nd ed. (New York: Oxford University Press, 1982), pp. 119–120.

[38]MOSHER, "The Public Service," p. 58.

[39]MOSHER, "The Public Service," p. 58.

[40]MOSHER, "The Public Service," p. 58.

[41]FRIEDSON, "Dominant Professions," pp. 71–92.

[42]FRIEDSON, "Dominant Professions," p. 84.

[43]FRANK LEVY, ARNOLD MELTSNER, and AARON WILDAVSKY, *Urban Outcomes: Schools, Streets, and Libraries* (Berkeley: University of California Press, 1974).

[44]LEVY, MELTSNER, and WILDAVSKY, *Urban Outcomes*, p. 186.

[45]LEVY, MELTSNER, and WILDAVSKY, *Urban Outcomes*, p. 217.

[46]GABRIEL A. ALMOND and SIDNEY VERBA, *Civic Culture: Political Attitudes and Democracy in Five Nations* (Boston: Little, Brown & Co., 1963), p. 70.

[47]CHARLES T. GOODSELL, *The Case for Beaucracy: A Public Administration Polemic*, 2nd ed. (Chatham: Chatham House Publishers, 1983), p. 75.

[48]JAMES D. THOMPSON, "Authority and Power in 'Identical' Organizations," *American Journal of Sociology*, 62 (1956), pp. 290–301.

[49]JAMES L. PRICE, "Use of Knowledge in Organizations," *Human Organization*, 23 (1964), pp. 60–73.

[50]WILLIAM E. TURCOTTE, "Control Systems, Performance, and Satisfaction in Two State Agencies," *Administrative Science Quarterly*, 19 (1974), pp. 60–73.

CHAPTER 7

Assessing the Reform Model:
Is It Really Neutral?

If parties were to be emasculated, what would be left save government
by the expert, government in the name of a public whose multitudes
could never speak except through interest groups—the very instruments
of that hidden government whose destruction constituted the
Progressive mission?

Grant McConnell, *Private Power and American Democracy*[1]

Reform movements have consistently sought to divorce administration from politics. The reformers, who saw politics as synonymous with party bosses and government corruption, tapped a powerful sentiment in the American public, which has
always mistrusted politics and politicians since colonial times. The colonial mistrust
of court politicians advising the King, the Madisonian mistrust of "factions" and
reliance on separation of powers, the frontier mistrust of politicians and emphasis
on limited government, all contributed to the popularity of the reformers' conviction that politics should be limited, and certainly kept out of administration.

As late as 1935, public administration experts continued to support the ideal
of the politics/administration dichotomy. J. M. Pfiffner wrote that politics was a
necessary aspect of government that must, however, "be confined to its proper
sphere," which is the "declaration of the will of the community." Administration,
on the other hand, is the carrying into effect of this will once it has been made clear
by political processes.[2]

THE REDISCOVERY OF POLITICS

When academic public administrationists were called to Washington during the
New Deal and World War II, the practical experience of managing the machinery
of government made them doubt the possibility of neutral administration. Paul
Appleby, for instance, was a New Deal administrator who left government after
World War II with the message that administration could not conceivably be
divorced from politics.[3] Appleby observed that legislatures do not and cannot state
policy so clearly and unambiguously that all discretion on the part of administrators

is eliminated.[4] In fact, much of the time Congress specifically resorts to ambiguously worded legislation because no majority can be found to support any unambiguous policy statement. In these cases, Congress "consciously" leaves the actual determination of the policy content of legislation to the courts, or much more frequently, to administrators.

However, administrators may initiate legislation as well. Appleby notes that more and more legislation is formulated by executive agencies, introduced by friendly legislators, and very often passed with active executive lobbying from the White House and/or agency lobbyists. This pattern of administrative dominance seems to prevail especially under active presidents. During the Kennedy–Johnson era, for example, major urban renewal and economic development legislation, including the Model Cities Act, the Safe Streets Act, the Elementary and Secondary Education Act, and the Economic Opportunity Act, were initiated and shaped by executive agencies.[5] The legislation of the 1960s was in large part shaped by the professionalized bureaucracies that were to manage the programs so authorized.

Administration, therefore, is not divorced from policy making, and it is impossible to imagine a system in which it could be. Administrators help develop, pass, interpret, and implement policies, and if policy making is essentially political, as the Progressives argued, then policy making by administrators must be as political as policy making by legislators, according to Appleby. Appleby points out that the modern bureaucratic agency has more contact with the public than do legislators. In a direct denial of Woodrow Wilson's claim that "the field of administration is a field of business," Appleby also argued that the political nature of governmental administration made it distinct from business administration, and therefore an inappropriate place for the simple application of neutral, scientific management techniques.[6]

All of this was heresy enough, from the standpoint of the classical reform model, but worse was to come. Norton Long argued in 1949 that since public administration is essentially political, "the lifeblood of administration is power. Its attainment, maintenance, increase, dissipation, and loss are subjects the practitioner and student can ill afford to neglect."[7] The classical theory had made no place for the role of administrative power, since administrators were to be the pliant tools of the policy makers, who had all the power. The classical theory of power derived from the hierarchical chain of command was inadequate, according to Long. "Power is only one of the considerations that must be weighed in administration, but of all it is the most overlooked in theory and the most dangerous to overlook in practice."[8]

Bureaucracies must cultivate power where they can find it, including those interests completely outside the chain of command. Long calls these "lateral" sources of power, which are crucial because no point in the administrative hierarchy, not even the presidency itself, can guarantee a constant flow of power down the chain of command. Long uses an example from the war to illustrate this fact:

> When the staff of the Office of War Mobilization and Reconversion advised a hard-pressed agency to go out and get itself some popular support so that the President could afford to support it, their action reflected the realities of power rather than political cynicism. It is clear that the American system of politics does not generate enough power at any focal point of leadership to provide the conditions for an even partially

successful divorce of politics from administration. Subordinates cannot depend upon the formal chain of command to deliver enough political power to permit them to do their jobs.[9]

If the cultivation of political support is so crucial to agencies during the war, when the whole government faced an external threat, it is even more likely to govern agency actions under normal circumstances of open disagreement and partisanship. Under these circumstances, it may be surmised, nothing important is done by public administrators *without* explicit political support.

WINNING POLITICAL SUPPORT

The article by Long in 1949 speaks to the importance of political alliances as a way in which an administrative agency can generate power necessary for successful action. But how do administrative agencies build the alliances on which power rests? An account of the Tennessee Valley Authority, published by Philip Selznick in the same year, provides an answer.[10]

The TVA had been set up in 1933, Franklin Roosevelt's first year in office. Its foremost congressional supporter was George Norris, an old-line Nebraska Progressive. The TVA was created to deal with a whole range of problems in southwest Appalachia: control of flooding, construction of parks, production of fertilizers, development of inland waterways, and (most controversial) production of cheap electric power. The agency was viewed with missionary zeal by the first TVA officials, who saw themselves as bringing economic salvation to one of the poorest sections of the country through scientific regional planning.

Almost immediately, the TVA faced strong opposition from some of the most powerful people in the country. The most notable opposition came from the utilities. The spokesman for the utilities was Wendell Willkie of the Commonwealth and Southern utility, who achieved such national prominence for his attack on the TVA that he received the Republican nomination for the presidency against FDR in 1940. With such powerful opposition, the TVA desperately needed its own source of political support; otherwise, it might go out of existence, as many of the other New Deal agencies were to do.

To meet the challenge, the TVA pursued a "grass-roots" policy that established special ties with a large number of existing local organizations and governments in the South, and through them to the agricultural elite which dominated the South's representation in Congress:

> A list of agencies with which the TVA has maintained some form of cooperative relationship includes nearly all of the governmental institutions in the area: municipal power boards, rural electric cooperatives, school and library boards, state departments of health, conservation and parks; state and local planning commissions, agricultural and engineering experiment stations, state extension services and others.[11]

These cooperative relationships were built on intergovernmental contracts. The TVA would coordinate, plan, and finance programs in health, recreation, education, and agriculture, and would pay the state and local agencies to provide the manpower and other facilities. Instead of competing with the TVA, therefore, state and local agencies actually become dependent on the TVA for funds in a period of financial stringency. State and local officials thus owed their jobs to the TVA, and the clients of these agencies (including the agricultural elite) depended on the TVA for vital services. These agencies and clients, along with the cities and farmers who were benefiting from the cheaper electricity provided by the TVA, provided a groundswell of local support that was sufficient to keep the TVA in existence, despite opposition from powerful utility companies.

The price of an implicit alliance with the South's agricultural elite, however, was tacit approval of the South's social system. As Selznick notes, "Emphasis on existing institutions as democratic instruments may wed the agency to the status quo."[12]

> The grass roots policy also meant acquiescing in white supremacy. In general, Negroes received short shrift from the TVA, as they did from many other New Deal agencies. Black agricultural colleges had no role in TVA's fertilizer program. Construction villages such as the model of Norris housed white families only. . . . [TVA] had a unique opportunity to ameliorate the racial situation. It made little effort to do so, despite repeated protests from the NAACP over Jim Crowism and abuses of black workers by white foremen.[13]

The development of grass-roots support from existing agencies turned the TVA from a crusading revolutionary organization into "just another power company." Early zealots who had hoped to transform the social system of the South left in discouragement.

This story has many implications for the administrative reform model, some of which will be developed later in this chapter. For the moment, it is enough to emphasize that an exchange of bureaucratic services for political support cut two ways: While the southern political leaders became obligated to the TVA and worked for its support in Congress, the TVA became obligated to the southerners as well. This suggests that administration is so embedded in the political environment that the potential for change through "rational administrative reform" is limited; if political realities do not change, then administrative reform by itself is not likely to force the change. Subsequent political changes in race relations in the South, for example, were not due to the professional expertise of planners, engineers, and other specialized experts working for the TVA, but to the development of new political forces such as the civil rights protest movement and the two-party competition for the votes that the protest movement generated.

WHICH INTEREST GROUPS ARE THE BEST ALLIES?

If the development of political support is crucial, an important question is, which interest groups are more valuable as allies? To answer this question, let us undertake the following thought experiment: Imagine that a state utilities commission is considering a proposal by the statewide telephone company to raise intrastate rates. It is estimated that the proposal would increase revenue for the phone company by $10 million. At the same time, of course, it would decrease the disposable income of the state's five million inhabitants by an average of $2 each. The phone company argues that the $10 million is absolutely necessary for its continued services. That amount of money could make the difference between a healthy dividend and happy stockholders, and a weak dividend and unhappy stockholders. Consequently, the phone company lobbies for the rate increase to the full extent of its very considerable powers.

On the other hand, consider Jane Doe, an average housewife who is faced with the prospect of a rate increase. She may or may not know she is faced with the increase, but if she were aware of that fact, how extensively would she lobby against it? She has only a $2 incentive to motivate her to go down to the state capital, write a letter, send a telegram, or lobby against the rate increase. This probably would not be a big enough incentive to get her actively involved in the dispute, even if she knew her letter would make a difference.

Because of the large number of people involved, it is very unlikely that her letter would make a difference. If a large number of other citizens were to send letters to their state representatives and the utilities commission, there is little doubt that they would have an impact; but each individual citizen would get the benefit of that massive lobbying effort *whether or not* he or she actively participated. On the other hand, if no one else were to write a letter, then one letter would not make a difference. No matter what everyone else decides to do, there is little reason for one member of this very large interest group to spend much in the way of resources to fight the rate increase. A similar logic applies to every large group in which the individual gets the benefits of collective action whether or not he or she participates. The incentive for nonparticipation seems overwhelming, and grows more overwhelming the larger the group involved.

For this reason, there is a drastic asymmetry in the amount of lobbying that the two sides will undertake before the utilities commission. The members of the large group (the phone company's consumers) have little reason as individuals to lobby; the phone company has every reason to lobby. The degree of financial involvement, although symmetric in the aggregate, is split up into tiny parts on the side of the phone users, but is felt by one powerful actor on the other side. What is more, the phone company is already mobilized for political action, having a large "public relations" branch with permanent connections to powerful political figures, while Jane Doe has none of these resources.

The implication of this thought experiment is that some interests are better potential allies for a bureaucracy than others. In general, a small cohesive, intense interest (like the phone company) speaks with a much more powerful political voice than a large, low-level, diffuse interest (like the aggregate of phone users).

In fact, the record does demonstrate that public utility commissions have accommodated themselves to the lopsided pressure from utilities such as the phone company. The advantages of such alliances are especially evident at election time, when the utilities are much more generous with campaign contributions than consumers are. (One Florida utilities commissioner, previously a Miami football coach, accepted a $24,000 contribution from the utilities with the justification, "They're old friends.")[14] Whether commissioners are elected or appointed, the intense lobbying from utilities makes an alliance with them by far the easier path, as is illustrated by the following commissioner's story. His first caller upon taking office was a Bell Telephone representative:

> He left enough printed material in my office to fill a bookcase. . . . He asked me to pick a date so they could fly me up to Murray Hill, New Jersey, to inspect the Bell Telephone Laboratories. He gave me a list of telephone numbers—home and

office—of his company's top executives and told me to call them any time, night or day, when I had a question about Bell, and to call collect.

I felt overwhelmed my first couple of years on the commission. The Bell men had a good sense of timing. About every three weeks or so they'd run with a proposal for rate reduction in some little out-of-the-way corner of the state, affecting maybe 150 people, and ask us to approve it. I'd ask questions of our own engineering and finance experts, and they'd come back with answers. After a while it dawned on me that they were just going down to the Bell lobbyist's office and asking them to come up with the information.

I got rather sore about all this—after all, I had practiced law for more than twenty-five years, and although I'm no genius, I wanted to do a serious job, for that's why the governor put me on the commission.

So I asked at one of our meetings, "Why can't we make our own studies of Bell? We're not regulating—we're just sitting up here in a nice boardroom and giving their decisions our blessings and putting the sanctity of the state upon them."

The other commissioners just laughed at me. "Go over to——," one of them said, mentioning the man who was Democratic majority leader in the legislature, "and ask him to give us the money we'd need to hire a competent staff."

I did just that, and ——told me I was out of my mind—— that he had more important things to do that session than to get into a hopeless fight with the Bell lobby. So I let it drop.

A year or so later we did have a young firebrand of a lawyer come onto our staff. He knew economics, and he had taken quite a few courses in public utilities. He lasted seven months. Bell hired him at a salary 69% percent over what he made for us, and the last I heard he's in one of their offices way out West.

I gave up trying to do anything in the telephone area and concentrated on bus fares. You can yell at the transportation companies without having the roof of the capital fall on your head. But Bell—well, my term was six years, and I'm too pragmatic a man to try to climb a mountain barefooted.[15]

This story gives us another clue to the importance of political power. Even in appointed commissions, the money for staff comes from legislators, and if utilities are major contributors to legislators' campaigns, then it may be impossible to get the staff necessary to challenge the information provided by the utilities: "A New York legislative committee on consumer protection, after a year-long study of that state's Public Service Commission, concluded that its control over power and telephone utilities was a 'fiasco' that cost citizens millions of dollars a year in excessive charges."[16]

Most regulatory commissions face united, intensely interested industries, and passive, fragmented, and large consumer groups: the asymmetry of political pressure in favor of the industries is a fairly uniform phenomenon, and has led to something called regulatory "capture," the regulation by commission in the interests of the industry regulated. One of the most striking cases is the Interstate Commerce Commission, whose origins and development during the Progressive era were discussed in Chapter 2. As early as 1936, a political scientist named Pendleton Herring was documenting regulatory capture in the various commissions. Herring introduced a chapter discussing the obedience of the ICC to industry interests with a quote from the Red Queen in *Alice in Wonderland*: "She never was really well brought up, but it's amazing how good-tempered she is: pat her on the head, and see how pleased she'll be."[17] Herring wrote, "Under the sheltering arm of the Interstate Commerce Commission, the railroads and the shippers have both found protection from the harsh impact of laissez faire. They have exerted themselves in their turn to protect the commission from assaults upon its independence."[18] The same pattern of mutual dependence between industry and the ICC continued after World War II. The ICC became a desirable appointment for individuals seeking a lucrative government job, with the regulated industry a potential next career step for commissioners who did not "rock the boat." Between 1958 and 1967, nine of the eleven commissioners who left the ICC received high-paying jobs in the transportation industry.[19]

CONGRESSIONAL SUPPORT FOR BUREAUCRACY

What can an interest group do for a bureaucracy, besides provide it with information? The most important service that an interest group can perform is to lobby Congress. If an agency like the TVA or the ICC alters its programs in order to attract the political support of an interest group, then both the interest group and the agency have a shared interest in adequate funding and authority to do what it is they both value. Both authority and funding, however, generally depend on congressional support. But how does this interest-group/bureaucracy alliance secure these benefits from Congress?

The way to influence Congress changed with the Progressive revolt. Before 1910, both houses of Congress were controlled by party machines, and the way to pass legislation through Congress was to obtain the support of the party machine. At the beginning of the 1910 session, George Norris and other Progressive Republicans voted with the Democrats to "unhorse" the Speaker. They were able to deprive the Speaker of his absolute control over the Rules Committee, and thus much of his dominance over legislation. The intended effects of Progressive reform were beginning to be felt. The spread of civil service, the consequent reduction in patronage, and the blow to the influence of the Speaker all led to a decline in the power of the party leadership in the House.

What was not intended or even foreseen was the subsequent rise in the committee system and committee chairmen as the primary force in congressional legislation. By the early 1960s, the committees had evolved into feudal power blocs, doing much of the work and exercising most of the authority of Congress. In the 1961–62 session, at the height of committee dominance of congressional decision making, 13,420 bills were introduced to Congress and immediately referred to some committee: the Agriculture Committee, the Armed Services Committee, the Appropriations Committee, the Ways and Means Committee, and so forth. Most bills never came out of their committees. Only 1,912 bills were reported out of committee to the floor of the House, and of these, 1,017 were enacted into law. That is, the committees constitute the largest obstacle to the passage of legislation, since they kill 86 per cent of the bills introduced to Congress; the House, Senate, and President, on the other hand, pass over half of the legislation that the committees pass.

Thus, the path to congressional influence for an interest group is the relevant committee. The Agriculture Committee, for example, can kill bills unfavorable to agricultural interests, and has a very good chance of passing into legislation bills favorable to agricultural interests. Consequently, these interests *must* be concerned about the composition of the Agriculture Committee. The Progressive reforms in Congress led to a decentralization of power to the committee system, and the committees have become the focus of lobbying efforts by bureaucracies and their interest-group allies.

What does the importance of the committee system mean for the average congressional committee member? Congressmen, who seek reelection every two years, certainly need the support of different interests among their constituents. Let us do another thought experiment to determine what kind of interests are likely to be most influential in Congress. If it turns out that congressional committees and bureaucracies are most responsive to similar kinds of groups, then the potential for a three-way alliance between interest groups, congressional committees, and bureaucracies exists.

Let us consider a proposal to raise first-class postage rates. Who in Congress would be concerned with such a proposal? Virtually every constituent of every congressman is a user of first-class mail, and therefore one might think that congressmen would be opposed to such increases. A proposal to increase the rate by 2 cents would increase the cost of first-class mailings by $2 to an average citizen who mails 100 first-class letters a year. On the other hand, there is no Association of First-Class Mail Users to object automatically to such an increase. Lacking such an organization, the citizen may not spend very much time objecting *as an individual*. If the citizen values his or her time at $5 an hour, then the simple act of writing a letter to a congressman is likely to cost more than the total cost of the rate increase. Furthermore, the effort of writing a letter is certainly likely to have very little impact by itself—if a lot of other people write letters objecting, then any one person's letter will be of no additional use; and if no other people write letters objecting, then that one person's letter will be of no use by itself. In either case, there is very little reason for a constituent to register an opinion with his or her congressman, or to investigate whether that congressman voted for or against the first-class rate increase, or to make a $5 contribution to the congressman who votes the right way, or even to take the time to vote for the congressman who votes the right way. The congressman who votes against a first-class mail increase is likely to find no benefits from that vote at the next election.

On the other hand, consider a third-class mail rate increase. Third-class (or "junk") mail users are businesses who operate on a thin profit margin by mailing out advertisements (and other "junk") at a rate that is actually lower than the cost of delivering the mail. Third-class mail is subsidized, then, by the first-class users, even though they may revile receiving it. A third-class rate increase certainly represents a major increase in costs to businesses who operate by this form of mailing, and could very well cause bankruptcy for some of them. The average third-class mail user is very happy, then, to make a sizable contribution to keep in Congress an active lobby which supports the reelection aspirations of key members of the Post Office Committee. Not only are the feelings of the third-class mail users much more intense than those of the first-class mail users, there are far fewer of them. It is much less likely that the third-class mail user will feel that his own objection will be meaningless because of the size of the group of which he is a member. Once again, the small, intense group is much more likely to be an active, organized political interest than the very large, diffuse interests.

There is another small, intensely concerned, highly organized group which is primarily concerned with the decisions of the House and Senate Post Office Committees. Besides the third-class mail users, the letter carriers themselves have an interest, because rate increases mean higher wages. Like the third-class users, their interest is intense rather than diffuse; and like the third-class users, they are highly organized and active politically.[20]

THE IDEA OF A SUBGOVERNMENT

Because *both* bureaucratic agencies and congressional committees value the same kind of intense, highly organized interest group as an ally, there is a potential for a three-way alliance between these actors. The interest group supplies electoral and political support for key congressional members, the congressmen provide budgetary and legislative support for the programs of the agency, and the agency supplies the services valued and demanded by the interest group and Congress. All three actors get what they desire most through this shared ability to "scratch each other's backs."

In a given policy arena, a three-way, stable alliance between an agency, congressional committee, and interest group has been called a "subgovernment." The alliance has also been called an "iron triangle" because of its durability and three-sidedness. A classic example of a subgovernment is the alliance between the Department of Agriculture, the House and Senate Agriculture Committees, and the Farm Bureau and other agricultural interests. These actors do not consitute a "power elite" capable of enforcing any policy through the federal government, but within the arena of agricultural policy, no actor or group of actors is powerful enough to stop the agriculture "iron triangle" when the three sides are united. For other examples of subgovernment alliances in the House of Representatives, see Table 7-1.

Consider the issue of tobacco price supports. One northern congressman recently reported that 93 percent of his constituents felt that less money should be spent on this form of subsidy to the tobacco industry. However, this congressman was not a member of the House Agriculture Committee, the agency with the first opportunity to support or kill any measure limiting tobacco price supports. The Agriculture Committee of the House tends to be dominated by members from rural districts, and the chairman of the Subcommittee on Tobacco tends to come from a tobacco-producing state like Kentucky.

A Congressman from a Northern port city might feel so opposed to tobacco price supports that he would seek a seat on the Agriculture Committee. However, the 93 percent of his constituents who oppose tobacco price supports are unlikely to reward him for spending his time and energy in that way. A much safer reelection strategy would be to get on the House Merchant Marine and Fisheries Committee, where he can serve the *intense* interests that his constituents have in port issues rather than their low-level opposition to tobacco price supports. Harold Seidman reports that:

> In the 90th Congress, only eight of the forty-nine members of the Senate and House Agriculture committees came from cities of over 25,000 population. . . . At least half of the members were actively engaged in agriculture or related occupations, and the Congressman Joseph Resnick asserted that a majority of the House committee members belonged to AFBF (American Farm Bureau Federation). In contrast, 28 of the 33 members of the House Merchant Marine and Fisheries Committee came from port districts which have a major interest in ship construction and maritime subsidies.[21]

TABLE 7-1 Subgovernment Alliances

ORGANIZED INTEREST GROUPS	EXECUTIVE AGENCIES	CONGRESSIONAL COMMITTEES
Farm bureaus Lumber companies	Department of Agriculture Forest Service Soil Conservation Service	Agriculture
Contractors Veterans groups Local governments	Department of Defense	Armed Services
Banks, savings & loan associations Insurance companies Brokerage houses	Treasury Department Federal Reserve System	Banking, Finance & Urban Affairs
Labor unions Teachers School districts	Labor Department Department of Education	Education & Labor
State & Local government Business corporations	Interstate Commerce Commission Transportation Department	Energy & Commerce
Foreign governments International business Council of Foreign Relations	State Department	Foreign Affairs
Contractors Developers State & local government Environmental groups	Army Corps of Engineers Interior Department	Interior & Insular Affairs
Lawyers Insurance companies State & local government	Justice Department	Judiciary
Shipbuilders Fishing industry Port cities	Bureau of Fisheries	Merchant Marine & Fisheries
Letter carriers Third-class mail users	Post Office	Post Office & Civil Service
Contractors Developers State & local government	Bureau of Reclamation Transportation Department	Public Works & Transportation

TABLE 7-1   (cont.)

ORGANIZED INTEREST GROUPS	EXECUTIVE AGENCIES	CONGRESSIONAL COMMITTEES
Contractors Universities Military	National Aeronautics & Space Administration National Science Foundation	Science & Technology
Small businesses	Small Business Administration	Small Business
Veterans	Veterans Administration	Veterans Affairs

Congressional committee membership tends to support the organization of subgovernments around intense, highly organized interests. Agriculture committees of Congress, like the Agriculture Department and American Farm Bureau, have been much more supportive of the tobacco industry than the anti-smokers' lobby.

Even though our northern congressman feels constrained to serve on the Merchant Marine and Fisheries Committee instead of Agriculture, he could oppose tobacco price supports on the floor of the House . . . or could he? There is a tacit understanding in Congress that individual members should not severely oppose on the floor the recommendations of congressional committees, except in unusual cases; this norm is known as "reciprocity." A northern congressman who opposes tobacco price supports on the floor, or western irrigation projects, or Mississippi flood-control projects, just because they do not benefit *his* constituents, might become known as a troublemaker. He might then find, when he looks for support for his special bills coming out of the Merchant Marine and Fisheries Committee, that the support is not there. The norm of reciprocity also operates from one house of Congress to the other, and even becomes an important consideration in the president's decision to sign bills into legislation.

Not every congressional committee is committed to the interests of a single, intense lobby. The Foreign Affairs Committee of the House, for example, is not associated with any strong lobby; but because it is neither a central procedural committee like the Rules Committee nor associated with a strong lobby, it is generally regarded as one of the weakest committees in the House. Committees with a strong interest-group backing, like the Agriculture Committee, the Armed Services Committee, or the Interior Committee, are more able to stand up to the president and bargain as equals, while the Foreign Affairs Committee is more subservient to the president. Said one congressman about the one-time chairman of the Foreign Affairs Committee, "Foreign Affairs is a disgrace because all Doc Morgan does, just like a rubber stamp, is give the Administration everything it wants."[22] In general, committee strength depends on the support of a strong political ally in the form of an organized, intense interest group.

Not every bureaucratic agency has a membership in an interest-based subgovernment. Like the Foreign Affairs Committee, the State Department lacks a strong domestic constituency; few people are intensely interested in the actions of the State Department. The exception is the Passport Office. Its director, Frances Knight, recognizing that travel agents needed quick, efficient service for their clients going abroad, turned to the travel industry as an ally. The presence of a strong interest-group ally inevitably led to friends in the House and Senate. Thus, while Congressman John Rooney of the House Appropriations Committee habitually bullied State Department officials when they asked for funds, "he consistently exempted the Passport Office from the customary budget cuts and interrogation. In fact, for several years Mrs. Knight simply refused to appear before the appropriations subcommittee. Rooney's potential for intimidation seemed to be inversely correlated with the strength of an official's power base.[23] Most of the State Department, however, represented a bureaucratic agency that was without subgovernment allies.

To recapitulate the argument of this chapter, political scientists claim that power is the first requirement of bureaucracy. Without power, agencies lose funding resources, favorable legislation, protection from opponents, and the cooperation of potential supporters. In the United States, public bureaucracies have sought power by forming alliances with active, organized interest groups and standing committees of Congress. These alliances, known as subgovernments, play an important role in the success or failure of agency programs. The result is a style of policy making that emphasizes minority interests and muffles low-level majoritarian interests. Thus, Post Office policy tends to be made in the interests of third-class mail users, defense policy tends to emphasize contractor needs rather than the taxpayers' interest in low-cost yet high military security, and pork-barrel politics tends to favor construction firms and grain and barge interests rather than overall water policy.

CHALLENGES TO SUBGOVERNMENT POLITICS

The dominance of specialized policy arenas by organized interests does not mean that majoritarian, low-level constituencies are powerless; rather, the power they have is mobilized *outside* the subgovernment policy arenas. Their power is exercised through party politics, public interest groups, and the courts, which represent arenas that define the limits of bureaucratic power. Majoritarian politics also employs different tactics and reveals different strengths and weaknesses than special interest politics. It is worthwhile, therefore, to examine these differences to better understand the power of subgovernments in relation to the political system.

A Theory of Majoritarian Politics

Low-level majoritarian publics constitute the most important potential outside threat to subgovernments. These publics are much larger in size than subgovernments and could easily overwhelm subgovernments if they were to become mobilized to exert influence in a policy arena. The involvement of majoritarian groups also changes policy outcomes because subgovernments do not adequately represent general interests in society. E. E. Schattschneider states, "The end product of party politics is inevitably different from that of pressure politics." Thus, subgovernments will lose in a contest with mobilized majoritarian groups, and therefore majoritarian groups are able to change government policy.

The problem for these large, amorphous groups is that they usually do not become involved because their individual members lack incentives to organize for political action. To become involved, the majority requires a mechanism to overcome individual disincentives to participate. In most democracies, the primary instrument that serves this purpose is the political party. However, in the American context, government reform over the decades has worked to weaken the political party, especially its role in governing through Congress and the executive. Schattschneider recognized the presence of majoritarian interest groups but expressed pessimism that they could counter the power exercised by special interests in the "pressure system." The only hope he offered for countering the upper-class, business bias of the pressure system is the political party.[24]

Under President Andrew Jackson, the political party did serve as the primary vehicle for organizing majoritarian publics for political action. However, the political party, especially at the state and local levels, often succumbed to control by special, business interests and became embroiled in bribes, fraud, and corruption. While the parties aided the poor immigrants with special benefits, the parties failed to promote the expansion of public goods. The mixture of populism and efficiency[25] that comprised the Progressive movement sought to recapture the vision of public-interest government as perceived by the middle classes. The consequence was the weakening of the political parties as a mechanism to represent majoritarian publics and an unintended strengthening of new "machines" or subgovernments built around the functional bureaucracies.

Schattschneider wrote his influential *The Semi-Sovereign People*, however, prior to the blossoming of certain highly significant, majoritarian political movements during the 1960s and 1970s. Although American parties are weaker than in other democracies, Schattschneider recognized that they play the dominant role in representing majoritarian interests during elections; candidates do not fare very well if they do not run on a Democractic or Republican ticket. Business interests need the Republican party just as labor needs the Democratic party if these interests expect to have influence on who gets into office. However, the strength of the parties in elections does not carry over into political power to make policy and govern the nation. This weak governing posture of the American parties has led to the periodic development of peculiarly American institutions that represent majoritarian publics outside the confines of political parties. While Schattschneider was aware of these institutions, he possibly underestimated their full potential for exercising power in the political system.

The Presidency

The most important institution in this respect is the presidency, which has increasingly taken on a plebiscitary character. The president is the only elected figure in the federal government who represents a national constituency. Schattschneider wrote that, "The Presidency has . . . become the principal instrument for the nationalization of politics."[26] In their contests with Congress for power and in their efforts to control the executive branch, presidents have had to appeal to public opinion as a primary weapon in their political arsenal. The advent of radio and television has greatly aided presidents in their quest for leading a national constituency. Franklin Roosevelt gave the nation comfort and courage through his "fireside chats"; later presidents such as John F. Kennedy or Ronald Reagan would use press conferences and TV addresses for communicating national purpose to the country.

Indicative of the national constituency of the presidency is the growing divergence between electoral results for congressional districts and Senate races versus the presidency. In 1984, Ronald Reagan won the presidency with an overwhelming majority, losing only the District of Columbia and Minnesota; at the same time, his party fared poorly in congressional races and the Republicans just barely held onto a majority in the Senate. Since the 1950s, the Democrats have controlled Congress, but the Republicans have won the presidency six times out of nine.

The policy programs of presidents have differed significantly from the policies favored by Congress. In the 1950s, Eisenhower resisted Democratic party pressure for social reform and macroeconomic policies by relying on a national constituency won by promises of stability, peace, and prosperity. The Kennedy–Johnson years of the 1960s, and to a surprising extent the Nixon years as well, saw the president ally himself with powerful party interests that wanted major social legislation in health care, unemployment insurance, civil rights, social security, housing, and welfare. The president worked to undermine the seniority system in the House and circumvent the old committee hierarchy that controlled the subgovernment pork barrel. Throughout this period, presidents tended to represent large, majoritarian interests against the special-interest biases of the legislature.

The budget also reflects these differences. In 1965, the defense budget comprised almost 50 percent of total federal spending, while the social-services budget constituted less than 25 per cent. By 1975, these proportions for defense and social services had exactly reversed: services greatly overshadowed defense as a proportion of federal spending. In this transformation, the president consistently allied himself with the forces favoring a shift in the direction of greater social services. The budget also underwent a change from being controlled by subcommittees of the Appropriations Committee to being dominated by entitlements, tax incentives, and loan guarantees. Nixon, in particular, pushed for this monetary approach to social-services spending. Currently, the Reagan administration is tilting the budget back in the opposite direction by building up defense and holding down social services.

Recall our earlier example of the Post Office subgovernment. The president is the only actor in the Post Office arena who is nationally elected. Unlike members of Congress, the president cannot base his reelection on the help of third-class mail users and letter carriers. He must win millions of votes by appealing to large masses of people, most of whom never participate in politics at all except to vote every four years in the national election. Without intense stakes in specific programs, most people respond to a president who promises efficient government, balanced budgets, and control of the bureaucracy. Consequently, the president is typically the only vocal leader who is willing to incur the displeasure of the third-class mail users and letter carriers.

In every case between 1955 and 1966, the president's proposal on postal wage increases was smaller than either the House or Senate committee's proposal, and normally the legislative proposal was within a few percentage points of the proposal by the National Association of Letter Carriers. The president was fighting for lower wages and higher third-class mail rates, and losing consistently because the committee was so subservient to union and interest-group pressures. Even the ultimate presidential weapon, the veto, was of little use: In 1960, a presidential veto of an 8.4 percent wage hike for postal workers was overridden by Congress.

The president has great difficulty challenging the combined opposition from interest groups, bureaucracy, and congressional committees. His main weapon against such a union is an aroused public opinion, and that is forthcoming primarily only in emergencies. Such an emergency was Christmas of 1966, when the Post Office machinery in various parts of the country simply broke down under the strain of the normal Christmas surge in mail. A single event

> . . . "triggered a public concern over postal issues that eventually shattered the monolithic, clientele-dominated environment of the Committee. Postal reform advocates seized upon the event to wrest the policy initiative from the clientele-Committee alliance, and the results were the formation of the Kappel Commission in 1967, the Commission's postal corporation proposal of 1968, President Nixon's appointment of a Postmaster General dedicated to the Kappel proposal, Nixon's subsequent reorganization bill of 1969, and the concomitant formation of a prestigious lobbying group, the Citizen's Committee for Postal Reform. The climactic environmental event was the ten-day postal strike in March 1970. The effect of all this activity was to increase the salience of postal issues nationally and to bring the executive branch to leadership of the policy coalition confronting the Post Office Committee.[27]

With the public behind him, President Nixon was successful in reforming the Post Office. What model of reform was chosen? As it happens, the model of reform was a perfect re-creation of the old Progressive model of reform: insulate administration from politics, organize the agency like a business corporation, and create an independent regulatory commission. The agency, now known as the Postal Service, is supervised by a Board of Governors analogous to a corporation's board. Beneath the Board of Governors is a hierarchical, bureaucratic staff headed by the Postmaster General.

Since the Postal Service was reorganized in 1970 with the intention of keeping first-class rates down by more efficient, neutral management, rates have increased from 6 cents to 22 cents. The political pressure and monopoly of information exercised by the intensely interested parties has served to dominate the independent regulatory commission as it did the Post Office Committees of Congress. The structural reform informed by the classical model did not change the political realities of the situation.

Public Interest Groups

A second major institution representing majoritarian interests that is peculiarly American is the public interest and single-issue groups.

Just as some congressional committees and some bureaucratic agencies are not part of subgovernments, some interest groups are also without subgovernment allies. Narrow-based interests can seek to influence the membership and decisions of single congressional committees. However, broad-based interests, like Common Cause, have interests that cut across many congressional committees. These interests may be powerful, but their influence does not derive from the relatively quiet, behind-the-scenes negotiation with congressional committees. Broad-based groups try to influence legislation by casting the spotlight of media attention on the issue—just the opposite technique of those interests who are safely part of subgovernment alliances and for whom media attention is anathema. The Congressional Reform Act, the Environmental Protection Act, and the reform of the Post Office are instances in which actors outside the subgovernment were able to mobilize sufficient resources to overthrow the entrenched subgovernment interests. Consequently, some interests operate by quite different means than those that institutionalize long-term, quiet alliances with congressional committees and bureaucratic agencies.[28]

These groups offer majoritarian publics an alternative to parties for influencing legislation directly. A public interest group is an organization that tries to mobilize a large number of diverse people to act politically on a set of issues (or sometimes just on a single issue) that involves such things as abortion, child abuse, civil rights, cheaper and more effective national defense, the environment, and health and safety. The distinguishing features of these groups are, first, that their leaders and the people they try to recruit do not necessarily benefit or suffer directly from the policy issue. This means that many people may push for child abuse laws who themselves have never experienced this problem or who don't even have children. This kind of ideological and issue-oriented involvement is distinguished from that of special interest groups who lobby for a specific monetary gain for themselves, such as milk producers or defense contractors. Second, these organizations try to get people involved in public-good issues, such as the environment, in which all of us are affected but only in a diffuse manner. They try to overcome the individual disincentives to take political action of consumers, women, the poor, and others.

Public interest groups usually get started by an individual or a small group of individuals who literally act as political entrepreneurs, mobilizing the mass publics into joining an action organization. Some famous political entrepreneurs of this type include Martin Luther King, Jr., who galvanized the civil rights movement into a national political force; Ralph Nader, who virtually single-handedly took on the giant corporations in the name of consumer protection and built a large and diverse lobbying organization that now concerns itself with a range of consumer and environmental issues; Betty Friedan, the founder of the National Organization for Women, which today is the largest women's organization in the country and had a hand in selecting Geraldine Ferraro as the running mate of Walter Mondale on the Democratic Presidential ticket; and Jerry Falwell, the fundamentalist preacher who started the Moral Majority movement, which had an impact in the election of the Reagan presidency.

Public interest groups have employed a variety of tactics in their efforts to overcome individual disincentives to participate in political action. Like the president, a valuable weapon in their favor is the news media. The media operate on profits that depend on selling their product. One kind of product that sells well is muckraking, scandal, and investigative journalism. Whether it is Watergate, General Motors' Corvair, or Anne Burford at the Environmental Protection Agency, the news media works as a willing ally of public groups seeking to expose behind-the-scenes deals or other shenanigans. Partly for this reason, public interest groups fought for the Freedom of Information Act and other "sunshine" laws that would open government agency records and decision making to public scrutiny.

The Courts

Public interest groups also have turned to the courts as a major ally in promoting social change. Two significant examples are the Clean Air Act of 1970 and the Environmental Impact Statement requirements. Repeatedly, public interest groups have brought suits against government agencies and corporations for violating the procedures and standards set up under these acts. Daniel Mazmanian and Jeanne Nienaber, for example, have argued that the threat of court suits has produced significant organizational changes in the way the Army Corps of Engineers goes about designing and planning projects. [29]

The greater involvement of courts in administrative policy making has led to a significant increase in the degree of judicial activism across a wide range of government policies. Donald Horowitz writes:

> Judicial activity has extended to welfare administration, prison administration, and mental hospital administration, to education policy and employment policy, to road building and bridge building, to automotive safety standards, and natural resource management. . . . Federal district courts have laid down elaborate standards for food handling, hospital operations, recreation facilities, inmate employment and education, sanitation and laundry, painting, lighting, plumbing, and renovation in some prisons; they have ordered other prisons closed. They have ordered the equalization of school expenditures on teachers' salaries, established hearing procedures for public school discipline cases, decided that bilingual education must be provided for Mexican-American children, and suspended performance requirements for automobile tires and air bags. [30]

Certain legal doctrines, prominent during the 1960s and 1970s, aided public interest groups in their use of courts to fight subgovernments. One particularly important doctrine concerns class-action suits. Under this doctrine, a private citizen can bring a lawsuit for money damages against another private person or a corporation. Usually the suing plaintiff is just one injured individual or a small number of injured individuals, but the class-action doctrine allows them to bring suit on behalf of all the other affected individuals. This kind of suit, therefore, directly overcomes the collective-action disincentive of large numbers of people when each has suffered some smaller loss which makes it not worthwhile to hire a lawyer. Under class action, one or two people may represent the whole class and bring suit that reaches into the millions of dollars. In 1974, however, the U.S. Supreme Court made a ruling which required that the plaintiff in a class-action suit must notify all the other members of the class before he could bring charges on their behalf. Since such a notification process entails huge expenses if the class consists of large numbers of people, the ruling effectively eliminates the action-forcing mechanism to overcome disincentives to participate.

The 1960s and 1970s also saw the expanded use of "private attorneys general" lawsuits which seek to get an agency or a corporation to initiate an action or stop an action that affects a major public interest, such as the environment, consumer protection, or safety. Unlike the class-action suit, plaintiffs may not bring these suits for money damages but use them to get the accused to pay for plaintiffs' legal fees and to invoke a standing to sue. This latter rule involves a demonstration by the plaintiff that a corporation or agency has committed a "legal wrong" against which the Constitution or common law offers protection. Initially, plaintiffs had to restrict their claims to physical or monetary losses, but in the 1970s legal doctrine liberalized the interpretation to include recreational, environmental, and aesthetic injuries. The vagueness of these criteria opened new areas for suits by a wide range of groups. Some of the more prominent groups that have employed this legal tactic include the NAACP, the American Civil Liberties Union, Common Cause, Ralph Nader, and the Sierra Club.

Concomitant with these developments, public-interest law firms proliferated in the 1970s. Young lawyers, especially, found the opportunity to represent poor people and environmental issues a challenging professional option. Yet the real support for these activities came from the generous practice in the 1970s of requiring that the defendant pay the legal feels of the plaintiff. In 1975, however, the Supreme Court limited this practice to only those statutes that explicitly provided for such plaintiff compensation. Since no legal protection exists for plaintiffs beyond the civil rights and environmental statutes, the continued energetic exercise of public-interest law may be threatened.

Besides the legal strategy, public interest groups have relied on protest demonstrations, sit-ins, and boycotts to get their message to the country. These tactics depend on cooperation from the news media as well as other methods of persuasion to get large numbers of people concerned. In 1973–74, for example, the oil embargo and the consequent steep rise in utility prices caused demonstrations at public utility companies in New York and California. In the California case, the Sierra Club chose utility regulation as a major issue in its environmental campaign. Under pressure, Governor Jerry Brown ended up appointing new utility-commission board members who were much more sympathetic toward changing the rate structure, and these changes eventually went through.

The Political Party

The fourth major institution supporting majoritarian politics is the political party. Parties have varied over the years in the extent to which they advocated a program for government that addressed the concerns of majoritarian publics, but clearly their influence became critical in certain stages of policy development. Up until the late 1960s, party power in Congress remained hamstrung by the seniority and committee systems. Powerful committee chairmen, many representing single-party interests in the South, dominated the key appropriations, rules, and commerce committees. New recruits might be elected across the country, but their partisan influence faded in the power of the committee system, the backbone of the subgovernment alliances.

When Congress passed the subcommittee bill of rights in 1971 and other pieces of legislation attacking the seniority and committee system, the power in Congress became increasingly diffused. The parties have moved slowly into this power vacuum, such that by 1985, the party caucus has replaced the old major committees as the main center of influence. David Rohde and Kenneth Shepsle report, for example, that the caucus has had difficulty finding members who want to serve on the Ways and Means Committee.[31] The reason is that under the committee's old glory days, members had to give up seats on all their other committees to serve on Ways and Means. Yet today, the Ways and Means Committee exercises such little power that this sacrifice of membership on other committees has deterred people who otherwise might have been willing to serve on this once-great congressional committee.

The parties have had a long history of majoritarian activism. The Democratic caucus under Hubert Humphrey in the 1950s devised much of the rationale and program substance to what became the Great Society of the 1960s. Humphrey had even advocated a national health insurance to go along with the other social policy changes.[32] In the 1960s and 1970s, the electoral rules changes which weakened the parties nonetheless often were motivated by desires to further majoritarian interests associated with the environment and the poor. Not unlike the Progressive attacks on the party at the turn of the century, contemporary public-interest reformers attacked the party as a way of getting at the congressional fiefdoms and remaining local party bosses. Both movements tended to rely on nonpartisanship as a symbol, thus weakening the beneficial aspects of party organization along with the detrimental aspects.

So far we have outlined the major actors and issues involved in the challenge to subgovernments; it remains to examine the dynamics of how subgovernments interact with majoritarian constituencies, including the consequences for policy outcomes. For this purpose, we will examine in some detail the challenge to the tobacco subgovernment that occurred in the late 1960s and early 1970s, as described by A. Lee Fritschler.[33]

THE DYNAMICS OF MAJORITARIAN POLITICS: THE SMOKING CONTROVERSY

The tobacco subgovernment looks very much like the other subgovernments described earlier in this chapter. The tobacco subgovernment, according to Fritschler, consisted of:

> paid representatives of tobacco growers, marketing organizations, and cigarette manufacturers; congressmen representing tobacco constituencies; the leading members of four subcommittees in Congress—two appropriations committees and two substantive legislative committees in each house—that handle tobacco legislation and related appropriations; and certain officials within the Department of Agriculture who were involved in the various tobacco programs of that department. This was a small group of people well known to each other and knowledgeable about all aspects of the tobacco industry and its relationship with the government.[34]

For many years, the subgovernment pursued a two-pronged strategy for promoting its own interests. It sought out government subsidies for the production of tobacco and it tried to deflect, and hopefully kill, any health or environmental attacks on tobacco advertising or on the sale and use of tobacco by the public. In both aspects of its strategy, the subgovernment had achieved remarkable success over a period of decades.

By 1961, however, independent scientific evidence had begun to accumulate that seriously posed the health threat of smoking, and a number of health groups and individual members of Congress attempted to pass legislation either warning people of the danger or prohibiting advertising and sales of tobacco products. The efforts of these health groups to get the government to take some action failed miserably. Between 1962 and 1964, various lawmakers introduced more than 15 bills into the House and Senate aimed at curtailing aspects of smoking; none of these bills received serious attention. In 1960, men from tobacco states chaired one-fourth of all the committees in the Senate; in the House, one-third of all committees had tobacco-state chairmen. Since the committees formed the authority in the Congress during this period, these men could effectively use their committee chairmanships to demand support from their colleagues through the reciprocity rule.

The resistance of the tobacco subsystem to any change in tobacco subsidies and regulation did not spell the end of the matter. In May 1962, at one of President Kennedy's major press conferences, a reporter asked what the president intended to do about the findings that cigarette smoking caused ill health. Kennedy, who was usually well prepared for questions, had received no briefing on the smoking and health issue and gave an awkward and noncommittal response. After the embarrassing conference, Kennedy had to do something. He decided to give the task to the Public Health Service (PHS) to appoint an expert advisory committee on the smoking issue. In January 1964, the advisory committee issued a report to the Surgeon General entitled "Smoking and Health," which stridently argued that the evidence overwhelmingly supports a link between smoking and a number of diseases, including lung and mouth cancers. Shortly thereafter, the Federal Trade Commission (FTC) entered the fray by announcing that it intended to hold hearings pertaining to rulemaking on the advertising and labeling of cigarettes.

The president's press conference, the publicity surrounding the Surgeon General's report, and the FTC hearings posed a major threat to the tobacco subgovernment. In responding, the tobacco powers in Congress succeeded in passing the Cigarette Labeling and Advertising Act, which mostly killed the FTC initiative and punished the FTC by denying it power to engage in rulemaking over cigarettes for the next four years. During the hearing on the legislation, the majority of witnesses testified against the FTC rule and the Surgeon General's report. It came out afterward, however, that many of the witnesses had received huge fees for their testimony from the tobacco institutes. In addition, the National Association of Broadcasters held its annual convention in Washington, D.C., during the hearings; over 400 of the 535 members of Congress were entertained by broadcasting executives at a reception at the convention.

In the ensuing four years, the FTC hardened its position against the tobacco interests. It set up laboratory studies of smoking and health and issued reports to Congress advocating cigarette labeling and the outright ban on cigarette advertising. The Public Health Service (PHS) and the Federal Communications Commission (FCC) also completed studies and issued reports unfavorable to the tobacco subgovernment. In 1967, for example, the Surgeon General created another panel called The Task Force on Smoking and Health, which included baseball star Jackie Robinson.

By 1969, the health interests and their allies in the FTC and FCC were preparing to issue new rules banning cigarette advertising on radio and television. In repsonse to this new challenge, the House Interstate and Foreign Commerce Committee, the Committee with direct jurisdiction over tobacco, reported out a bill that would have prohibited any action against cigarette advertising by the states permanently, and by the federal agencies for the next six years. In exchange, the Committee bill granted a slightly stronger cigarette warning on the package.

This time around, the subgovernment had gone too far. The Senate favored federal regulation of tobacco and some states, such as California, went ahead on their own and passed legislation. Even *The New York Times* said it would no longer carry cigarette ads without health warnings. Finally, eight years after the Surgeon General had issued its report, the FTC's ban on cigarette advertising on TV and radio was accepted.

The smoking and health controversy reveals various reasons why subgovernments have difficulty at times restricting policy decisions within their boundaries. Many of these reasons concern changes that take place in the broader political, social, and economic systems of the country. Depending on the circumstances, changes may be initiated either by members of the subgovernments themselves or by outside forces.

A change in technology, demography, or knowledge about harmful effects may lead to a realignment of interests concerned with a policy area.[35] For decades, the tobacco subgovernment operated unchallenged by majoritarian constituencies affected by smoking. As evidence of the carcinogenicity of smoking mounted, health groups turned to the news media, the presidency, and sympathetic agencies such as the FTC or the PHS. In the cigarette case, President Johnson stayed in the background, which weakened the health interests and postponed the success of a ban on advertising. Yet by 1969, public opinion had shifted away from viewing tobacco as merely an economic issue, as the subgovernment preferred to cast it. The majority forced the subgovernment to accept a new definition of tobacco policy that included health and the environment. While it did not overthrow the subgovernment, the majority was able to change the equilibrium of forces operating in the tobacco arena.

ASSESSING THE CHALLENGE

Do the actions of public interest groups, the parties, and other national institutions challenge the dominance of the subgovernment system of bureaucratic politics? There is little doubt that majoritarian politics challenges subgovernments in a powerful manner at given points in time. The civil rights movement altered party politics in the South; the environmental movement produced dramatic legislation promising to clean the water and air within a decade; between 1965 and 1975, the defense budget declined significantly as a proportion of total federal spending, while social spending skyrocketed; the courts have altered the way pork-barrel agencies, prisons, schools, and other public institutions do business.

The durability of these challenges to subgovernments remains in question. David Stockman has documented that social policy aimed at helping the poor seems to devolve over time into a social pork barrel.[36] Large segments of the middle class and even the rich end up getting government subsidies in housing, social security, loans, food, travel, and tax expenditures. Stockman shows that in farm subsidies, education subsidies, and other areas subgovernments gradually come to dominate policy making, even when the initial program is aimed at a broad consituency.

Similarly, the resignation of Anne Burford at the Environmental Protection Agency highlights the change in politics surrounding the social regulation passed in the early 1970s which dealt with health, safety, and the environment. One of the main lessons of the implementation literature in public policy is that the coalition that succeeds in passing the initial legislation has difficulty sustaining its activism over time as the spotlight of public opinion shifts to new issues.[37] Those groups most directly affected, however, retain a high interest in influencing the outcomes after the legislative battle. Usually these groups represent producer and other highly organized interests.

The effect of majoritarian politics on public policy, therefore, is probably more volatile and erratic than subgovernment politics. It often possesses a "flash-in-the-pan" character with no lasting, major change in outcomes. Challenging a subgovernment such as tobacco takes considerable time and repeated efforts:

> While the struggle goes on—it can last for years—it is difficult to say *who* controls *what* in the policy area affected. It becomes easier to bring about change while the subsystem is in a state of disarray. Eventually things settle down and a new subsystem emerges. Often it is different in terms of size and membership from the one that existed when the controversy started. The success of the challenge can sometimes be measured by the permanence of any realignment that might occur within a subsystem.[38]

Since, as Schattschneider states, *"organization is itself a mobilization of bias in preparation for action,"*[39] no governmental structure is neutral to the basic question of politics: who gets what? One organizational structure excludes some groups, while another organizational structure excludes others. This political question—who has the power and who gets the resources?—is thus fundamentally more important for organizational design than the question of efficiency, and it makes irrelevant the various reform quests for neutral structures and procedures for policy making.

Accepting the non-neutrality of administration complicates the final goal the orthodox reformers sought to promote: accountability. Since they assumed administration to be neutral, only political executives at the top of organizations had to be held accountable through the electoral system. Denying this assumption raises serious questions about whether and to whom administration is accountable. These questions are addressed in the next chapter.

NOTES

[1]GRANT McCONNELL, *Private Power and American Democracy* (New York: Alfred A. Knopf, Inc., 1966), p. 47.

[2]Quoted in DWIGHT WALDO, *The Administrative State* (New York: Ronald Press, 1948), p. 115.

[3]PAUL APPLEBY, *Policy and Administration* (University, Ala.: University of Alabama Press, 1949).

[4]APPLEBY, *Policy*, pp. 5–10.

[5]RANDALL B. RIPLEY and GRACE A. FRANKLIN, *Congress, The Bureaucracy, and Public Policy*, 2nd ed. (Homewood: Dorsey Press, 1980), pp. 219–220.

[6]PAUL APPLEBY, *Big Democracy* (New York: Alfred A. Knopf, 1945), pp. 1–10.

[7]NORTON LONG, "Power and Administration," *Public Administration Review*, 9 (1949), p. 257–264.

[8]LONG, "Power," pp. 257–258.

[9]LONG, "Power," pp. 259–260.

[10]PHILIP SELZNICK, *TVA and the Grass Roots* (Berkeley: University of California Press, 1949).

[11]SELZNICK, *TVA*, p. 39.

[12]SELZNICK, *TVA*, p. 72.

[13]THOMAS K. McCRAW, *TVA and the Power Fight, 1933-1939* (Philadelphia: J. B. Lippincott, 1971), p. 142.

[14]JOSEPH C. GOULDEN, *Monopoly* (New York: Pocket Books, 1968), p. 283. Copyright © 1968 by Joseph C. Goulden. Reprinted by permission of Brandt & Brandt Literary Agents, Inc.

[15]GOULDEN, *Monopoly*, pp. 284–285.

[16]GOULDEN, *Monopoly*, p. 280.

[17]PENDLETON HERRING, *Public Administration and the Public Interest* (New York: McGraw-Hill, 1936), p. 179.

[18]HERRING, *Public Administration*, p. 210.

[19]ARI HOOGENBOOM and OLIVE HOOGENBOOM, *A History of the ICC: From Panacea to Palliative* (New York: W. W. Norton & Co., 1976), p. 183.

[20]RICHARD F. FENNO, JR., *Congressmen in Committees* (Boston: Little, Brown & Co., 1973).

[21]HAROLD SEIDMAN, *Politics, Position and Power: The Dynamics of Federal Organization*, 2nd ed (New York: Oxford University Press, 1979), p. 40.

[22]FENNO, *Congressmen*, p. 114.

[23]DONALD WARWICK, *A Theory of Public Bureaucracy* (Cambridge: Harvard University Press, 1975), p. 77.

[24]E. E. SCHATTSCHNEIDER, *The Semi-Sovereign People: A Realist's Guide to Democracy in America* (New York: Holt, Rinehart and Winston, 1960), p. 56.

[25]THEODORE J. LOWI, "Machine Politics—Old and New," *The Public Interest*, 9 (Fall 1967), pp. 83–96.

[26]SCHATTSCHNEIDER, *Semi-Sovereign People*, p. 14.

[27]FENNO, *Congressmen*, p. 282.

[28]JEFFREY M. BERRY, *Lobbying for the People: The Political Behavior of Public Interest Groups* (Princeton: Princeton University Press, 1977).

[29]DANIEL MAZMANIAN and JEANNE NIENABER, *Can Organizations Change?* (Washington D.C.: The Brookings Institution, 1979).

[30]DONALD HOROWITZ, *The Courts and Social Policy* (Washington D.C.: The Brookings Institution, 1977).

[31]DAVID ROHDE and KENNETH SHEPSLE, "The Ambiguous Role of Leadership in Woodrow Wilson's Congress." Delivered at the Annual Meeting of the American Political Science Association, New Orleans, 1985.

[32]JAMES L. SUNDQUIST, *Politics and Policy: The Eisenhower, Kennedy, and Johnson Years* (Washington D.C.: Brookings Institution, 1968).

[33]A. LEE FRITSCHLER, *Smoking and Politics: Policy Making and the Federal Bureaucracy*, 3rd ed. (Englewood Cliffs: Prentice-Hall, 1983).

[34]FRITSCHLER, *Smoking*, p. 4.

[35]ROBERT D. BEHN and MARTHA A. CLARK, "The Termination of Beach Erosion Control at Cape Hatteras," *Public Policy*, 27,1 (Winter, 1979) pp. 99–127.

[36]DAVID STOCKMAN, "The Social Pork Barrel," *Public Interest*, 37 (1974), pp. 3–30.

[37]EUGENE BARDACH, *The Implementation Game: What Happens After a Bill Becomes A Law* (Cambridge, Mass: The MIT Press, 1977).

[38]FRITSCHLER, *Smoking*, p. 6.

[39]SCHATTSCHNEIDER, *Semi-Sovereign People*, p. 30.

CHAPTER 8

Assessing the Reform Model:
Is It Accountable?

The New Machines are machines because they are relatively
irresponsible structures of power. That is, each agency shapes important
public policies, yet the leadership of each is relatively self-perpetuating
and not readily subject to the control of any higher authority.

Theodore J. Lowi, "Machine Politics—Old and New"[1]

The previous chapter described patterns of politics that have evolved around professionalized, supposedly "neutral" public bureaucracies. In this chapter, we argue
first that the patterns of politics that have evolved create a major problem of accountability in American politics. The subgovernments discussed in the previous
chapter are accountable to narrow interests, but whether there is any power capable
of aggregating these narrow interests into a composite that represents the public
interest is an open question.

Second, we argue that the classical model of "executive management" has not
been sufficient to guarantee any broader accountability on the part of subgovernments. Progressive reformers believed that a single chief executive is more visible
and more easily held accountable for agency actions. They also felt that greater
central control of agencies would reduce overlapping and achieve budget savings.
More importantly, the New Deal reformers had great optimism that centralization
and increased staff resources would produce long-range, coordinated decisions. We
argue, however, that this hope has been largely in vain.

This is not to imply that subgovernments are, in fact, the sum total of American politics. There are sources of political power that challenge the power of
professionalized bureaucracies and their allies. However, as we saw in the last
chapter, these sources of influence center on majoritarian institutions such as the
political party, which administrative reformers have continuously sought to weaken
or circumvent.

THE PROBLEM OF ACCOUNTABILITY

Contrary to popular belief, the problem is not that bureaucracies are accountable to no one. Professionalized bureaucracies must rely on the political support of the relatively narrow interest groups they serve; this political reliance means that bureaucracies cannot "go their own way." However, at both the local and national levels, the narrow base of political support for professionalized bureaucracies has created similar problems of fragmentation. The problem is that the summation of a lot of narrow interests, to which bureaucracies are narrowly accountable, does not necessarily add up to policies that serve the broader interest.

Functional Fiefdoms in Local Government

The classical administrative model assumes that the top managers are fully responsive to public interests and, in turn, have complete policy control over their subordinates: "Electoral mechanisms of popular control are predicated on the assumption that the officials voted into office are in full command of policy and program, and that the other components of governmental machinery are little more than executors of their collective will."[2]

The Progressives proposed to give top officials control of governmental machinery by centralizing responsibility in professional managers. Managers came initially from the business community as temporary volunteers who served on public commissions and boards. In the New Deal, the commission form gave way to the professional, full-time manager, including a city-wide manager, whose responsibilities were modeled after the private business corporations. The city council acted in the role of the board of directors and the city departments in the role of line divisions. Managers were expected to hire professionals who would replace the political party appointees from the city wards. Accountability would be maintained from the lower level professionals to the top managers. The latter were held responsible to the public through their appointment by the city council.

What has happened to these reform expectations? Have they produced coordinated and accountable urban policy? We will first address the issue of the responsiveness of professional managers to elected officials.

David Hammack's account of the history of power in New York City argues that narrow special interests have had *more* influence after World War II than they had at the turn of the century.[3] The fragmentation of political power today, asserts Hammack, coincides with the historical evolution of a dispersion and competition among the city's economic and social elites; yet he believes that the Progressive reforms, far from retarding these decentralizing trends, actually reinforced and accelerated them. By the postwar era, the city government consisted of decentralized and competing "islands of power."

How could this happen? Hammack argues that Progressive reformers, frustrated by their inability to exercise more political influence, sought to require literacy tests for voters and entrance exams for civil service employees. The source of their frustration was the growing dominance of a centralized political machine at the turn of the century: "The regular political organizations of New York City, Brooklyn, and the state as a whole mobilized the greatest concentrations of power . . . and they grew increasingly independent of the economic elites during the last years of the nineteenth century." Hammack adds that "Increasingly during the nineties, party leaders derived their power from their ability to organize coalitions, mediate and conciliate among competing groups, and win elections."[4]

By attacking the political parties, the Progressives had intended to make the city government more efficient and accountable to the middle and upper classes. While the party machine's corruption and violence motivated the progressive attack, the reformers had less of an understanding of the brokerage, coalition formation, and electoral functions that the party had performed. Although the city manager (or the mayor) in the Progressive scheme of government sat as the formal head of the administration, he could not galvanize a broad political coalition to govern the city.

Instead, power flowed to the professional agencies and their constituencies. Wallace Sayre and Herbert Kaufman describe New York City government in the postwar era as a multiplicity of decision centers, each composed of a "core group" made up of "functionally specialized officials" in the agencies and departments and a "satellite group" made up of leaders of interest groups, professional societies, contractors, suppliers, and others intensely affected by government decisions. Despite the presence of overlapping memberships in these various decision centers, the activism of the press, the wide jurisdiction of the courts, and the executive authority of the mayor's office, the authors conclude that "the autonomous nature of the core group and satellite groups in each decision center is striking."[5]

Sayre and Kaufman clearly indicate the decentralized nature of government in New York City:

> Most participants are galvanized into action by only a relatively narrow range of issues and ignore most others no matter where they occur; as a result, most of the actors in any center share very special interests in the problems at hand. . . .
>
> What is perhaps most surprising is the failure of the central organs of government to provide a high level of integration for the city's system. The Council has been weak, the Board of Estimate inert, the Mayor handicapped. . . .
>
> State administrative supervision of city agencies has encouraged many city officers and employees to develop close links with their functional counterparts in the state capital, and to rely on these to buttress their resistance to leadership from the city's central institutions. The nature of the judicial process renders the courts incapable of performing an integrative function. Thus, despite the opportunities for integration presented by the formal powers of the city's central institutions, they have generally officially ratified the agreements reached by the active participants in each decision center, which are offered to them as the consensus of experts and interested groups, or, on an ad hoc basis, have chosen one or another alternative suggested when the experts and interested groups have been divided on an issue. . . .
>
> Seldom have they imposed, on their own initiative, a common set of objectives on all the centers of decision.[6]

Sayre and Kaufman refer to this semi-autonomous bureaucratic decision-making structure as "islands of functional power."[7] Interest groups no longer have to go through the party bosses in order to secure favors, concessions, and subsidies from the city bureaus; they now have direct access. Contractors, real estate developers, construction unions, and finance corporations have an intense interest in becoming involved in city development policies; their small numbers and high vulnerability to policy give them strong incentives and the capacity to lobby city agencies. They have become the natural allies of these city agencies in the quest for more funds and expanded policies.

The agencies also have the power of information and expertise at their disposal. Many elected officials, in contrast, are generalists who are not familiar with the intricacies of agency policies. This contributes to the weakening of political authority over the decisions of the professionalized agencies.

Certain statutory developments bolstered the political decentralization of power. The Progressives had supported executive centralization, but they also had promoted independent local districts with separate sources of income. In the post-Progressive and New Deal era, cities never fully discarded the commission form of government, despite the growing reliance on city managers. A prominent manifestation is the semi-autonomous school district, which enjoys its own tax millage and authority structure, independent of the central administration.

A second statutory reinforcement of decentralized power was the growth of independent authorities with their own sources of revenue. Port authorities, park commissions, sewerage and housing authorities, and other such institutions gained the power to collect fees for their services and issue long-term bonds to finance new projects. Robert Moses, who held chairmanships of park and port authorities in New York City, Long Island, and New York State, used these independent sources of revenue to build a financial and construction empire unmatched by any other public figure in the nation's history. The central administrative hierarchy exercised only limited and sporadic control over Moses' independent policy-making and revenue-collecting centers. Instead, Moses led the government component of a large development-oriented coalition of interests.

Moses' biographer poignantly chronicles how poor and lower-middle-class citizens in the Bronx fought a valiant yet ultimately losing battle against the route for the Cross Bronx expressway.[8] Thousands of citizens affected by the proposed route could not force Moses to alter it even one inch to save their neighborhoods and their homes, schools, and churches. (This despite the fact that an alternate route would be cheaper and straighter.) Moses did not need these peoples' votes in order to stay in office; neither did he require their money in order to continue to build his projects. With semi-independent statutory authority and his own revenue source from tolls and bonds, he could follow his own engineering preferences without interference from anyone.

A third factor was the growth after World War II of categorical grants from state and federal governments. City departments could establish independent sources of grant revenue that allowed them to operate outside of the normal budget purview of the city administration. Some grants were tied to specific forms of revenue, such as the gasoline tax, that could only be used for the activities of a given agency. Agencies that showed skill at procuring grant money from higher governmental levels could hold functional control over policy in their own areas independent of broader, city-wide interests. The city found it difficult to turn down the money, even though it exercised only indirect control over the consequences. Furthermore, capital expenditures financed by initial grants gave rise to operating costs that had to be met from local sources of revenue, thereby further constricting the policy and budget discretion of the city government.

The fragmentation of local government, however, has proven to be an obstacle to federal grants that involve several local agencies. Jeffrey Pressman, for example, cites a lack of concentrated political power as a major impediment to redevelopment grants in Oakland, California.[9] Oakland is a reform city with a mayor/

city manager/council form of government. Power is highly fragmented in many fundamental ways. The city government is a city-wide authority only in name—it excludes such important areas of public policy as aid to the poor, redevelopment, economic growth, housing, the port operations, and the schools. Each of these areas is controlled by an autonomous commission, such as the Oakland Housing Authority and the Oakland Redevelopment Agency.

Oakland also has no active and vigorous political parties or even organized political groups. Pressman states that nonpartisanship in Oakland "constitutes a grave limitation on local political leadership." Labor groups have not played a significant role since the 1940s, turnout at local elections is very low, and student groups have played no role in electing the city government. Pressman asserts that "It often appears as though politics in Oakland does not exist."[10]

However, a more fundamental fragmentation of power which separates politics from administration occurs between the council, the mayor, and the administration of the government. The council members and the mayor are part-time employees, while the city manager receives a large salary and basically runs the city. The manager, in turn, has a belief that his job is not political but administrative, yet his conception of administration is very wide. The manager stated: "A policy decision would be that policemen in Oakland should carry guns. Administrative decisions would be when they should carry guns, where they should carry guns, and how they should use those guns."[11]

Pressman concludes that the main problem for successfully implementing a grants program is a lack of political capacity at the local level to aid minorities and poor people. He supports Duane Lockard's notion that "the dispersal of local power to non-elected bureaucracies has made it extremely difficult for poor and black people to influence policy outcomes."[12] He notes the parallel between cities in the U.S. and the "vicious circle of weak authority" in developing countries. Local governments lack control over many other institutional actors in the region, such as in Oakland where many of the main activities of redevelopment are outside its jurisdiction and the bureaucracy sits independent of the elected council and mayor. In other words, no institutional mechanisms exist to channel political demands of poor people to the real decision makers in government due to weak or nonexistent party and other political organization. In addition, the political component of the government lacks institutional mechanisms to influence the decisions of the budget office and the departments, much less the independent authorities in the city.

The growth of autonomous, expert bureaucracies as a means for insulating policy making from party politics backfired against the Progressive's goal of greater centralized coordination and executive control. As Frederick Wirt says in his critique of reform institutions in San Francisco, "the price for achieving . . . honesty was to make San Francisco's governors impotent, robbing them of coordinated instruments for meeting crucial urban problems as they emerged."[13]

Had the party bosses retained their power, they would never have allowed bureaucracies to emerge as autonomous centers of power outside of their influence; but as the party machines declined, in their place have emerged the professional bureaucracies, which Theodore Lowi has dubbed "the new political machines." He argues that while the Progressives cleaned up much of the corruption of the old machines, they also "destroyed the basis for sustained, central, popularly-based action." This ability to take concerted action, which the old machines were beginning to exercise at the turn of the century, "was replaced by the power of the professionalized agencies. . . . The Triumph of Reform really ends in paradox: Cities like New York became well-run but ungoverned."[14]

Fragmentation in Independent Regulatory Agencies: The Case of the Fed

The problem of fragmentation in government based on autonomous, professional agencies is not confined to the cities. Beginning in the latter part of the nineteenth century, but accelerating greatly during the Progressive era, the Congress and the president created numerous independent agencies. Of particular interest in this regard are the independent regulatory agencies that manage much of the federal government's relations with the private economy.

An example is the Federal Trade Commission (FTC), which, like other products of the Progressive era, was created with the intention that it should be operated independently of partisan politics. The commissioners are appointed by the president and ratified by the Senate. During the New Deal, President Roosevelt tried to redirect various government agencies, including the FTC, in his attempt to turn around the spiraling inflation and depression. Relying on a 1926 Supreme Court decision, he fired a conservative FTC commissioner named William E. Humphrey. However, the Supreme Court reversed itself in 1935 by arguing that the independent regulatory commission "cannot be characterized as an arm of the executive" and that the president could not fire a commission member. Thus, the fourth branch of government was removed from direct presidential control.

The independence of the regulatory commission is indicated clearly by the Federal Reserve Board (the Fed). Members of the Board are appointed by the president with the consent of the Senate, but once they are in office, the Board members may not be removed for fourteen years. The chairman of the Board is also appointed by the president, in this case every four years. But the president must wait two years into his term before the previous chairman's term of appointment is over. The founders of the Fed deliberately staggered the chairman's term with the election of the president precisely to prevent the president from exercising too much influence over monetary policy. Since 1935, the Federal Reserve also enjoys independence from the normal budgetary process. This situation is possible because the Fed earns billions of dollars in income from the management of the government securities portfolio.

The formal ability to appoint the chairman of the Federal Reserve Board does not mean that the president can always choose someone whose policies he prefers. In 1979, for example, *Business Week* maintained that President Carter's choice of Paul Volcker as chairman was strongly influenced by the collapse of the dollar on the foreign exchanges:

> Shattered confidence in the Carter Administration left the President no choice but to select a man who would be instantly hailed as the savior of the dollar, even though that meant bringing in a chairman far more conservative than Carter would have preferred.[15]

Like other government agencies, the Fed must cultivate a congressional committee and interest groups as allies. In building a defensive alliance against the president, the Fed possesses several organizational advantages besides budgetary independence and the long tenure of Board members. Of critical importance is the peculiar organization of the Federal Reserve banking system. Each regional Federal Reserve Bank, such as in Chicago or Denver, is legally a private institution that has stock owned by member banks of the Federal Reserve System and a private Board of Directors composed of nine members. In addition, the local branches of the regional Federal Reserve Banks each elect five to seven members to their Boards of Directors, which brings the total number of private directors to around 250 people.[16]

Francis Rourke argues that the variable power of a public agency depends on the prestige, wealth, geographic dispersion, and organization of its clientele.[17] The private directors of the Federal Reserve banks meet all these criteria. Usually the directors are local financial institution presidents or vice-presidents; often they are prominent local business executives. A former staff economist with the Federal Reserve Board emphasized this point:

> The Fed has its tentacles stretched into all parts of the country. The regional bank presidents carry a great deal of prestige, and the Boards of Directors are made up of local dignitaries and VIPs. Anybody who is anybody in the local community over time has a chance to serve on the Board of Directors.[18]

This prestigious group carries considerable weight in Washington politics and is relied on by the Fed to sustain its independent position.

A second major strategy that the Federal Reserve uses to remain independent of the president is to hide behind its professional expertise. This strategy is illustrated by the operations of the Federal Open Market Committee (FOMC), the Federal Reserve body responsible for monetary policy. In 1975, for example, the Congress passed Resolution 133, which required that the FOMC publish the money supply target agreed upon at its last meeting. The FOMC responded by publishing several different money supply targets. On professional grounds, these various components of the money supply may deserve independent consideration; but if the FOMC missed one target, it was sure to hit one of the others. Hence, the multiple-target regime preserved FOMC professional judgment and did not increase congressional or presidential control over monetary policy.

In its dealings with the outside, the FOMC regularly tries to vote unanimously. John Woolley has argued that the consensual decision making of the FOMC makes the decision appear more technical and professional.[19] Since the target agreed upon in the decision is subject to varying interpretations, a consensual vote keeps the real decision making on monetary policy out of the spotlight of public opinion or the watchful eyes of the president and the Congress.

How, then, does the president put pressure on the Fed to follow his wishes? The approaches that the president takes are threefold. All are indirect; none use the formal hierarchy envisioned by the classical reformers. The most common approach is to publicly voice a position on monetary policy that criticizes the Federal Reserve. The spokesman is usually not the president himself (although in particular situations the president has become directly involved), but rather either the Secretary of the Treasury or a member of the Council of Economic Advisors (CEA). Presidents also send messages to top officials at the Treasury stating whether they will tolerate criticism of the Fed and of what kind.

The president has urged that the CEA include language in the Annual Report of the Council that specifically discusses monetary questions. The Reagan administration, for example, included a gradual slowdown in money growth as one of the top points in its written documents about the president's macroeconomic policy. A related strategy of the administration is to threaten to set up expert commissions to study either monetary policy or the organizational independence of the Federal Reserve. Under the Reagan administration, the Treasury publicly announced that it was considering a study of monetary policy instruments. The visibility of such commissions and studies brings public pressure to bear in favor of the administration's preferences. This strategy is designed to sway public opinion and the relevant interest groups to support the president's position on monetary issues. At other times, the purpose is to cast blame on the Federal Reserve, thus lessening the administration's own perceived culpability. Another major purpose of this strategy is to convince members of Congress not to support the Fed over and against the policies of the president.

Private channels of influence serve the president better for communicating his true meaning to the Federal Reserve Board. The most known channel of this sort is the Treasury lunch, where members of the Fed and the Treasury discuss mutual policy issues, especially the financing of the debt. Participants believe, however, that the meetings of the "Troika" and the "Quadriad" produce franker discussions of monetary policy and the economic outlook. These meetings involve the Secretary of the Treasury, the Fed chairman, the CEA chairman, and the Director of the Office of Management and Budget. However, administration participants complained that, even in these private settings, the Fed chairman was not entirely open about monetary policy.

The president always reserves the option of meeting directly with the Fed chairman and other members of the Board. Most presidents have exercised this option on the larger questions of monetary policy. Advisors also believe that direct meetings with the president are more effective than meetings with other top administration officials, because "the President carries a certain aura about him that makes others not want to disagree too strongly with his preferences."[20]

The key point is that the power the president exercises over regulatory agencies is not through the executive management movement's conception of the Chief Executive Officer, but rather that his influence appears much closer to Richard Neustadt's view of presidential power as resting on bargaining, persuasion, and political alliance building.[21] John Woolley compares the Federal Reserve's formal independence to other independent regulatory agencies by stating, "It was conceived in the same progressive reform spirit embued with faith in expertise, faith in the effectiveness of tinkering with 'the machinery of government,' and distrust of politicians."[22]

Fragmentation in Subgovernments: The Pork Barrel

Most of the federal government's programs are carried out within the cabinet departments, such as Defense or Interior. Can there be a problem of fragmentation and accountability in these large, hierarchical departments? While these departments look monolithic on paper, evidence suggests that neither the president nor the department secretaries have had much success in controlling the activities of these agencies. They remain accountable primarily to the special interests in the subgovernments of which they form a part.

The poor administrative record of the implementation of water projects is an example of how agencies can remain unaccountable to the formal hierarchical authority of cabinet departments directly under the control of the president. The cause of administrative failure in water agencies, like the Corps of Engineers, is not that they lack popular and political support—they are among the most popular and politically powerful agencies in the country; instead, most problems seem to arise over a lack of central coordination across subgovernments, for example, between the Corps of Engineers and the Bureau of Reclamation.

The Corps of Engineers, housed within the Department of Defense, is primarily concerned with flood control and is supervised by the House Public Works Committee, a committee composed in large part of congressmen from southern and midwestern states, where flooding is a problem. The Bureau of Reclamation is an agency within the Department of the Interior, concerned primarily with irrigation, and is supervised by the House and Senate Interior Committees composed largely of legislators from those western states which have large amounts of land in the public domain and where lack of water is a serious problem.

Both agencies have strong interest-group support. The Corps of Engineers, for instance, has a very close relationship with the National Rivers and Harbors Congress, "a thriving voluntary association with more than 7000 members, 50 state groups, and affiliations by state, city and county agencies, water and land development associations, business firms, and various other groups. Among the individual members are government officials at all levels, members of Congress . . . officers of the Corps of Engineers engaged in rivers and harbors work, and contractors."[23] The contractors are those firms which actually do the work of building the projects designed by the Corps of Engineers, and for whom a new contract often means the difference between profit and loss. Hence, these contractors provide much of the "political muscle" of the Corps.

The Bureau of Reclamation has similar close ties to the National Reclamation Association, which is composed of arid-land ranchers and farmers as well as contractors. Both interest groups "are very jealous of special relationships with their Government sponsor. Interlopers are not treated kindly. Programs which dilute the sponsor's single-minded concern with their interests are vigorously opposed."[24]

One of the people viewed as an interloper is the president. If he tries to insert himself too vigorously into the policy-making process with respect to either flood-control projects, or irrigation projects, or even the coordination of flood control with irrigation, he finds himself the object of abuse by interest groups and their congressional allies. For instance, in 1923, President Harding thought it would be nice to move the Corps of Engineers into the Department of the Interior along with the Bureau of Reclamation in order to coordinate the work of the two major water-development agencies. Congress rejected the proposal. In 1932, President Hoover issued an executive order effecting the same transfer; Congress nullified the order. Since that time, most presidents have favored the same move, but none have succeeded in bringing it about.

Because Congress kept the two agencies apart, they were in no position to cooperate in the development of the Kings River in central California during the Roosevelt administration. Administration of this development project by the Corps would have pleased the flood controllers and major contractors; administration by the Bureau of Reclamation would have pleased the large farmers. FDR wrote to the Secretary of War, who was supposedly in a direct line of hierarchical authority between the president and the Corps, "I want the Kings and Kern River projects to be built by the Bureau of Reclamation and not by the Army Engineers." However, the dam was built by the Engineers, after a dramatic showdown in Congress between the two groups of legislative supporters.

After the Kings River conflict, sharp criticism of the lack of cooperation between the two agencies led to an administrative agreement. The occasion for this agreement was the development of the huge Missouri River system. Once again, the two agencies were in the process of creating mutually inconsistent plans for development, and a major "war" between the two subgovernments seemed to be in the making, with the Corps proposing flood-control dams and the Bureau proposing irrigation projects. The agreement between the two agencies "was a simple consolidation of almost all the projects proposed by both agencies, with none of the inherent conflicts of purpose resolved and with specific glaring inconsistencies retained. The rationale of the reconciliation was very simply and transparently political."[25] The Corps would be allowed to have its flood-control projects on the tributaries, and both would support the other's projects:

> It was the sort of agreement that would not have been surprising had it been made by two sovereign powers confronted by a third at whose expense the two could collaborate for their mutual benefit. In the Missouri Basin, however, the third party consisted of the United States and those members of its broad constituency whose interests were not served by either agency within the territories that the jurisdictional settlement allotted to each.[26]

The result was a development program whose overall benefits were doubtful, and whose individual projects were often patently inefficient. In short, the agreement produced projects that the popular press likes to portray as bureaucratic bungles. For instance, the *Reader's Digest* printed an article on a 300-mile irrigation canal in North Dakota "designed to bring irrigation water to about 1200 farm families that are already growing good crops without it. Total cost: $500 million—involving about $300,000 worth of irrigation subsidy per family. The project will literally take more land out of production than it puts into production. . . . Its significance is that it's an average, run-of-the-mill worthless project, typical of many others now being built in the name of irrigation, flood control and barge transportation."[27] The *Digest* also cited this project as an example of bureaucratic knavery, pointing out that the economic analysis supporting it was based on gross distortions and unsubstantiated claims. Ultimately, however, this was not a bureaucratic failure, but a political one. The project's cost and absurd organization can only be blamed on committee fiefdoms responding to the intense interests of contractors and others.

While the Bureau got a dozen projects like this one in North Dakota as its share of the deal, the Corps was allowed to build six dams on the main branch of the Missouri River. This arrangement had the added advantage of extending the inland barge transportation system, which is yet another element in the Corps' political influence. The inland waterway is the only transportation system that is entirely built and operated by public monies. The subsidy amounts to more than $300 million a year in support of barge lines and coal and grain companies. Presidents since Franklin Roosevelt have tried to get the barge companies to pay part of the cost, but the strength of the Corps' subgovernment has prevailed.

One of Jimmy Carter's first lessons in office, after running on a platform of controlling the bureaucracy, was that even a president does not easily challenge the Corps. His plan to scrap seven of the Corps' more inefficient projects provided the first major battle of his administration, demonstrating why the Corps, a military bureau, calls itself an "agency of Congress" rather than an agency of the Commander in Chief. As recently as 1985, President Reagan tried to consolidate the Corps of Engineers and the Bureau of Reclamation, only to have his proposal rejected by the bureaus themselves and their congressional supporters.[28] In summary, as one political scientist has written,

> The Corps has not actually been responsible to the national constituency represented by the President. It has repeatedly been able not to respond to demands to coordinate its activities with other programs. . . . (It has) virtual autonomy within the bureaucratic structure. . . . If the Corps has been responsive to the wishes, even the orders, of the presidency, a quite different pattern of power would have existed, and the consequences in distribution of benefits of the Corps' activities within various areas might also have been different.[29]

THE LIMITATIONS OF EXECUTIVE CONTROL

Why shouldn't the president (or the governor or mayor) be able to better coordinate the apparently fragmented efforts of professionalized bureaucracies? After all, isn't the president the boss of the two million federal civilian bureaucrats, and the Commander in Chief of the Armed Forces?

One of the misconceptions that Americans often have is that the president is "boss" of the federal government, in the same way that a chief executive is "boss" of a private company. Indeed, many government reformers in public administration and business management have pressed for the implementation of a corporate model of the president as chief executive officer (CEO). We expect a chief executive to set goals for his company and to carry them out through the efficient management of people and organizational structures. He will try to hire the best people available and fire those that do not produce. He will be able to offer a number of incentives and perquisites to subordinates to induce them to work hard, including bonuses, company cars, trips, salary, and perhaps most important, the possibility for fast advancement to the top. He may also have to restructure the company in response to changes in personnel, technology, and the market for his products.

Organizationally, private companies are often set up with clear lines of authority to the chief executive. The chief executive relies on a top management team and several vice presidents to help him monitor subordinate performance. At central headquarters, the top management is grouped into broad functional responsibilities, such as sales, marketing, production, and finance. Below top management is the divisional or regional management that also is grouped on functional lines. Profit is a primary measure of subordinate performance, and a regional or divisional manager who does not reach profit goals comes under pressure to do better. If he fails, he will lose his job.

In the time of Woodrow Wilson, when the president had no authority to even review the budget requests of executive departments, a move toward a more corporate model of the presidency made good sense. Even in Franklin Roosevelt's time, when the president had only a handful of staff aides, strengthening the Executive Office and the White House staff served a useful purpose. However, continuing further down this reform road, while at the same time weakening other majoritarian institutions such as the political party, began to show signs of trouble by the 1960s.

While the corporate model of executive control does give the president greater expertise and other staff resources, in the public sector it is an insufficient solution to the accountability issue and, in fact, creates its own lack of accountability. First of all, the corporate model cannot directly restructure the fragmentation of subgovernments which depend on political alliances outside the control of presidential resources. Yet every president in the postwar period has run on a platform attacking subgovernments and advocating administrative centralization for the presidency as the solution to this fragmentation problem. However only a wholesale change in the American Constitution downgrading the role of the Congress and the courts would give the president the power to use administrative restructuring to attack subgovernments directly.

Second, while it may be possible for the presidency over time to usurp this power, it would be a mixed blessing for him and a net loss for public accountability. The kinds of institutions that the corporate model has created add to the presidential bureaucracy as the means for controlling the executive branch bureaucracy. The White House staff has grown to around 400 to 500 employees, and the Executive Office of the President has risen to over 2000 employees, and includes the Office of Management and Budget. In addition, the numerous other independent agencies that are supposed to serve the president in policy making and management have also grown rapidly and include such agencies as the Arms Control and Disarmament Agency, the Central Intelligence Agency, the Federal Emergency Management Agency, the Selective Service Commission, the Office of Personnel Management, the General Services Administration, and others.

Many of these offices, agencies, and councils surrounding the president are supposed to display a neutral, professional competence and other traits of the reform model of administration. But as we learned in Chapters 6 and 7, the reform model is not necessarily neutral or efficient. Many officials in the Office of Management and Budget or the Selective Service Commission develop loyalties and allegiances other than to the president; inefficiencies also develop in this presidential bureaucracy parallel to those in the executive branch generally. Terry Moe argues that the reform tradition surrounded the president with more expertise but did not improve responsiveness to the President's program.[30] He maintains that each president from Kennedy to Nixon found that "presidential institutions and their routine processes for policy making and management were inadequate for his needs." Moe's explanation for this inadequacy is that "the separation of politics and administration was formalized in the structure of government."[31] Presidents discovered that they had authority to make policy but much less authority to manage policy to respond to their wishes. Administration was in the hands of independent commissions, neutrally competent civil servants, interdepartmental committees, and regional field offices.

Finally, the larger the president's bureaucracy, the more layers of hierarchy there are between him and the people actually running the government's programs. He thus becomes more insulated from the broader government and runs the risk of making himself less accountable to the public. While trying to create a neutral, hierarchical accountability to the president, reformers lost sight of the mechanisms for keeping the president politically accountable to the rest of the government.

In the next two sections we will discuss the corporate approach to the president's management of people and organizational structures in the executive branch, as illustrated in the Nixon and Carter presidencies. We will save the discussion of alternative approaches to presidential management for the last chapter, where we will discuss two presidents from the opposite ends of the political spectrum who have been perceived as strong leaders: Franklin Roosevelt and Ronald Reagan. Both tended not to follow in practice the tenets of the classical management model.

Managing Subordinates

If one assumes that bureaucrats act rationally in their own self-interest, each with his or her own goals, then the president is in a good position to enforce compliance if he controls the "benefits" that motivate the subordinate. In a bureaucracy, the benefits which might motivate subordinate responsiveness are promises of job security, promotion and advancement, salary increases, and perquisites of office. The superior who can dispense or withhold these benefits will be in a more commanding position than a superior who has no control over such major facets of his subordinates' jobs.

However, in his book on public management, Gordon Chase, an experienced public manager, raises doubts about the ability of public managers to exercise leverage over employee benefits. Throughout his career, Chase served in public managerial positions in several areas of government at various levels, including positions in the Foreign Service and the White House, as Head of the Equal Employment Opportunity Commission, and as chief administrator of New York City's Health Services Administration. He makes this observation about managing personnel:

> Personnel agencies handle issues fundamental to management control: who can be hired, who is promoted, and how much each is paid. Normally managers will want as much control over these decisions as possible, so they can have the people they want and wield the carrot and stick to control them and ensure performance. Typically, however, the public manager will find few of these decisions within his or her authority.[32]

Other managers who have worked in both the public and private sectors echo Chase's comment about the exercise of control over public employees. Michael Blumenthal, for example, served as Secretary of the Treasury under President Carter. Before that, he was chief executive officer at Bendix. Upon leaving government, he became head of Burroughs Corporation. He states that "The head of a government department or agency is not like the chief executive of a large corporation who has control over the personnel system, who can manage it, can instill a certain spirit, can hire and fire. In government that kind of control does not exist." He claims that a top public manager has "almost no control over selection. Hiring goes off a list. And to go outside that system involves more bureaucratic footwork than it is worth." Blumenthal concludes that "Out of 120,000 people in the Treasury, I was able to select twenty-five maybe. The other 119,975 are outside my control."[33]

Bureaucracy has evolved in the twentieth century into a mismatch between formal authority and actual hierarchical control of subordinate incentives. While a superior in a "rational" bureaucracy has the responsibility for dictating subordinate behavior, "rational" bureaucracies operate to a large extent by a system of general rules and regulations which govern, among other things, subordinate benefits. Superiors cannot fire subordinates immediately, and perhaps not at all; pay levels are governed by another set of rules, and advancement in the bureaucracy by yet another. Most bureaucracies in the federal government work under civil service rules which guarantee that superiors cannot dismiss subordinates for arbitrary or political reasons. These rules serve to protect subordinates from partisan political influence, but also from executive leadership. A staff aide in the White House remarked in 1971: "President Nixon does not run the bureaucracy; the civil service and the unions do. It took him three years to find out what was going on in the bureaucracy."[34]

The president has more control over the upper-level members of the executive branch, those political appointees who are cabinet secretaries and undersecretaries and members of the White House staff. However, the subgovernment alliances between interest groups and congressional committees are not formed by these high-level officials but by the permanent bureaucrats beneath the political appointees. Each of these individuals knows that he will still be there when the present administration has come and gone. Gordon Chase remarks, for example, that, "For public managers the most important fact about their elected chief is likely to be that the chief has had little or no prior management experience."[35] The average tenure in office of cabinet secretaries, for example, is only approximately one to two years.

Furthermore, the congressional committee members are the ones who most clearly control the flow of benefits to the permanent civil service in the form of budgets and program authorizations. Thus, J. Edgar Hoover as "neutral" bureaucrat was nominally subordinate, through the Attorney General, to the president. For much of his career, however, he was above control by either one. Hoover knew he had the strongest degree of congressional support, making it politically impossible for a president to fire him, or even to alter the flow of resources to the FBI. "His relations with Congress were, quite simply, the most successful in the history of American public bureaucracy. Until the year before his death, no public hearing had ever been held on his budget, and never in his career as Director was any budget request denied."[36] When subordinates are guaranteed some standard benefits through the neutral, automatic procedures of the civil service, and other benefits through close relationships with Congress, no wonder the president cannot directly command the executive branch.

The upper-level departmental leaders and the presidential staff are the only individuals whose actions the president can attempt to control directly. While his legal authority to fire these individuals is clear, his power to overcome the political constraints is not. A president normally hires some departmental secretaries in order to secure the political support of a party faction or interest group, such as agriculture or business. Firing these secretaries would alienate these groups and decrease his political influence rather than increase it. These departmental secretaries are, of course, aware of this, and consequently consider themselves, at times, as the lobbyists for these groups as much or more than they consider themselves the president's agents of control. John Ehrlichman, President Nixon's White House aide, remarked that after the cabinet and subcabinet officers are appointed, "they go off and marry the natives."[37]

Presidential staff people are certainly thought to have no interest but the president's to represent, but even here there may be unpleasant consequences for a president if he fires one of his own staff. Such firings disrupt the orderly flow of business and call into question that which must not be questioned: the president's ability to run his own house. For these reasons, if a member of the president's staff is not doing his job as well as the president wishes, there is a tendency to shuffle him to a harmless position rather than fire him outright.

Lyndon Johnson once said that he didn't just want a particular individual's support, he wanted his "balls in his pocket." The president has that degree of support over very few subordinates. Neustadt wrote that if a president is to lead, he must use his power to persuade other people, because he does not have the power to command. The "persuasive task" is to induce people to "believe that what he wants of them is what their own appraisal of their own responsibilities requires them to do in their interest, not his."[38] This is a far cry from what Johnson and other strong presidents might like.

There are other reasons why the president has limited control over the executive branch. A superior who can control the incentives of a subordinate must also be able to monitor the subordinate's behavior. The superior who cannot monitor the subordinate may well find out after the fact that the subordinate was pursuing his or her own interests. However, many superiors have only limited ability to monitor subordinate behavior because of distance, lack of expertise, or simply because there are too many subordinates. The classic case of a monitoring problem is the on-duty patrolman. Police departments tried many ways to keep patrolmen from spending their time asleep in a warehouse or drinking with friends. Before the invention of the patrol car with a two-way radio, the most successful technique was the call box, from which the patrolman had to check in at various hours.

The president is burdened with all the problems that limit monitoring. None of the operational programs in the executive branch are housed in the White House or the Executive Office Building. Most of the president's subordinates are a much greater distance from the White House than a patrolman ever was from the precinct station. Furthermore, many of them are engaged in technical tasks which he cannot monitor because of a lack of understanding. Morton Halperin has described ways in which the military was able to use its expertise to influence presidential decisions, including the use of expert advisory committees stacked "to influence the President and his principal counselors. For example, in an effort to get the strategic missile program moving over the opposition of the Air Force (which was more concerned with bombers), the civilian director of the program in the Pentagon, Trevor Gardner, created a Strategic Missiles Evaluation Group whose members were appointed on the basis of their commitment to ICBMs and their influence with senior officials."[39]

Managing Organizational Structures

Problems with operational distance, monitoring, and span of control have encouraged presidents from Johnson to Reagan to use administrative centralization to increase presidential control of the bureaucracy. Many of these centralization drives have adopted the corporate model. One of the most elaborate and well-documented efforts to centralize management along these lines was President Nixon's reorganization proposals of the early 1970s.

Nixon's Reorganization Strategy.   In 1969, Nixon established an Advisory Council on Executive Reorganization, chaired by Roy L. Ash, then president of Litton Industries. Ash put together a series of organization proposals that would have basically transformed the White House into a corporate CEO model: organization of major departments by function; acceptance of the policy/administration dichotomy; limited span of control; and straight lines of authority. The original reorganization plans moved cautiously in this direction by establishing a White House Office for the Director of the Bureau of the Budget (now changed to the Office of Management and Budget) and the creation of a Domestic Policy Council in the White House headed by John Ehrlichman. The Council's structure would parallel the organization of the National Security Council chaired by Henry Kissinger. These moves served as an attempt to consolidate power over policy formulation in the White House rather than the bureaucracy.

The next set of Ash Council proposals went further toward the orthodox model. They recommended consolidating the clientele-oriented departments of Agriculture, Commerce, Labor, and Transportation into four goal-oriented super-departments of Community Development, Economic Affairs, Human Resources, and Natural Resources. In conjunction with these consolidations, the Ash council proposed to incorporate into the four super-departments many independent agencies, such as the Small Business Administration and the Farmers Home Administration. Opposition from farmers organizations, labor, and other constituencies, however, made these proposals stillborn in the Congress, and Nixon quickly abandoned them when he realized their political costs.[40]

The president then proceeded on another tack. In January 1973, he proposed to create his own corporate structure through the use of assistants to the president. Features of the plan included that access to the president would be limited to five assistant presidents; four assistants to the president would be responsible for integrating policies in domestic affairs, foreign affairs, executive management, and economic affairs; and access to the assistant presidents would be limited to only three "Counsellors"—the secretaries of Health Education and Welfare (HEW), Agriculture, and Housing and Urban Development. The plan created a three-tier structure, with the other departmental secretaries at the bottom.[41]

Nixon's model of the presidency followed Woodrow Wilson's view of power: "There is no danger in power if only it be not irresponsible." But what makes power irresponsible? According to Wilson, power that "is divided and dealt out in shares to many" makes for irresponsible power. Wilson believed that power centralized in chief executives could be "easily watched and brought to book." Likewise, Nixon felt that the cabinet officers and especially the agency heads must come more closely under the control "of the man who must serve *all* of the people as their president." However, the disadvantages of this system (and the blind side of Wilson's argument) became apparent during Nixon's administration: The departmental secretaries who should have had direct access to the president were frustrated to find themselves two levels down in the hierarchy, and the president himself became so insulated that there was a question as to whether he was getting sufficient information to perform his job adequately. The Watergate affair, in fact, may stand as the tragic culmination of this kind of administrative thinking. The president became increasingly unaccountable to other parts of the government and more and more dependent on his own large staff for information and advice. Such unaccountable power easily led to its abuse. With the Watergate disclosures, Nixon decided to abandon his assistant-presidents idea and reinstitute direct contact with cabinet members.

Reorganization was not the only component of Nixon's administrative strategy to control the bureaucracy. Standard operating procedures, those rules by which agencies run themselves, can be another impediment to a superior's control over subordinates. When a subordinate can object to a superior's orders by claiming that "rules require a different course of action," then a superior is going to have to convince or persuade the subordinate, rather than simply command. That standard operating procedures can limit even the president is evident from the case of the naval blockade discussed in Chapter 6.

The existence of hierarchy itself, while intended as the instrument of control, can serve as a means for subordinate noncompliance. When a superior has to convince only one subordinate, it is easier than trying to get an entire hierarchy to comply, since intermediaries in the hierarchy can send a matter down for further study and subordinates can send it back up for guidance or clarification. For the president, it can often be frustrating trying to get commands through departmental secretaries, undersecretaries, and assistant secretaries down to the operational, program level for action; and once it is transmitted, the president may be unclear whether the directive was transmitted in its original version. Said one of FDR's aides:

> Half of a President's suggestions, which theoretically carry the weight of orders, can be safely forgotten by a Cabinet member. And if the President asks about a suggestion the second time, he can be told that it is being investigated. If he asks a third time, a wise Cabinet officer will give him at least part of what he suggests. But only occasionally, except about the most important matters, do Presidents ever get around to asking three times.[42]

Perhaps this is what was meant by a former Nixon appointee who commented: "No decision in government is made only once."[43]

Especially in his second term, Nixon attempted to place people in cabinet and sub-cabinet positions that were loyal to him. He tended to choose people who had little independent political standing, which made transferring positions or firing appointees possible without creating a political protest in the country. Nixon also greatly increased the use of the budget impoundment power in his second term. He made efforts to stop whole programs through the withholding or postponement of funds. Finally, Nixon increased the use of regulation writing to influence the way the bureaucracy carried out program mandates. Social-services rules were modified, for example, to restrict the discretion exercised by social workers in the granting of aid to the poor.

A panel of the National Academy of Public Administration, in its written report to the Erwin Committee of the United States Senate, expressed concern about the Nixon plan for presidential management:

The United States Government (under Nixon) would be run like a corporation—or at least a popular view of the corporate model—with all powers concentrated at the top and exercised through appointees in the President's Office and loyal followers placed in crucial positions in the various agencies of the Executive Branch. . . . No one can guess how close the American government would be to this closed hierarchical model had not Watergate exposures halted the advance toward it—at least temporarily.[44]

The panel made these comments despite its close philosophical ties to the traditions of a strong and vigorous presidency originally espoused by the Brownlow Committee and the Hoover Commission. Perhaps the experiences of Watergate and the actual practice of strong administrative management by President Nixon reawakened interest in the advantages of a "pluralistic" executive, as so eloquently expressed by James Madison, for holding the president accountable for his actions.

Carter's Reorganization Strategy. Despite Watergate and all the debate about the dangers of a strong presidency, when Jimmy Carter ran for president in 1976, he espoused the very same administrative doctrines put forth by the Ash Council under Nixon.[45] He supported a simplification of the administrative structure and an introduction of zero-base budgeting in order to achieve the goal of "eliminating duplication and overlapping of functions." In restructuring the Defense Department, Carter proposed to "remove the overlapping functions and singly address the Defense Department toward the capability to fight." Along these same lines, Carter recommended the consolidation and reduction in the number of government agencies and departments—a nine-tenths reduction in the number of units at the federal level from 1900 down to only 200. His comprehensive plans attempted to consolidate diverse programs in four areas: economic and community development, natural resources, food and nutrition, and trade.

President Carter also shared Nixon's view of the presidency as a plebiscite for the people over and against the influence of special interests. He expressed opposition to incremental policy making in which the "special interests can benefit from the status quo." He believed that the president should make comprehensive, bold policy that sets long-range goals for the nation. He felt that this planning approach to goals would remove conflict and disharmony from his cabinet and his relations with the Congress. Thus, as Seidman points out, Carter's initial approach to administration seemed to rest on almost meaningless generalities: eliminating duplication, consolidating functions, increasing efficiency, and improving planning and coordination.[46]

In practice, administration by Carter turned out differently. Carter never enjoyed the same degree of political support as the Nixon administration, and from his early days in office, Carter found his political position in the country steadily eroding. His overall plans for consolidation never got off the ground, and his one concrete consolidation proposal, to create a Department of Natural Resources, encountered strident opposition in the Congress. Within a short time, Carter abandoned his major reorganization plans altogether.

Interestingly, however, the few reorganizations carried out by the Carter administration contradicted orthodox principle but faithfully adhered to the political realities of his interest-group support. Carter established the Department of Education by breaking up (not consolidating) the Department of Health, Education and Welfare. He received strong endorsements from the National Educational

Association, which supported the creation of a separate education department. He also created the Department of Energy, which was a consolidation of sorts, by bringing together energy-related activities from several other agencies; yet the motivation for the Energy Department came from the need to do something visible in support of his declaration of the "moral equivalent of war" against the energy crisis. The establishment of the Energy Department pleased the energy groups enormously and made it appear that Carter was doing something new and different to stave off the energy problem. Ronald C. Moe, a specialist in American government with the Congressional Research Service, concluded: "On balance, the President's reorganization effort has resulted in more, not fewer, agencies, and in more agencies and programs being placed outside direct accountability to the President."[47]

According to Seidman, Nixon's and Carter's grandiose reorganization plans reveal the presidents' continuing, unthinking reliance on orthodox administrative principles as a value independent of any policy or political goals.[48] Yet Presidents Nixon and Carter clearly benefited politically from their espousal of orthodox administrative principles. It made them appear managerial to the public, cemented solidarity with the business elites, and portrayed them as interested and capable of achieving economy and efficiency in government. More than that, the administrative orthodoxy serves the national coalition that elects the president. Since the president usually runs against the interest-group triangles of Congress, the administrative orthodoxy, with its emphasis on centralization and comprehensiveness, serves his political and policy strategies to appeal to this broader, national constituency. In addition, both Nixon and Carter saw themselves as running against the Washington bureaucracy. Administrative reform that aims to bolster central clearance and White House power is intended to further this cause as well.

Presidents have not applied administrative orthodoxy unthinkingly and without consideration of political or policy goals, but they have failed to fully recognize the limitations of orthodox administrative ideas to successfully achieve these goals in practice. The administrative orthodoxy recommends fighting bureaucracy with more bureaucracy. It advocates adding more layers of hierarchy, new administrative rules, and additional central staff supposedly loyal to the president. Yet none of these reforms changes the essential structural characteristics of bureaucracy which themselves can be the impediments to presidential control.

None of the characteristics of bureaucracy is unambiguously beneficial from the standpoint of the individual at the top of the executive branch. Expertise may enhance bureaucratic efficiency, or it can become a power base for subordinates wishing to change the president's mind. Rules and regulations can create a neutral, objective method of operation, but they can also serve as a constraint on presidential freedom of action. Division of labor can increase the span of control so that the president cannot control the entire range of governmental functions, but increased hierarchy can become a method of avoiding responsibility. When one combines these facts with the omnipresence of strong political alliances between bureaucrats at the program level with congressional committees and interest groups, it is not surprising that the president must resort to the "power to persuade" as the main element of leadership. The political game of alliance formation and bureaucratic noncompliance belie the claim of bureaucratic neutrality and, more importantly, bring into question the Progressive claim for accountability through a neutral bureaucratic structure.

In the next chapter, we bring together the various themes of efficiency, neutrality and accountability into a general assessment of the administrative reform tradition. We will try to show the interrelationships between the various explanations for bureaucratic dysfunctions we have discussed and the implications for the conduct of policy making and administration.

NOTES

[1] THEODORE J. LOWI, "Machine Politics—Old and New," *The Public Interest*, 9 (Fall 1967), p. 87.

[2] WALLACE S. SAYRE and HERBERT KAUFMAN, *Governing New York City: Politics in the Metropolis* (New York: Russell Sage Foundation, 1960), p. 720. Reprinted by permission of Basic Books, Inc., Publishers.

[3] DAVID HAMMACK, *Power and Society: Greater New York at the Turn of the Century* (New York: Russell Sage Foundation, 1982).

[4] HAMMACK, *Power*, pp. 316–317.

[5] SAYRE and KAUFMAN, *Governing*, p. 714.

[6] SAYRE and KAUFMAN, *Governing*, p. 715.

[7] SAYRE and KAUFMAN, *Governing*, p. 719.

[8] ROBERT CARO, *The Power Broker: Robert Moses and the Fall of New York* (New York: Vintage Books, 1975), pp. 837–894.

[9] JEFFREY L. PRESSMAN, *Federal Programs and City Politics: The Dynamics of the Aid Process in Oakland* (Berkeley: University of California Press, 1975).

[10] PRESSMAN, *Federal Programs*, pp. 28 and 30.

[11] PRESSMAN, *Federal Programs*, p. 36.

[12] PRESSMAN, *Federal Programs*, p. 146.

[13] FREDERICK M. WIRT, "Alioto and the Politics of Hyperpluralism," *TRANSaction*, 7 (1970), pp. 46–55.

[14] LOWI, "Machine Politics," p. 86.

[15] JOHN WOOLLEY, *The Federal Reserve and the Politics of Monetary Policy* (Cambridge: Cambridge University Press, 1984), p. 202.

[16] LAWRENCE S. RITTER and WILLIAM L. SILBER, *Principles of Money, Banking and Financial Markets*, 3rd ed. (New York: Basic Books, 1980).

[17] FRANCIS E. ROURKE, *Bureaucracy, Politics and Public Policy*, 3rd ed. (Boston: Little, Brown & Co., 1984).

[18] JACK KNOTT, "The Federal Reserve's Political Support Network" (unpublished manuscript, Michigan State University, 1984).

[19] WOOLLEY, *Federal Reserve*.

[20] KNOTT, "The Political Support Network," 1984, p. 10.

[21] RICHARD E. NEUSTADT, *Presidential Power: The Politics of Leadership from FDR to Carter* (New York: John Wiley, 1980).

[22] WOOLLEY, *Federal Reserve*, p. 106.

[23] GRANT McCONNELL, *Private Power and American Democracy* (New York: Vintage Books, 1966), p. 219.

[24] HAROLD SEIDMAN, *Politics, Position, and Power: The Dynamics of Federal Organization* (New York: Oxford University Press, 1980), p. 127.

[25] McCONNELL, *Private Power*, p. 224.

[26] McCONNELL, *Private Power*, p. 224.

[27] JAMES NATHAN MILLER, "Half a Billion Dollars Down the Drain," *Reader's Digest* (November 1976), pp. 143–144.

[28]PHILIP SHABECOFF, "Water Agency Merger Plan Rejected," *New York Times*, February 6, 1985, p. 11.

[29]McCONNELL, *Private Power*, p. 216.

[30]TERRY MOE, "The Politicized Presidency," in *New Directions*, John Chubb and Paul Peterson, eds. (Washington: Brookings Institution, 1985).

[31]MOE, "Politicized Presidency," pp. 255–256.

[32]GORDON CHASE and ELIZABETH C. REVEAL, *How to Manage in the Public Sector* (Reading: Addison-Wesley Publishing Co., 1983), p. 69.

[33]W. MICHAEL BLUMENTHAL, "Candid Reflections of a Businessman in Washington," in *Public Management: Public and Private Perspectives*, James L. Perry and Kenneth L. Kraemer, eds. (Palo Alto: Mayfield Publishing Co., 1983), pp. 24–27.

[34]RICHARD P. NATHAN, *The Plot That Failed: Nixon and the Administrative Presidency* (New York: John Wiley & Sons, 1975), p. 83.

[35]CHASE and REVEAL, *How to Manage*, p. 25.

[36]EUGENE LEWIS, *Public Entrepreneurship: Toward a Theory of Bureaucratic Political Power: The Organizational Lives of Hyman Rickover, J. Edgar Hoover, and Robert Moses* (Bloomington, Ind.: Indiana State Univeristy Press, 1980), p. 154.

[37]SEIDMAN, *Politics*, p. 91.

[38]NEUSTADT, *Presidential Power*, p. 114.

[39]MORTON HALPERIN, *Bureaucratic Politics and Foreign Policy* (Washington D.C.: Brookings Institution, 1974), pp. 162–163.

[40]SEIDMAN, *Politics*, pp. 114–115.

[41]SEIDMAN, *Politics*, p. 121.

[42]NEUSTADT, *Presidential Power*, p. 32.

[43]RICHARD P. NATHAN, "The Administrative Presidency." *The Public Interest*, 44 (Summer, 1976) 44.

[44]NATHAN, *Plot*, p. 89.

[45]JACK KNOTT and AARON WILDAVSKY, "Jimmy Carter's Theory of Governing," *Wilson Quarterly*, 1 (1977), pp. 49–67.

[46]SEIDMAN, *Politics*, p. 128.

[47]SEIDMAN, *Politics*, p. 131.

[48]SEIDMAN, *Politics*, p. 132.

CHAPTER 9

Explaining Bureaucratic Dysfunctions:
Two Models

I am plagued with doubt—I am not quite sure whether the world is run by incompetents who are sincere or by wise guys who are putting us on.

Laurence J. Peter, *Why Things Go Wrong*[1]

Reformers over the decades set great store in the possibility of guaranteeing efficient, neutral, and accountable administration through their general recipe for professionalized bureaucracy. They were also remarkably successful in instituting their recipe and in getting the public to go along with their view of bureaucracy. The "efficiency expert" became a heroic public figure in the Progressive years, while the party boss became an object of suspicion and derision. City managers achieved a prominent position in the public eye, and professionals achieved a high-status position in society. The forest ranger, the agricultural extension agent, the highway engineer, the public health official, and other occupations became respected bureaucratic professions. By the time of World War II, professional bureaucracy had become the norm for government administration.

Today, however, seventy years after the Progressive Era, bureaucrats have joined, if not replaced, party bosses in the ranks of unpopular public officials. Indeed, "antibureaucratic sentiment has taken hold like an epidemic."[2] Voters have supported tax revolts whose organizers have charged bureaucracy with the responsibility for governmental inefficiency and waste. Congressmen have run campaigns charging that bureaucracy is "out of control," either out of ineptitude or avarice, and Congress has invested heavily in congressional staff as a way of improving its own oversight of bureaucracy. Nixon felt that the bureaucracy was subverting his administration's goals, while Carter's presidential campaign was based in large part on his ability to reform bureaucracy as demonstrated in his previous experiences as governor of Georgia. Most striking of all is the Reagan campaign's assault on bureaucracy as a central element of "big government," and Reagan's interpretation of his election as a mandate to "cut bureaucracy down to size."

TWO VIEWS OF BUREAUCRACY

On closer inspection, however, the "problem of bureaucracy" is somewhat difficult to pin down. At times, one hears that bureaucrats are "out of control" in the sense that they are stuck in inefficient bureaucratic routines, and no way can be found to break them of the laziness or timidity that keeps them in that routine. In this case, the image is of bureaucrats arriving at their offices at late hours in the morning only to drink coffee and read *The Washington Post*. When difficult decisions need to be made, they desperately try to find ways to avoid taking any responsibility.

At other times, one hears that bureaucrats are "out of control" in the sense that they are grasping for political power beyond what is legitimately theirs. In this case, the image is of forceful bureaucrats pushing themselves, unwanted, into private lives and public policies beyond their rightful scope of administration, in a power-hungry megalomania. The problem with bureaucrats in this view is not their laziness, but their ambition.

These two criticisms are, of course, to some extent inconsistent. As Charles Goodsell notes in his defense of public bureaucracy, "Bureaucrats are portrayed as fear-ridden yet arrogant, incompetent yet ominous, Milquetoasts yet Machiavellians. Bureaucracy is rigid and at the same time expansionist."[3] One view asserts that the bureaucracies are unaccountable because they are rigid and unresponsive; the other view claims it is because they are too dynamic and power-mad. The first depicts bureaucracies as havens for inefficient paper-pushers who can't summon the initiative to fulfill the minimum that is asked of them by political leaders. The second depicts bureaucracies as fortresses for power-grabbers who can't restrain themselves from imperialistic action beyond what is asked of them by political leaders. The first popular view we will call "red-tape bureaucracy," and the second we will call "imperialistic bureaucracy." Both popular views have been supported in the press, and in various academic writings as well; but how can they both be right?

Bureaucracy as Red Tape

In 1976, residents of the Love Canal area of Niagara Falls, New York, found that their grade school, their playground, and their homes had been built on a toxic-waste dumping ground. The sludge their sump pumps had been pumping from their basements contained some of the most harmful substances known to man.

The response of bureaucrats to this discovery was ambivalent. The head of the county health department demanded that residents stop pumping the substances from their basements into the sewage system on the grounds that it was polluting the sewage system; at the same time, the department claimed that the health threat to residents was slight. Finding their own bureaucracies unresponsive, residents brought in their own outside experts who documented the relationship between the toxic wastes and the high incidence of birth defects, miscarriages, and serious health problems among children in the area.

The New York State Department of Health, which was oriented toward traditional health problems such as sanitation and contagious diseases, resisted the evidence connecting the toxic wastes to health hazards and refused to do much about the problem. The residents felt that the bureaucrats were too dense or too timid to recognize the government's responsibility in this new area of hazardous waste control.

Relations between the residents and the state bureaucracy became so difficult that a panel of federal bureaucrats from the Environmental Protection Agency (EPA) and the Department of Health, Education and Welfare was asked to arbitrate the dispute. The federal panel found that the residents were right and the state agency was wrong, but (like the state bureaucrats) used such cautious language that no action was forthcoming. The head of the Federal Disaster Assistance Administration was reluctant to interpret existing regulations in a way that would allow him to respond to the emergency for fear of setting a precedent that would require his agency to intervene in some unknown number of future toxic-waste cases. "To the people of Love Canal, his reasoning was similar to that of a lifeguard who might refuse to pick up a struggling, drowning person because the act might impede the development of a good water-safety program in that person's community at some time in the future."[4]

By 1980, when the Environmental Protection Agency announced that residents had suffered chromosome damage that might indicate danger for themselves and their offspring, frustration with federal bureaucracies had mounted to such an extent that the residents took two EPA bureaucrats hostage. This action brought President Carter, in the midst of a reelection campaign, to Love Canal to declare that Love Canal did, in fact, constitute an emergency that the federal government could respond to under existing law. This allowed over 700 families to be removed from the area, four years after the problem had become known.

Throughout the affair, local, state, and federal bureaucrats left the impression with residents that they valued the security of their standard operating procedures more than the health of the citizens they were supposed to serve. The residents regarded bureaucratic intransigence as an obstacle that had to be overcome, and taking the EPA officials hostage symbolized this attitude. The residents were joined by other officials in this view, including one New York state senator who charged that the residents had been the "victim of a cover-up involving public and private entities including the State's Department of Health."[5]

This pattern of citizen dissatisfaction with bureaucratic response has been apparent in other cases, some involving hazardous-waste pollution and others not. In the case of foreign policy, the federal State Department has frequently left its client (in this case the president) with much the same feeling of frustration that the health departments engendered in the Love Canal residents. Shortly after President Kennedy was inaugurated in 1961, he faced a confrontation with the Soviet Union over Berlin. He asked the State Department to draft a response to the Russians. The State Department did not respond for a month, and the response, when it came, was an unusable compilation of old position statements. Thereafter, Kennedy increasingly avoided the State Department, relying on individuals outside that bureaucracy for much of his foreign policy advice. "The president used to divert himself with a dream of establishing . . . a secret office of thirty people to run foreign policy while maintaining the State Department as a facade in which people might contentedly carry papers from bureau to bureau."[6]

This was a dream which was, in fact, largely realized under Nixon, who used the National Security Council and the National Security Advisor, Henry Kissinger, instead of the State Department to make top-level foreign policy decisions. This is a pattern which has been followed in large part by subsequent presidents, leading to continued tension between the Secretary of State and the National Security Advisor in subsequent presidential administrations, including that of Ronald Reagan. The structure of American foreign policy has been fundamentally transformed by the presidential perception that State Department officials are bureaucrats who are too bound up in trivia to face up to big problems, and so timid that they are content to "carry papers from bureau to bureau."

Both the chemical poisoning of a residential neighborhood and the long-term inadequacies of the State Department are instances in which the well-being of Americans are at stake, either as individual citizens or as a nation. The clients of these governmental agencies, whether homeowners or presidents, have experienced a deep dissatisfaction with the behavior of these agencies, and they have attributed the inadequacies to "red-tape" ridden routines established by rules, regulations, and standard operating procedures. This is one common point of view about bureaucracies. Just as often, however, one hears a completely different and apparently contradictory view: that of the imperial bureaucracy.

The Imperial Bureaucracy

According to this second view, bureaucrats are dangerous because of their capriciousness and power, rather than contemptible because of their preference for carrying irrelevant papers around. Far from being incapable of original thought and energetic action, bureaucrats always seem to be thinking of new ways of extending their reach into areas where they have no legitimate business. The problem, in this view, is not to urge bureaucrats to respond more energetically to crises, but to rein in a runaway bureaucracy.

Once again, history supplies a number of instances that seem to support this view. One of the most dramatic is the Federal Bureau of Investigation, especially the FBI under J. Edgar Hoover, who served as director from 1924 until his death in 1972. As director, Hoover was so powerful that presidents feared to fire him. Hoover's power was partly indicated by his refusal to perform tasks that his nominal superior, the Attorney General, might require of him. When Robert Kennedy was Attorney General, he asked Hoover to send FBI agents to police civil rights demonstrations in the South. Hoover's personal antipathy to the civil rights movement was well known, and he refused Kennedy's directive, forcing Kennedy to deputize Immigration Officers and others to perform the job.[7]

Even more telling was Hoover's ability to do things that were *not* asked of him. For instance, the FBI ran its own campaign against Martin Luther King between 1963 and King's death in 1968. King's famous "I have a dream" speech inspired the rest of the nation, but it convinced Hoover and the FBI that King was "the most dangerous Negro leader in America," and must be taken "off his pedestal." The FBI planned to promote their own "safe" candidate for leadership of the civil rights movement, and engaged in extensive surveillance of King in an attempt to blackmail him. As late as 1968, the FBI was still directing the field offices in this campaign. One observer notes that "the King persecution is but one vivid example of relatively commonplace Bureau behavior."[8]

In Washington, it was questioned whether this clandestine surveillance and blackmailing by the FBI also extended to members of Congress. Various members believed in the existence of "secret files" on members of Congress, containing discrediting information which Hoover "kindly" agreed to keep quiet in return for cooperation from Congress. At any rate, Hoover never ran into serious opposition from Congress.

No one ever criticized Hoover's FBI as being timidly bound by its own red tape, or unable to undertake bold new responses to difficult or crisis situations. On the contrary, the question was whether the FBI's bold responses were under control by the rest of the federal government.

The Reform Model Challenged

Neither the State Department's affinity for red tape nor the FBI's grab for power is adequately explained by the original reform prescription. The State Department had been revamped completely by the Progressive reform model in 1924, with legislation creating a professionalized foreign service officer corps, and eliminating the old "spoils system" which had previously staffed the State Department with political hacks. This corps controlled the rest of the State Department through a complex system of specialized departments, integrated under a strict chain of command and a well-developed system of rules. To all appearances, it was a perfect model of a reformed bureaucracy, yet presidents increasingly have regarded it as an inefficient bunch of paper-pushers.

Similarly, the FBI is a child of the Progressive reform prescription. Hoover took control of the FBI in 1924 on condition that he could run it as a nonpartisan, professionalized agency. The FBI agent was the standard for the professional law enforcement officer, incorruptible and businesslike, as far from a Tammany Hall cop as a city manager was from Tweed himself. To all appearances, it was a perfect model of a professionalized law enforcement agency, yet presidents found it running its own unauthorized campaign of harassment and intimidation against the civil rights movement.

It is experiences such as those with the State Department, the Love Canal crisis, and the FBI, along with countless other citizen confrontations with Internal Revenue Service officials, Social Security officials, and other bureaucrats, that have revised the public's estimation of what to expect from a professionalized bureaucracy. The simple explanation for the State Department case is that bureaucrats are doddering fools who are incapable of rational action—persons with more intelligence and initiative are in private business. However, this simple explanation conflicts with a similarly oversimplified explanation of J. Edgar Hoover, which suggests that bureaucracies attract psychopaths with an uncontrolled lust for power, as the more extreme critics of Hoover's career have suggested.

We reject both of these oversimplified explanations. We argue that different kinds of bureaucratic behavior can be understood in terms of quite normal preferences for success within the system of incentives created by the administrative reform institution. The problem, in short, is that *reform institutions create incentives for either red tape or imperialistic behavior, depending on conditions that are left out of the reform model.* Ultimately, we will argue that the key explanatory variables for understanding red tape or imperialistic behavior are political variables, which reformers have continuously overlooked because of their assumption that bureaucracy could and should be nonpolitical. This assumption of political neutrality was the central flaw which led from the creation of Progressive reform institutions such as the reformed State Department and the FBI to the problems which became manifest in the reform movements of the 1960s.

EXPLANATION ONE: INDIVIDUAL COGNITIVE LIMITS

While sociologists were documenting the existence of the rigidity cycle, goal displacement, and other disturbing bureaucratic behaviors, scholars in the field of public administration were developing explanations for such behaviors. The first, and in many ways the most influential, of these was Herbert Simon's explanation, articulated in *Administrative Behavior*,[9] and later elaborated upon by James March and Herbert Simons in *Organization*.[10]

Simon's main contribution was the concept of "bounded rationality." Simon believed that the classical model does not serve as an adequate science of organization. He argued that it is extraordinarily difficult to design an organization that fully achieves the societal goal people have set for themselves. The reason is that people confront various kinds of uncertainties, including not even knowing the probability distributions of outcomes, that limit their choice. He therefore argued that organizations are usually simplified, approximate, and limited models of the "objective" rationality required to reach the societal goal. March and Simon write:

> Because of the limits of human intellectual capacities, in comparison with the complexities of the problems that individuals and organizations face, rational behavior calls for simplified models that capture the main features of a problem without capturing all its complexities.[11]

Instead, people and organizations operate under a bounded rationality. In everyday life, individuals rationally take much of their world for granted as they go about their business. People do not have to "decide" each day on what side of the street to drive or how to knot their necktie. These matters are based on habit and established routine, such that they become little more than reflex actions. In this manner, individuals are free to focus their problem-solving attention on pressing concerns. Trying to comprehensively investigate all issues is not rational because of the constraints on human cognition, time limits, and lack of resources. However, organizational decision making also reflects individuals' dependence on a set of "givens" or premises that influence attention, energy, and skills.

In an organizational setting, Simon believed that the organization's structures and procedures operate to determine the premises for the decisions of its members. The organization constitutes a kind of filter that defines the boundaries within which individuals make rational choices. Standard operating procedures (SOPs) determine the sequence of attention, how the problem is divided, and relations with outsiders. To explain what decisions people in an organization make (and to explain why they seem to make inefficient decisions), it is necessary to examine the structures and standard operating procedures that set the premises for their limited choices. In a bureaucracy, these premises are comprised of a limited set of programs that make up the organization's repertoire of alternative actions, and these premises change very slowly over time.

People also use adaptive search strategies to deal with their limited problem-solving capacity. They give their attention to problems sequentially, so that they will not have to think of everything at once. One key feature of this is *selective attention*, in which decision makers appear to ignore information that seems to attack their preconceived notions, and respond favorably to information that seems to support their biases. The "cognitive limits" explanation for his behavior is obvious: It is not rational for people with limited cognitive capacity to continuously make wholesale revisions in their orientations and outlook.

Another empirical phenomenon explained by cognitive limits is *satisficing*. This is a term that refers to decision makers who do not engage in an endless search for what Taylorites called "the one best way," but "make do" with satisfactory alternatives. Again, satisficing is explained quite easily from the cognitive-limits approach as stemming from individual inability to search for and evaluate all possible alternatives. If satisficing still leaves room for improvements, they can be attacked again later in an iterative fashion. In other words, people keep chipping away at problems rather than trying to solve them all at once.

If organizations evolve to compensate for individual cognitive limitations, why should we still observe inadequacies in bureaucratic performance? In other words, where do bureaucratic dysfunctions come from, according to this explanation? In March and Simon's work, it is often difficult to tell whether they are speaking of an organization or an individual, for during much of their discussion of limits on rationality, an organization acts just like a cognitively limited individual. Cognitive limits, therefore, provide an explanation for some of the organizational dysfunctions discussed so far.

Trained Incapacity.   One link is between Simon's notion of "bounded rationality" and the bureaucratic dysfunction of "trained incapacity." Prior training constitutes an important premise for an official's technical decision making. This kind of technical decision making is so fully absorbing in its own right that the individual has no time or energy left for considering broader aspects or other technical processes in the organization. He rationally limits his attention to his own field, letting other aspects of organization act as "givens." Once an official has learned how to analyze certain types of situations in a certain way, it is difficult— and certainly very costly—to learn a new set of premises. Hence, the cognitively limited bureaucrat will solve new problems in old ways, seeing only the partial and the specialized aspects of the problem rather the problem as a whole.

Goal Displacement.   Having accepted a set of standard operating procedures by which to achieve an organizational goal, and therefore operating under a bounded rationality, an individual in an organization will not rethink this system repeatedly; he will take the SOPs as given—as the premises for decision—in order to concentrate on the day-to-day issues. This means that the individual will not concern himself with the original design of the organization, but will rather be satisfied with following the means that had at one time been determined to be appropriate for the goal. The individual will thus come to pursue these means as if they were goals.

Dual System of Authority.   From the perspective of bounded rationality, the "trained expert" is someone who has invested a large proportion of his cognitive talents in developing a certain view of things. Along with other professionals with the same training, these individuals will resist efforts to get them to abandon that investment and think of problems from entirely different perspectives. For instance, getting a doctor to think of a problem from a legal or an engineering perspective would be difficult. Consequently, when a superior attempts to use hierarchical authority to force the trained expert to do something in a way that is contrary to his or her training, the expert will resist. Hence, there is a conflict between the hierarchical authority of the superior and the bounded rationality of the trained expert.

The Solution: Smarter People?

What would happen if the cognitive capacity of the average bureaucrat were suddenly twice or ten times as great? If the limits on individual cognition are the key determinant of organizational behavior, then bureaucratic behavior would suddenly improve. Bureaucrats could process information faster and consider decisions from different angles. Doctors could afford to try to think like engineers part of the time. Individuals would be more likely to perceive when it is appropriate to follow routines and when it is inappropriate. When routines are perceived as inappropriate, they would be able to consider more innovative alternatives. Organizations would be more flexible because individual bureaucrats would be more innovative and better decision makers. There would be less conflict because individual bureaucrats could see things from each others' point of view. There would be less goal displacement because individuals would be able to reconsider the premises of their decisions more frequently, and to readjust the means to make them more appropriate to the organization's goals.

However, a different explanation for bureaucratic dysfunctions would argue that *making individuals smarter would not necessarily improve bureaucratic performance, and might well make it worse*. The reason is that, according to this view, bureaucratic problems are not caused by limits in individual cognitive capacities. Individuals are generally smart enough to do what is in their self-interest, according to this view. The problem is that individual self-interest and bureaucratic performance often require different behaviors. In other words, *the problem with bureaucracies is that they have structured a system of incentives that guides rational individuals to the wrong behavior*.

EXPLANATION TWO: RATIONAL INDIVIDUALS, IRRATIONAL STRUCTURES

The second explanation for bureaucratic dysfunctions assumes that the structural rules operating in a given organization determine what behaviors are required of individuals who hope to "succeed" in those organizations. In other words, organizational rules fix a set of incentives that shape the behavior of goal-oriented or success-oriented members. This explanation further assumes that organizational members are generally smart enough to be able to interpret those incentives correctly; that is, they are generally doing the best that they can do in a given organization to further their own personal goals. This assumption is known as the "rational actor" assumption or the "maximizing" assumption, and it generally conflicts with the notion of bounded rationality that people probably can't process information well enough to pursue their own goals in a maximizing way.

If people are able to pursue individually rational strategies, then how can we explain the existence of bureaucratic dysfunctions? The explanation rests with the observation that *it generally is very difficult to structure an organization so that individuals, in pursuing their own self-interest, are always working for the organization's best interest at the same time.* In fact, according to this explanation, bureaucracies structured according to the classic formula of hierarchy, specialization, professionalism, and written rules and regulations may well create incentives that virtually *require* smart individuals to behave rigidly, to define problems narrowly instead of broadly, to abuse or ignore clients, or to engage in conflicts with superiors, subordinates, or other organizational divisions.

Incentives and Bureaucratic Pathologies

From this perspective, there is a quite different explanation of each of the bureaucratic dysfunctions. They are seen as being the rational response of individuals to the incentives created by hierarchy, specialization, rules and regulations, and professionalized staffing.

Rigidity Cycle. From the perspective of structural incentives, bureaucratic rigidity does not follow from having individuals with limited cognitive capacity. Rather, individuals with unlimited cognitive capacity would be just as likely to behave in a cautious, rule-following manner, if any other behavior would lead to the end of their careers. In fact, the smarter the bureaucrat, the more able he or she is to figure out the incentives.

Goal Displacement. The managerial orthodoxy doesn't try to motivate individuals to pursue organizational goals as such. Rather, it builds incentives that motivate individuals to follow hierarchical orders and standard operating procedures. It is not surprising, then, that bureaucrats *do* follow orders and standard operating procedures so persistently; nor is this goal displacement evidence of individual cognitive limitations.

Trained Incapacity. Suppose a military problem develops, and the Navy wants to deploy a fleet, the Air Force wants to launch an air strike, and the Marines want to storm the beaches. Each views the problem from its own specialized perspective, and claims to see no value in the solutions proposed by the other specialists. Is this an example of bounded rationality? From the perspective of the incentives explanation, it is important to note that if the Marines get to storm the beaches, their Corps will get the front-page publicity and the credit with Congress, their officers will get the medals, commendations, and promotions, and their budget will do better in the next allocation of defense funds. According to the incentives explanation, specialists have a biased view of the world because they have biased incentives, not because of the limits of bounded rationality.

Dual System of Authority. Similarly, when an expert rebels against the hierarchical authority of the non-expert, that is not due to the expert-subordinate's inability to see a superior's point of view, but to incentives built into the bureaucracy to resist the reduction of one's influence. From this perspective, Admiral George Anderson's resistance to President Kennedy's advice on how to run the Cuban missile blockade was not because he could not see the President's point of view; rather, he did not want to establish a dangerous precedent of having a non-

Naval officer tell the Navy how to run its ships. Anderson's plans for the blockade were different from the president's because he had different goals. In order to preserve the autonomy of his bureaucracy, Anderson felt bound to resist outside invasion of what he regarded as his domain. His reference to the Navy regulations was simply a standard technique by which subordinates seek to justify and explain their behavior to superiors, especially in cases in which the subordinate knows that his knowledge of the rules is better than his boss's.

Bureaucratic Dysfunctions in the State Department

An example of an author who uses this perspective is Donald Warwick, in his *Theory of Public Bureaucracy*.[12] In this book, Warwick documents the bureaucratic dysfunctions present in the behavior of the State Department. However, his explanation for those dysfunctions does not rely on the cognitive limitations of the individual State Department officials—he never cites Herbert Simon. Quite the contrary, his explanation is based on rational individuals responding as best they can to a difficult set of incentives. He also links the problems in the State Department to what he calls the "managerial orthodoxy"—the accepted use of hierarchy and rules in reformed administrative agencies.

Until World War I, patronage characterized the way the State Department hired personnel. This style of staffing came to a halt with the Rogers Act of 1924. The Act created the Foreign Service, which is not an organization, but an elite personnel system for the merit staffing of leadership positions in the foreign embassies and Washington offices of the State Department.

Following the creation of the Foreign Service, the State Department became a professionalized bureaucracy, hierarchical in structure, with a strict chain of command leading up through the bureau heads and the office of the secretary to the President. It was also specialized, with geographical bureaus as well as functional bureaus (cultural affairs, military affairs, political affairs, etc.) It also had an extensive body of rules and regulations specifying how tasks were to be carried out. National security considerations alone required rules for specifying access to files, clearances for intradepartmental memos and public documents, and even the disposal of papers.

Within a few decades of its transformation by the Progressive reform model, it was already being criticized by its main client, the President. Franklin Roosevelt remarked, "The Treasury is so large and far-flung and ingrained in its practices that I find it is almost impossible to get the action and results I want. . . . But the Treasury is not to be compared with the State Department. You should go through the experience of trying to get any changes in the thinking, policy, and action of the career diplomats and then you'd know what a real problem was."[13]

Kennedy and later presidents gradually shifted the focus of foreign policy formation away from the State Department, in the belief that it was too inefficient and clumsy a tool for modern crisis management. This diagnosis has been confirmed by numerous journalists and social scientists. The latter pointed to incidents such as one during the Czechoslovakian crisis in 1968. As a sign of our disapproval of the Czech government, we ordered the American embassy to slash its staff from 78 to 22 people. To everyone's surprise, the embassy was reported to be functioning much more effectively with less than one-third of the people.

The large size of American embassies and the commitment to maintaining an

American life style abroad means that a large proportion of their work consists simply of maintaining themselves. What is more, despite the size of the embassies, they normally can't undertake any major decisions on their own, unlike Russian embassies, which are much smaller yet are delegated the authority to make fairly large commitments. This means that a great deal of communications must pass back and forth from the State Department to the embassies, and each of these must receive numerous clearances, according to standard operating procedures. One Undersecretary of State "was startled to learn that a routine cable on the subject of milk exports required twenty-nine separate signatures."[14] Since a spot-check revealed 1,238 telegraphic messages within the State Department (more than the Associated Press and the United Press International combined), the total number of signatures required for a day's worth of cables is staggering. No wonder Kennedy decided the State Department consisted entirely of paper-pushers!

One State Department official, Deputy Under Secretary William Crockett, determined to improve the Department's effectiveness. Crockett headed the huge State Department division called Area O, which is responsible for administrative and housekeeping functions and which employs half of the stateside employees in the Department. Crockett was convinced that administrative inefficiency in Area O was the result of an overload of rules and levels of hierarchy which hurt bureaucratic initiative and flexibility. He therefore drastically reorganized Area O by eliminating the constraints of hierarchy and rules on many of the subordinates in the Department. For instance, he eliminated six levels of hierarchy in the chain of command between himself and the program managers in charge of employment, training, and supplies. In addition, he moderated the number of rules and clearances to give subordinates more freedom.

Subsequent evaluation of Crockett's experiment supported many of Crockett's hopes. The evaluators observed a "marked reduction in the number of clearances required for action as well as in the amount of direction received from superiors." The program managers felt that communications were flowing more smoothly and that actual performance was improving. The regional bureaus of the State Department, which depended on Area O for technical details and supplies, "reported greater speed and flexibility in their work as a result of the decentralization of functions. They also noted slight improvements in the quality and speed of services obtained from the restructured O units."[15] Supply of services within Area O offices also improved as a result of the change.

Shortly after Crockett's departure in 1967, however, much of the hierarchy and red tape that he had eliminated had reappeared in Area O. According to Warwick, this return to an earlier, more inefficient level of bureaucratization was the result of demands from both superiors and subordinates. The question that Warwick finds most fascinating is why superiors and subordinates would agree on the desirability of bureaucratic hierarchy and rules that outsiders felt inhibited the performance of the organization. Why does bureaucracy persist?

Superiors, according to Warwick, promote hierarchy and rules as a means of asserting their control over a difficult situation. The State Department was charged with the foreign affairs of the most powerful country in a nuclear age. Congress, especially, demanded accountability from State Department superiors, and has harbored strong critics of the Department's performance since the days of Joe McCarthy and the Red Scare. This problem of control is exacerbated by the ambiguity of organizational goals and the necessity of cooperating with other governmental agencies, such as Defense and Agriculture. Given this difficult control problem, how was a supervisor to manage? The answer, according to Warwick, was forthcoming from the "managerial orthodoxy."

> A further prop for bureaucracy lies in the managerial philosophy pervading the federal executive system and for the most part shared by Congress. The basic tenet of this orthodoxy is that efficiency requires a clean line of authority from top to bottom in an organization. The central responsibility of the superior is the faithful implementation of policy directives sent from above and accountability to his own superiors; the key responsibility of the subordinate is obedience. . . . As is true of many social theories, the deep penetration of administrative orthodoxy into the collective consciousness of government creates a tendency toward self-perpetuation.[16]

In other words, superiors felt a positive pressure from Congress to control the State Department or face the consequences. They also felt a pressure to control it using the orthodox means of hierarchy and rules. Thus, when charged with the responsibility of "coordinating" the overseas activities of the Department of Agriculture or Labor, the response of State Department officials was to write a pamphlet of "regulations" for employees of those departments, and to appoint embassy assistants in charge of coordination in each relevant country. Thus was a new level of hierarchy and a new mass of red tape added to the bureaucracy.

At the same time that superiors felt pressure from Congress and elsewhere to control their subordinates by means of hierarchy and rules, the subordinates were facing incentives to go along. Subordinates realized that success depends on following hierarchical directives and rules.

Warwick discusses one situation in which a State Department subordinate was grilled by the Congressional Appropriations Committee because he approved a risqué play as a sample of American culture for presentation abroad. This kind of adverse criticism from Congress can threaten careers, not to mention the embarrassment of the grilling itself. How can a subordinate protect himself from this kind of situation? One way is to say, "My superior approved the play as well," and show a paper with the superior's signatures. A second way is to point to a set of standard operating procedures which cover that situation and show how those regulations support the decision in question. In the former case, it is hierarchy that legitimizes subordinate behavior; in the latter case, it is rules and regulations. The moral of the story is not to take any action that is not covered by an order from one's hierarchical superior or by the rules and regulations.

But what if your rules and regulations don't cover a particular situation, and your boss is too busy to provide guidance? Then the subordinate is likely to demand that one's boss have an assistant who is more accessible, or that more rules and regulations be written to provide guidance. In either case, the result is more hierarchy or more rules.

The pressures for conformity, combined with the inherent ambiguity of the task facing the State Department, created a situation in which the normal official craved guidance. Again, in the context of the orthodox administrative style, the demand for guidance became converted to a demand for hierarchy and rules as the only feasible way in which "guidance" and "safety" could be delivered to a bureaucrat.

Incentives and Imperial Bureaucracy

The incentives framework has the added attraction that it has the ability to explain how, under different circumstances, the problem of "runaway bureaucracy" might develop. The conditions, of course, are the opposite of those that would lead to bureaucratic stodginess and red tape: a safe political environment, a concrete task, an internal reward system shaped to reward innovativeness. While those bureaus with weak political support and difficult tasks to administer are forced to use their internal reward systems as control mechanisms (as with the State Department), bureaucracies with strong interest-group and congressional support have no need to use rules to protect themselves. Instead, they can use a strategy of aggressive bureaucratic expansion as a way of maintaining a friendly environment and a constant flow of resources. The pursuit of these goals may well lead to a reputation of a bureaucracy that is "out of control" by people other than the bureaucracy's special clientele.

A fascinating example of this alternative strategy occurs within the State Department. The head of the Passport Office within the State Department for several years "simply refused to appear before the appropriations committee" headed by John Rooney, the same congressman who made the rest of the State Department tremble. The Passport Office, unlike the rest of the State Department, had developed strong political allies among the travel bureaus that were dependent on quick passport service and cooperation from the Office for its clients. These travel bureaus had expressed their pleasure with the Passport Office's director, Frances Knight. Knight, in turn, had a much more concrete, definable task—processing passports—than the rest of the State Department. With a friendly external environment, Knight was able to pursue the performance of this concrete task aggressively, rather than use the hierarchy and rules to avert political criticism. As a result, the Passport Office under Knight was unique in the State Department for its efficiency, as well as for its lack of servility to Congress. "Under the direction of Frances Knight it developed a reputation as the most efficient operation in the State Department and one of the best in the federal government."[17]

Thus, with a different political environment and a different task creating different incentives, the reformed bureaucracy's hierarchy and rules can become either a source of red tape and bureaucratic inefficiency or a means of harnessing energy for an "imperialistic," runaway bureaucracy. An array of bureaucratic dysfunctions can be explained by rational individuals responding to bureaucratic incentives.

THE AMBIGUITY OF ALTERNATIVE EXPLANATIONS

While both the "bounded rationality" and "incentives" models can explain various bureaucratic dysfunctions, the models appear to be inconsistent. It is unlikely that Admiral George Anderson was both too dumb to see President Kennedy's reasons for wanting the blockade run his way, and also so smart that he figured out why it was in his and the Navy's best interest to block Kennedy.

While the explanations seem to be inconsistent, they both predict similar kinds of bureaucratic behavior. If both explanations predict that Admiral Anderson will resist Kennedy's attempts to run the blockade (although for very different reasons), then the fact that Anderson does so provides no evidence as to which theory is right.

In fact, it is amazing how many instances of bureaucratic pathology are explicable from both perspectives. While we explained the State Department's rigidity in terms of smart bureaucrats obeying incentives not to "make waves," Simon might have explained the same behavior in terms of individuals with limited cognitive capacity (but the best intentions) who are simply unable to imagine alternatives other than following standard operating procedures and orders.

Similarly, Air Force General LeMay's plaintive wish—after the crisis had been averted—to bomb Cuba anyhow, might have been evidence of the limits of his cognitive processes, and many observers would swear that that was the reason. On the other hand, it may have been simply the envious observation that the Navy was getting all the credit, and an air strike would bring some of the credit (and personal glory) in his direction.

The lack of response by the New York State Health Department to the Love Canal crisis may have been due to the inability of the individual bureaucrats to dream up appropriate responses to new situations—cognitive limits; or it could have been the result of precise calculations by scheming bureaucrats that there was no reward to them for using scarce resources on this new problem—if the state legislature wanted them to do something about toxic wastes, they should give them larger budgets and more personnel. Was bureaucratic rigidity due to lack of cognitive ability, or to a clever plan to blackmail the legislature for more funds?

Even the most mundane and simple examples of bureaucratic ineptitude do little to solve the problem. As an example of bureaucratic stupidity, organization theorist Lawrence Peter offers the example of a street-painting crew who paint a white line down the center of a road, right over the carcass of a dead dog.[18] Are the members of the street crew really so stupid that they can't see the value of moving the body of the dog? On the other hand, what's in it for them? They have a certain number of miles to paint in a day, and if they take the time to move the animal, they will certainly get no reward, and may be late for supper. If they do stop, will the person that touches the smelly, rotting carcass catch rabies or some other dread disease? Will they be covered by insurance if they do get sick? Besides, it is not their job to clean dead animals off of streets, and the department whose job it is has the proper equipment to avoid catching an illness. A smart street painter might well decide that the smart thing to do is paint over the dead dog. The same behavior can be explained as either bounded rationality or a smart response to bureaucratic incentives.

AN INTEGRATED EXPLANATION: A RATIONAL-CHOICE MODEL OF IGNORANCE AND BIAS

The last example of the street painter suggests a way out of the dilemma of choosing between "cognitive limits" and "bureaucratic incentives" as the fundamental explanation for why things go wrong. This example suggests that smart individuals often have incentives to act dumber than they are. If we can explain why organizations sometimes create incentives that lead individuals to remain ignorant, use biased information, and satisfice, then we will have reached a parsimonious theory; that is, one that shows how a *single* set of assumptions can lead to the kind of behaviors predicted by *both* models.

Until fairly recently, rational-choice theorists had made the assumption of compete information in which decision makers confronted no or very limited uncertainty. This led them to construct models of decision making that looked very different from those proposed by March and Simon. In fact, March and Simon reacted against this "no uncertainty" assumption in developing their cognitive-limits approach, that is, an approach which assumed that decision makers confront large amounts of unknowns or uncertainties in solving problems or reaching goals. It also led them, we believe, to place too much emphasis on cognition as the overwhelming variable in choice, and too little emphasis on political incentives.

What has happened more recently is that rational-choice theorists have begun relaxing the "no uncertainty" assumption, thus belatedly discovering the kinds of rational behaviors which March and Simon over two decades ago attributed to limited cognition. However, an important difference still remains: Rational choice under uncertainty shows that these behaviors—selective attention, satisficing, sequential search, assumed premises—may really be optimal self-interested behavior under the constraints of uncertainty, and not necessarily the result of cognitively limited people who may not see their best interests.

Rational Ignorance in Large Organizations

Randall Calvert is one rational-choice theorist who has demonstrated that the two explanations can be integrated by showing that the basic assumptions of one model (the bounded-rationality model) can be derived from the other model (the model of maximizing actors responding to incentives).[19] In particular, Calvert shows that there are situations in which rational actors will face incentives that make it desirable for them to *prefer biased information* over unbiased information. By searching for and passing on biased information, bureaucrats constrain themselves and others to act as though they were constrained by bounded rationality; but their behavior derives ultimately from the maximizing behavior of individuals responding to incentives.

In Calvert's model, a decision maker who is faced with two alternatives also has two available sources of information. One is unbiased, while the other one is biased in the sense that it is likely to exaggerate the relative benefits of one of the alternatives. Calvert shows that the decision maker will have good reasons to prefer the information from the biased source of information, *whether or not he or she has any personal bias in favor of one alternative*. In a world of uncertainty, the advice of an unbiased observer, Calvert shows, is likely to make little difference to the decision maker; the unbiased advice merely reflects the uncertainty of the situation and serves as no guide for action. This is even more true if the decision maker is already biased toward one of the alternatives.

This "selective attention" to narrow and biased sources of information is often given as evidence for the bounded-rationality assumptions and models in political science and public administration. However, Calvert shows that this kind of behavior can be derived as the *optimal* choice of maximizing decision makers in a world of imperfect information. As Calvert says, "strange things can happen when we actually model rational decision making under imperfect information."[20]

As strange as the Calvert result is, it was anticipated by a similar result developed by an earlier expert on rational behavior named Anthony Downs. This result argued similarly that rational, maximizing individuals would, at times, have incentives to remain ignorant of alternatives which are best for them. In particular, this condition, which Downs calls "rational ignorance," applies when individuals are part of a large organization and will have only a small impact on the organization's decision. An individual might be better informed about the relative advantages of two mayoral candidates than anyone else in the electorate, but his or her vote will only influence the election if all the other voters happen to be tied. Realizing this, voters generally spend their time, money, and energy on activities that are guaranteed to have an impact on their personal happiness, such as bowling or watching television. Thus, voters "do not bother to discover their true views before voting, and most citizens are not well enough informed to influence directly the formulation of those policies that affect them."[21]

While "rational ignorance" is generally applied to large mass electorates, it is clear that it applies just as well to the behavior of individuals within large bureaucracies. The individual health official may realize that the Love Canal toxic-waste problem is a serious one that requires further study. On the other hand, if one state health official becomes informed about the problem, that is not going to change the fact that the bureaucracy has no resources to do anything about it. Furthermore, time spent on the toxic-waste problem is time taken away from the study of projects for which there is already an organizational commitment, and for which the individual bureaucrat will be individually rewarded. Just as in mass electorates, the tendency is for individuals in large organizations to become experts on projects for which there is an incentive to be expert. Specialization within organizations is a way of guaranteeing that individuals have no incentive to become expert on the "big picture." The bureaucratic dysfunction known as "trained incapacity" is virtually synonymous with the notion of "rational ignorance."

Satisficing

Having argued that organizations can create incentives that guide rational individuals toward partial ignorance and biased information, it remains to demonstrate that similar processes can guide rational maximizers toward "satisficing" behavior.

Economists Richard Zeckhauser and Elmer Shaefer have a demonstration of this phenomenon. They consider an individual who is facing a large number of alternatives, each of which has an unknown value between $1 and $100. It costs him $1 to discover the value of each alternative. If the individual pays one dollar, evaluates one alternative, and finds that it is worth $10, he could stop and choose that one; but chances are that he could find a better alternative by spending one more dollar. On the other hand, it would be silly for this individual, if he wants to maximize his return in the long run, to keep spending dollar bills until he has found one of the $100 alternatives. Assuming that each of the values between $1 and $100 is equally likely, the individual should be "satisfied" if he has found an alternative worth at least $87. If he hasn't found an alternative that high yet, it is probably going to be worth his while to evaluate one more alternative. If he has found an alternative worth $87 or more, then he probably isn't going to get lucky with an extra dollar spent for more evaluation. The maximizing individual will "satisfice" at an alternative worth $87.[22]

This point generalizes quite easily. Evidence of "satisficing" does not mean that individuals have cognitive limits; even an individual with no cognitive limits will satisfice in a world with a certain amount of uncertainty.

Summary

The most important point made in this chapter is that a single, relatively parsimonious explanation is possible for a *range* of bureaucratic behaviors, from the stodgiest to the boldest. As information becomes more costly, as organizations become larger, as the incentives in organizations are more rewarding of rule-following behavior, then we can expect individuals to follow bureaucratic routines more closely, evaluate new alternatives more rarely, and remain ignorant of the big picture more completely. As the reverse conditions apply, we can expect bureaucrats to take more chances, invest more resources in innovation, and develop the capacity to see farther and more broadly. In either case, they may well display a tendency to rely on biased information for their decision making, and they will almost certainly pass on biased information in the hopes of convincing members of Congress, interest groups, and other bureaucrats of the correctness of their position.

CASE STUDY: WEAPONS ACQUISITION

The integrated explanation for bureaucratic behavior set forth in this chapter can be illustrated by the case of weapons acquisition. Here is an instance in which bureaucrats have been accused of acting very dumb, and also accused of acting very smart. They have been described as searching for biased information and of "satisficing" in policy-making, but of maximizing political advantage. This combination of characteristics can best be explained by assuming that in responding to political incentives, bureaucrats have incentives to search out the best information available on some aspects of the weapons acquisition process, and to produce and pass on biased information in other cases.

The C-5A Transport. The C-5A, built by Lockheed, was not only an extremely expensive airplane—costing about twice the original estimates—but was also ineffective and unsound. Lockheed started producing the planes before testing was finished. One engine fell off a plane while it was taxiing for take-off. In addition, the instrumentation was so unreliable that the C-5A was prohibited from flying in very bad weather, and the payload was much less than originally planned because of structural problems. Nor could the plane take off on anything but hard-surface runways, contrary to specifications. From 1965 to 1971, the cost per plane rose from $28 million to $60 million, while the comparable Boeing 747, sold to commercial airlines, cost about $23 million.

What was the Pentagon's reaction to this failure on the part of Lockheed? Was it outraged that its scarce funds were being used up on a costly, unreliable aircraft? On the contrary, the Pentagon reaction was one of defensiveness. One Pentagon official said, "We probably won't use the airplane as much as we intended." In 1968, a Pentagon efficiency expert named A. Ernest Fitzgerald told a congressional committee about enormous cost overruns in the development of the Air Force's C-5A transport. Twelve days later, he was notified that a unique computer error was responsible for his belief that he had civil service tenure. He was stripped of his responsibilities and assigned to investigate cost overruns on a twenty-lane bowling alley in Thailand. He was investigated by the Office of Special Investigations, which turned up nothing but a lot of hostile comments by other Pentagon officials. A year later, he was fired. The Air Force told members of Congress who had been impressed with his performance that he was fired for economic reasons. The Air Force officers who handled the Fitzgerald case were promoted. At about the same time, Henry Durham, a Lockheed production-control engineer, released a detailed statement about Lockheed's inefficient management. Durham received so many death threats that six federal marshals were assigned to guard him.[23]

Fitzgerald went through four years of lawsuits and almost $1 million in legal fees to get his job back, only to find that he was given an office and no responsibilities. Eight more years went by, and in 1981 the court ordered the Air Force to give Fitzgerald a job with real responsibilities. Fitzgerald said, "I hope the Air Force will accept it this time. I'd like to do something worthwhile. Things are worse than ever around here. Unit costs are going up at four or five times the rate of inflation."[24]

One year later, Fitzgerald got his original job back, and by 1984 he was subpoenaed to testify before yet another congressional committee, investigating yet another round in defense overruns. He described practices used by Pentagon officials that allowed such overcharges as $1,118.26 for the nylon cap for an airline stool; the cap should have cost just 26 cents. He testified under subpoena because the Pentagon had refused to allow him to testify as a Pentagon spokesperson, claiming that "bad management has shot down more airplanes, sunk more ships and immobilized more soldiers than all our enemies in history put together."[25]

The Viper. The anti-tank rocket, called the Viper, was built by General Dynamics. In 1976, General Dynamics proposed that the Viper should cost $78. It would be cheap enough and light enough for every infantryman to have one, making the infantryman the equal of his most feared enemy, the tank.

By 1982, the Viper was projected to cost $787 each. Worse, a General Accounting Office report on the Viper pointed out that the Viper was developed to combat 1960s-generation Russian tanks, and that current Russian tanks have more armor on the front than the Viper can penetrate. Infantrymen would have to try to ambush a tank from the side or the rear, where a miss would mean annihilation by the tank's machine guns. Moreover, it was not clear how a column of tanks could be ambushed by infantrymen. One critic said that the Viper should come with a "pop-up Medal of Honor," since it will take extraordinary heroism to use it at all. The GAO report convinced the Marines to cancel their order for the Viper. One Marine spokesmen said they wanted a weapon that would defeat modern Soviet tanks, "not just piss them off."

The Army, however, was evidently satisfied with the Viper's more limited capability. The Army ordered 60,000 Vipers from General Dynamics for 1982 alone. One retired Army general wrote, "The generals who promote weapons like the Viper tend to be the bravest guys in the world because they know they're never gonna get shot at. But they're not worried about putting some 19 year old in a position where he's not even gonna be able to fight."[26]

A Rifle for Vietnam. Weapons for the U.S. Army are the responsibility of the ordnance corps, which consists of the Army's weapons laboratories, the Army Material Command, and private weapons contractors. The ordnance corps has traditionally argued that the army infantryman was first and foremost a sharpshooter, and built guns accordingly. The corps has fought for weapons with heavy bullets that will remain steady in flight for hundreds of yards, even during a wind.

During World War II, it became apparent to some people that the sharpshooter was no longer the best role for the infantryman. Studies demonstrated that four-fifths of combat soldiers never fired their weapons during a battle. Much of the reason seemed to be that the sharpshooter's rifle they were issued, the M-1, took time to lift and aim; in the heat and confusion of modern warfare, individual infantrymen were convinced that their single bullets would not make much of a difference. The 20 percent of combat soldiers who did shoot were those with Browning automatic rifles, one or two per squad; these fighters felt that their ability to "hose down" an entire area made it important that they shoot.

After World War II, there was some demand for automatic rifles that would be lightweight and cheap enough for every infantryman to use. The ordnance corps, faced with this request, produced a monstrosity: the M-14, a heavy sharpshooter's rifle capable of automatic fire. The rifles and ammunition were both so heavy that the weapon's recoil was dangerous and the soldier was unable to control the aim. It was useless, both as a sharpshooter's weapon and as an automatic rifle.[27]

Nevertheless, it was adopted as the standard Army rifle in 1957. The M-14 was the weapon that infantryman began the Vietnam War with. The principal competition was a weapon known as the AR-15, a reliable, lightweight automatic. It used lightweight bullets that tumbled when they hit the enemy's body, causing a great deal more damage. From the perspective of the ordnance corps, however, it had a severe drawback: It was not the product of the ordnance corp's own weapons labs and Army Material Command, but of outside competition. Its success, therefore, meant failure for the ordnance corps and a slap in the face to everything the corps had stood for. The corps had every incentive to try to kill the AR-15, despite its advantages, and it made every attempt to do so.[28]

However, John Kennedy overruled the ordnance corps and required that the AR-15 be made available to the Special Forces. It worked so well for them that Secretary of the Army Cyrus Vance tried to find out why the ordnance corps had rejected the weapon. He found out that the ordnance corps had rigged the tests, with the printed minutes of the meetings stating that the ordnance corps would report only tests that "reflect adversely on the AR-15 rifle." The corps was forced to proceed with the AR-15.

They proceeded to modify the AR-15 for the infantryman's use, in order to justify their own existence as a bureaucratic entity. In doing so, they destroyed most of its advantages. They transformed the AR-15 into the M-16—a heavier, less effective, and unreliable rifle.

The army added a manual bolt closure and made the bullet twist faster. The first modification made the gun heavier, and the second made it less lethal. Most importantly, the army changed the gunpowder in order to use the Army's "sole-source" supplier of ball powder, a company known as Olin-Mathieson. Using the Army's protected supplier was good politics, since that kept an important established lobbyist happy. However, the powder supplied by Olin-Mathieson—although fine for a sharpshooter's weapon—fouled up the automatic M-16. Secondly, the powder caused the weapon to shoot faster than it was designed to shoot, which made a completely reliable weapon into one that would jam repeatedly. Engineers reported in 1965 that the weapon would never fail with the original powder, but would jam half the time with Olin-Mathieson's ball powder. The Army replied that the producer of the weapon, Colt, could use any powder it chose just to pass the tests, as long as it shipped the weapon to Vietnam with the Olin-Mathieson powder. The M-16 passed the tests fine with the appropriate powder, but was shipped to Vietnam with powder that caused jamming.[29]

Infantrymen in Vietnam were found dead with their M-16s jammed or broken down as the soldier tried frantically to correct the problem while under fire. Soldiers were disgusted with the weapon, and wrote to their congressmen, reporting that most of their dead friends had been found with ammunition jammed in the chamber. The Army hierarchy took the position that the problem was due to the soldiers who were inadequately cleaning their weapons; but they never supplied enough cleaning materials, and never addressed the question of whether the powder was making the weapons fire too fast. Congressional investigators found that one Marine had died running up and down the line in his squad, unjamming the rifles, because he had the only cleaning rod issued to the entire squad.

The M-16 still has the new twist that reduced its lethality, and still uses the Olin-Mathieson powder. It is still the official weapon of Army infantrymen.

Explaining Failures in Weapons Acquisition: Incentives and Information

What are the incentives facing officials in the weapons acquisition process, and do those incentives trigger the kinds of decision making that were evident in the Viper, the C-5A, and the M-1 cases? The key incentive, as we mentioned in Chapter 7, is to create a base of political support among interest groups influential in Congress. While peace movements come and go, by far the most influential interest group in the weapons acquisition process is the weapons firms themselves. Lockheed, General Dynamics, and McDonnell Douglas, along with a lot of smaller suppliers, all derive over two-thirds of their sales from defense contracts. They and their subcontractors also employ large numbers of defense-plant workers in a large number of congressional districts all over the country. They are the most intensely interested group of lobbyists in any congressional battle over defense spending, and a major reason why the Department of Defense is such a strong bureaucratic agency in Congress.

Defense contracts are a very lucrative form of business for firms. The reason is that the Pentagon contracts pay all documented costs of producing an airplane and a percentage of those costs as profit. Thus, the firms have every reason to escalate costs as far as possible, by paying high salaries, by paying suppliers and subcontractors excessively, and by working inefficiently. For Pentagon contracts, increases in cost merely serve to increase profits rather than decrease them, as is the case with the private market. As the C-5A whistle-blower, Ernest Fitzgerald, notes, "We are not buying airplanes; we are buying the contractor's costs."[30]

Lobbying activity, except for entertainment, is billed as an administrative expense of defense contracting and counted as a "cost" in a "cost-plus" contract, guaranteeing that taxpayers underwrite contractors' lobbying efforts in Congress. Furthermore, a percentage of such costs are also added as profit. Entertainment expenses of lobbying are tax deductible, and therefore partially supported by the taxpayer.

Lobbying activities are multiplied in congressional districts all across the country by making sure that the subcontracts for major weapons systems are in as many different congressional districts as possible. During the controversy over the B-1 bomber, Rockwell International mobilized 114,000 employees and 3,000 subcontractors in 48 states to write to Congress describing the economic effects of cancelling the bomber. Rockwell spent $1.35 million on the effort.

Watching the weapons firms' expenditures is the military's job, but the military may have very little incentive to keep costs down. The route to a successful career in the military is getting larger budgets from Congress, not blowing the whistle on expenditures; Fitzgerald found this out in the case of the C-5A. Senator Chuck Grassley, an Iowa Republican, notes that "The problem is a Federal system that rewards high costs. The bureaucrat gets promoted by raising a larger budget from Congress. And the government contractor, whose profit is a percentage of costs, has an incentive to raise his costs."[31] Grassley might have added that the incentive for members of Congress is to guarantee reelection by protecting local defense firms.

Thus, while it is impossible to deny the existence of limited cognitive abilities on the part of all humans, military weapons experts included, it is difficult to see how this has fundamentally affected the weapons acquisition process. If they were smarter, would Pentagon bureaucrats not respond to incentives to protect their weapons-firm allies with biased tests? If they were smarter, would members of Congress fail to see the reelection advantages of logrolling for larger weapons contracts? If they were smarter, would weapons firms no longer respond to the built-in incentives of the cost-plus contract to keep costs up, instead of down?

The integrated theory of incentives and information would suggest that individuals will ignore whatever information would lead them to make a decision they don't want to make anyhow. In fact, they will try to produce information that supports the action that will reward them the most, and screen out information that would suggest they have a duty to do something that is less than rewarding to themselves.

"Everyone is Behaving Perfectly Rationally"

If this is true, then it is not the limits on individual bounded rationality that are the ultimate cause of bureaucratic pathologies, because *better information and better decision making will just be distorted to fit the incentives.* Even if people were perfectly rational, with unlimited cognitive powers, bureaucratic pathologies would persist because of the structure of incentives in a bureaucracy. Whistle-blower Ernest Fitzgerald specifically denies that there is any bureaucratic bungling or stupidity involved in weapons-acquisition disasters like the C-5A. "In fact, everyone is behaving perfectly rationally by responding to the real rewards in the system."[32]

Mr. Fitzgerald's critique is, of course, the most drastic possible criticism of the weapons acquisition process. It implies that things cannot be improved by adding a few computers, hiring smarter bureaucrats, or replacing corrupt officials with honest ones. It implies that the most elaborate and sophisticated cost-control system in the world, combined with a professionalized military and a clear system of hierarchical control leading up to the Commander in Chief, has not eliminated incentives for inefficiency. If this is true, then the reformed bureaucratic structure is not sufficient to guarantee good administration, because of overlooked incentives. In the case of weapons acquisition, hierarchy, rules, and professionalization promote an incentive system that rewards "passing the buck," "trained incapacity," bureaucratic rigidity, and other manifestations of bureaucratic dysfunction.

While we don't regard the question of cognitive limits versus incentives as firmly settled, instances such as the M-16 rifle lead us to believe that the most important way to understand the bureaucratic pathologies occurring in reformed administrative agencies is by understanding the incentives that the use of hierarchy, rules, trained experts, and specialization have built into modern bureaucracies. This is the perspective that is most firmly associated with the political scientists who have studied modern bureaucracy. For as individual bureaucrats, legislators, and interest groups bargain with each other in furtherance of their own individual incentives, they are, by definition, engaging in politics.

From this perspective, reformed administrative agencies may be nonpartisan in that political parties are excluded from influence; but they can never be politically neutral, because the individuals in the organizations will always be playing political games in response to the incentives that they perceive. From this perspective, the important question is, "What are the incentives leading people to support the institutions of the Progressive reform movement, and to continue to support those institutions after various bureaucratic pathologies became apparent?" This is the problem investigated in the next chapter.

NOTES

[1]LAURENCE J. PETER, *Why Things Go Wrong; or, the Peter Principle Revisited* (New York: William Morrow, 1985), p. 11.

[2]HERBERT KAUFMAN, "Fear of Bureaucracy: A Raging Pandemic," *Public Administration Review*, 59 (1981), p. 1.

[3]CHARLES T. GOODSELL, *The Case for Bureaucracy: A Public Administration Polemic*, 2nd ed. (Chatham: Chatham House Publishers, 1983), p. 12.

[4]ADELINE GORDON LEVINE, *Love Canal: Science, People, Politics* (Lexington: Lexington Books, 1982), p. 64.

[5]LEVINE, *Love Canal*, p. 156.

[6]ARTHUR M. SCHLESINGER, JR., *A Thousand Days* (New York: Fawcett World Library, 1967).

[7]VICTOR S. NAVASKY, *Kennedy Justice* (New York: Atheneum, 1977), p. 20.

[8]EUGENE LEWIS, *Public Entrepreneurship: Toward a Theory of Bureaucratic Power* (Bloomington: Indiana University Press, 1980), p. 147.

[9]HERBERT A. SIMON, *Administrative Behavior: A Study of Decision Making Processes in Administrative Organizations* (New York: Free Press, 1945).

[10]JAMES G. MARCH and HERBERT A. SIMON, *Organizations* (New York: John Wiley, 1958).

[11]MARCH AND SIMON, *Organizations*, p. 169.

[12]DONALD P. WARWICK, *A Theory of Public Bureaucracy: Politics, Personality, and Organization in the State Department* (Cambridge: Harvard University Press, 1975). Reprinted by permission.

[13]MARRINER S. ECCLES, *Beckoning Frontiers* (New York: 1951), p. 336.

[14]GEORGE BERKELEY, *The Craft of Public Administration* (Boston: Allyn and Bacon, 1981), p. 124.

[15]WARWICK, *Theory*, pp. 46–47.

[16]WARWICK, *Theory*, pp. 69–70.

[17]WARWICK, *Theory*, p. 77.

[18]PETER, *Why Things Go Wrong*.

[19]RANDALL CALVERT, "The Value of Biased Information," *Journal of Politics*, 47 (1985), pp. 530–555.

[20]CALVERT, "Value of Biased Information," p. 553.

[21]ANTHONY DOWNS, *An Economic Theory of Democracy* (New York: Harper & Row, 1957), p. 259.

[22]RICHARD ZECKHAUSER and ELMER SHAEFER, "Public Policy and Normative Economic Theory," in *The Study of Policy Formation*, Raymond A. Bauer and Kenneth J. Gergen, eds. (New York: Free Press, 1968), p. 94.

[23]CHARLES PETERS and TAYLOR BRANCH, *Blowing the Whistle: Dissent in the Public Interest* (New York: Praeger Publishers, 1972), pp. 196–204.

[24]RICHARD REEVES, "Pentagon Whistle-Blower Wins Only When in Court," *Detroit Free Press*, March 12, 1981, p. 9A.

[25]CHARLES MOHR, "Subpoenaed Official Aide Assails Pentagon on High Military Costs," *The New York Times*, June 26, 1984, p. A15.

[26]*Detroit Free Press*, June 2, 1982, sec. B, p. 1.

[27]JAMES FALLOWS, *National Defense* (New York: Vintage Books, 1981), p. 79.

[28]FALLOWS, *National Defense*, pp. 80–82.

[29]FALLOWS, *National Defense*, pp. 81–88.

[30]CHARLES MOHR, "Critics See Key Flaws in Arms Cost Controls," *New York Times*, May 18, 1985, p. A1.

[31]WINSTON WILLIAMS, "Bungling the Military Buildup," *New York Times*, January 27, 1985, p. III-1.

[32]MOHR, "Critics," p. 8.

CHAPTER 10

The Politics of Administrative Reform:
Individual Rationality vs. Social Irrationality

> The bureaucracy serves as a convenient lightning rod for public frustration and a convenient whipping boy for congressmen. But so long as the bureaucracy accommodates congressmen, the latter will oblige with even larger budgets and grants of authority. Congress does not just react to big government—it creates it.
>
> Morris P. Fiorina, *Congress:*
> *Keystone of the Washington Establishment*[1]

The previous four chapters have argued that the classical administrative principles of hierarchy, specialization, written rules, and merit staffing fail to deliver the efficiency, neutrality, and accountability that were the formally espoused goals of the reform movement. However, we have also argued that the reform model, presupposing the separateness of politics and technical administration, has been the orthodoxy throughout much of the twentieth century. How can these two facts be reconciled?

One possible reconciliation is that there are political reasons why political actors adopt the classical model, apart from its presumed efficiency and neutrality. That is, the classical reform model has been popular in the twentieth century because it is good politics; and it is good politics because it provides unique political advantages to legislators, interest groups, and to administrators themselves.

While support for the classical administrative model has been and continues to be individually rational, this does not imply that it is socially efficient. There are numerous instances in politics in which the sum of individually rational actions is an outcome that is bad for everyone. We will examine this phenomenon at the end of this chapter.

THE POLITICAL ADVANTAGES OF
THE REFORM MODEL FOR ADMINISTRATORS

Administrators have probably gained the most from the classical reform model. Countless times since the Progressive era, administrators have used the Wilsonian notion of a politics/administration dichotomy to justify imposing their own policy preferences instead of those of elected officials. The politics/administration dichotomy has served as an umbrella for bureaucratic political influence under the guise of neutral expertise or neutral implementation of legislative mandates. It is difficult to imagine an idealogy that could have done more to justify bureaucratic politicization than the idealogy of bureaucratic neutrality. When used by a canny bureaucratic politician, it is a powerful weapon.

J. Edgar Hoover: Reforming the FBI

Perhaps the foremost example of a bureaucrat who consciously used the classical model of administrative reform to his own political advantage, and provided a link between the 1920s and later eras, was J. Edgar Hoover. When Hoover was first asked to take control of the Federal Bureau of Investigation during the scandal-ridden Harding administration, he said he would do it only under certain conditions: "that the agency be nonpolitical, that appointments and promotions be based on merit, and that the Bureau be responsible only to the Attorney General."[2] From the moment that he took charge of the Bureau on these reform terms, he began to implement every aspect of the classical model: hierarchy, professional specialization, extensive written rules, and merit appointments. Hoover made the Bureau "a professionalized agency composed of career civil servants appointed and promoted on merit. Clear lines of authority ended in the Director's office, not in the hands of politicians nor in the sway of any other department of government."[3] He instituted strict rules of procedure involving every aspect of agency performance, including the strictest dress codes and codes for off-duty behavior. Local offices throughout the country were administered under these rules, making possible the greatest standardization of behavior and performance. "Such standardization of procedure down to seemingly trivial detail made possible iron-handed supervision and oversight unknown outside of some military units."[4]

Hoover used to his advantage the scientific management movement's faith in technical, "scientific" solutions. He made sure that the Bureau was in the forefront of new scientific developments in crime-fighting, and made sure this aspect was publicized as the major component of the Bureau's public image. His reports to Congress relied heavily on "scientific statistics," and indeed he invented the Uniform Crime Reports in 1930. Congress was delighted with the very first figures: they seemed to admit of 'efficiency' or of today's 'cost-benefit' analysis for an organization which produced services rather than goods."[5]

Because the Crime Reports were the prime source of information about crime, they allowed the FBI to define and measure the reality that they were charged with handling. The FBI could use charts, tables, and large numbers to document the "need" for larger FBI budgets. They could also selectively focus on certain types of crimes in order to enhance the appearance of their own effectiveness. For instance, Hoover made sure that the FBI concentrated on bank robberies and kidnappings, which were often undertaken by amateurs and were therefore easier to solve, yet sure to get large amounts of favorable publicity. At the same time, Hoover kept the FBI out of the way of professional "mob" crimes like prostitution, drug abuse, and gambling, which were more difficult to deal with and which offered a larger threat of agent corruption. In fact, Hoover continued to deny the existence of the Mafia long after other law enforcement officials were actively concerned with its activities. The Crime Reports de-emphasized the crime areas that the FBI avoided and thus guaranteed favorable statistics for reports to Congress.

The professionalization of the FBI provided Hoover with a way of winning interest-group support from what might have been antagonistic competitors of the Bureau: the local police departments. Hoover established the FBI Academy as a way of legitimizing the professional claims of the Bureau, and made it available to local law enforcement officials.

> Professionalization . . . was a part of the current set of received values which typified the reformer, the civil servant, the academic and, increasingly, the middle class as a whole. With the Academy Hoover got into the creation of the police version of these values "on the ground floor" and used them to tremendous advantage. The [local law enforcement] officers who graduated and became strong (and successful) candidates for upward mobility constituted a potent "old boy" network. They owed their rise in no small way to the beneficence of J. Edgar Hoover.[6]

The classical model of reform served Hoover well in dealing with his primary constituency, the Congress. From the first, Congress seemed eager to buy the image of professional toughness, scientific expertise, and political neutrality, and just as eager to overlook the Bureau's weakness in wartime intelligence and in fighting organized crime. Congress helped maintain the myth of Hoover's absolute incorruptibility even though Hoover accepted gifts from people who had business with or were under investigation by the FBI.[7] Congress seemed to want to share in the popular public image of the Bureau, and Hoover was willing to comply by, for instance, publishing a booklet called *The Story of the FBI* listing the members of the appropriations subcommittee that handled the FBI budget. The members of that committee sent copies to their constituents and urged Hoover to reissue it when new members were appointed to the committee.[8]

The payoff to Hoover from this support in Congress, in the public, and in local law enforcement agencies was tremendous. First of all, Hoover had a more secure flow of budgetary resources from Congress than virtually any other agency. Said Congressman John Rooney, for many years the head of the appropriations subcommittee dealing with the FBI, "I have never cut his budget and I never expect to. The only man who ever cut it was Karl Stefan, Republican from Nebraska who held this job before me. When Stefan went home for election that year, they nearly beat him because he took away some of Hoover's money."[9] In fact, when the President's Bureau of the Budget would cut FBI budget requests, the Appropriations Committee would always restore them.

Interestingly, the political influence of the FBI was used to insulate Hoover from presidential supervision. Hoover was allowed to maintain his position long after the normal retirement age. Presidents knew that the Bureau was personally controlled by Hoover, and that firing him would cause disruption of the Bureau's operations. They also knew that firing Hoover would alienate large portions of Congress. As mentioned earlier, Hoover was able to resist requests from his nominal superior, the Attorney General, that he became more involved with protecting the civil rights movement, because he disliked the black civil rights movement and hated Martin Luther King. Hoover led a campaign to "neutralize" King as head of the civil rights movement up until King's death. In that year, FBI headquarters told field agents that Dr. King must be destroyed because he was seen as a potential "messiah" who could "unify and electrify" the "black nationalist movement."[10] Because of Hoover's unwillingness to help the civil rights movement, Robert Kennedy, as Attorney General, had to use federal marshals and other federal law enforcement officials to protect civil rights demonstrators.

In sum, Hoover's faithful use of Progressive reform structures provided him with a political power base in the FBI. The use of hierarchy, specialization, merit selection, and written rules of procedure gave Hoover a formula for administrative effectiveness and political influence. As one political scientist wrote, "Never in American history had a bureaucrat so thoroughly capitalized on being resolutely 'apolitical.' The seemingly neutral competence of the FBI would, for a generation, always be posed against the somehow less altruistic claims of political appointees."[11]

Robert Moses: New York's Construction Coordinator

At the level of state and local administration, the biography of Robert Moses stands as a model of the usefulness of the "neutral" Progressive reform model to an essentially political bureaucrat. Robert Moses was himself one of the theoreticians of the Progressive reform movement, working for New York's Municipal Research Bureau in the heyday of municipal ferment. When New York City elected a Progressive reform mayor in 1910, Moses was appointed to implement a merit-system reform of New York's personnel system. Moses failed at that attempt, but was more successful in reorganizing New York's state government in an unlikely coalition with the Tammany Hall governor, Al Smith.

Smith made Moses a key figure in New York state park administration. Moses moved from there into New York City park administration, highway construction, bridge construction, and housing. The story of Moses' rise to power is told in Robert Caro's *The Power Broker*.[12] For our purposes, the story is significant because it is a distinctly twentieth-century tale: the political influence of a supposedly neutral bureaucrat.

Moses aggressively defended his claim to being politically neutral. He was never elected to public office, and his public image was uniformly that of a nonpartisan public servant using his expertise to make policy decisions in the public interest.

The reality was that Moses, like Hoover, used his hierarchical control over his bureaucratic organization, his monopoly on expertise, and his public reputation for political neutrality as resources to build a political "machine" that outmaneuvered even that of Tammany Hall.

Moses built his own organization on Progressive administrative principles. As one of his aides emphasized, "Everything was by the 'chain of command.' Everyone had to go through that chain. If you sent him a note with a suggestion or a complaint, he would send it right back to you with a note scribbled on it: 'Have you talked to your superior about this?' "[13] This chain of command gave Moses strict control over his subordinates, an authority he reinforced with an overbearing personal attitude. He was well known for ordering people out of bed at night to deal with a special issue, for making them work long hours of overtime, even for humiliating them in front of an audience. The people who could not handle this pressure responded with alcoholism, marital difficulties, and even, in one case, suicide.[14] The others were strict Moses loyalists.

Moses also used specialization and division of labor. "He didn't want engineers wasting time debating legal points or lawyers discussing engineering problems. If a legal problem arose at a staff meeting and an engineer ventured an opinion on it, he would cut him short with a curt 'Stop practicing law. Leave that to the lawyers.' "[15] Moses' control of expert professionals became one of his power bases. He was hired and retained by mayor after mayor, despite personal antagonisms, simply because he was successful at putting together a stable group of engineers, architects, and lawyers that was absolutely essential for dealing with New York City's transportation problems.[16]

Another reason mayors were afraid to fire him from his numerous parks, transportation, planning, and housing positions was that he had so successfully wrapped himself in the cloak of nonpartisanship. Moses was able to get his way by threatening to resign because mayors, as partisan political leaders, knew that the press would be convinced that only cheap politics would drive a mayor to get rid of a valuable "neutral expert" like Moses. Thus, in every one of his numerous conflicts with mayors, governors, and even presidents, Moses was able to get the upper hand because the public had accepted the Progressive definition of expertise as "good" and partisan politics as "bad."

Despite this appearance of nonpartisanship, Moses used his position and his expertise to wield vast influence over political decisions in the city and state of New York. Virtually every important political actor in New York politics—in the banking industry, the construction industry, labor unions, the insurance industry, the Catholic Church, and the parties themselves—became obligated to Robert Moses through a conscious process of co-optation and exchange.

For example, every Moses construction project allowed Moses to hand out construction contracts, banking business, and insurance policies to contractors, banks, and insurance companies selected by Moses himself. He carefully chose contractors who had influence with key political figures, banks with political muscle in the state legislature, and insurance companies with representatives in the state legislature. Through this network of obligations, he had an impressive amount of control over the political decisions of the state legislature itself.

When the Catholic Church needed to expand Fordham University, Moses, as Slum Clearance Committee chairman, forced hundreds of tenants from six acres of downtown Manhattan and turned the site over to Fordham. In return, the Catholic Church became an ally of Moses. "Time and again, when a project he was sponsoring was stalled, the Catholic hierarchy—religious or secular—interceded with the politicians, providing the push that was needed to get it rolling again."[17]

Most ironical of all, Moses, the Progressive reformer, was able to provide the resource that Tammany politicians needed most in order to get them into the Moses camp. That resource was patronage. As head of the New York City Parks Department, and as construction coordinator for the city, Moses was able to hand out temporary and summer jobs to politicians' supporters. He was also able to decide which boroughs of New York would get the highway and housing construction projects that their borough politicians desired. This placed the Tammany politicians in debt to Moses, so that Moses was able to have his way with the City's Board of Estimate.

By playing the game of politics under the guise of a neutral administrator, Moses was able to have the best of both worlds. He had the influence of a top politician and the public respect of an expert civil servant.

Other Administrators

We find it significant that a bureaucrat like Moses, who was ultimately re-vealed to have a strong taste for power, found the Progressive model of administra-tive reform a useful structure for his ambitions. Moses' credentials as a Progressive administrative reformer were impeccable, and he was able to maintain the struc-tural appearance of the ideal reform bureaucrat throughout his career. J. Edgar Hoover, too, when asked to take over the FBI, gave the characteristics of the Progressive reform model as the only conditions for accepting the job.

In addition, both Hoover and Moses used classical administrative principles internal to their organizations to maintain a strong, top-down control. They even imposed their own racial and other prejudices through the hierarchy. This combi-nation of internal control and external autonomy gave them extraordinary political success.

This is not to argue that all bureaucrats were able to use the Progressive reform model to become as powerful as Moses and Hoover. On the contrary, it is clear that Moses and Hoover were the exceptions among bureaucrats. Rather, we would argue that the structural characteristics emphasized by Progressive reformers were and are useful to top bureaucratic officials who seek to have autonomous political influ-ence. Furthermore, to the degree that top-level bureaucrats do have autonomous political influence, it is generally because they are able to use the cloak of neu-trality, the aura of professional expertise, and the hierarchical control of their organizations as political resources.

All of these things were true of other powerful top-level bureaucrats. Admiral Hyman Rickover, the developer of the nuclear submarine, had a managerial style similar to that of Moses and Hoover. He also had a reputation for tremendous engineering expertise, as well as for political neutrality, despite the fact that he was an expert at playing the press, the public, and Congress for his own policy goals.

Warwick found that higher-level bureaucrats in the State Department chose to support the "managerial orthodoxy" of control through hierarchy and rules rather than an alternative managerial style because the managerial orthodoxy served their own purposes. When Truman's Secretary of State Dean Acheson shifted opera-tional responsibilities down to the assistant secretaries, these assistant secretaries faced the problem of controlling their own subordinates. The result was a vast increase in the volume of communication.

> If the Assistant Secretary for African Affairs becomes overloaded, he appoints a trusted deputy to screen the 'really important' messages going to and from his bureau. If the trusted deputy cannot handle the message flow, he may add a layer beneath him (which may be obscured by the designation of 'Special Assistant'). . . . The new screening layers typically increase the total volume of communications in the system. The official originally appointed to be a consumer of paper rapidly becomes a pro-ducer.[18]

The State Department official sees increased hierarchy as part of the solution to his problem, and increased rules as another part of the solution. He generates rules and SOPs as ways of keeping subordinates in line, and other rules develop for handling the flow of communication between branches of the Department. The result is an increasing cycle of rules and hierarchy. This may not be efficient for the organization as a whole, but no individual administrator has an incentive to do anything but try to keep up with the rising tide of bureaucracy by contributing to the hierarchy and rules. The progressive model of reform is the individually rational solution to the administrator's problem, even though it may not be efficient for the organization overall.

Numerous city managers have found that they are able to play a dominant role in their cities because they have followed the same pattern. Professional expertise and hierarchical control over their agencies give them the resources to play a good game of politics, and the aura of nonpartisanship provides them with a cover for playing it and for objecting to "political" interference from city council members and other politicians.

This strategy of political influence was not invented by Progressive administrators. It seems that whenever societies have developed bureaucracies based on neutral expertise, the bureaucrats have been able to use their positions as a power base. Max Weber claims that, "Under normal conditions, the power position of a fully developed bureaucracy is always overtowering. The 'political master' finds himself in the position of the 'dilettante' who stands opposite the 'expert.' "[19]

What is important is that the succession of reform movements in the United States provided the opportunity and legitimation for the use of that strategy as it had never been used in American politics. The Jacksonian frontier mentality had generally exalted amateurism, sneered at experts, and feared professionals seeking to make a career out of public employment. Before the Progressives, it would have been impossible for a bureaucrat to appeal for public support against an elected official on the grounds that he, the bureaucrat, represented the public interest better than the elected official. It was the successive reform movements' legitimation of hierarchy, expertise, and political neutrality that made possible the Hoover/Moses strategy of political influence for top-level bureaucrats. It is also fairly clear that it is for this reason that engineers, scientists, and technical administrators of all sorts supported and continue to support the classical reform model of administration.

Low-Level Bureaucrats

It is not just the high-level bureaucrats who have something to gain by supporting and acting on the classical model of administrative reform. The low-level bureaucrats find it serves their purposes as well. Their purposes, of course, are generally nothing so grand as gaining large amounts of autonomous political influence or controlling large organizations. Their goals are likely to be something more like securing a long and successful career in the bureaucracy. This goal, itself, was made possible by the civil service notion that it should be possible to make a career out of government employment, a notion that Jacksonians repudiated.

Given that bureaucrats support the general civil service notion of a career bureaucracy, the particular structural features of the classical model provide a strategy for securing that goal on the individual level. As we discussed in Chapter 9, the low-level bureaucrat in the State Department *supported* the regeneration of hierarchy and rules because hierarchy and rules specify in detail the behavior that will minimize the risk of "selection out" and other sanctions.[20]

Without hierarchy and rules, the individual bureaucrat would have no behavioral directive programming his or her behavior. However, most bureaucracies, whether the State Department, the Forest Service, a police department, or a state highway department, provide more than adequate signposts indicating acceptable behavior and, more importantly, exactly what behavior is sufficient to terminate a career. Not all bureaucrats follow these signposts—individual bureaucrats may "buck the system" by rate-busting, leaking information to the press, or whistle-blowing. But the rule book provided the forest ranger and the standard operating procedures drilled into a Foreign Service officer give a clear map to what is "safe behavior" for those low-level bureaucrats who choose to follow it.

CONGRESS AND THE ADMINISTRATIVE REFORM MODEL

Warwick argues that an agency, once created by Congress, may be shaped in the image of the "managerial orthodoxy" by the shared interests of the upper-level bureaucrats seeking organizational control and political influence, and the lower-level bureaucrats seeking a safe career pattern. However, this leaves the question, why should Congress cooperate by creating new bureaucracies in the first place? In particular, why should Congress indicate apparent agreement with such notions as a politics/administration dichotomy by delegating independent decision-making authority to administrative agencies?

The most striking example of this is the delegation of regulatory authority to independent regulatory commissions. The public explanation for congressional delegation to independent agencies is pure Wilsonian Progressivism: Having established that some aspect of the economy or society should be regulated "in the public interest," Congress delegates the implementation of that policy goal to a panel of nonpartisan experts who will make the detailed decisions.

An alternative explanation can be generated, however. This alternative explanation is that the politics/administration dichotomy served the electoral interests of Congress.

Neutrality and Expertise: The Delegation of Authority

As we discussed in Chapter 5, the Progressive era had legitimized the legislative delegation of authority to independent bureaucratic experts. This delegation has become a pattern that is troubling to many.[21] However, the political advantages of delegating "hot" issues to independent regulatory agencies staffed with neutral experts continue to the present day.[22] The recent history of the FDA serves as a case in point.

During the late 1950s, Senator Estes Kefauver investigated price-fixing and deceptive advertising in the drug industry. He failed to gain much popular interest in the problem. When his staff leaked information to the press about the thalidomide disaster in Europe, in which an unsafe sedative had led to a large number of horrible birth defects, the press publicized the issue, creating a public uproar about drug safety.[23] Congress responded with greater delegations of authority to the Food and Drug Administration, but Kefauver's issues of price-fixing and deceptive advertising were ignored.

In the ensuing decades, various legislators found it politically useful to keep drug safety in the public attention and to emphasize this issue in their oversight of the FDA. "For two decades a number of congressmen—especially Senators Estes Kefauver, Gaylord Nelson, and Edward Kennedy and Representatives Lawrence Fountain and Paul Rogers—have headed almost continuous investigations of the FDA and the drug industry. These investigations have often gained national attention and have helped the congressmen involved rise in prominence. With rare exceptions, these congressional hearings have criticized FDA decisions and enforcement as lax, have attributed this laxness (directly or by implication) to agency subservience to industry, and have demanded tougher regulation."[24]

One may ask why Congress has continued to support the FDA with budget increases and continued expansion of regulatory authority. The evidence indicates that the FDA has a record of being extremely cautious about approving new drugs for American markets, even to the point of denying American physicians drugs that are already in use in other countries. The FDA seems to have been quite responsive to congressional wishes in this matter. Thus, the most politically astute course of action for Congress has been to maintain its delegation of authority to the FDA while running a campaign of criticism against it.

The Politics of Oversight and Delegation

Since Congress can and does oversee independent regulatory agencies, as with the FDA, the question may arise, why should it persist in delegating regulatory authority? If it is so concerned about issues such as drug safety, automobile dealer regulations, and broadcasting licenses, why doesn't it eliminate the FDA, the FTC, and the FCC and legislate on these matters directly?

One answer to this question is that Congress lacks the necessary expertise, time, and information. To routinely make decisions regulating new drugs, trade, and nuclear utilities requires trained experts and the processing of a lot of complex information. Rather than take this burden upon itself, the Congress prefers to set up an independent agency to do the work for it. This delegation of authority frees Congress from having to routinely make all these regulatory decisions.

However, while agency expertise is valuable for congressmen, delegation of authority for this reason is not the whole story. On various occasions, Congress has overruled the decisions of regulatory agencies when it felt it was politically necessary to do so. For example, Congress stopped the FTC from requiring used-car dealers to reveal defects in their autos; Congress stopped the FTC from regulating the meatpackers during World War II; and Congress overruled the FTC's original antismoking regulation in the 1960s. As the FDA example makes clear, they also "second guess" the FDA on drug regulation.

Furthermore, as political scientist Morris Fiorina points out, Congress does reserve the right to make its own judgments on matters that are sufficiently important to it. Congress has refused to delegate decision making on the structure of taxes, despite the fact that the issue is highly complex. The reason for this is that taxation is an important political asset, rather than a threat. By passing complex tax legislation, members of Congress retain the explicit authority to do favors for key interest-group supporters. Delegating authority to create a tax code in the "public interest, convenience and necessity" would deprive Congress of its most lucrative opportunity to do favors in the private interest.[25]

Similarly, agricultural subsidies are as complex as many economic, energy, or environmental issues delegated to independent agencies. Again, Congress has maintained primary decision authority in these areas because of the political advantages of doing so.

Thus, while Congress does gain the advantage of agency expertise and information processing in many complex policy areas, there are also important political reasons for congressmen to decide to delegate authority or not. The political explanation for Congress's delegation decisions is that Congress can force regulatory agencies to make the hard decisions, overturning them by methods of oversight when it is politically advantageous to do so. As a study of broadcast regulation by the FCC concluded,

> In a field such as communication, where the interests of powerful industry forces frequently collide, nothing is more unsettling to many lawmakers on Capitol Hill than the prospect of making a law! Thus, rather than enact new laws or amend the Communications Act, the Congress has preferred to use a variety of informal techniques in directing and overseeing the activities of the FCC. Such informal controls are naturally more pervasive since they are not subject to review by the whole Congress and enable legislators to advance personal and constituent interests without the need for a full-scale political battle.[26]

Rules and Regulations: Constituency Service

The discussion of congressional delegation to regulatory agencies explains why Congress might find it advantageous to support the classical administrative reform elements of neutrality and expertise. Buy why should Congress support the reform prescription of administration by written rules?

At first glance, one might feel that Congress would be opposed to written rules of procedure in a bureaucracy. After all, Congress is a political institution, whose actors are dependent, at least in the popular view, on "back-scratching" and the dispensing of personal favors. Wouldn't the administration of an agency by neutral, faceless bureaucrats following written procedures ruin its own ability to influence bureaucratic decision-making authority?

In fact, as we discussed in Chapter 3, congressmen became increasingly dependent on the services provided by bureaucracies in order to get reelected. Public agencies generated interest-group support which translated into organized political support for members of Congress. Large-scale bureaucracies operate through standard operating procedures and rules that make the mass provision of services possible to a wide range of constituencies.

Interestingly, however, congressmen have also capitalized politically on the negative side effects of standardized written procedures of bureaucracy. Fiorina points out that in recent years, members of Congress have increasingly committed their staff members to the task of providing "ombudsman" services for constituents.[27] For the most part, this means that staffers field requests from constituents who want their member of Congress to do something about a problem they are having with a federal bureaucracy. They may want to inquire about finding a missing Social Security check, or getting a relative into a Veterans Hospital, or some other procedural matter. Many congressional staff persons have become quite expert at locating the correct bureaucratic office to get a problem looked into, and at using congressional influence to spur a bureaucratic response. Congress members have also found that handling a large number of such requests is a good way to win an even larger number of votes.

If this is the case, then the important thing to notice is that members of Congress benefit doubly from large-scale bureaucracies, which provide mass services to large numbers of citizens and which use a strict, routinized procedure for providing those services. They benefit largely because the bureaucracy is able to provide mass constituencies with government services. They also benefit in part because the routinization of procedure is sure to generate a large number of constituents who will feel the bureaucracy's impersonal, bureaucratic routines have generated an inappropriate response in their unique case. When the bureaucracy refuses to deviate from its bureaucratic rules, the citizens regard this as a manifestation of bureaucratic red tape and turn to their members of Congress for assistance. Thus, the more hidebound and routinized the bureaucracy's procedures, the better the personalized response of a congressman's staffer looks in comparison. The ideal response of a congressional staffer should be to show a human, personal response to the citizen's problems, and a commitment to wage war with the bureaucrats in the citizen's name. Thus, congressmen need to establish bureaucracies and to wage war against them at the same time.

Fiorina, together with economist Roger Noll, has developed a mathematical model of the relationship between bureaucrats, legislators, and citizens.[28] The model suggests that legislators will encourage bureaucrats in their commitment to a formal, routinized mode of operation on the ground that it will offer the legislators a chance to improve their chances for reelection by means of providing services to constituents. They point out that this campaign strategy is one which is not available to a challenger, who has no grounds or opportunity to intervene with the Veterans Administration on behalf of a voter.

On the other hand, the incumbent can do this at the taxpayers' expense. As Fiorina and Noll note, "The number of staff workers operating in district offices rose from fewer than one per district in 1960 to about four per district in 1974."[29] They also point out that this was the period in which incumbents were widening their electoral advantage over challengers. They claim that legislators gain politically as popular ombudsmen from the growth of large-scale governmental agencies which provide routinized services to constituents.

Some more recent evidence that congressmen can have it both ways with bureaucracy occurred in the wake of the Reagan administration budget cuts. Congressmen were able to vote for budget cuts and then turn around and take credit for trying to help constituents find other sources of service. Congressional offices were flooded with complaints from citizens who had had their Social Security checks eliminated or other services cut. Congressional staffers made substantial efforts to help constituents, not only by appealing their cases to federal agencies, but by providing information about alternative state, local, and private charity sources of assistance for the needy. What is more, members of Congress did not suffer at the polls for the budget cuts they had, after all, approved in appropriations bills—House incumbency reelection rates were just as high in 1982 and 1984 as they had been in recent years, despite the fact that a major recession occurred in 1982 and a Republican President had won a landslide relection in 1984. The constituency services of incumbents allowed them to play the role of protector of the public vis-a-vis the bureaucracy, despite the fact that Congress had itself approved (or had the power to veto) the major policy decisions that had caused the citizens' problems.

Specialization

While members of Congress have much to gain from a model of administrative reform that emphasizes the politics/administration dichotomy, bureaucratic expertise, and bureaucratic rules, they also have much to gain from the reform element of functional specialization. The reason for this is that bureaucratic specialization is compatible with the internal structure of influence in Congress, which is itself based on specialization. Members of Congress have found that the way to gain influence in the House is to become known as the expert on some program. Becoming an expert on a program means becoming an expert on a bureaucracy's program.

This has been especially the case in the wake of the "subcommittee bill of rights" in the early 1970s, which gave each committee's subcommittees more autonomy to pursue their own legislative and oversight goals. While this increased fragmentation has done little to enhance the legislative function of Congress, it has evidently increased the ability of individual legislators to have an impact on a bureaucratic agency. By 1984, there were 326 committee and subcommittee chairmanships in the House and Senate, held by 202 different individuals. Most members of the majority party now chair some subcommittee. The increasingly large staffs are specialists, too. "Staff allegiance is to the subcommittee chairman rather than to the overall purpose of the legislature, and bickering with members of other staffs becomes a primary means of self-advancement.'[30] These staffs may make it actually harder to come to grips with a large, integrative problem such as budget deficits, as some have charged. However, their specialized program expertise makes it easier for an individual member of Congress to have an impact on a bureaucracy.

While specialization is present everywhere in the industrial world, in order to facilitate division of labor, members of Congress tend to protect and enhance peculiar federal agency structures that make the bureaucracy permeable to subcommittee investigations and constituency service requests. As a specialist on executive-branch organization has written, "What may appear to be structural eccentricities and anomalies within the executive branch are often nothing but mirror images of jurisdictional conflicts within the Congress. Congressional organization and executive branch organization are interrelated and constitute two halves of a single system. . . . To understand the organization of the executive branch, one must first understand the organization and culture of the Congress and the high degree of congressional involvement in administrative decisions."[31]

As we mentioned in an earlier chapter, the administrative reform model is somewhat ambiguous, especially as regards the prescription for "specialization" in organizational structure. However, this very ambiguity itself is an asset to Congress. Congress has resisted reorganization plans drawn up by technicians who were unconcerned with congressional political requirements. On the other hand, one can resist a reorganization plan that one doesn't like just by proposing an alternative principle of organization—say, organization by clientele instead of organization by function. Thus, members of Congress can justify keeping the Bureau of Reclamation separate from the Corps of Engineers on the grounds that the clientele of the two agencies are geographically separated. The ambiguity of the classical model of administrative reform only enhances its usefulness to Congress.

INTEREST GROUPS AND ADMINISTRATIVE REFORM

Not only bureaucrats and legislators, but also interest groups themselves have much to gain by a general acceptance of the classical model of administrative reform. The reason is that the classical model has served to decrease the emphasis on political parties and partisan affiliation, and increase the influence of those resources that interest groups have the most of—insider access and expertise.

Political scientist E. E. Schattschneider pointed out in 1960 that political parties have a monopoly on the ability to get elected.[32] Interest groups, no matter how large or powerful, cannot effect their policy goals by nominating an AFL–CIO or a Farm Bureau candidate for the presidency and hoping to get that candidate elected, nor can they hope to run candidates for office and hope to get a majority of the members of the House or Senate. Only parties can hope to win elections in this way, and Schattschneider concluded that parties have a natural advantage over interest groups. If one interest group makes unreasonable demands on the policy platform of a political party, the party can always form an alternative coalition of interests. Schattschneider argues that the Republican Party, therefore, has an advantage over the business interest groups it represents—where else can they go for their candidates other than to the Republicans? Similarly, the Democratic Party has a degree of autonomy from the labor and other interest groups in its coalition. Interest groups need parties more than either party needs any interest group.

But is this, in fact, the case? Does an interest group really need a political party at all, or does it have other strategies it can pursue? Schattschneider implicitly points out that interest groups can win if they can define the game in a way that makes the political parties irrelevant. If party competition becomes increasingly irrelevant for policy outcomes, then interest groups can win their policy goals autonomously from political parties.

The reform tradition has changed the rules of the game in an explicit attempt to weaken the influence of political parties on policy formation. Reformers believed that the political party was an institution that distorted the public interest as it represented it in Congress and the other institutions of government. Many of the reforms of the Progressive era—the party primary, the initiative and referendum, registration laws, nonpartisan ballots, and cross-filing—were directly motivated by an attempt to change the rules of the game to make political parties less important. The administrative reforms of the era—civil service, the city-manager form of government, regulatory agencies—were intended to insulate the impact of political parties on administration. Progressives sought a separation of politics from administration, and for them "politics" meant "parties." In large part, they succeeded in weakening both the electoral and administrative roles of parties. The administration of the FBI, the Corps of Engineers, the Post Office, the Defense Department, and most other federal agencies is still political, as was discussed in an earlier chapter; but the politics of these agencies has little to do with political parties.

Furthermore, even members of Congress, who are still consistently members of political parties, may find that much of their political activity is divorced from political parties. Whole committees (such as the Post Office committee) pursue their legislative and oversight functions in a nonpartisan, though still political, way.

Members of Congress may construct reelection strategies that are based on constituency service, interest group contributions, and personality, while depending on their political party for little in the way of campaign contributions or other resources.

The argument of many political scientists is that interest groups have stepped into the political vacuum created by the diminution of political parties. This theme was first advanced by Grant McConnell.[33] In a chapter entitled "The Progressive Legacy," he summarizes the Progressive attack on political parties, then asks, "If parties were to be emasculated, what would be left save government by the expert, government in the name of a public whose multitudes could never speak except through interest groups . . .?"[34]

While political parties must necessarily trade one interest group off against another, interest groups have found government by "expert" to be quite conducive to their narrow interests. As was discussed in an earlier chapter, "experts" often have as narrow a perspective on problems as the interest groups themselves. Thus, when highway engineers advance more and better highways as a solution to every transportation problem, the highway lobby has cheered them on.

McConnell points out that regulatory agencies demonstrate this dynamic most clearly:

> These appointive, determinedly nonpartisan bodies were to be the solution to the dilemmas of Congress when it was faced with the problem of regulation in highly technical and complicated areas. But almost nowhere were these commissions equipped with guides to their conduct other than the very general Congressional admonition that their rules and decisions should be "in the public interest.". . . The lack of principled guides to action led to a sense of the arbitrary character of the situation.   In sheer self-defense, if nothing else, the commissioners were forced into a search for accommodation, and accommodation slipped imperceptibly into corruption.[35]

What was true of regulatory agencies was true of other administrative agencies as well. The specialization of bureaucracies narrowed their focus to one that was commensurate with narrow interest groups. The veil of nonpartisanship meant that administrative agencies lacked any substantive policy guidance from partisan debate, but left those agencies open to the influence of private interest groups. What is more, the ideology of "bureaucratic expertise" meant that only interest groups who commanded enough resources to hire their own experts could hope to influence bureaucratic agencies.

Thus, the Department of Agriculture has consistently been open to the expert advice of farm lobby economists and lawyers. The education professionals (but certainly not students or parents) have sufficient expertise to advise the Department of Education. The aura of professional expertise united the FBI with its client support groups—the local law enforcement agencies.

Thus, in its nonpartisanship, its specialization, and its emphasis on professional expertise, the new administrative state is ideally suited to influence by organized interest groups.

THE PRESIDENCY AND ADMINISTRATIVE REFORM

It might appear that since the president has a broad-based constituency, he would be the only governmental actor not to support the narrow interest-group politics of professionalized bureaus. In one important sense, this assessment would be correct: The president often runs on a platform aimed at attacking the special interests and their alliances in the subgovernments of the federal government.

Indeed, the president's political weakness, which is in part a result of the administrative reform movements' success, has led him to seek political solutions to his problems. For the most part, however, this has meant that presidents have adopted the reform ideology of the executive management movement. They have done so for at least two reasons: First, they have benefited electorally from the movement's emphasis on central coordination, elimination of duplication and overlap, consolidation of departments and agencies, and in general more effective and efficient government. It is possible and often desirable for the president to run on a platform of attacking the bureaucracy and showing how his new management techniques or reorganization proposals will make the difference. Thus, the administrative reform values of efficiency and central coordination have been good presidential politics.

Second, presidents have sought to strengthen the presidential institutions of government. In doing this, they have relied on private expert commissions or on public administrationist thinking. These reform efforts produced a corporate form of presidential administration which Richard Nathan has called the "administrative presidency." In earlier times, when no central clearance existed and the president needed basic administrative help, strengthening these professional institutions contributed to presidential power.

However, since the model of executive management reform relied exclusively on neutrality, hierarchy, and specialization with no role for the political party or other political institutions, the cumulative result over time has been to strengthen the institutions of neutral competence surrounding the president. These institutions give him the formal trappings of more central power, while at the same time creating newer forms of professional and bureaucratic interests outside of his control. Even the White House itself came to be filled with various offices and commissions responsive to the professional interests of subgovernments and only indirectly loyal to the political program of the president. So, as the president gained more formal professional expertise and administrative capacity, he also seemed to lose ground in his fight to control the bureaucracy. Indeed, his own White House organization and executive office became part of the problem rather than the solution.

We would argue that this kind of vicious circle prompted presidents to go even deeper in their commitment to executive management ideology, believing that past dosages had not done the trick. By the middle 1970s, presidential administrative capacity was stronger than ever before, yet the president seemed weaker than ever before. President Carter, following his predecessors, advocated more consolidations, newer budget techniques, and further reductions in duplication and overlap.

Frustrations with the cumulative effects of classical executive management reforms prompted some presidents to break out of this pattern. In his second term,

President Nixon abandoned the classical approach in favor of an ill-fated attempt to politicize the bureaucracy. Nixon had discovered that his "corporate" White House, set up on classical administrative lines, did not guarantee political responsiveness to his program. Franklin Roosevelt also espoused the classical model of reform while personally pursuing a quite different management style (discussed in Chapter 13). Most recently, President Reagan has rejected the classical model in some aspects of his administration (also discussed in Chapter 13). Thus, while most presidents have found the classical model good politics, the cumulative frustrations of the model have caused important exceptions to the rule.

ADMINISTRATIVE REFORM AND THE PUBLIC INTEREST

This chapter has argued that the classical model of administrative reform, based on nonpartisanship, hierarchy, routinization of procedure, specialization, and professional expertise, has benefited a variety of important political actors—interest groups, presidents, members of Congress, and administrators themselves. If all of these groups benefit, then who can be the losers? Is it possible that an institutional reform that benefited so many actors could be contrary to the public interest? To answer this question, it is necessary to distinguish between individual rationality and collective welfare.

The Prisoners' Dilemma: From Decentralization, Inefficiency

In the past few years, social scientists have become increasingly aware that a group of individuals, all acting in a way that is faultlessly logical from an individualistic point of view, can each end up worse off than before. One class of situations that exhibits this unpleasant possibility is the "prisoners' dilemma," as illustrated below.[36]

A very simplified example of a prisoners' dilemma would be an imaginary society composed of two interest groups—we'll call them the farm lobby and the education lobby. Each interest group is in favor of a federal subsidy of benefit only to its own members. Each subsidy is worth $50 million to each interest group, but costs $60 million. The costs are divided equally among the two groups. If the farm lobby gets its own subsidy while blocking the education subsidy, it gets $50 million less $30 million, or $20 million in net benefits, while the education lobby is simply out $30 million in taxes. If neither subsidy passes, both get a net benefit of zero. If both subsidies pass, both groups get a net benefit of $50 million less two times $30 million, or a loss of $10 million. This information is summarized in Table 10-1.

Now let us imagine that the social process is decentralized so that each interest group gets to decide *on its own* whether or not it gets its own subsidy. What will happen? If the education lobby forbears, then the farm lobby can get $20 million instead of nothing by passing the farm subsidy. If the education lobby passes its own subsidy, then the farm lobby loses $10 million instead of $30 million. *No matter what the education lobby does, the farm lobby is better off protecting the farm subsidy.* The same thing is true for the education lobby. Both will end up fighting for their inefficient subsidies, even though the final outcome is worse than if both did the individually irrational act of vetoing their own subsidies. Individual and collective rationality are at odds.

TABLE 10-1   An Illustrative Prisoners' Dilemma

Education Lobby

	Protects education subsidy	Gives up education subsidy
Protects farm subsidy	Farmers = −$10 million Educators = −$10 million	Farmers = +$20 million Educators = −$30 million
Farm Lobby		
Gives up education subsidy	Farmers = −$30 million Educators = +$20 million	Farmers = 0 Educators = 0

The problem only gets worse if there are more interest groups, each with special influence over their own subsidies. It is important to note that it is decentralization, or specialization, that creates the possibility of the dilemma. If society were to use centralized majority rule voting on whether to have the entire package of subsidies, or none at all, then everyone would vote for none at all;[37] or if specialization were to be divorced from self-interest, there would be no problem. If the farm interest group got to decide on the merits of the education lobby's subsidy, and vice versa, then the efficient outcome would be achieved. The problem occurs to the extent that special interest groups achieve special influence over the projects that they have a special interest in.

Administrative Reform and the Prisoners' Dilemma

It is because of this possible dilemma, in which the public interest seems to suffer at the hands of individual rationality, that we must consider whether the aggregation of a variety of individually rational actions makes society better off or worse off. It was individually smart for a variety of bureaucrats to fight for greater autonomy for their own agencies, in the name of expertise and political noninterference. It was individually smart for congressional oversight committees to delegate legislative authority to agencies, while asking in return for responsiveness to individual legislator requests for constituents and interest groups. It was individually smart for interest groups to support the creation of the administrative state, because they were able to enhance their own access and influence to the delegated sources of policy-making power. But in the aggregate, have these changes made us all better off or worse off?

Numerous authors claim that we are collectively worse off as a result of the institutional changes that have given narrow interest groups special influence over decisions in which they are especially interested. The decline in political parties, the fragmentation of Congress into specialized committees, and delegation of decision-making authority to specialized professional bureaucracies are all institutional transformations that have tended to maximize the influence of organized special interest groups in decisions that concern them.

In the case of administrative reform, the "external" effects that make individually rational actions bad for society as a whole may include the fact that, collectively, we have less control over our government's actions than before. The bureaucratization of the Department of Agriculture gave farmers more control over farm policy, but decreased the decisiveness of the electoral process over farm policy. The creation of the Department of Education tightened the education lobby's control over education policy, but did not increase the ability of the government as a whole to come up with a comprehensive social-welfare service reform.

This is very much the theme of political scientists Theodore Lowi,[38] Grant McConnell,[39] Harold Seidman,[40] and Morris Fiorina.[41] Individually, a variety of interests may have been served by the insulation of professionalized experts from partisan control. Collectively, the price all of those interests pay is the fragmentation of government and the subsequent loss of accountability. Fiorina argues that this has led to immobility, since the government cannot deal with the problems that transcend the narrow boundaries of any bureaucracy's specialized professional expertise. It has also led to alienation from the public, which sees government as performing the narrow, technical tasks very well, but unable to solve such major political problems as the deficit. Lowi's cry that the bureaucratization of our cities has made them "well-run but ungoverned" is applicable to the nation as a whole. Our professionalized bureaucracies constitute "functional fiefdoms" of autonomous political influence, so masked that even the professionals who dominate the bureaucracies are not aware of themselves as political actors.[42]

It is this masking of political power that needs to enter the consideration of administrative reform in the future. In the past, the implications of reform for the collective well-being remained in the background; short-term gain for congressmen, administrators, and interest groups dominated decision making. While expertise and professionalism are indispensable to competent government, how to harness these qualities to the political will of the broader community without destroying them is the heart of the reform problem.

Budgeting is a foremost example of both the persistence of the classical model of administrative reform and the distance between individual rationality and collective well-being. It is to this topic that we turn in our next chapter.

NOTES

[1] MORRIS P. FIORINA, *Congress: Keystone of the Washington Establishment* (New Haven: Yale University Press, 1977), p. 49.

[2] EUGENE LEWIS, *Public Entrepreneurship: Toward a Theory of Bureaucratic Political Power* (Bloomington: Indiana University Press, 1980), p. 104.

[3] LEWIS, *Public Entrepreneurship*, p. 105.

[4] LEWIS, *Public Entrepreneurship*, p. 107.

[5] LEWIS, *Public Entrepreneurship*, p. 118.

[6] LEWIS, *Public Entrepreneurship*, p. 121.

[7] VICTOR S. NAVASKY, *Kennedy Justice* (New York: Atheneum, 1977), p. 30.

[8] RICHARD F. FENNO, JR., *The Power of the Purse: Appropriations Politics in Congress* (Boston: Little, Brown & Co., 1966), p. 377.

[9] NAVASKY, *Justice*, p. 34.

[10] LEWIS, *Public Entrepreneurship*, p. 146.

[11] LEWIS, *Public Entrepreneurship*, p. 122.

[12] ROBERT A. CARO, *The Power Broker: Robert Moses and the Fall of New York* (New York: Vintage Books, 1975).

[13]CARO, *Power Broker*, p. 271.

[14]CARO, *Power Broker*, p. 273.

[15]CARO, *Power Broker*, p. 272.

[16]CARO, *Power Broker*, p. 622.

[17]CARO, *Power Broker*, p. 741.

[18]DONALD P. WARWICK, A *Theory of Public Bureaucracy: Politics, Personality, and Organization in the State Department* (Cambridge: Harvard University Press, 1975), p. 125. Reprinted by permission.

[19]MAX WEBER, *From Max Weber: Essays in Sociology*, H. Gerth and C. Wright Mills, eds. (New York: Oxford University Press, 1946), p. 232.

[20]WARWICK, *Public Bureaucracy*, pp. 69–71.

[21]THEODORE J. LOWI, *The End of Liberalism: The Second Republic of the United States*, 2nd ed. (New York: W. W. Norton & Co., 1979).

[22]MATHEW D. McCUBBINS, "The Legislative Design of Regulatory Structure," *American Journal of Political Science*, 29 (1985), pp. 721–748.

[23]PAUL J. QUIRK, "Food and Drug Administration," in *The Politics of Regulation*, James Q. Wilson, ed. (New York: Basic Books, 1980), p. 199.

[24]QUIRK, "Food and Drug," pp. 215–216.

[25]FIORINA, *Congress*.

[26]ERWIN G. KRASNOW and LAWRENCE D. LONGLEY, *The Politics of Broadcast Regulation* (New York: St. Martin's Press, 1973), p. 70.

[27]FIORINA, *Congress*, pp. 58–60.

[28]MORRIS FIORINA and ROGER NOLL, "Voters, Bureaucrats, and Legislators: A Rational Choice Perspective on the Growth of Bureaucracy," *Journal of Public Economics*, 9 (1978), pp. 239–254.

[29]FIORINA and NOLL, "Voters," p. 252.

[30]GREGG EASTERBOOK, "What's Wrong With Congress," *Atlantic Monthly* (1984), p. 59.

[31]HAROLD SEIDMAN, *Politics, Position, and Power: The Dynamics of Federal Organization* (New York: Oxford University Press, 1980), p. 40.

[32]E. E. SCHATTSCHNEIDER, *The Semi-Sovereign People: A Realist's View of Democracy in America* (Hinsdale, Ill: The Dryden Press, 1960), p. 59.

[33]GRANT McCONNELL, *Private Power and American Democracy* (New York: Alfred A. Knopf Inc., , 1966).

[34]McCONNELL, *Private Power*, p. 47.

[35]McCONNELL, *Private Power*, pp. 49–50.

[36]See, for instance, the readings in *Rational Man and Irrational Society: An Introduction and Sourcebook*, Brian Barry and Russell Hardin, eds. (Beverly Hills: Sage Publications, 1982).

[37]RUSSELL HARDIN, "Collective Action as an Agreeable n-Prisoners' Dilemma," *Behavioral Science*, 16 (1971), pp. 472–479.

[38]LOWI, *Liberalism*.

[39]McCONNELL, *Private Power*.

[40]SEIDMAN, *Politics*.

[41]FIORINA, *Congress*.

[42]THEODORE J. LOWI, "Machine Politics—Old and New," *Public Interest*, 9 (1967), pp. 83–92.

CHAPTER 11

The Quest for Technical Efficiency:
Budget Reform

> Far from being a neutral matter of "better budgeting," proposed reforms
> inevitably contain important implications for the political system; that
> is, for the "who gets what" of governmental decisions.
>
> Aaron Wildavsky, *The Politics of the Budgetary Process*[1]

The Progressive reformers sought to change and improve public budgeting in response to widespread corruption and mismanagement. The executive management
movement of the Roosevelt era also made budgeting a major feature of its design for
improving central administration. However, the capstone of budget reform came
during the 1960s and 1970s. Budget reform emerged with almost every new administration. The Congress also introduced its own budget reform: the 1974 Budget and
Impoundment Control Act. Each reform was supposed to bring a new era in
government management and profoundly alter the setting of objectives and the
efficient allocation of resources. The results of these reforms instead proved to be
mixtures of failures interspersed with some solid achievements.

Executive-branch reforms seemed to come and go with depressing regularity.
The Reagan administration discontinued Zero-Base Budgeting (ZBB) just as the
Nixon administration had abandoned Planning-Programming-Budgeting Systems
(PPBS) ten years earlier. Similarly, the Carter administration discontinued the
Nixon system of Management by Objectives (MBO).

Critics of congressional budgeting have also grown in number in recent
years.[2] A recent critic of budgeting in the Department of Defense, where PPBS is
supposed to have succeeded more than anywhere else, observes that "Many critics
accuse the Department of Defense (DOD) of the same kind of mismanagement that
PPBS was supposed to eliminate."[3]

All the reforms evidenced a similar decision logic that may roughly be described as "rational comprehensive." This means that they attempted to integrate
the various functions of governing into one grand budget design for planning,
managing, evaluating, financing, and controlling programs. In many respects, the

reforms represented the conflux of the classical administrative model with the newer disciplines of systems analysis and managerial economics. Policy makers often adopted this abstract logic of reform, however, less for its known efficacy in management improvement than for its political expediency. Consequently, in some cases the reforms served as window dressing, having less to do with the real political rationality at work in policy making than with the appearance of rationality.

This chapter seeks to demonstrate the origins of budget reform in the classical model, to show why the overblown expectations of these reforms could never be fully realized, and to point out those aspects of budget reform that have proved to be valuable and enduring.

THE STAGES OF BUDGET REFORM

Not until the 1921 Budget and Accounting Act did the executive have any mechanism for reviewing the budget proposals of the departments. The departments had sent their budgets directly to the relevant committees in Congress. For much of the nineteenth century, the Congress had reviewed budget and tax measures in the powerful Ways and Means Committee; but in 1865 Congress decided to separate the review of expenditure and revenue by establishing an Appropriations Committee. By 1885, the single Appropriations Committee had evolved into eight subcommittees that recommended appropriations to the Congress as a whole. This decentralized structure facilitated the kind of patronage and corruption practiced by Boss Platt and led to rapidly growing expenditures and deficits in the early twentieth century. The 1921 Act thus established the Bureau of the Budget (BOB) as an arm of the Treasury Department and created the General Accounting Office for auditing executive accounts. The Act improved the control function of the budget and opened the door for more central coordination and planning of programs. Although this was only a beginning, as Allen Schick states, "budget reform meant executive budgeting."[4]

The Executive Budget Movement

In the first decade of the twentieth century, muckraking exposés of public corruption and the lack of systematic budget accounts prompted reformers to argue for a centralized, executive budget as an instrument of government planning. Schick states that the Taft Commission of 1911 and its three leading experts, Cleveland, Goodnow, and Willoughby, viewed budgeting as consisting of three basic functions:

1. the *planning* function, whereby the chief executive imposes a "comprehensive and consistent set of judgments on all government spending";
2. the *management* function, in which, through the "functional consolidation of the agencies [and] the elimination of independent boards and commissions," the chief executive can coordinate the activities of government; and
3. the *control* function, under which the executive controls waste and fraud through better and uniform accounting procedures, centralized purchasing, and expenditure audits.[5]

The Taft Commission, in a remarkable foretaste of the planning and budgeting movements of the 1960s and 1970s, rejected line-item or "object-of-expense" classifications for the budget (such as supplies, salaries, travel, capital purchases, and so forth) in favor of activity or functional classifications according to class of work. Schick emphasizes that the program preferences "conformed to the prevailing ideas of separation of politics from administration" and "grew out of their vision of the budget as a planning instrument and was consistent with the contemporary drive to organize departments along functional lines."[6]

The application of these modern-sounding Progressive ideas to the practice of budgeting took several decades. During the 1920s and 1930s, budget reform swept through the state capitols and local city halls, but the focus of attention was on the control function through improved accounting procedures. Accountants devoted their efforts to improving methods of control through line-item objects of expenditure. According to Schick, "technique triumphed over purpose."[7] The first director of the newly created Bureau of the Budget in Washington wrote, "The Bureau of the Budget is concerned only with the humbler and routine business of government. Unlike Cabinet officers, it is concerned with no question of policy save that of economy and efficiency."[8]

The depression in the 1930s fundamentally changed the conception of the role of the federal government in social and economic affairs. The concept of a weak executive no longer fit the reality. The Roosevelt administration had boldly enacted a wide-ranging legislative program that included the creation of numerous new agencies and executive activities. The resistance of the Congress to a stronger executive had succumbed to a call for a strengthened executive to meet the country's pressing needs.

The president's 1937 Committee on Administrative Management, known as the Brownlow Committee, proposed several new functions for the BOB that centered on the coordination and management of the budget. The Committee was able for the first time to bring together the various strands of administrative-reform ideas into a new, workable design for the president and other executives. Seedling Progressive ideas of the early twentieth century, which confronted dangerous political hazards to growth and development, finally reached maturity by the end of the second World War. The Committee's recommendations led to the passage of the Reorganization Act of 1939, which established the Executive Office of the President. The Act required the transfer of the BOB from the Treasury Department to the new Executive Office. In addition, the giant expansion of the federal budget in the 1930s led to broader expenditure classifications and a greater emphasis in BOB on programs and cost accounting. During World War II, Harold D. Smith, the Director of BOB, wrote, "The main function of the Bureau is to serve as an agent of the President in coordinating operations and in improving the management of the government."[9]

One further impetus to budget reform developed out of the Reports of the two Hoover Commissions of 1949 and 1955. The first Commission led to the Budget and Accounting and Procedures Act of 1950. The Act gave the president increased authority to define accounts and determine budget presentations as well as workload and other management measures of performance. Hoover coined the term "performance budgeting" to describe the Progressive emphasis on activity or functional classification in budgeting. Though the new phrase stuck, the adoption of performance measures did not spread very far.

Scientific Management and Budgeting

The scientific management movement, associated with the pioneering efficiency studies of Frederick Taylor in industrial and mechanical engineering, constitutes the other major thread in the development of modern budget-reform systems. The question of efficiency hinges not only on procedures for implementing certain tasks, but even more directly on the choice and design of alternative projects. This latter dimension of the scientific management movement came to depend less on mechanical engineering than on the growing disciplines of operations research, welfare and managerial economics, and systems analysis. The manner in which these disciplines were applied to budgeting conformed closely with the organizational principles of the classical, bureaucratic model of administration. While other social sciences had begun to undermine the tenets of the classical model (discussed in Chapters 6 through 8), these disciplines were working to add new support.

At the turn of the century, some cities were already employing a technique that tried to compare costs and benefits of public-works projects. This technique traces its development to the nineteenth-century French economist, Jules Dupuit, whose concepts defining social welfare formed the basis for the seminal work of the Italian social scientist, Vilfredo Pareto. However, the idea of measuring social costs and benefits did not attain much application in the United States until the 1930s and 1940s. A special boost to the use of cost-benefit analysis came in 1939, when the U.S. Flood Control Act specifically stated that, "the benefits to whomsoever they may occur (must be) in excess of the estimated costs." Other agencies, including the Tennessee Valley Authority and the Department of Agriculture, also adopted rudimentary forms of cost-benefit analysis. By the early 1960s, the Inter-Agency Committee on Water Resources and the Bureau of the Budget began to adopt a set of cost-benefit criteria for evaluating river projects.

The practical application of these ideas had been greatly enhanced in 1949 by the work of two British economists, Nicholas Kaldor and Sir John Hicks. According to Pareto's definition of efficiency, a project is efficient if it will make either everyone better off or at least no one worse off than he would have been without the project. Pareto optimality thus required a calculation of the individual benefits and costs to people affected by a public project. Discovering individual preferences, however, was often difficult, if not impossible. Kaldor and Hicks addressed this problem by arguing that only total costs and total benefits need to be compared. They got around the difficult political problem of distribution by simply assuming it away: The gainers could compensate the losers through some undefined form of redistributive policy. They also restricted the calculations to dollar amounts so that comparisons could be made between diverse benefits and costs.[10]

Applied welfare economics, therefore, complemented and furthered the traditions of the scientific management movement in public administration. Schick states: "They hoped that marginal analysis of spending alternatives (battleships versus poor relief in Pique's classic case) would enable governments to adopt a mix of programs that maximized the welfare of their citizens. The quest for a welfare formula led to ingenious methodologies for bypassing the problems of interpersonal comparisons (Pareto rules and compensation schemes, for example)."[11] The welfare formula of Kaldor and Hicks is thus little different than the "one best way" of the Taylorites: There exists a mix of programs that makes everyone better off and no one worse off. Likewise, cost-benefit analysis assumes a separation of politics from administration. The objectives (projects, programs, policies) are given by the political process, but the optimal choice among them is a purely technical operation based on efficiency criteria.

While cost-benefit analysis tries to meet objectives at the lowest cost, it does not attempt to change organizational structures or the objectives themselves. This bolder understanding of efficiency, whereby both objectives and structures become subservient to the efficiency criterion, did come to dominate reform in the 1960s and 1970s. Just as Taylor eventually was not satisfied with tinkering with the mechanical components of the work process, but extended his studies to organizational structures and procedures, so welfare economics extended its reach into analyzing government systems and decision structures.

Before examining specific budget systems in more detail, it should be noted that the original theoretical treatise underpinning a budget reform may be much more sophisticated than the eventual application of the reform in government practice. In fact, one of the lessons of these reforms may be that considerable distortion is introduced as a reform is diffused into practical use. We mention this diffusion problem because of the differences between the two managerial budget techniques that were introduced in the 1960s and 1970s, PPBS and ZBB. In its original theoretical form, as propounded by Peter Phyrr, ZBB treats allocation decisions in a very unsatisfactory way;[12] in contrast, the theoretical bible of PPBS, written by Charles Hitch and Roland McKean, develops very sophisticated reasoning on budget allocation decisions.[13]

In addition, although we believe that both ZBB and PPBS follow a similar underlying logic and that this logic is a faulty way to approach budget reform, we do not want to reject everything in these two systems. Some components of PPBS, especially, have proved to be useful and enduring.

PLANNING-PROGRAMMING-BUDGETING SYSTEMS

The most prominent expression of the ambitious attempt to organize decision processes around marginal utility analysis was the Planning-Programming-Budgeting Systems (PPBS) introduced into government under the Johnson administration. PPBS combined cost-benefit and systems analysis with the main features of the clasical model of organization. The PPB system required "institutional reorganization to bring relevant administrative functions under the jurisdiction of the authority making the final program decisions."[14] Schick also states that "the first and final elements of POSDCORB [Brownlow Committee, 1937] were packaged into a new budgetary formula: the Planning-Programming-Budgeting System (PPB)."[15]

The logical structure of PPBS, as well as other welfare economic decision procedures, may be summarized as consisting of the following properties:

1. List all values relevant to a problem under consideration.
2. Specify precisely and carefully the objectives derived from these values.
3. Comprehensively list alternative ways of achieving the objectives.
4. Evaluate each alternative in terms of its ability to achieve the objectives.
5. Choose the alternative that maximizes the achievement of the objectives.

The rationality embodied in these decision properties is comparable to the rationality of the classical model of organization. The procedure is deductive; that is, the properties are arranged in a hierarchy such that the conclusions are contained in the premises. Once a decision maker knows the values and objectives and has the relevant information and theory to test the alternatives, the best choice is simply a matter of computation. The procedure is also comprehensive, meaning that it presumes to control all the relevant variables within its sequence of steps. Finally, the procedure assumes that objectives and values are known in advance and can be separated from the sequence of steps designed to carry them out in an efficient manner. Thus, the procedure embodies the familiar properties of hierarchy, comprehensiveness, and the separation of politics from administration.

Procedures and Structures

The building blocks of PPBS are the new program categories for the budget. Financial data are collected on functionally related activities that oftentimes cut across more traditional organizational structures. In addition, PPBS creates new program evaluation and review organizational units to replace or sometimes supplement the traditional budget offices. Usually, however, a "crosswalk" system is also installed that operates to translate the new budget data into the old categories for comparison purposes.

The program budget operates through program memoranda that contain much more elaborate information than the traditional budget and involve budget managers in a more demanding review process. Program goals are supposed to be quantified and supported with performance measurements as far as is feasible. After program objectives are identified, "alternative methods of meeting them are to be subjected to systematic comparison."[16] Budgeters are required to rank their various programs in order of priority, even for comparison across agencies in a department. Finally, the program memoranda must include multi-year analyses of the impact of current spending.

A persistent political difficulty with the setting up of a PPBS was the restructuring of the agencies into new program categories. The United States Department of Agriculture (USDA) initially established 14 program categories with names like Farm and Forest Products, Protection of Human Health, Housing in Rural Areas, and so forth. Within a few years, however, these program categories had evolved into fewer and entirely meaningless generalities with names like Communities of Tomorrow, Dimensions for Living, Resources for Action, Growing Nations/New Markets, Income and Abundance, and Science in the Service of Man. Other agencies had taken the opposite tack—they increased the number of categories to such a large number that any activity found a niche. Agencies quickly learned to either recommend numerous categories so that everyone gets a piece of the action, or to have a few general categories so no one feels threatened.[17]

Political competition among agencies also influenced the choice of categories. The Soil Conservation Service (SCS), for example, opposed the creation of a program category entitled "Rural Community Development" because it felt that this title de-emphasized resource conservation and would give the Department of the Interior an advantage in the struggle over which department had jurisdiction over natural resources. Instead, the SCS made a plea for a program category that would preserve or even enlarge the clientele of the SCS.

What the designers of PPBS failed to realize, but what the practitioners recognized right away, was that how the categories are defined has implications for power relations. Some categories reveal information previously obscured; other categories conceal; others promote different values. The choice depends on the objectives and purposes in setting up the categories. A dam, for example, can be used for recreation, fishing, electric power, irrigation, and drinking water. The category of building it falls into will have implications for the kinds of measurements used in determining performance: extensiveness, visitors, hydroelectric power, and so forth. What category it falls into will thus make a difference in how it is perceived by the evaluators.

It was also unfortunate that the way PPBS became institutionalized in various government agencies tended to make it more static and sequential than the original theory. Many of the proponents of PPBS, for example, had a sophisticated view of objectives which included the realization that objectives are often multiple and vague, and hence difficult to state in priority lists. Charles Hitch wrote, "We have never undertaken a major system study at RAND in which we are able to define satisfactory objectives at the beginning of the study."[18] Some developers of PPBS thus emphasized the feedback and interactive relation between properties of the decision logic and saw the decision logic not as a closed system, but as a learning process that must be repeated over and over again.

PPBS has made significant contributions. The classification of budget accounts on functional lines serves a valuable program-evaluation purpose, inside and outside government. Analysis of alternatives at the margin is also an invaluable activity for making efficient budget allocations. Finally, multi-year projections, although not always accurate in forecasting the future, do give policy makers important information on the possible consequences of alternative courses of action and their long-run costs for the budget. In such areas as weapons development, but also in social security and utilities, these projections are necessary for policy planning.

Where PPBS seems to fail most pointedly, therefore, is not in the specific techniques of budgeting or in its emphasis on more analysis, but in its call for *comprehensive* and *deductive* procedures for analysis. Routine, multi-year projections in most accounts, listings of all possible alternatives, and lists of goals serve no sound budget-management purpose, yet characterize PPBS in practice.

Evidence from studies of PPBS reveals that practitioners had great difficulty making routine five-year projections, considering systematically all other alternatives, and comprehensively ranking programs in order of priority. Some supporters of PPBS claim that the inability of departments like the USDA or Interior to accomplish these analytical tasks in budgeting stems primarily from two factors: the rather vague goals and low-level technology of these and other agencies and the lack of trained, analytical personnel. While undoubtedly both of these claims contain some validity, the operation of PPBS in the Defense Department, where neither of these technical or personnel liabilities exists, raises serious questions about the hope that if we only try harder (improve technology, hire more analysts, etc.), PPBS will succeed as a comprehensive system of budgeting.

PPBS in the Defense Department

In the Defense Department, PPBS contains three components: the planning phase, which "assesses the threat and articulates the direction in which DoD should head"; programming, which "designs the composition of forces by allocating funds to every DoD activity"; and budgeting, which "takes the first year of the five-year plan and examines it in detail so that when the budget is submitted to Congress, it is as accurate and complete as possible."[19]

While these procedures sound sensible and rational, Mark Cancian, who recently completed an analysis of them, claims they do not work very well and may even cause considerable harm in the way DoD allocates resources. Cancian states that the planning phase "focuses on what is needed rather than what is affordable or executable."[20] In other words, PPBS in practice (and Zero-Base Budgeting in both practice and theory) separates planning from budgeting: agencies are supposed to set plans and goals first, *before* they consider budgets.[21] This decision procedure rests on the decision logic outlined above. People are assumed to be able to articulate and plan values and objectives in advance of any consideration of means for achieving them. Studies of budget behavior, however, clearly show that budgeters cannot follow these sequential planning-programming-budgeting phases without ending up ignoring the plans or altering in an iterative fashion the relationship between plans and resources. Cancian concludes that such a separation between plans and budgets "generates wants but not priorities. Assuming a fiscally unconstrained world for planning is like designing an airplane while assuming that gravity does not exist."[22]

Rather, the planning process meets the needs of responding to an enemy threat by "multiplication" types of plans. By this Cancian means that the planners simply add numbers of ships, planes, or whatever in order to meet the hypothetical threat. They do not engage in thinking that explores realistic alternatives. The plan becomes advocacy for more of everything, a matter of dividing up the pie among the services. When the results of the planning phase were leaked to the press a few years ago, even Secretary Caspar Weinberger disassociated himself from the plans, calling them the "services' unconstrained wants."

Programming is supposed to turn the ideas of the planning phase into concrete, five-year budget projections. Cancian argues, however, that since the plans are so unrealistic, little incentive exists to make the transition to practical budget projections. Instead, the programming documents are drafted by numerous committees working through a consensus process that finds a "justification for virtually any defense program." In addition, operations and support costs are regularly underestimated, and this is especially the case for systems that do not yet exist. Inflation has also been routinely underestimated in the projections. The result is a situation in which there is "a lack of clear direction and severe doubts about fiscal executability."[23]

Not until the budgeting stage do any realistic adjustments to cost take place. Since the programming phase takes a long time and is always running behind schedule, it overlaps considerably with the budgeting phase. The only benefit of this is that now the budgets and programs begin to adjust to each other. Cancian observes that, "With programming decisions being made so late, the budget is, in effect, written over and over again." Cancian does admit, however, that at this point the plans are finally set on realistic assumptions. The budget document represents the "most authoritative statement on defense strategy" and "alone embodies all the hard trade-offs through which U.S. strategy unfolds."[24]

The Staff Report on defense organization of the Armed Services Committee echoes these criticisms. It complains that the planning phase is unconstrained by resources, which gives plans an unrealistic quality. The report quotes Admiral Elmo Zumwalt, who complains that, "I found this particular document (the strategic planning document) to be almost as valueless to read as it was fatiguing to write." The report also attacks the comprehensiveness of PPBS procedures: "The PPB system completely rewrites all strategic planning documents and conducts reviews of all programs and budgets each year. The workload associated with these tasks is enormous." The report quotes a defense management resources study concerning: "the utter impossibility of the assumed tasks (comprehensive annual assessments of national military strategy and force structure), and most seriously, an inability to grapple with alternatives linked to resources."[25]

The Defense Department was the first government organization to introduce PPBS. It also was supposed to have had the greatest success with its operation. Failure here cannot be blamed on inadequate technical levels or untrained personnel, yet Cancian concludes that, "Many of Secretary McNamara's problems are still present after 20 years of PPBS. . . . Ultimately, a failing PPBS is not an economic problem; it is a military problem."[26] This is not to say that PPBS is the sole cause of these problems; rather, the example shows that PPBS cannot easily eradicate, and may even contribute to, those underlying organizational pathologies described in Chapters 6 through 8, despite the high expectations of its proponents.

ZERO-BASE BUDGETING

The Nixon administration decided to discontinue PPBS as the budgeting system for the federal government and introduced a new management procedure called Management by Objectives. This reform, however, did not outlast the Nixon/Ford administrations—Jimmy Carter replaced it with a more comprehensive budgeting and management technique known as Zero-Base Budgeting. Since ZBB incorporates many of the features of MBO, it is worthwhile to focus on ZBB as the prototypical budget reform of the 1970s.

PPBS attempted to extend the logic of welfare economics to rationally allocating government expenditures at the margin; it ranked and compared new projects. In contrast, ZBB sought to examine every budget every year "from scratch." The reform's procedures did not focus on incremental spending, but on the "base"— those programs already in the budget from previous years. ZBB operated as a tool for curbing and controlling expenditures through rational analysis of cutbacks.

Unlike PPBS, ZBB does not require new organizational units or an exclusive focus on programs. ZBB begins with the identification of the decision units which will prepare the first parts of the budget. The choice is based on size and structure of the organization, but virtually any expenditure activity will suffice: capital projects, work assignments, or any fairly major organizational activity that possesses accounting support. In this respect, ZBB need not be as threatening to existing organizational interests as PPBS, which attempts to create new program categories.

The next step in ZBB procedures is to draw up the budget documents, known as decision packages. The packages form the basic building blocks for the rest of the ZBB procedures. A decision package provides a justification for and a description of various activities and programs of the decision units. Each decision package must contain the following information:

1. a statement of the objectives of the program,
2. a description of the activities of the program,
3. a listing of the benefits and costs of the program,
4. workload and performance measures, and
5. alternative ways of accomplishing the objectives.

A decision unit could have only one decision package, but usually a unit will draw up several decision packages for each of its activities. These decision packages, taken together, constitute the unit's budget document.

Decision packages must be of two types. The basic type must identify the lowest expenditure at which the program would still be viable. This package is known as a "minimum level of effort" (MLE) decision package. The expectation is, of course, that the MLE package would be lower than last year's budget, which is why this procedure is termed "zero-base." In addition, budgeters must draw up incremental decision packages that show levels of expenditure above the MLE amount. Usually each decision unit draws up many packages, including one MLE for each activity and two or three incremental packages for each activity.

After the decision packages are put together, the organization must rank them in order of priority. The only criterion for ranking is that MLE packages must rank higher than their associated incremental packages, although an incremental package of one activity may rank higher than the MLE of another activity. Usually this procedure produces thousands of decision packages in government-sized agencies. Consequently, the ranking of the packages that is carried out at the lowest levels of the agency must be grouped (or consolidated) at successively higher levels, so that top management will only consider a reasonable number of packages (around 50 to 100). This means that lower-level rankings may be completely changed by the time they reach the top management committees. Indeed, studies of the Consumer Products Safety Commission, an agency designated by the Carter administration as a testing ground for ZBB, demonstrated that top management had made major changes in the priority rankings of the decision units.

Budgeting takes place under the ZBB system by adding up in sequence the various costs of the decision packages, beginning with the highest ranked priorities. When the entire amount of available money is allocated in going down the priority list, a cutoff line is drawn. Those budget items above the line receive funding; those below the line do not receive funding. Suppose, for example, that the priority list contains 100 decision packages, with each package costing $5,000 (an unrealistic figure, of course). If the total available funds equal $400,000, then the first 80 decision packages will receive funding under the ZBB budgeting procedure; the remaining 20 decision packages at the bottom of the priority listing will receive no funding. The ZBB system does not determine how large the budget should be, but only calculates how any given amount should be allocated among a set of priorities.

Unlike the theory behind PPBS, ZBB baldly adopts the rational comprehensive decision logic. It assumes programs can be analyzed from scratch each year and that goals can be set prior to knowledge about resources or feasible alternatives. Since these assumptions are wholly unrealistic, ZBB quickly developed into a form of incremental budgeting. It is worthwhile to examine some of the difficulties associated with three features of ZBB: ranking, minimum level of effort, and objective setting.

Ranking

A critical problem with ZBB is the requirement that programs be ranked in order of priority not only in subfields, but across agencies. Such ranking schemes involve questionable measures of performance, uncertainty over the benefits of programs that have vague objectives, and difficult political choices that an agency may not want to face. Furthermore, even under assumed conditions of complete information and no political conflict, a priority listing of objectives does not always produce the right decisions. Capital projects, in particular, cannot easily be ranked in any rational manner, given a specified budget. Capital projects are usually lump-sum public expenditures in the sense that they cannot easily be broken up or mixed with each other. Rather, they form discrete packages that must be taken more or less as whole entities, which leads to what operations researchers call the "knapsack" problem.[27] The problem is summed up by Jack Hirschleifer, a well-known economist:

> Unfortunately, it is not in general true that investment opportunities can be uniquely ranked; the desirability of any one may be affected by the other project elements in any overall package into which it enters. Thus a correct ranking rule for individual projects is not generally possible.[28]

The two economists who developed PPBS in the Defense Department also express some skepticism of any ranking procedure: "The use of listings (of priority rankings) does not solve the allocation problem and can even trap us into adopting foolish policies."[29]

Many other government programs, such as welfare assistance, do have divisible properties, meaning that managers can decide to allocate more or less money to each one. The way ZBB handles this issue is through the incremental decision packages. Here again, however, ranking the incremental packages in order of priority, even assuming full rationality and information of managers, cannot be easily accomplished.

Imagine three individual programs. Economists assume that for each program, the marginal rate of production of benefits decreases. Consequently, no matter how steep the benefit curves were initially, eventually marginal benefit production should be equal for all three programs. Indeed, economists recommend that budgeters allocate money proportionately, so that each additional dollar spent is equal in benefits for all three programs.[30]

Consequently, only in a special sense can each incremental package in ZBB be ranked in order of priority. The total benefits of each program are different, yet the marginal benefits, on which the incremental packages depend, should be the same for a given increase in expenditure. Decision packages based on these increments, therefore, would be equal in importance, and could not be ranked. The significance of this result is that, even given the ideal, rational world often assumed by budget reformers, the procedures of ZBB cannot be carried out as intended.

But ranking also involves important political considerations. Many program elements are actually interdependent and cannot be listed separately, or they can be presented as interdependent for political purposes. The hearings in Congress concerning the space shuttle reveal that Dr. Fletcher, then head of the National Aeronautics and Space Administration (NASA), argued that the shuttle program could not be ranked independently of the proposed space station or the proposed space telescope. According to congressional testimony, these three major space projects depended on each other for success. In effect, NASA argued that the committee had to accept its whole budget as a total package or not at all. The members of the congressional committee never did receive a priority ranking of these programs.[31]

In carrying out the ZBB procedure, moreover, evidence shows that those programs ranked around the cutoff line are the only ones that receive serious attention; the others do not need to be carefully ranked and often cannot be carefully ranked because their existence is not in jeopardy. A great deal of political strategizing, therefore, goes into keeping certain decision packages away from the cutoff line.

Minimum Level of Effort

The heart of the ZBB process is the MLE decision packages. As Schick states, "Of course, the minimum level of effort packages are the distinctive 'zero-base' component of the system, and their elimination would convert the Georgia system into incremental budgeting."[32] Once again, however, evidence strongly suggests that budget managers have difficulty carrying out this requirement.

Even under conditions of complete information and no political conflict, some government programs may contain no feasible MLE budget amount. In this respect, capital projects fare quite well: building a bridge over a river would seem to entail some minimal spending level below which the bridge could not be built. However, for programs that have a continuous nature to them and therefore cannot be presented as a single, discrete expenditure, the designation of a MLE decision package becomes problematic. Consider a food-stamp or soup-kitchen program to feed the poor and hungry. Conceivably, ten million people might be involved if the need were great enough; on the other hand, if only a hundred people receive food, the program would still serve some purpose. The elastic nature of spending and benefits means that there may be no theoretical MLE at which the program no longer is viable, other than the obvious point where no money is spent. Nonetheless, numerous government programs possess this elastic feature, especially those in the social services area.

The difficulty with setting a MLE amount is revealed by a survey of state governments that have adopted ZBB procedures. The most common practice takes last year's budget, or possibly a current services budget, to serve as the MLE amount; or, somewhat more in keeping with the spirit of ZBB, some states adopted a rule of using 90 percent of last year's budget as the MLE amount. In either case, the designation of a MLE rule is completely arbitrary and smacks of incremental budget procedures. In a state such as New Mexico, which participated fully in the Sunbelt's growth during the 1970s, the idea of setting a minimum level of effort substantially below last year's budget seemed ludicrous.[33] Hence, budgeters set the MLE at a percentage above the previous year's budget. In keeping with its general opposition to ZBB, NASA also resisted setting a MLE amount for its space centers in Houston and Florida. Elmer Groo, the NASA spokesman, stated, "I really do believe it is a matter of judgement. I don't think there's any final definition of a core capability at any given space center."[34]

Setting Objectives

ZBB requires that budgeters first identify what they want to do and then rank their priorities. Only subsequently will money amounts determine the cutoff line for the budget. Such a budgetary expression of the old politics/administration dichotomy is both technically and politically unwise.

First, consider the technical problem. The amount of money available has a significant impact on the design of spending programs and their order of priority in the budget. If a professor makes less than $40,000 per year, it is unlikely that a Maserati sports car would rank very high in his list of budget priorities. Yet if that same professor were to win the state lottery of $5 million, the same sports car, given his tastes, might jump very close to the top of his spending list. Likewise, albeit on a less dramatic plane, differences in budget amounts change the priority ranking of objectives in government budgets. Evidence for this appeared very early in the ZBB saga in Georgia. During ZBB's first two years there in 1973–74, revenue estimates turned out to be erroneous, in part because of the oil embargo and its impact in the U.S. The consequence was the redoing of the state's budget several times over as each new revenue estimate was issued. Agency heads did not prefer to keep the same rankings under different income assumptions. Economists refer to this technical problem as the "income effect."

The political problem with separating planning and budgeting is that, in government, the means for accomplishing a task and the ends of the task are both political. The building of a new military helicopter is supposed to serve the end of national defense, yet the way the helicopter is produced—either by this company or that one, in this state or another state, with these components or different ones— becomes a political goal for certain participants. Which way is chosen is not a politically neutral decision that can be made solely on efficiency grounds. Consequently, political decision makers need to know the means simultaneously with the ends they are considering.

Finally, it might be noted that routinely listing objectives for every activity in government cannot easily be carried out. Even the Office of Management and Budget's circular on ZBB, which gives the example of the construction of new mental health institutions across the country, did not succeed at stating a policy objective for the activity. Rather, the OMB circular focuses on the building of alternative numbers of institutions as the budget choice, leaving completely open the question of whether these entities are good public policy or not. As has been shown, a routine that requires objective lists often ends up merely recording outputs of government (more of this, more of that) rather than stating the supposed purpose for these activities.

CONGRESSIONAL BUDGET REFORM

The legislature remained mostly immune to the centralization and management movements and the rational-comprehensive reforms taking place in the administrative branch. The institutional structure of Congress depended upon a patchwork of political fiefs centered around certain powerful committee chairmen. The House Ways and Means Committee controlled revenues, and the Appropriations Committee exercised dominance over expenditures. However, the Appropriations Committee devolved into several subcommittees whose chairmen held the keys to the budgetary treasure chest. The number and focus of these subcommittees did not correspond to any coordinated assessment of related government functions; rather, they reflected the political interests and power of members of the committees.

This feudal structure gave rise to periodic interest in congressional budget reform. A typical budget reform, proposed by Arthur Smithies in 1955, decries the fragmented patchwork of budget committees in Congress. His remedy was to create a Joint (Congressional) Budget Policy Committee which would be empowered to consider all revenue and expenditure proposals at a single time. The Committee would have the authority to pass a joint budget resolution that would be binding for the other members of the legislature. As Wildavsky emphasizes, Smithies presented this reform as "a moderate proposal to improve the rationality of the budgetary process."[35]

The real political implications of such a proposal, however, are far from moderate. Such a powerful budget super-committee would constitute a cabinet government that could defy the president's budgetary programs. This example, and the assessment of it, leads Wildavsky to conclude that the most direct way to change budgeting is to "introduce basic political changes."[36] He suggests giving the president more powers to control the votes in the legislature; or allowing a small minority of congressmen to control the votes of other members of the legislature. A second conclusion is that every real change in the budgetary process will also produce changes in the political process, and hence in who has influence in the legislature. Changes in influence, in turn, lead to changes in budget outcomes. Budget reform is, therefore, not just a matter of decision-making rationality, but inherently involves political value changes and conflict.

The 1974 Budget and Impoundment Control Act

In the 1960s, efforts by liberal presidents to promulgate new domestic spending programs ran afoul of the vested interests of the powerful committee chairmen. Two forms of resistance emerged against the president's programs: a conservative fiscal interest, represented by Wilbur Mills and the Ways and Means Committee, which insisted upon tax increases *and* budget cuts; and an organized interest-group alliance with the appropriations subcommittees, which wanted to maintain spending patterns in the areas under their jurisdiction. This latter resistance developed because the congressional appropriations structure tended to reinforce the subgovernment alliances that emerged during the passage of new legislation. Although the appropriations subcommittees took a more conservative fiscal stance than the authorizing committees, close ties did develop between the appropriations subcommittee chairmen and especially favored programs affecting their districts. Subcommittee chairmen also used their budget positions to build policy reputations in the Congress and often became identified with certain programs as the legislative initiators. With relatively continual economic growth during much of this period, conflict over the committee fiefdoms remained manageable.[37]

By the late 1960s, and especially in the 1970s, several developments led to the breakdown of this stable, incremental budgetary system. The most important development was the abuse of executive budget power by the Nixon administration.[38] Impoundments, budget ceilings, and budget transfers worked to undermine Congress' budget authority. A second factor was the growing institutional rivalry between the Ways and Means Committee, the appropriations subcommittees, and the authorizing committees. Each of these committees brought a different set of interests to the budget process and each was engaged in trying to expand its own interests by gaining control over larger areas of expenditure.[39]

The authorizing committees sought to greatly reduce the number of permanent budget authorizations, thus forcing agencies to seek re-authorization on a multi-year or even an annual basis. These committees also tried to write budget requirements into authorizations, thereby tying the hands of the appropriations subcommittees. By the late 1970s, Schick and Wildavsky report that budget authorizations were running around 40 percent above the budget appropriations for the same agency programs. In addition, nearly 10–15 percent of the total budget, including the State Department, Justice Department, and numerous defense agencies, faced annual authorization requirements for their budgets.

The Ways and Means Committee expanded its jurisdiction through the "back door." Loan guarantees, entitlements, and tax expenditures fell within its purview, and these aspects of the budget were growing by giant leaps during this period. Entitlements, in particular, held certain advantages for those who wanted to increase their spending jurisdiction. To alter entitlement amounts requires a change in the law, making cutbacks much more difficult to achieve. Entitlement growth also followed demographic changes in the society. An expanding population plus inflation ensured spending and program growth. Schick estimates that by the time of the 1974 Budget and Impoundment Control Act, over 70 percent of the budget fell into the "uncontrollable" category of expenditure; that is, those areas requiring legislative as opposed to appropriation decisions in order to effect change.[40] The once all-powerful appropriations subcommittees found themselves overseeing an increasingly smaller proportion of the federal budget.

The internal rivalry for jurisdiction and power left the Congress weakened in its struggle with the Nixon administration over control of the budget. The Congress possessed no analytical capacity to challenge the president's estimates or to propose an alternative set of budget totals. The wide use of impoundment by the Nixon administration abnegated the decisions of Congress that ran counter to the administration's preferences.

The Congress responded to this situation by passing the 1974 Budget and Impoundment Control Act. The congressional forces arrayed against the Nixon administration's budget practices transgressed partisan and institutional lines. Liberals opposed the president because of his spending cuts; conservatives opposed him because of his intrusion on Congress' prerogatives with the budget. Each of the institutional power centers also opposed the president, and each center was needed for a successful passage of reform legislation. Thus, budget reform could not be used

to severely attack the interests of any of the finance, budget, or legislative committees. Their interests were "grandfathered" into the new process.[41]

The Budget Act established new House and Senate budget committees that
would be responsible for broad functional and policy dimensions of a unified
congressional budget. Assignments to these committees would be in addition to the
other assignments of congressmen and were not perceived as the basis for a legislative career. The reformers also established the nonpartisan Congressional Budget
Office (CBO) to produce projections and fiscal analyses comparable to those OMB
provided the White House. Finally, the reform set up a budget timetable to reconcile the broad budget targets established by the budget committees with the decentralized appropriations and authorizations procedures of the subcommittees. (See
Table 11-1.) In the initial versions of the timetable, the first Budget Resolution in
May was to have had the authority of a budget ceiling; but in the wider congressional negotiations, the first resolution was reduced in importance to merely a
recommended set of functional totals. The appropriations and other committees
still could build the budget in their own way.

Besides these internal legislative changes, the Act also included a separate
section on dealing with the executive. This section addressed the impoundment
problem by distinguishing between recisions and deferrals and by making the former
action dependent on congressional approval. The data presented to the Congress by
the executive had to include several new features that enhanced policy analysis and
long-range planning. These are as follows:

1. a statement of current tax expenditures, including revenue lost;
2. five-year projections of future proposed spending;
3. spending projections for new presidential legislative proposals;

TABLE 11-1   Congressional Budget Timetable

Late January: President submits budget (15 days after Congress convenes).

March 15: All legislative committees submit program estimates and reviews to budget committees.

April 15: Budget committees report first resolution.

May 15: Deadline for receipt of authorization bills from committees.

May 15: Congress completes action on first resolution. Before adoption of the first resolution,
neither house may consider new budget authority or spending authority bills, revenue
changes, or debt limit changes.

May 15 through the seventh day after Labor Day: Congress completes action on all budget
and spending authority bills.

September 15: Congress completes action on second resolution. Thereafter, neither house
may consider any bill, amendment, or conference report that results in an increase over
outlay or budget authority figures, or a reduction in revenues, beyond the amounts in the
second resolution.

September 25: Congress completes action on the reconciliation bill or another resolution.
Congress may not adjourn until it completes action on the second resolution and reconciliation measure, if any.

October 1: Fiscal year begins.

4. budget figures formatted by national goals, agency missions, and federal programs; and

5. a one-year lead time for authorization requests prior to appropriation legislation.[42]

The loss of budget authority to the Nixon administration led Congress belatedly to copy in legislative guise the major features of the executive budget reforms of the twentieth century. The budget committees would take responsibility for the main policy direction and planning of the unified budget; the appropriations and authorization committees would play the role of the budget examiners in OMB; and the CBO would adopt the part of the fiscal, economic, and forecasting functions of the Council of Economic Advisors (CEA) and the OMB. The reform attempted to make congressional budgeting more analytical, rational, and comprehensive.

The CBO has proven to be a high-quality, reliable fiscal agency that significantly enhances the analytical power of the Congress to deal with the executive's budget and economic projections and assumptions. The new budget committees, and especially the Senate Budget Committee, faced institutional challenges to their operation which they successfully overcame. In addition, the provisions restricting the initiation of new entitlement programs has had the desired effect. Most of the growth in entitlement spending since 1976 has occurred because of program expansion in already existing titles.

By the time of the Reagan administration, however, it had become apparent that the new procedures did not alter the underlying manner in which Congress makes the budget. The First Resolution increasingly had little impact on budget decisions, and the Second Resolution merely reflected the totals built up in the committee decision process over the summer. Economic growth slowed somewhat, while spending continued to escalate; deficits grew larger, and conflict over distributing the smaller pie grew sharper. By the 1980s, Congress typically could not find the consensus to pass the budget on time nor stick to its budget timetable. The current services budget, which was supposed to be Congress' "base" for making comparisons with the president's proposals, in reality became the "continuing resolution" by which Congress allowed executive agencies to continue spending even though a new budget had not yet passed.

The Reform of the Committee System

During the same period that reformers sought to rationalize the congressional budget process in response to the challenge of the Nixon administration, congressmen continued to face individual electoral pressures to provide local constituency benefits. These contrary pressures produced a sort of congressional schizophrenia: Members of Congress sought to reinforce the comprehensive and unified features of the Budget Act to gain control over totals, yet at the same time they sought to strengthen the decentralized benefits of the subcommittee system, which worked to undermine the control of totals.

The most significant changes occurred in the structure of the committee system in Congress and in the procedures and norms for appointment and advancement in committee membership. The 1971 Subcommittee Bill of Rights gave the subcommittees much greater independence from their parent committees by not allowing committee chairmen to choose the subcommittee chairmen. Seniority would no longer determine who would dominate the committees. The large influx of new democratic congressmen in 1974–76, following the Watergate affair, further reinforced this trend toward democratization of power among numerous subcommittees populated with newer members. Between 1965 and 1973, the number of subcommittees had grown from 113 to 125; by 1975, the number had climbed to 151.[43] Each subcommittee also enlarged its staff and came to exist much more independently of the parent committee. In the House in 1973, one of every two democrats chaired a subcommittee, and in the Senate, each democrat chaired an average of two subcommittees.

Ken Shepsle has written that these decentralizing developments have worked to reinforce the "tugs of geography and jurisdiction" that dominate budget decision making in the Congress.[44] Congressmen find themselves in the situation that they must support increased spending for their district in order to be assured of reelection next time around, yet the collective consequence of this myriad of small decisions is a lack of overall budget control and planning. The congressmen are caught in a "prisoners' dilemma" in that all would be better off if they could cooperate to control overall spending, but each member asks why he should be the one to sacrifice, when the other members benefit from his restraint. Consequently, each member "defects" from the overall cooperative solution of responsible budgeting in favor of assuring his own reelection at home. The result is an inability to make responsible budget decisions.

In his initial budget, President Reagan attempted to exploit this decentralized decision making in Congress to his own advantage. He effectively worked with the Republican party caucus and leadership to enforce the First Budget Resolution as a budget ceiling for all the detailed appropriations accounts. Instead of reconciling the totals to the details, he sought to reconcile the details to the prearranged totals. For the first year, this strategy proved surprisingly successful. The more atomized decision making in Congress made the problem of coalition building more open and fluid. A strong and popular president could lead a budget coalition to victory; the old committee seniority no longer stood in resistance. As Jacobson agrees, "The Congress, as it now operates, *can* be led."[45]

The problem is that this leadership is not institutionalized in any sense. Coalitions of decentralized players are enormously unstable. President Reagan's initial victory did not last very long and he has been unable to reconstruct a majority budget coalition. His 1985–86 strategy is quite different. He makes no attempt to interfere directly in the congressional budget process, nor does he work closely with the Republican congressional leadership. Rather, he has so structured his proposals that an effective congressional response requires the "single super budget committee" to actually make an alternative budget package. The Reagan budget arrives in Congress with giant-sized deficits, further drastic cuts in domestic spending, and large, real increases for defense. His strategy is to "hang tough" on defense, relying on Congress's disinclination to raise taxes significantly. The only meaningful role for the budget committees, therefore, is to try to cut the domestic part of the budget, or to accept the outsized deficits—something that most congressmen feel is politically dangerous.[46]

The plight of Congress over the budget in the 1980s reveals that the more significant "budget reform" of the 1970s was not the 1974 Budget Act: Instead, the decentralization of the committee structure; the diffusion of the budget to entitlements, loan accounts, tax expenditures, and other uncontrollable spending; and the demise of the power of the appropriations committees constitute the more important budget "reform." This is not to say that the CBO and other features of the 1974 reform have had no impact. While these features provided more and better information on which to make comprehensive budget decisions, they did not alter the underlying individual and institutional incentives for making budgets. Even though the parts have changed, they still dominate the whole.

BUDGET REFORM AND AMERICAN POLITICS

Budget reform has had an illustrious history in the United States. Many significant innovations came out of the New York Bureau of Municipal Research as well as other institutions of the Progressive era. In addition, the scientific management movement, by including budgeting in general management functions, made budgeting an integral feature of the modern presidency. Accounting procedures, coordination, program evaluation, and budget control have all benefited from the reform tradition.

In the postwar era, however, the striving to produce the ultimate, ideal system that would tie all the components together in one grand design revealed the limitations and contradictions of the reform approach. While the reform tradition savored accountability and especially efficiency, it ignored power. Centralized coordination of the budget requires knowledge, but it also requires the organizational and political incentives to sustain central control. However, who is to say that this central power will be used for benign ends? Decentralized access to the budget devolves power to numerous and diffuse interests most affected by government spending. Under this kind of system, the budget totals and their effect on the general welfare no longer remain accountable to anyone.

A way of stating this in general terms is that power conflicts with accountability. Giving a single committee in Congress the power to decide revenues and expenditures in a binding fashion achieves the coordinated macro-budget so desired by rationalists, but this same concentration of power imposes a particular political will on all others. Conversely, the democratizing decentralization of budget power in Congress today allows for innumerable points of access for almost every conceivable interest. Each budget subsidy has its subcommittee that generates organized interests in that arena, so the power to make collective decisions to control the budget is diminished. Similarly, the concentration of budget power in the White House is what the reform tradition had sought. However, when Nixon seemed close to achieving the "administrative presidency," the public administrationists, who for several years prior had been its main advocates, now learned to fear what they had wrought.[47]

Why Are Budget Reforms Implemented?

Given the limitations of the classical approach to budget reform, why have so many governments persisted with reform efforts? In other words, if the reform model doesn't work, why is it so popular?

One reason for budget reform is the political benefit of looking rational.[48] Politicians such as Jimmy Carter can campaign on the basis of introducing new,

rational budget procedures, and thereby controlling bureaucratic sprawl and inefficiency. However, politicians often stay on the national scene for only a relatively
short period of time, which means that they gain the short-term political benefits of
a fancy new procedure, but have left office by the time the costs start to mount up.
Supporting the latest new budget technique, therefore, is good partisan politics and
helps to increase the legitimacy of the new administration to the populace.

A second political reason for adopting these techniques is to give respectability
to something you want to do for other reasons. A state government, for example,
that needs to cut the budget because of severe economic conditions is tempted to
adopt Zero-Base Budgeting as a rationalization for asking for cuts. ZBB makes the
process seem like it is not a political choice, but rather a matter of a new
technique—how can anyone argue with a scientific method that will make government operate more efficiently? This kind of ploy also throws the permanent agency
officials off guard temporarily, which gives an advantage to the budget office and the
political officers who want to cut programs.

The rapid turnover among top political executives means that they are often
not the ones to bear the costs of implementing and coping with the ultimate failure
of a new reform technique. The benefits to top executives materialize quickly, since
they are largely symbolic in nature; the costs affect others much later. In addition, it
is time consuming and difficult to actually measure the supposed benefits of a new
procedure. The results are often ambiguous, especially with regard to the expected
budget savings and greater policy effectiveness. Rapid turnover among top executives may mean, therefore, that very little substantive learning takes place. Even
useful knowledge about what doesn't work may be lost.

The prestige of the federal government also induces many budget reforms to
spread nationwide. If top executives had initially introduced these reforms for political and symbolic reasons, the routine application of the new procedures to
thousands of political jurisdictions across the country entails the loss of this political
advantage but the increased likelihood of efficiency costs.

Finally, administrative reform is difficult because it is harder to think about
the rationality of decision procedures than it is to think about the rationality of
substantive government programs. Altering administrative procedures is much like
writing a new constitution—both involve the selection of rules to govern the activities of government over a long period of time. The rules must accommodate
changes in technology, political ideology and power, and demographics. The altering of budgetary rules, while certainly not as broad as constitution writing, seems to
be extremely complex, if one judges from the checkered history of budget reform in
the U.S. and elsewhere.

Rationality and Budget Reform

Many people still cling to the idea that the set of steps—define objectives,
consider alternatives, evaluate the alternatives, and choose the best alternative—is
the most rational way to approach budget and other administrative problems.
Budget reform is based on this kind of deductive rationality. Given a set of objectives, a closed and known set of alternatives, complete information regarding their
consequences, and criteria for choosing among them, the choice is deductive; that
is, in a logical sense, the premises imply the conclusion. Decision making of this

form is very much like the solving of an algebraic equation—given certain assumptions and the rules of algebra, the solution is a matter of computation.

Some problems are amenable to this reform view of rationality, especially those in which goals can be specified and outputs objectively measured, and in which it makes sense to speak of maximization. However, many other problems are not amenable to this approach. These are problems in which goals and success or failure are ambiguous or in conflict, in which outcomes are unclear, and in which causality of events is difficult to untangle.[49]

Public budgeters are both too dumb and too smart to approach ill-structured problems in the classical manner because (1) they can't do what is called for, and (2) they use another mode of thought that is more inductive in character. Budgeters rely on pattern finding and experiential and historical analogies to make sense of conflicting and ambiguous stimuli. They behave, in many respects, like Herbert Simon's description of master chess players who "recognize" the current game situation by comparing it to the thousands of game situations they have in their memory. In effect, the chess players make an analogy between the current game and other games they have played. Budgeters rely on the context, comparisons with a historical base amount (generally last year's budget), and particular problem areas.

Second, public budgeters are in a political situation which does not allow them the time nor the freedom to comprehensively explore all alternatives and to set objectives precisely. Other actors control different dimensions of the budget process and the interaction among the participants is what determines the final outcome. Hence, a kind of strategic rationality, similar to that found in competitive board games, dominates the thinking and calculations of players. Information is not something freely divulged, and when it is available, it will be used as part of a partisan discussion of the budget. The rules of budget procedure, therefore, must take into account the kinds of power plays the rules foster—not a particularly easy thing to figure out or agree upon.

The open-ended, political nature of the budget process makes simple, deterministic procedures unworkable. The problem is, what kind of reform works better? Unfortunately, there are no recipelike answers to this question. A couple of guidelines, however, need to be emphasized.

First of all, any budget reform must address the political and organizational incentives of the participants. For example, if participants are caught in a prisoners' dilemma over agreeing on responsible total amounts for spending due to the decentralization of committee decisions, then some form of centralization is called for. This does not mean that everything in the budget process must be centralized or placed in a hierarchy. In fact, specialization through decentralization is a highly valuable strength of the current system. Generally, these choices of organizational incentives will entail trade-offs. Centralization may favor one value, decentralization another. The most direct way to change budgeting, therefore, is to change the political decision process.

Better information alone will not suffice to improve budgeting. Without coupling information with incentives to use it, information may be ignored or even get in the way of good decisions. This latter possibility is real because information generated outside of political constraints often tends to be too comprehensive to be of much value. An example is the planning phase in the Defense Department discussed earlier. In budgeting terms, this guideline means that reform should emphasize the simultaneous character of planning and budget decisions; yet the "knapsack" and incremental-ranking illustrations demonstrate that working with budget constraints often makes the procedures of the rational model unworkable, even assuming complete information and perfect measurement. Thus, analysis and information must be seen as supplements to, not substitutes for, the political decision process.

Aside from political incentives, reformers should recognize the inductive character of government decisions. Reform has attempted to apply rational logic to decision making by standardizing and routinizing procedures in systems of bureaucratic control. While setting a few salient objectives makes sense for an organization, routinely requiring a "laundry list" of objectives from all corners of the organization on a yearly basis invites red tape. Similarly, doing a zero-base review of certain programs at intermittent intervals is wise management, but routinely requiring zero-base reviews every years brings cynicism and superficial data. Reforms should aid calculation, not overwhelm it.

For these reasons, many of the deficiencies of bureaucratic hierarchy manifest themselves in budget reforms. However, budget reform is not the only area of government administration in which the classical bureaucratic model has dominated thinking. As we will explore in the next chapter, the conceptualization and reform of personnel have also followed the classical tradition.

NOTES

[1]AARON WILDAVSKY, *The Politics of the Budgetary Process*, 3rd ed. (Boston: Little, Brown & Co., 1979), p. 127.

[2]THOMAS D. LYNCH, "Federal Budgetary Madness," *Society*, 20 (1983), pp. 11–15; Naomi Caiden, "The Myth of the Annual Budget," *Public Administration Review*, 42 (1982), pp. 516–523.

[3]MARK F. CANCIAN, "PPBS: Rude Awakening," *Proceedings* (Annapolis: United States Naval Institute, 1984).

[4]ALLAN SCHICK, *Budget Innovation in the States* (Washington: The Brookings Institution, 1971), p. 17.

[5]SCHICK, *Budget Innovation*, p. 16.

[6]SCHICK, *Budget Innovation*, p. 20.

[7]SCHICK, *Budget Innovation*, p. 21.

[8]LARRY BERMAN, *The Office of Management and Budget and the Presidency, 1921–1979* (Princeton: Princeton University Press, 1979), p. 6.

[9]SCHICK, *Budget Innovation*, p. 29.

[10]JOHN A. FEREJOHN, *Pork Barrel Politics* (Palo Alto: Stanford University Press, 1975), pp. 28–29.

[11]SCHICK, *Budget Innovation*, p. 33.

[12]PETER A. PHYRR, *Zero-Base Budgeting: A Practical Management Tool for Evaluating Expenses* (New York: John Wiley & Sons, 1973).

[13]CHARLES HITCH and ROLAND McKEAN, *The Economics of Defense in the Nuclear Age* (Cambridge: Harvard University Press, 1961).

[14]This is a statement taken from the RAND corporation and quoted in Aaron Wildavsky, "The Political Economy of Efficiency: Cost-Benefit Analysis, Systems Analysis, and Program Budgeting," *Public Administration Review*, 26 (1966), p. 302.

[15]SCHICK, *Budget Innovation*, p. 31.

[16]U.S. Bureau of the Budget memo.

[17]AARON WILDAVSKY and ARTHUR HAMMANN, "Comprehensive versus Incremental Budgeting in the Department of Agriculture," *Administrative Science Quarterly*, 10 (1964), pp. 321–346.

[18]HITCH AND McKEAN, *Economics*.

[19]CANCIAN, "PPBS," p. 44.

[20]THOMAS H. HAMMOND and JACK H. KNOTT, *A Zero-Based Look at Zero-Base Budgeting* (New Brunswick: Transaction Books, 1981), pp. 33–35.

[21]This is also a criticism made by the Senate Staff Report on defense organization. See "Defense Organization: The Need for Change," *Staff Report to the Committee on Armed Services, United States Senate,* (Washington, D.C.: U.S. Government Printing Office, 1985), p. 499.

[22]CANCIAN, "PPBS," p. 46.

[23]CANCIAN, "PPBS," p. 48.

[24]CANCIAN, "PPBS," p. 52.

[25]Senate Staff Report, "Defense Organization," pp. 496 and 507.

[26]CANCIAN, "PPBS," p. 52.

[27]HAMMOND and KNOTT, *A Zero-Based Look,* pp. 53–54.

[28]JACK HIRSCHLEIFER, *Investment Interest and Capital* (Englewood Cliffs: Prentice-Hall, 1970), p. 47.

[29]HITCH and McKEAN, *Economics,* p. 53.

[30]For a formal analysis of this problem, see Hammond and Knott, *A Zero-Based Look,* pp. 111–114.

[31]HAMMOND and KNOTT, *A Zero-Based Look,* p. 49.

[32]ALLAN SCHICK, "Zero-Base Budgeting and Sunset: Redundancy or Symbiosis," *The Bureaucrat,* 6 (1977), pp. 12–32.

[33]JOHN D. LAFAVER, "Zero-Base Budgeting in New Mexico," *State Government,* 47 (1974), pp. 108–112.

[34]HAMMOND and KNOTT, *A Zero-Based Look,* p. 38.

[35]WILDAVSKY, *Politics,* 4th ed., p. 133.

[36]WILDAVSKY, *Politics,* 4th ed., p. 132.

[37]JACK KNOTT, "Political Theory and Budget Reform," *Society,* 20 (1983), pp. 27–32.

[38]LOUIS FISHER, *Presidential Spending Power* (Princeton: Princeton University Press, 1975), pp. 175–226.

[39]ALLEN SCHICK, *Congress and Money* (Washington: The Urban Institute, 1980), pp. 17–49.

[40]SCHICK, *Congress,* p. 27.

[41]SCHICK, *Congress,* pp. 78–89.

[42]THOMAS D. LYNCH, *Public Budgeting in America* (Englewood Cliffs, NJ: Prentice-Hall, 1979), pp. 37–38.

[43]GARY C. JACOBSON, *The Politics of Congressional Elections* (Boston: Little, Brown, 1983); and Morris P. Fiorina, *Congress: Keystone of the Washington Establishment* (New Haven: Yale University Press, 1977).

[44]KENNETH A. SHEPSLE, "The Failure of Congressional Budgeting," *Society,* 20 (1983), pp. 4–10.

[45]JACOBSON, *Congressional Elections,* p. 182.

[46]*National Journal,* February 9, 1985.

[47]RICHARD P. NATHAN, "The Administrative Presidency," *The Public Interest,* 44 (1976), pp. 40–54.

[48]HAMMOND and KNOTT, *A Zero-Based Look,* p. 102.

[49]JAMES G. MARCH and JOHANN P. OLSEN, "The Uncertainty of the Past: Organizational Learning Under Uncertainty," *European Journal of Political Research,* 3 (1975), pp. 147–171.

CHAPTER 12

The Quest for
Neutral Competence:
Personnel Reform

Thus began the quest for neutral competence in government officials. . . . The core value of this search was ability to do the work of government expertly, and to do it according to explicit, objective standards rather than to personal or party or other obligations and loyalties. The slogan of the neutral competence school became, "Take administration out of politics."

Herbert Kaufman, "Emerging Conflicts"[1]

Personnel administration has served as a target for reform from the nineteenth century until the present. Throughout this reform history, reformers sought to reduce or even eliminate completely the influence of political parties on the personnel practices of all three levels of government. Reformers since the Progressives, in addition, have tried to replace the party-based system with bureaucratic civil service procedures that supposedly incorporated "scientific" personnel practices. In a strictly formal sense, the reformers achieved these goals. The vast majority of employees in government are not appointed by political parties, but are covered by standardized civil service procedures.

Throughout this period, reformers did make one significant, positive contribution. They recognized that political loyalty alone is not sufficient to guarantee successful, democratic government. The Progressives, in particular, realized that the government sorely needs competence and expertise, especially in technical fields such as health or engineering. Today, for example, one would be hard pressed to find anyone who would not support the employment of highly qualified biologists in the Food and Drug Administration. Government pursues policies in numerous, very technical fields that demand qualified experts, and the personnel reforms of the Progressives made it possible to find, hire, and retain these experts.

Nonetheless, personnel reform has had a checkered history, and dissatisfaction with personnel procedures has continued over the years. By the administration of Jimmy Carter, the general perception among personnel experts as well as among many political leaders was that the personnel system required a major overhaul.

The rhetoric for this more recent reform sounded very much like the rhetoric at the turn of the century: Employee incompetence, political manipulations, and corruption require a renewed commitment to "neutral competence."

We wonder, however, why a greater commitment to the orthodox principles of neutral competence will be any more successful in the next seventy years than it has been in the past seventy years. Perhaps what is needed is a change of direction, rather than renewed commitment to the orthodoxy of neutral competence.

We will argue in this chapter that, while the reformers made a positive contribution, they also committed two serious errors. The most fundamental error has been the belief that it is possible to create a neutral, nonpolitical administration based solely on expertise and professionalism. This approach to personnel omits important social and political variables from administrative practice. Second, the premise of neutrality led the Progressives to adopt a "scientific" view of personnel management which assumes a technically based body of knowledge for managing personnel relations. In point of fact, no such technical body of knowledge exists, which makes personnel science a kind of pseudoscience which serves as a mask for other, real social and political purposes.

To date, the continued dissatisfaction with personnel reform has yet to provide the basis for any systematic challenge to orthodox principles of personnel administration. The various calls for "reform" of the civil service are, for the most part, calls made in the spirit, if not the original letter, of the orthodox doctrine of reform. Recent reform proposals have continued to insist on political neutrality for all but the upper-level positions, efficiency as the primary goal of personnel administration, and objective standards of merit evaluation. In 1971, the foremost student of public personnel administration claimed that "What is really needed is a PPBS-type analysis of public personnel practices in terms of their long-range costs and benefits towards government objectives."[2] This illustrates the continued desire to replace politics with more technical, rationalistic analysis.

The foremost recent reform attempts have not charged that the orthodox reform model is wrong, but that the practice of civil service administation has never completely fulfilled or deviated from the orthodox norm of scientific, neutral competence. In personnel administration, the intellectual heritage of the reform tradition stands as accepted doctrine, a doctrine that fails to have any well-developed competitors.

ORIGINS OF PERSONNEL REFORM

Nineteenth Century Reform

To the reformers of the nineteenth century, moral outrage over the corruption and patronage abuses of the political machines served as the primary impetus for change. They wanted to depoliticize the government service by reducing the tie between employment and party affiliation. Their strategy for achieving this goal was for people entering the civil service to take a competitive examination; only those with the highest scores would receive employment. The reformers wanted promotion to depend on merit and competency, not political affiliation. Agencies were expected to hire employees at the lowest grades and then promote them to higher positions from within the service. Employees were expected to use "neutral competence" in the performance of their duties.

This concept of depoliticization was first officially recognized in the Grant administration. On the last day of the session for the Forty-first Congress, Senator Lyman Trumbull attached a rider to an unrelated appropriations bill that gave the president the power to establish civil service procedures. The recent exposés of corruption in Boss Tweed's New York political machine had stirred the necessary votes to pass the bill with the rider. The bill was conceived as a weak gesture to the reformers, but to everyone's surprise, President Grant went ahead and appointed a Civil Service Commission.[3]

Once Congress realized that the president meant to proceed with civil service reform, the Congress abruptly cut off appropriations for the newly-formed commission. By 1875, the Commission no longer existed, but the policies it had begun to enact remain to the present day as accepted practices in personnel management. The Commission, for example, instituted the "rule of three" (meaning the Commission must have at least three members), the policy of restricting lateral entry, and the practice of promotion only from within the service through competitive examination.

In the decade after 1875, further impetus for civil service reform came from the examples of Great Britain and Germany. The latter country had just achieved imperial unification and used civil service laws to promote a standardized bureaucracy. In Britain, civil service laws hastened the decline of the aristocracy's influence over the bureaucracy and strengthened the link between the rising national leadership of the political parties, the newly enfranchised commercial classes, and the university intellectuals. In both cases, civil service reform furthered the interests and power of the dominant political forces in the country.[4]

The American reform setting differed significantly. Leading proponents of the reform included the clergy, professionals, lawyers, academics, and journalists who formed a reform coalition much like the single-issue public interest groups of today. Business interests halfheartedly supported the reform for the sake of efficiency, but showed wariness of the potential for an independent and powerful bureaucracy. Unlike Britain or West Germany, the American political parties only reluctantly and sporadically supported personnel reform in the nineteenth century. Government employment as a form of payoff for partisan loyalty had grown into a way of life for American political parties. Unlike their European counterparts, these parties represented loose coalitions of local interests that controlled election to the Congress as the primary mode of influence over national policy. The president often acted as the "manager" of these loose coalitions, and found himself trying to make bargains between southern interests, reform interests, and the urban political machines.[5] The civil service reform movement thus constituted a single-issue campaign of independents inimical to these core interests of the political parties.

In this highly partisan setting, civil service legislation passed because of electoral competition rather than through agreement on the need for a neutral civil service. By 1882, the electoral prospects of the Republican party looked dim. The party seized on the notion of promoting civil service reform both as a way of freezing their supporters in office, as well as taking the political wind out of the Democrats' reform sails. The final bill reflected the political compromises needed for passage. Passed in 1883, the Pendleton Act established an independent, nonpartisan body called the Civil Service Commission (CSC) to oversee a merit-based personnel system. The Act included geographic representation to appease the South, rejected the principle of appointing people only at the lowest grades, appointed only three members to the Civil Service Commission (the Grant administration's Commission had five members), and made their appointments subject to approval by the Senate.

As Stephen Skowronek argues, the "merit system was born a bastard in the party state. The support it had gained among the party professionals was that of another weapon in the contest for party power."[6] Between 1884 and 1900, the number of federal positions under the civil service rules rose from 11 percent to 46 percent. The president and the Congress had control over expanding or contracting these figures, which fluctuated with the electoral prospects of the party in power. By 1900, the federal service had grown in numbers from 113,000 persons to almost 210,000, with over 100,000 positions still available for party patronage.

The Progressives

After 1900, the Progressive reformers took up the banner of civil service reform, but they wanted more than depoliticization of personnel administration. Unlike the reformers of the previous century, they worked for greater efficiency and productivity in the public service through the application of scientific management principles in government. A fascinating example of this progressive preoccupation with the science of personnel management is given in Robert Caro's account of Robert Moses' proposal for reform of the New York City civil service system:

> All government service could be divided into sixteen categories. . . . Each category could be divided into specific jobs. . . . Each job could be scientifically analyzed to show its "functions" and "responsibilities." Each function and responsibility—and there were dozens of them for most jobs—could be given a precise mathematical weight corresponding to its importance in the over-all job. And the success of the employee in each function and responsibility could be given a precise mathematical grade. These grades would, added together according to weight and combined in service records for each employee, "furnish conclusions expressed in arithmetical . . . terms" and these conclusions and these alone should be "used as a basis for salary increase and promotion."[7]

While today Moses' proposals appear as almost a parody of scientific management in government, during the Progressive era public administrationists had great optimism that such a science could succeed. Moses, for example, studied public administration at Oxford, England, and also at the New York Bureau of Municipal Research. His civil service reform proposals for New York City derived from his Ph.D. thesis at Oxford, entitled "The Civil Service of Great Britain." One person who had read the thesis was H. Elliot Kaplan, later the president of the New York Civil Service Commission and executive director of the Civil Service Reform Association. Kaplan evaluated the thesis some years later by simply remarking, "It was a masterpiece." He added, "There were very few people in the United States in 1914 who knew much about civil service. Bob Moses really knew."[8]

While Moses' proposals were rebuffed by the New York machine, elements of a science of personnel management began creeping into government. These elements included standardization of position classifications for all employees, the relating of examinations to job requirements, and the embedding of rank in positions rather than in people. In the following years, this quest for a science of personnel management has characterized the civil service at all three levels of government. If the civil service in actuality did not correspond to this ideal, the fault seemed to always be placed on "politics."

The Progressive era also witnessed a growing conflict over who controlled the new civil service system. By the time of the Wilson administration, the contest for control of civil service wavered back and forth between the president and the Congress. To the extent that a president needed the reformers to hold his coalition together, he pushed for further reform extensions. Skowronek maintains that Woodrow Wilson, for example, faced considerable political opposition in Congress, both to his civil service ideas and his substantive policy program. Despite his avowed support of a strong central administration that would control the civil service system, Wilson gave up this control in favor of political support in Congress for his legislative policy program, called the New Freedom.[9]

It was left to the Harding administration in 1921 to attempt to reassert some presidential control over civil administration with the passage of the Budget and Accounting Act. This Act established the Bureau of the Budget (BOB) and the General Accounting Office (GAO) as well as made several changes in the personnel system. The GAO and the independent Bureau of Efficiency (a separate oversight body of the civil service created by Congress) responded to congressional prerogatives, while the BOB and the CSC seemed closer to presidential control. Thus, the consolidation of civil service reform during the Progressive era carried with it growing institutional politics.

Post-Progressive/New Deal Reform

Much of the patronage efforts of the political parties centered on local political interests that did not coincide with presidential policy concerns. Patronage did not offer the president administrative or political control over his administration; it had the contrary effect of strengthening ties of the administration to Congress and state and local political interests. Thus, until the time of Franklin Roosevelt, presidents saw the advance of neutral competence in the civil service as a means of gaining more control over administration. Theodore Roosevelt, for example, made bold efforts to dominate the Civil Service Commission.

Teddy Roosevelt and Woodrow Wilson did not achieve their goals of centralized control over the civil service. Not until the first term of Franklin Roosevelt did the various functions of personnel management become consolidated under a centralized commission. Prior to this time, the commission's main function had been the policing of spoils and nonpolitical hirings. Position classification, efficiency ratings, and retirement programs were administered in other agencies. In addition, the various dimensions of employee relations did not come under the Commission's purview. By 1934, however, the Commission had received new authority to carry out these various functions.[10]

The new, consolidated commission, however, faced difficult problems of reconciling its past policing role with the more positive management functions of employee relations and evaluation. This internal tension eventually led to proposals by the President's Committee on Administrative Management (the Brownlow Committee) in 1937 for the establishment of a single personnel manager appointed by and responsible to the president, with a separate administrative board assigned to policing functions. This modern-sounding proposal, however, failed to pass in

Roosevelt's administrative reform, and in fact, did not pass Congress until the 1978
Carter personnel reforms. Instead, the Roosevelt administration went in the opposite direction by decentralizing employee relations, recruitment, evaluation, and
position classification as the responsibility of individual federal agencies. This decentralization eventually led to a questioning of the ambiguous role played by the
Civil Service Commission.

Two other developments took place during the Roosevelt administration that
have had an impact on the Civil Service Commission to this day. One was Executive Order #8802 in 1941, which for the first time established rules concerning
discrimination according to race, religion, and national origin. This order eventually became the basis for further executive orders dealing with equal employment
opportunity. For example, in 1948 President Truman's executive order created the
Fair Employment Board, and the legislation of 1972 for the Equal Employment
Opportunity Act gave authority for this policy to the Civil Service Commission.

Second, in 1944 Congress passed the Veterans Preference Act, which gave
veterans the right to appeal dismissal to the CSC. Prior to the passage of this act,
civil service laws had taken great care in ensuring apolitical hiring of employees, but
the dismissal of employees continued to follow a less standardized format. By 1944,
however, almost 50 percent of federal employees had served in the armed forces;
half the civil servants now had the right to appeal dismissal to the CSC.

Personnel Politics

While civil service reform attacked partisanship in the name of political
neutrality, it really created a new and different kind of personnel politics centered
on institutional rivalries and policy politics. This underlying politics of personnel
administration goes to the heart of the problem of reforming personnel administration today.

The first reform issue today is efficiency. While it is the case that the reduction in partisan patronage increased the competency and efficiency of civil administration, many of the problems remain with us. As we have seen in previous
chapters, the perceived inefficiency of government agencies is partly the fault of
bureaucratic routines and red tape; but it also represents the political power of
public-employee alliances with powerful interest groups and the Congress. These
alliances have supported policy expansion and have promoted professional autonomy from the executive.

Beginning in the Progressive era, public employees over the years developed
political ties to Congress either directly, as with the postal workers, or indirectly
through private contractors, unions, and other powerful interest groups. A similar
development occured at the local level. Public employee unions came to constitute
an important political constituency for many local governments. Seeking efficiency
through neutral competence "created a thrust toward fragmentation of government,
toward the formation of highly independent islands of decision making occupied by
officials who went about their business without much reference to each other or to
other organs of government."[11] Trying to perfect the system of employee autonomy
and supposed neutrality will thus not solve the efficiency problem and may, in fact,
exacerbate it.

Neutrality raises the second question of accountability. The history of obfus-
cation of control over the civil service system, coupled with strong congressional

intrusion into personnel practices of government agencies, leaves the president in a weakened position vis-à-vis the bureaucracy. A significant problem of presidential leadership in the postwar period revolves around efforts to strengthen or weaken executive direction of government employees through the morass of civil service rules and regulations. Similarly, a major complaint of mayors is their inability to influence the decisions and practices of their own administrations. It is no coincidence that every president since Roosevelt has sought to politicize sections of the bureaucracy. Indeed, the Hatch Acts passed by the Congress, which prohibited any partisan political activity by federal employees, may be seen as efforts by local political coalitions to thwart Roosevelt's attempt to try to control the federal bureaucracy through a stronger national party. As Herbert Kaufman has observed, "In forming alliances with legislative committees and clientele groups, [public employees] succeeded in carving out for themselves broad areas of discretion free of real supervision by their political chiefs."[12]

In general, under the banner of neutrality, public employees have striven for political and professional autonomy through public-employee unions, professionalization, and alliances with Congress. The Congress, for its part, has responded to local political coalitions which often include public employees and their supporters—contractors or national professional associations. The president, in contrast, has sought stronger central control of the civil service in order to gain loyalty and direction to his program.

These contests for accountability, neutrality, and efficiency have led to continuous efforts to reform personnel administration. Rather than seeing the underlying political dimension as the cause of the controversy, public administrationists have continued to strive for a neutral and competent service. As Kaufman has shown, however, neutral competence conflicts with the other central administrative values of accountability and executive leadership. Unfortunately, the real question is not one of neutrality—it is which set of institutional structures and rules causes whose policy and political interests to prevail.

STATE AND LOCAL CIVIL SERVICE: THE FALSE SCIENCE OF PERSONNEL MANAGEMENT

A Progressive reformer of the 1910 era would feel quite at home in the personnel systems of our contemporary state and local governments. The civil service laws and regulations in our state governments and in over three-quarters of our cities are known as "merit systems" because they are designed to protect against partisan influence on hiring and other personnel practices, and to assure that the primary requirement for entry into the system is a "merit exam." Local government personnel systems also rely heavily on a standardized classification system for employee positions, standardized pay scales, and standardized procedures for promotion that include written examinations. While no one still proposes to give mathematical weights to the components of employee tasks, the system does adopt the assumption that task performance and task interrelationships are known well enough that standardized procedures may be followed to assign rewards and punishments.

E.S. Savas and Sigmund Ginsburg have undertaken a thorough study of the New York City civil service system.[13] As envisioned by the early civil service reformers, applicants must take written merit examinations to enter the system. Managers must hire those people with the top three scores on the exam. There is no way for partisan politicians to intervene in the hiring process to reward their supporters or to fire opponents, as was the intention of the Progressive reformers. Promotions, too, are made primarily on the basis of merit exams. Jobs are specialized, with a clear, written description of narrow responsibilities and of lines of accountability. All personnel practices are governed by an independent, three-person civil service commission. On the surface, at least, the New York civil service system seems a perfect embodiment of the orthodox vision of civil service.

However, the formalities of a science of personnel cannot hide the realities of numerous social and political variables that impinge on employee performance and distort the actual operation of the system. These variables are not included in the civil service model. In fact, employees in the system have a virtual lifetime guarantee for their jobs. Savas and Ginsburg state, along with many other analysts, that "the system prohibits good management, frustrates able employees, inhibits productivity, lacks the confidence of the city's taxpayers, and fails to respond to the needs of the citizens."[14] In sum, civil service reform has performed in a way that is quite contrary to the original hopes and expectations of the civil service reformers. The reasons for this failure will provide an understanding of why similarly motivated personnel reforms might also be expected to fail.

The Rigidities of Examinations and Classifications

One basic reason for dissatisfaction in personnel systems is that merit examinations often have little to do with on-the-job performance. As Savas and Ginsburg point out, "Not a single case could be found where the validity of a written test— with respect to predicting performance on the job—was even proven." But managers are not allowed, under the rules, to consider previous job performance or special skills when making personnel decisions. They are required to pass up individuals with a good record or the right skills in favor of someone who might have scored only a few thousandths of a point higher on the merit exam.

Furthermore, specialization in job descriptions has resulted in narrow, constraining job definitions for positions such as photostat operators, doorstop maintainers, and foremen of thermostat repairers. Gordon Chase, the former Director of New York's Health Services Administration, concurs that personnel systems rely on "exaggerated, misleading, or irrelevant standard job descriptions."[15] The result of this narrow job definition is that individuals who hold such jobs recognize them as unsatisfying, boring, and unworthy of close attention and care. The orthodox tenets of specialization and written rules have resulted in institutionalizing job dissatisfaction.

The written procedures required of the civil service, along with protests and appeals, mean that often people who are better trained and more marketable have found other jobs by the time the city actually is able to hire someone for a job, often months after the merit exam has been given. Gordon Chase states, "Good people seek nongovernmental opportunities rather than contend with the frustrations of the hiring process."[16] Overall, Savas and Ginsburg found that there was a rough inverse correlation between test scores and hirings; the lower the test score, the larger the number of people hired from that score. The people who score well on exams end up finding other jobs. Savas and Ginsburg therefore charge that the civil service procedures have instituted an inverse merit system, where the least capable people are hired and promoted.

Furthermore, the existence of civil service rules and the independent civil service commission mean that the lines of accountability are nearly severed. Managers in municipal agencies cannot influence pay raises, have little to say about hirings or promotions, and must defer to the head of the civil service commission on all matters of personnel. Understandably, they have little to say, therefore, about the on-the-job performance of their employees.[17] If a manager's employees prefer to spend their time studying for irrelevant civil service promotion exams rather than perfecting job performance, the manager can do little to penalize them, and can hardly even blame them. In other words, civil service rules, examinations, and job specialization have not guaranteed the kind of efficient meritocracy envisioned by the Progressives.

Political Self-Interest

One must ask, as we did in Chapter 10, why has the system been maintained for so long? Who stands to gain by the system, and who protects it?

In some ways, the civil service employees and their unions have found the civil service system quite compatible with their own goals. For example, the civil service regulations require current employees to be considered for promotion before outsiders. This means that outsiders can normally get jobs in the civil service only at the lowest entry levels. Limiting access in this way protects the job security and promotional opportunities of existing employees.

Furthermore, the civil service system has been compatible with the seniority goal of employee organizations. Vacancies are filled from the people in the next lower grade in the same agency, by preference. Individuals who are looking for a promotion can study for and retake the examination, so that promotion on the basis of the examination system looks very much like promotion based on seniority.

It is difficult to argue that the current municipal civil service system in New York City or elsewhere is the ideal one as regards efficiency, accountability, or neutrality; yet it has been maintained because it serves the interests of those who are most concerned with maintaining the system.

Nevertheless, even the most severe critics of the New York civil service, like Savas and Ginsburg, have done little to imagine an alternative model of municipal personnel. Savas and Ginsburg conclude that reform is called for, but their reforms accept the basic orthodoxy of a merit civil service, and do not address the political realities that orthodox reform represented. They say, "A true merit system must be constructed anew, one that provides the opportunity for a qualified citizen to gain access nonpolitically, to be recognized and rewarded for satisfactory performance, and even to be replaced for unsatisfactory service."[18] In other words, we must return to the orthodox ideal, try it one more time, and see if we can really make it work. To make it really work, Savas and Ginsburg make a series of proposals. They argue that "performance appraisals" should be the basis of raises and promotions. Positions should be reevaluated regularly to weed out unnecessary jobs. Written examinations should be replaced in large part by oral examinations.

However, it is not clear why an altered structure, based on performance appraisals or oral exams instead of written exams, would eliminate politics and solve the underlying problem of bureaucratic inefficiency. The reforms Savas and Ginsburg suggest sound much like the personnel system used in the State Department's Foreign Service, which is also criticized for red tape and inefficiency.

Other reforms suggested by Savas and Ginsburg cannot be criticized—for instance, their suggestion that "positions should be evaluated regularly to weed out rampant credentialism." But who is to do the weeding? As long as the distribution of political influence is the same, why should the outcome of such a procedure be any different than it is under the current structure? And if reforms were undertaken to change the distribution of political influence (away from municipal employee unions, for instance), wouldn't those changes be fought by those who benefit from the current distribution of political influence? Furthermore, if the distribution of political influence were changed, would that necessarily guarantee that "the qualified citizen" would be allowed "to gain access nonpolitically," or would the beneficiaries of the new distribution of political influence bias the new procedures in such a way as to secure favorable decisions for themselves?

We believe that Savas and Ginsburg seem to make the same fundamental error that was made by the early Progressives who devised the original civil service schemes: basing reform on the desirability of a "nonpolitical" personnel system, and devising a set of structural rules that will promote efficiency and accountability if people agree to act nonpolitically. This pattern fails when individuals refuse to act nonpolitically. One can propose "neutral performance-appraisal" systems, but where do we find the neutral bureaucrats to conduct them? One can propose "specialization to promote efficiency," but will specialization really promote efficiency or will it create specialized subunits working at cross-purposes toward their own specialized goals? One can propose "hierarchy to promote accountability," but how do we guarantee it won't promote buck-passing? Savas and Ginsburg propose their own structure for personnel reform that is intended to promote efficiency, accountability, and political neutrality, but one is left wondering if their structural reform will really promote the desired ends any more than the structure they so effectively criticize has.

An alternative approach might include some of the following elements. First, a reform should recognize a trade-off between political leadership and a system controlled by a civil service commission. Placing personnel power in the hands of an oversight agency like the civil service commission inevitably reduces the ability of the appointed bureau chiefs to direct their own employees. We would like to see a tilting toward more political control by elected and appointed chief executives. This shift would recognize that none of these civil service systems are neutral with respect to public policy.

Second, we would like to see a less standardized performance and position classification system. In more routinized job categories, perhaps a rigid position classification system is beneficial, but for many jobs in government, such standardization just stifles innovation and productivity. Gordon Chase states, " 'Objectivity,' in the form of standardization is the backbone of the civil service philosophy. While such an approach may work well with routinized and technically specialized jobs, it often fails miserably with the more ambiguous, policy-oriented positions."[19] He goes on to argue that the simplified standards that are applied to "simpler, less complex jobs" are "applied across the board."

WATERGATE AND THE FEDERAL CIVIL SERVICE

Many of the issues that Savas and Ginsburg raised with regard to the New York civil service have been raised over the years about the federal civil service. It has been seen as impeding managerial control over agencies, hindering the hiring of the most expert employees, and promoting overspecialization through job descriptions. These personnel issues neared crisis proportion for the first time during the Watergate scandal of the Nixon administration.

The federal bureaucracy is split between a small number of political appointees who hold the key policy-making positions at the top of the executive departments, and the vast majority of civil service appointees. The distinction is clearly a manifestation of the Weberian notion of a politics/administration dichotomy, since the theory holds that the policy decisions will be made by the administration officials at the top and implemented in a politically neutral way by the nonpartisan civil servants at lower levels of the government hierarchy. The political appointees are partisan members of the administration in power, while the civil servants are appointed for lifetime positions through the merit system.

During the Watergate crisis, it became apparent that Nixon appointees in the bureaucracy had tried to "politicize" the nonpartisan civil servants. As Frederick Mosher wrote in his commission report on Watergate and public administration, "The critical error of the present (Nixon) administration apparently has been to assume that, since large numbers of the senior career officers were appointed during regimes of the other political party, old loyalties were so fixed that they could not be transposed to the objectives of a new and different administration. This was a miscalculation with serious consequences."[20]

In other words, Nixon appointees believed that their supposedly nonpartisan (but largely Democratic) civil service subordinates would try to subvert the goals of the Nixon administration. Nixon himself felt that the bureaucrats who had made their careers building the programs of his Democratic predecessors were the enemies of his own program. He complained to his chief domestic adviser, John Haldeman, "We have no discipline in this bureaucracy. We never fire anybody. We never reprimand anybody. We never demote anybody. We always promote the sons-of-bitches that kick us in the ass."[21] On that occasion, he wanted to fire the director of the San Francisco office of the Small Business Administration, a career bureaucrat supposedly protected by civil service regulations. He wanted that bureaucrat publicly punished "as a warning to a few other people around in this government, that we are going to quit being a bunch of God damn soft-headed managers."[22]

The Nixon administration increasingly began to try to intervene in personnel policy as a way of enforcing what it regarded as the lines of accountability from the bureaucracy through the elected administration to the people. To do this, the administration tried to make regional directors, who are often the key program managers, political appointees; it added political appointees to the Office of Management and Budget; it replaced career bureaucrats serving as Assistant Secretaries of Administration with political appointees, and used what leverage it had under civil service regulations to put political pressure on civil service officials whose actions were contrary to the administration's purposes.

As investigations of the Watergate scandal proceeded and as Congress moved toward impeachment, there was increasing dissatisfaction with the Nixon personnel practices. A respected public administrationist, Frederick Mosher, headed a panel which studied the personnel practices of the Nixon administration and made several recommendations for reform of the civil service. Once again, however, the reforms suggested were straight out of the orthodox guidebook. First of all, the panel reaffirmed the goal of keeping career civil servants completely separated from political influence: "The Panel recommends that the Committee urge the Congress, the President, and the U.S. Civil Service Commission to require and superintend strict enforcement of the laws and regulations forbidding political considerations in career personnel actions."[23]

In addition, the panel proposed several structural reforms for the political appointees. They recommended

> The President maintain an assistant on personnel, with adequate staff, who would, among other duties, develop and maintain a continuing roster of the best qualified possible appointees to executive and judicial offices. The primary authority and responsibility for political appointments be vested in the heads of the departments and agencies who would work with the assistance of the presidential staff suggested above, and whose choices would be subject to presidential veto. . . . Proposed appointees to the more specialized political posts be reviewed and approved or vetoed prior to their appointment by nonpartisan panels of experts in their fields.[24]

Ironically, the blue-ribbon panel of public administrationists was proposing a series of structural changes that would make the political appointees look like a miniature, high-level civil service. Their proposals would weaken presidential and democratic control over political appointees by imposing structural requirements, yet leave the president with veto power over names suggested by personnel assistants, the department heads, and "nonpartisan panels of experts."

A similar kind of response to Watergate came from Bernard Rosen, a former head of the Civil Service Commission.[25] He proposed to insulate the CSC even more completely from presidential influence. The CSC would report to and seek funds directly from Congress and achieve the statutory authority to discipline individual employees anywhere in the government. The emphasis in Rosen's proposal is on strengthening the institution's neutral competence.

This is a weak and unimaginative response to the problem of Watergate, unnecessarily bound by the orthodox personnel principles. The problem of Watergate raised the question of what to do when the president was unfit for office. One obvious answer to the question is for Congress to remove an unfit president through constitutional proceedings, and this is what happened in the case of Nixon. However, it seems unnecessary to bind the hands of all future presidents by limiting their control over the bureaucracy through imposition of a civil service model incorporated on political appointees. To the extent that the structural changes proposed by the Mosher panel and Rosen report could really stand in the way of a president who intends to enact bad policies (whatever they might be), they would also certainly stand in the way of a president determined to enact good policies. Giving department heads the primary authority over political appointees would certainly increase the fragmentation of the federal government, as would giving veto power to "nonpartisan panels of experts." In addition, giving even more independent power to the CSC would undoubtedly, as Hugh Heclo states, lead to a situation in which "the responsibility of top political executives seems bound to be diluted."[26]

THE CARTER CIVIL SERVICE REFORM

The most important attempt to transform the civil service system since its creation by the Pendleton Act in 1883 occurred under the Carter administration with the 1978 Civil Service Reform Act. Carter himself called this "the centerpiece of government reorganization during my term in office." The act eliminated the Civil Service Commission, replacing it with the Merit Systems Protection Board (MSPB) and the Office of Personnel Management (OPM). The MSPB is charged with guaranteeing the neutrality of the civil service and protecting individuals in the civil service from political abuses. The OPM serves as the president's staff agency on personnel in the same way that the Office of Management and Budget serves him for budgeting.

In addition, the Act replaced the Federal Labor Relations Council with an independent Federal Labor Relations Authority. In 1962, President Kennedy had issued Executive Order #10988, known as the "Magna Carta of labor relations," which established a system of labor relations for federal employees, including the right to form labor unions (but not to strike). The new Authority has responsibility for regulating and overseeing the conduct of labor relations in the federal government. At the same time, the equal employment opportunity responsibilities of the Commission, which derived from the 1972 Equal Employment Opportunity Act, were given over to the Equal Employment Opportunity Commission.

Perhaps the most innovative part of the 1978 Act created the Senior Executive Service (SES), which was intended to create a pool of mobile senior executives who can move from agency to agency. This would give political appointees in the agencies a larger pool of senior civil service executives to choose from as they staffed their offices. Another key element of the reform was a performance appraisal system, in which civil service employees were to be rated on the basis of written "job-related performance standards based on objective criteria," rather than on the basis of traits not necessarily linked to job performance, such as loyalty and maturity.

The rationale and main components of the 1978 Civil Service Reform Act clearly represent an approach to personnel reform far superior to the proposals of the Mosher panel or the Rosen report. In concept, the Act derives from a reform proposal put forth by Hugh Heclo in 1975, which he hoped would create a Third Force in government in addition to the traditional dichotomy between politicians and administrators. He envisioned an elite group of civil servants called Federal Executive Officers who would possess many of the characteristics of the Carter SES group. Heclo also supported a compromise, "middle way" for solving the problem of institutionalizing executive leadership and neutral competence in government. In this respect, the Act, at least in part, recognizes the legitimacy of executive, political leadership and proposes a different solution.[27]

However, a close inspection of the Civil Service Reform Act reveals a strong reluctance to really modify the early nineteenth century and Progressive personnel principles. The reform seems unable to come to grips with the political problem that the president faces in putting a national program together. In addition, the reform appears to continue to accept, for the most part, a dichotomy between politics and administration and a reliance on a set of standardized rules and regulations for institutionalizing merit in government. Thus, the reform carries the hubris of a nonpolitical scientism which is at the root of the personnel management problem. This orthodox orientation can be seen in a number of ways.

First, the reform is based on a continuing belief in the possibility and desirability of a politics/administration dichotomy, despite the fact that academic political scientists have repudiated this idea for years. The dichotomy appears in the rationale for the separation of the OPM and the MSPB—the OPM is supposed to be the political advisor on personnel matters for the presidency, while the MSPB is to maintain strict political neutrality. The mechanism for maintaining the neutrality of the MSPB is the independent commission, with its three members' long terms of office serving to insulate them from political influence.

In principle, the idea of institutionally separating the administrative values of executive leadership and expertise makes some sense. On the other hand, the assumption that the MSPB is guaranteeing neutral competence is false. Rather, we would like to see this Board worry more about expertise and less about neutrality, or if that proves unworkable, to at least recognize that it does serve self-interested seniority and union or other personnel interests contrary to presidential leadership. This may not be bad in itself, and could serve as a kind of institutional competition among administrative values.

Second, with the confirmation of the belief in the politics/administration dichotomy, it was inevitable that the Civil Service Reform Act of 1978 would also confirm a belief in the merit system. While the measurement of merit would differ under the reform, the civil service reform upheld the notion that objectively measured merit, rather than political sympathy for administration goals or some other criterion, would be the basis of civil service employment.

The concern with technical efficiency that motivated the civil service reforms closely paralleled the Progressives and the Taylorites. The primary motivation for the reforms, according to President Carter, was the public "suspicion" that public employees are "underworked, overpaid, and insulated from the consequences of incompetence."[28] This was regarded as the primary reason for a presumed bureaucratic inefficiency in the federal government.

The original Progressive model assumed that business administration was the natural model for administrative efficiency. The staff report on which the 1978 reform was based repeatedly claimed that government personnel administration can be improved by imitating the methods "that are used widely and effectively in private administration."[29] One such method was the use of performance appraisals, used by a large number of private corporations. Hence, the 1978 civil service reforms instituted performance appraisals, based on "objective criteria." It did not specify what those objective criteria were or how they were to be objectively discovered and determined.

While we are not opposed to performance appraisals per se, we do object to across-the-board mandating of these kinds of "merit" procedures. Some fields are highly technical and a performance standard is fairly easy to identify. Laboratory technicians, for example, need to know a prescribed set of techniques for testing substances. However, many other more policy- or people-oriented jobs pose great difficulties for merit measurements by way of simple, standardized tests. They inevitably involve a great deal of personal judgment and discretion.

Hugh Heclo claims that a benefit of the civil service idea is the "capacity to respond effectively to a succession of different political leaders. . . ." Nevertheless, he believes that in the United States the civil service has come instead to be "synonymous with a body of procedural rules: the formal classification of specific job duties, competitive examinations open to all job seekers, numerical scoring of the applicants' merits, impersonal rankings, protection for an individual's hold on a given job, and all the rest of the civil service apparatus."[30] We do not see how the merit system installed by the Carter reform changes this perspective on personnel management.

Finally, one exception to the continued reliance on a set of rules may be the creation of the Senior Executive Service. In this instance, however, the emphasis has been placed almost wholly on the original scientific-management view of motivation, Theory X. That is, the civil service reform of 1978 was based on the Taylorite notion that civil servants are fundamentally lazy and must be motivated by factors such as bonuses (the carrot) and swifter dismissals (the stick). Senior executives were given a cap on salaries and were forced to compete for a limited number of bonuses of different sizes that were to be handed out as rewards for good job performance. Indeed, one of the primary complaints of the Carter administration was that not enough civil servants were fired for inefficiency.

In concept, the SES also was supposed to foster greater movement of top civil servants among jobs to facilitate matching the best people with the right tasks. It included expanding and improving the pool of people recruited into top positions. These other nonmonetary dimensions of the SES, however, never really materialized.[31]

EVALUATION OF THE CARTER CIVIL SERVICE REFORM

The civil service reformers of 1978 were in the ironic position of condemning the efficiency and accountability of the civil service system created by the turn of the century, yet confirming their devotion to the principles established by those early reformers. We are left asking, is there reason to believe that a reform which departs little from orthodox principles will provide the means for significant improvement in the civil service system? In other words, does the Carter civil service reform escape the logical contradictions and false assumptions of the original reform movement? Despite the reform's mixture of old and new, on balance there is little reason to think so.

It became apparent very early that the first premise of the Carter reforms—the desirability of a politics/administration dichotomy—was still an impossible dream. Politics reared its head in the passage of the legislation and in its implementation. Congress was suspicious of the large bonuses which could be handed out to senior executives in the SES program, in part because these executives would be making more money than members of Congress. When, under the 1978 reform, agencies made large numbers of large bonuses, "there was a real possibility that angry legislators would scrap the entire bonus system. Strong lobbying by the Carter administration, however, salvaged a compromise: retention of the bonus program, but reduction of the percentage of SES members eligible from its original level (50 percent) to only 25 percent."[32] This, of course, angered the senior executives and increased the number who opted for retirement or a move to the private sector. Thus, the reform had an immediate effect that was exactly opposite to the desired one: Instead of encouraging the best senior executives to stay with the public service, it encouraged the most senior and most capable ones to leave.

Further, there is no reason to believe that a civil service reform so firmly based on Theory X motivation will escape the problems identified with that approach. To recapitulate the discussion in Chapter 6, it was argued that Theory X motivation runs the risk of increasing bureaucratic intransigence and rigidity, since employees are unwilling to identify with an organization that holds sanctions over their heads. If this is true, then of course the reform would once again be counterproductive in that it would hurt employee morale and create more bureaucratic intransigence rather than less. There is evidence that this is indeed the case. For instance, the senior executives who signed up for the SES did so with the lure of the 50 percent bonus rate; when that bonus rate was eliminated, morale declined.

Furthermore, the key to success of the reform lies, as it so often does in these cases, with the implementation of a technical requirement that may turn out to be surprisingly difficult. This is, of course, the definition of "objective criteria" as the basis for job-related performance appraisals. As administrators discovered when the PBBS system was mandated for budgeting, defining "objective criteria" for evaluating the productivity of the public sector—whether a budget item or an employee's performance—is often difficult or impossible. Even in the private sector, accountants have discovered that it is difficult to parcel out the contributions to productivity of various interactive workers in a team. Indeed, the most successful organizations may be the ones where it is most difficult to sort out the contributions of the members, precisely because they are working together so well. As a General Motors official has noted, "We measure absenteeism, we measure profitability, we measure scrappage rates, we measure energy use, and every one of them can be called part of productivity. But it's difficult to measure productivity period."[33]

For this reason, it is difficult to imagine that managers in the civil service will suddenly be able to hand out standardized rewards to individuals on the basis of objective criteria that truly measure employee contributions to abstract organizational goals such as military security or social welfare. And if they cannot develop such objective criteria, then they will very likely use bonuses for normal, internal political reasons: to reward supporters, cooperators, and allies and to punish ratebusters and troublemakers. Whether this use of bonuses, in fact, contributes to organizational productivity is, of course, dubious.

On the other hand, the idea of creating greater flexibility in work assignments, the opportunity to reward personnel for performance in some manner, and the need to pay to personnel competitive salaries all deserve further attention. Even the notion of blurring the sharp distinction between political appointees and bureaucrats has its value. Heclo, in particular, has argued for a strategic approach to the relations between bureaucrats and political appointees.[34] By this he means that politicos should approach the bureaucracy neither from a wholly negative Theory X viewpoint, nor from the passive, conciliatory Theory Y viewpoint. Instead, political appointees should recognize the important expert and other resources that the bureaucracy can bring to policy making and implementation. At the same time, the political appointees should use their political standing to benefit the bureaucrats when possible. This mutual dependence offers the opportunity for exchange. In some ways, the Carter reforms attempted to establish this perspective but did not fully succeed.

The Carter reformers also rightly recognized that no central administration source could, for instance, specify the "objective criteria" which would be used to fix the performance appraisal standards for civil service employees. Consequently, this job was passed to the individual agencies. Indeed, the legislation required that the president's Office of Personnel Management was to decentralize personnel as much as possible, letting the agencies evaluate their own employees and reward the deserving as they chose.

What the Carter reforms did not resolve was the problem of the balance between expertise and political loyalty to the president and other chief executives.

Reagan's approach to personnel has gone in the opposite direction from the orthodox tradition, making political loyalty the prime criterion for hiring and advancement.

REAGAN'S CIVIL ADMINISTRATION

A major feature of the controversy over the role of the presidency in American government has centered on the relations between the president and the bureaucracy. Presidents since Franklin Roosevelt have struggled with this issue. Herbert Kaufman foresaw these developments when he wrote:

> For though the mechanisms of neutral competence were remarkably successful in reducing the influence of the political parties on the administrative hierarchy, they did not necessarily increase the President's control over administration. Rather, they encouraged the development of "self-directing" groups within the bureaucracy, and these groups in turn cultivated their own sources of support among professional groups concerned with the subject matter over which the services have jurisdiction, among their clienteles, and among appropriate Congressional committees and subcommittees.[35]

The question of greater presidential leadership is, at heart, a political issue, not simply a matter of coordination, program planning, and policy direction. Kaufman shows that doctrines in public administration tended to follow the political interests of those favoring the kinds of policy programs sponsored by the president or the Congress. Starting with Roosevelt, those favoring an expansion of government programs, especially to the urban poor, generally favored stronger central leadership.

The institutionalization of the two conflicting doctrines of neutral competence and executive leadership came to full expression in Franklin Roosevelt's second term. The Brownlow Committee recommended moving the BOB to the newly created Executive Office of the President (EOP). At the same time, these agencies grew enormously in size; the BOB, for example, grew from 40 employees to more than 500. During the Truman and Eisenhower years, these changes established themselves firmly as the White House itself also started to grow in size and sophistication. The president became increasingly dependent on these permanent institutions for interacting with the rest of the government. Terry Moe describes the flowering of this traditional system:

> In formal terms, "politics" was confined to the fledgling White House organization, the very highest levels of the bureaucracy, and the director of the Budget Bureau. The system was, in great measure, an institutional embodiment of neutral competence and the politics-administration dichotomy.[36]

Moe argues that the political support for these reforms derived from expectations of an activist and strong presidency which would promote social change and progress. Similar to Kaufman, Moe describes the intensifying conflict between leadership expectations for the president and his lack of capacity to direct changes in his administration. Moe believes that from President Kennedy on, presidents have not found neutral competence enough; to effect their policy and program goals, they have preferred "responsive competence."

By the 1970s, political appointees had dwindled in number to only around 2,500 persons, 700 of these situated at the very top of government departments.[37] Donald Devine maintains that at the outset of the Reagan administration there were about 2,359 government appointees in noncareer positions in the federal government, a decline from 3,773 prior to the Carter administration. However, he asserts that even at the *high point* "of noncareer appointments, career employees still represented 99.85 percent of federal employment." He then states, "How one can be concerned with the 'pollution' of the career civil service when political appointees represent only 0.15 percent of all appointments is beyond comprehension."[38]

The people whom the president has the right to appoint and dismiss generally stay in office a very short time, on average only about a year and a half. They also tend to be younger and much less experienced in the operations of government than their civil service counterparts. In the past, many of them have had ties to interest groups associated with the agencies they are appointed to administer. Consequently, presidents have invariably faced the prospect of these appointees coming to identify closer with their own agencies' pet projects than with the president's program. For this reason, Nelson Polsby has argued that presidents in their second terms have increasingly turned away from interest-group representatives in favor of generalist managers and the political faithful who have few loyalties except to the president himself.[39]

The insulation of the president from the rest of the executive branch based on institutions of neutral competence conflicts with the expectation that the president should lead the nation, define a legislative program, and manage the bureaucracy. Some of the consequences of this incongruence between expectation and capacity were examined in Chapter 8. Kennedy and Johnson, as well as Nixon in his first term, attempted to expand the policy and administrative capacities of the White House through the creation of centralized White House councils and offices. These presidents also sought policy advice and support by creating task forces composed of experts from outside research institutes and from what Heclo refers to as "issue networks."[40] In other words, presidents sought to improve their capacity for leadership by circumventing the established bureaucracy.

However, these strategies for capacity building failed to recognize the potential for creating in the White House itself the kinds of bureaucratic pathologies—parochialism, infighting, inefficient routines—that the presidents had tried to overcome. Presidents, in effect, had attempted to fight bureaucratization by establishing the bureaucratic model in the White House. The contradictions of this strategy came to a head under President Nixon, who found himself too isolated from the rest of the government; and though he created these structures and procedures, he also fell victim to them. Nixon appeared to recognize the weakness of this bureaucratic strategy when, at the start of his second term, he fired all his cabinet members in order to embark on an effort to politicize top administrative posts, including those in the OMB. This political strategy came crashing to a halt with the Watergate scandal.

Neither Presidents Ford nor Carter made any significant changes in the situation, although Carter's personnel reforms laid the foundation for the more thoroughly political strategy adopted by President Reagan. Both of these presidents were seen as rather weak actors in the government system, which for a time was exactly what an American public preferred after the excesses of the Nixon administration. Nevertheless, by the second half of the Carter Presidency, the perception that Carter could not lead the government came to dominate the news media and popular opinion. By 1980, Reagan was able to sweep into office on the tide of popular discontent with Carter's "lack of leadership."

When President Reagan assumed office, he set about pursuing a personnel policy that angered many of the public-administration proponents of neutral competence. In his efforts to carry out his program, Reagan tilted personnel policy away from competence toward responsiveness to presidential directives as the primary appointment criterion. Chester Newland states that the Reagan administration used three main tests for appointing people to political posts: a proper conservative ideology, loyalty to Reagan, and membership in the Republican Party.[41]

The Reagan administration also pursued some other personnel tactics that furthered its efforts to get the bureaucracy to respond to presidential initiatives. In its first year, the Reagan administration took several months to fill vacant political posts in the bureaucracy. This tactic served the dual purpose of giving the administration more time to assure that the appointees would be loyal to Reagan and to proceed with its initial budget and tax programs for economic recovery, unimpeded by any bureaucratic opposition from the agencies involved. The administration also made numerous dual appointments in the Executive Office of the President (EOP), such as in OMB and the Office of Policy Development, and in the White House proper. In effect, these posts became an extension of the White House organization. The administration even took the unprecedented step of removing secretarial and clerical staff from Executive Office and White House positions and filling them with people loyal to the new administration.

In many respects, the Reagan administration attempted to fulfill the intent of the Keep Commission under Taft and the efforts by Theodore Roosevelt to control the Civil Service Commission during the time of the Progressives. Both Presidents attempted to create a civil service responsive primarily to executive interests rather than to those of local parties or Congress. Both presidents did not believe that Congress should exercise control over personnel matters. The legislation that actually passed, however, failed to support these presidential ambitions, largely because the Congress exerted its power to block such changes.

The Reagan administration, however, has taken considerable steps toward gaining control of the Office of Personnel Management *and* the MSPB. Newland maintains that while the OPM is used explicitly for political loyalty checks of appointees, the MSPB is also influenced by White House preferences. Ironically, the Carter reforms, which attempted to embody a Theory X mode of personnel management, have offered the Reagan administration the flexibility to use political criteria in moving people out of positions and determining their salaries and duties. Newland quotes Bernard Rosen, a former U.S. Civil Service Commission Executive Director, who maintained that the Civil Service Reform Act has been a "disaster for merit."[42]

The Reagan administration has even skirted the legality of the Hatch Act by permitting certain members of the OPM to quit their jobs during the campaign, but then return to them afterward. OPM's Director, Donald Devine, states that such rehirings do not violate the Hatch Act so long as "no agreements are made beforehand." Likewise, Devine appointed regional representatives across the country who appeared to combine personnel management and political campaign duties.

Public-administration observers argue that the president has deinstitutional-
ized and politicized the federal bureaucracy.[43] Bernard Rosen, who had also sharply
criticized the Carter administration for increasing the number of political appointees, especially attacked the Reagan administration for using the SES as a means to
further politicize the top managerial levels.[44] These charges concern the attack the
administration has made on the independence of personnel practices and the replacement of career people and stable, nonpartisan institutions with politically
oriented supporters of the current administration. These critics worry about the loss
of institutional memory, career experience, and professional norms. They fear that
this will lead to a decline in institutional capacity and expertise in favor of ideologi-
cally motivated personnel decisions.

On the other hand, one might argue that the Reagan administration has
learned from the experiences of earlier administrations that further bureaucratization of the personnel system does not serve the interests of an activist president—he
gets expertise but not responsiveness to his program. Reagan also eschewed the
strategy of building a mini-bureaucracy in the White House, thus attempting to
circumvent the career bureaucracy. This does not mean, of course, that Reagan's
strategies had no faults or worked one hundred percent as anticipated. As Moe
points out, the Reagan approach produced such politically harmful choices as
James Watt in Interior and Anne Burford at the Environmental Protection
Agency.[45] The Reaganites also took a very negative view toward the career bureaucracy and contributed to a further decline in employee morale.

Given the Reagan administration's intention to cut the size of the domestic
government, antagonism between the administration and the bureaucracy seems
almost inevitable. Nevertheless, Moe believes that the Reagan approach reinforces
and builds on the kinds of developments toward greater presidential leadership
inaugurated during the Kennedy, Johnson, and Nixon years.

PERSONNEL PROBLEMS AND SOLUTIONS

Since the Progressive period, reformers have perceived the problem of chief executives as a problem of building neutral competence.[46] Mayors needed city managers
with expert staff support, expert commissions, and professional department heads.
Reformers defined many areas of government as even too specialized for these
general managers and created special districts or authorities independent of central,
city-government institutions. Similarly, reform efforts to develop the presidency
worked to create independent civil service institutions and support organizations not
directly controlled by the president but based on norms of professionalism and
neutral competence. Initially, both presidents and mayors welcomed these developments because the kinds of patronage operated by the political parties did not
always conform with chief executive interests, but rather responded to the needs of
local political bosses and their cronies. By the time of the Franklin Roosevelt
presidency, however, chief executives increasingly came to recognize the divergence between the values of neutral competence and executive leadership.

Public administrationists continued to resist the idea that a political conflict
over administrative values undergirded the persistent controversies in personnel
administration. They made the opposite argument that the chief executives them-

selves were to blame, and lamented the fact that chief executives, for whatever reason, could not seem to grasp the great value of neutral competence and instead behaved in undesirable, political ways. Since their diagnosis of the problem centered on their perception of incompetent chief executives, their solution hinged on furthering and perfecting the institutions of neutral competence.[47]

However, if we make a different kind of argument—namely, that the causes of the problem center not on the individual personalities and foibles of presidents, but rather on the institutional incentives of the executive branch in its relations with Congress—then further pursuit of neutral competence misses the mark and may even be a cause of the problem rather than the solution. Moe states in this regard: "It is hard to think of [a misunderstanding of administrative organization] that could be more fundamental—standard evaluations tend to be quite off the mark, and their proposed reforms, as a result, fail to address the basic causes of the problem."[48] Continued efforts to bureaucratize the White House or to proceed with attempts to insulate the president from directly influencing the main personnel practices of his own administration, while at the same time demanding the president's leadership of the government, will work only to further destabilize the presidential system, not create a more effective presidency.

The question is whether politicization and centralization of personnel administration constitute a problem for chief executives. The public administration literature really offers no answer to this question, other than to admit that neutral competence and political leadership represent two competing, highly incongruent administrative values (although it took until after World War II for reformers to understand this fact). Once the divergence between these values came into the open, reform advocates tended to take one position or the other, depending on their political affiliations. Liberal reformers, for example, have tended to applaud the activist presidential exertions of Roosevelt, Kennedy, and Johnson in the field of personnel management, while at the same time they have decried similar political moves by Nixon and Reagan. Administrative effectiveness to carry out a chief executive's program is not a value shared by those who oppose what the President intends to do.

If the furthering of neutral competence fails to address the real issues facing chief executives, then reformers need to face up to the underlying political dimension of personnel administration. If presidents with completely different ideologies, styles, and personalities all strive for similar administrative and personnel changes, the weight of evidence falls on the side of a need for somewhat more politicization and centralization of personnel practices than has existed as standard practice over the past few decades.

The president is the one actor in our system of government who represents a national constituency; he is also the focal point of the national party system, to the extent that national parties exist independently of local political coalitions; and he represents the single center of executive authority in a fragmented and decentralized federal government. Continuing to take away from the president his ability to direct personnel changes in his administration, or insisting that he adopt the private, corporate model of bureaucratic hierarchy in the White House, works to create enormous tensions due to the political demands placed on him by these governmental, national party, and popular constituencies.

NOTES

[1]HERBERT KAUFMAN, "Emerging Conflicts in the Doctrines of Public Administration," *American Political Science Review*, 50 (1956), p. 1060.

[2]FREDERICK C. MOSHER, "The Public Service in the Temporary Society," *Public Administration Review*, 31 (1971), p. 59.

[3]JAY M. SHAFRITZ, ALBERT C. HYDE, and DAVID H. ROSENBLOOM, *Personnel Management in Government: Politics and Process*, 3rd ed. (New York: Marcel Dekker, 1986), p. 13.

[4]STEPHEN SKOWRONEK, *Building a New American State: The Expansion of National Administrative Capacities 1877–1920* (Cambridge: Cambridge University Press, 1982), p. 82. Reprinted by permission of Cambridge University Press.

[5]SKOWRONEK, *Building a New American State*, pp. 58–59.

[6]SKOWRONEK, *Building a New American State*, p. 68.

[7]ROBERT CARO, *The Power Broker: Robert Moses and the Fall of New York* (New York: Vintage Books, 1974), p. 75.

[8]CARO, *Power Broker*, pp. 72–75.

[9]SKOWRONEK, *Building a New American State*, pp. 194–198.

[10]SHAFRITZ, HYDE, and ROSENBLOOM, *Personnel Management*, pp. 32–43.

[11]KAUFMAN, "Emerging Conflicts," p. 1062.

[12]KAUFMAN, "Emerging Conflicts," p. 1062.

[13]E. S. SAVAS and SIGMUND G. GINSBURG, "The Civil Service: A Meritless System?," *The Public Interest*, 32 (1973), pp. 70–85.

[14]SAVAS and GINSBURG, "Civil Service," p. 72.

[15]GORDON CHASE and ELIZABETH C. REVEAL, *How To Manage in the Public Sector* (Reading: Addison-Wesley, 1983), p. 70.

[16]CHASE and REVEAL, *How To Manage*, p. 69.

[17]CHASE and REVEAL, *How To Manage*, p. 69.

[18]SAVAS and GINSBURG, "Civil Service," p. 291.

[19]CHASE and REVEAL, *How To Manage*, p. 70.

[20]FREDERICK C. MOSHER, *Watergate: Implications for Responsible Government* (New York: Basic Books, 1974), pp. 74–75.

[21]RICHARD P. NATHAN, *The Plot That Failed* (New York: John Wiley & Sons, 1975), p. 69.

[22]NATHAN, *Plot*, p. 69.

[23]MOSHER, *Watergate*, p. 155.

[24]MOSHER, *Watergate*, p. 151.

[25]BERNARD ROSEN, *The Merit System in the United States Civil Service* (Washington: U.S. Government Printing Office, 1975).

[26]HUGH HECLO, *A Government of Strangers: Executive Politics in Washington* (Washington: Brookings, 1977), p. 245.

[27]HUGH HECLO, "OMB and the Presidency," *The Public Interest*, 38 (1975), pp. 80–98.

[28]FREDERICK THAYER, "The President's Management 'Reforms': Theory X Triumphant," *Public Administration Review*, 38 (1978), pp. 309–314.

[29]THAYER, "President's Management," p. 311.

[30]HECLO, *Government*, p. 246.

[31]MARK ABRAMSON, RICHARD SCHMIDT, and SANDRA BAXTER, "Evaluating the Civil Service Reform Act of 1978: The Experience of the U.S. Department of Health and Human Services," in *Legislating Bureaucratic Change: The Civil Service Reform Act of 1978*, Patricia W. Ingraham and Carolyn Ban, eds. (Albany: State University of New York Press, 1984), pp. 117–121, 125.

[32]CHASE and REVEAL, *How To Manage*, p. 328.

[33]THAYER, "President's Management," p. 311.

[34]HECLO, *Government*, pp. 194–232.

[35]KAUFMAN, "Emerging Conflicts," p. 1070.

[36]TERRY M. MOE, "The Politicized Presidency," in *New Directions in American Government*, John Chubb and Paul E. Peterson, eds. (Washington: Brookings Institution, 1985), pp. 253–272.

[37]HECLO, *Government*, p. 36.

[38]DONALD J. DEVINE, "Escape from Politics," *The Bureaucrat*, 11 (1983), p. 18.

[39]NELSON POLSBY, "Presidential Cabinet Making," *Political Science Quarterly*, 93 (1978), pp. 15–26.

[40]HUGH HECLO, "Issue Networks and the Executive Establishment," in *The New American Political System*, Anthony King, ed. (Washington: American Enterprise Institute, 1978), pp. 87–125.

[41]CHESTER A. NEWLAND, "A Mid-Term Appraisal—The Reagan Presidency: Limited Government and Political Administration," *Public Administration Review*, 43 (1983), pp. 1–21.

[42]NEWLAND, "Mid-Term Appraisal," p. 15.

[43]MARGARET JANE WYSZOMIRSKI, "The De-Institutionalization of Presidential Staff Agencies," *Public Administration Review*, 42 (1982), pp. 448–458.

[44]BERNARD ROSEN, "Federal Civil Service Reform: A Disaster for Merit," *The Bureaucrat*, 11 (1982), pp. 8–17.

[45]MOE, "The Politicized Presidency," p. 262.

[46]HECLO, "OMB," pp. 80–88.

[47]MOE, "The Politicized Presidency," p. 267.

[48]MOE, "The Politicized Presidency," p. 267.

CHAPTER 13

Institutional Choice:
Reassessing the Alternatives

The dream of reason did not take power into account.

Paul Starr, *The Social Transformation of American Medicine*[1]

A power to advance the public happiness involves a discretion which may be misapplied and abused.

James Madison, *The Federalist Papers*[2]

Madison was aware that any governmental institution that is powerful enough to get something done is also powerful enough to be dangerous. This seems to pose a dilemma for theorists: Either hem in the institutions of government so that they are very likely to get nothing done, or else concentrate power at the risk of unaccountable government.

Wilson, on the other hand, seemed to believe that the problem could be solved by borrowing a certain institutional design—the institution that has been the focus of study in this book. Scientific, hierarchical administration, he argued, would be a means of concentrating power without the potential for abuse. Progressives supported the institutional choice of city managers, independent regulatory agencies, and a professionalized military, State Department, and other federal bureaucracies with this faith explicitly in mind. Subsequent administrators have advocated program budgeting, civil service, a politically neutral presidential staff, and additional independent regulatory agencies for much the same reasons. It is now time to reassess this institutional choice.

POWER AND ACCOUNTABILITY

It must first be said that administrative reform has brought lasting, positive changes in the way our country is governed—budget accounting, training techniques, professional expertise in crucial positions of government. No one, ourselves included, would want to turn the clock back on these advances.

However, public bureaucracies continue to create dissatisfaction because of a lack of efficiency and a lack of accountability. According to the orthodox view, this disparity between the promise and performance of the reform model is that the reform model must have been applied incorrectly or insufficiently. According to this perspective, a failure of an independent regulatory agency calls for a renewed search for a structural formula based on professionalism and neutral competence that *this time* will guarantee efficiency. If program budgeting was a failure, then this calls for a search for a structural formula for budgeting that *this time* will guarantee an efficient allocation of budget resources. If past reorganizations of the Department of Defense fail to control interservice bickering, then this calls for a search for a structural formula that *this time* will guarantee smoothly coordinated defense decision making.

These efforts may be referred to as "tinkering" with the classical reform model, because none of them challenge basic assumptions of this model. They continue to insist that politics, especially party politics, is bad and needs to be restricted further. Such tinkering with the administrative reform model continues to ignore the realities of organized politics. This fact is evident in the continued tinkering with the civil service system, regulatory agencies, and the Office of Management and Budget. Furthermore, proponents of reform insist that greater efforts to achieve comprehensive system rationality will succeed where they have been shown to fail in the past. Technical improvements (such as computerization of budgeting) encourage the advocates of comprehensive rationality in their hopes to combine efficiency and accountability under a framework of technical neutrality. That is, they claim that technical neutrality is a means for getting efficient outcomes that are accountable to the needs of the public.

Our approach to the classical values is different and calls for something more revolutionary than tinkering with the classical model of administrative reform. We believe that the first of the classical norms—technical neutrality—is impossible on the face of it; and we believe that the second and third norms—efficiency and accountability—cannot both be maximized in a single institution.

The Impossibility of a Neutral Hierarchy

Our perspective in this book is that politics is the strategic interaction of individuals responding to incentives defined by their institutions. It is impossible to imagine an institution that is neutral in this sense, because every institution creates incentives, and there will always be conflicts among individuals based on those incentives. Because of this, the interesting question is how institutions shape outcomes by creating incentives that lead to one decision or another. As long as different institutional arrangements lead to different outcomes, then those institutional arrangements cannot be regarded as neutral.

Furthermore, the theoretical work by Thomas Hammond and Paul Thomas demonstrates that hierarchies are not neutral because different ways of organizing hierarchies necessarily bias the outcomes toward one outcome or another.[3] The important question to ask, then, is, "Who gets what with different institutional arrangements?"

The Trade-Off Between
Accountability and Efficiency

Different institutional arrangements bias outcomes in one way or another. That is why contractors lobby for keeping the Corps of Engineers outside of the Transportation Department, while environmentalists lobby to move the Corp inside the Transportation Department. However, it is possible to think of institutional arrangements involving larger trade-offs between larger societal values, including a trade-off between accountability and efficiency.

Organizations that are closely monitored to guarantee their accountability seem often to create incentives for individuals to behave in a way that results in inefficient organizational behavior. Faced with constant, hostile supervision from Congress, State Department bureaucrats sought to guarantee organizational control through hierarchy and rules. Subordinates sought to justify their own behavior through hierarchy and rules. The net result was an organization that was caught in a bureaucratic rigidity cycle. The very closeness of monitoring seemed to generate inefficiency even as it guaranteed accountability.

On the other hand, we have examples like those of Robert Moses, who created an extraordinarily efficient organization for realizing his own dreams for New York City. This organization was just the opposite of the State Department. It was innovative where the State Department was stodgy; it was imperialistic where the State Department was timid; it rewarded bureaucratic innovativeness and excellence, rather than bureaucratic conformity. However, the conditions for creating this kind of incentive system in the Moses organization seemed to be the same conditions that guaranteed a loss of public control over the organization. Moses' "deals" with strong political actors guaranteed him freedom of action, freedom which he used to create an incentive system that made subordinates responsive to his own wishes.

Moses' organization was ideal from the standpoint of efficiency, but there were evidently costs associated with loss of public control. While Moses had succeeded in co-opting the relevant political actors in his environment in order to provide a basis for energetic pursuit of the organization's goals, the same co-optation made it possible for the organization to be unaccountable. Because Moses was a racist, his parks were segregated. Because he disliked the urban poor, his parkways were designed just low enough that buses could not use them. Because he disliked mass transit, there was no room in the public-works agenda for New York City to develop it. Because of the requirements of his political machine, expressways went where he planned for them to go, regardless of the effect on the stability of the neighborhoods.

The same thing could be said of other bureaucrats who developed records as hard-driving, efficient administrators. Discovering striking parallels in the lives of Robert Moses, J. Edgar Hoover, and Admiral Hyman Rickover, Lewis finds a similar loss in public control over these men and their organizations as they gained bureaucratic political power.[4] "In Hoover's case, and in Moses' as well, the entrepreneurial leaps always resulted in a diminution of the traditional prerogatives and controls of democratic government. The relevant loss of control in Rickover's case was in the traditional hold the Navy brass had to surrender."[5]

Defining a public entrepreneur as "a person who creates or profoundly elaborates a public organization so as to alter the existing pattern of allocation of scarce public resources," Lewis is concerned with an area that is of the utmost political significance. It is significant that Lewis finds that the "internal logic of the process of public entrepreneurship always and everywhere seems to imply a buffering and boundary creation that seals relevant parts of the organization off from what otherwise would have been decisive elements in its task environment."[6] In other words, Lewis finds a link between bureaucratic initiative and a loss of accountability.

The "buffering and boundary creation" that Hoover, Rickover, and Moses worked so hard to create are built into the city manager's office. Assuming that public preferences are captured by the socioeconomic characteristics of the population, Robert Lineberry and Edmund Fowler demonstrate that the public's preferences are less determinative of public policies in cities with city managers and reformed elections than in cities with partisan political patterns.[7] While the city manager reform was intended to insulate administration from politics, it has also evidently insulated key political decisions—now made by bureaucrats—from public preferences.

Taken together, the problems of bureaucratic dysfunctions and of bureaucratic accountability comprise a trade-off. As bureaucracies are subject to institutions of democratic control, they tend to become increasingly subject to rigidity cycles and other dysfunctions; as bureaucracies are free of democratic control, they tend to exhibit greater efficiency and effectiveness. While it might be possible to imagine organizations that are both efficient and accountable, it is difficult to point to examples. Furthermore, Donald Warwick's theory of bureaucratic dysfunctions argues that such examples would be unstable, since close outside supervision is the instigating "trigger" that sets off the rigidity cycle;[8] and, according to Lewis, breaking an organization out of a rigidity cycle seems to require the organizational "buffering" or "co-optation" that insulates the organization from the broadest public control.

Stated in this way, the problem of bureaucracy is exactly the same as the classic problem of political power that has been addressed by democratic theorists throughout history: how to make power accountable.

SOLUTIONS TO THE TRADE-OFF:
MORE HIERARCHY? MORE PROFESSIONALISM?

As the potential for bureaucratic inefficiency and bureaucratic unaccountability became clear during the twentieth century, various solutions to the problem have been proposed. Virtually none of them involves acceptance of the inevitability of a trade-off between these two values. Instead, the classic solutions seem to involve yet more applications of the Progressive ideals.

A striking case is Carl Friedrich, who started by rejecting the classical dichotomy between policy formation and policy execution, but ended by putting his faith in the neutral competence of administrators. Friedrich stated that "Public policy, to put it flatly, is a continuous process, the formation of which is inseparable from its execution."[9] Bureaucrats must necessarily have some discretion over policy. "But are there any possible arrangements under which the exercise of such discretionary power can be made more responsible?"[10] Friedrich feels that one such check on bureaucrats is "internal." He quotes John Gaus on the "inner check" of the professional:

> The responsibility of the civil servant to the standards of his profession, in so far as those standards make for the public interest, may be given official recognition. . . . Certainly, in the system of government which is now emerging, one important kind of responsibility will be that which the individual civil servant recognizes as due to the standards and ideals of his profession. This is "his inner check."[11]

Thus, while there may be no dichotomy between policy formation and policy execution, Friedrich is put in the odd position of claiming that there is a dichotomy between the political man, who may use his discretionary powers in his own interest, and the professional administrator, whose inner check impels him to use discretion in the public interest.

Of course, Friedrich's position is ultimately no more tenable than that of the original Progressives, and Herbert Finer was quick to point that out.[12] The problem with trusting administrative accountability to professional responsibility, according to Finer, is that there is no guarantee that professional standards are identical to the needs of the public as determined by political institutions. Worse yet, Finer sees in official responsibility to the profession the potential for "the enhancement of official conceit and what has come to be known as 'the new despotism.' "[13] When democratic control is weak, Finer believes that professional responsibility may "fall away into all sorts of perversions." The evidence of bureaucratic dysfunctions in professionally dominated bureaucracies supports Finer's argument.

Consequently, according to Finer, one cannot make any solutions to the problem of administrative accountability that do not include hierarchical authority to reward and/or punish subordinates, even if those subordinates are professionals. Finer can thus be seen as emphasizing the hierarchical aspects of the classical model, while Friedrich emphasizes the element of trained professionalism. On the other hand, we have seen that strict use of hierarchical authority can lead to its own dysfunctions, in the form of the rigidity cycle.

The debate between Friedrich and Finer, which became a classic in the public-administration literature, leaves the impression that each is right in criticizing the other. Ultimately, neither approach to accountability is completely adequate. Finer seems to be correct in claiming that professionalism is an insufficient safeguard, while Friedrich is correct in claiming that no system of hierarchy can hope to be capable of enforcing absolute accountability; and if it were able to enforce absolute accountability, the Warwick argument would still suggest that it would be at the expense of flexibility and efficiency. The Friedrich/Finer controversy elaborates in detail the trade-offs involved in the classical reform model.

ALTERNATIVES TO THE REFORM MODEL

This book has advanced the theme of institutional choice: that the organizational structure of typical twentieth-century bureaucracies resulted from particular choices of particular political actors responding to various incentives. The overwhelming preponderance of the classical bureaucratic structure in modern bureaucracy, it is argued, is best understood as resulting from the overwhelming political advantages of that particular form to such political actors as interest groups, legislators, executives, and the bureaucrats themselves.

For this institutional choice to have been a choice in any meaningful sense, however, there had to be an "alternative" to the classical model of structure, with its hierarchy, non-overlapping division of labor, written rules, and merit staffing. But is it possible to imagine any realistic alternatives to this model? Friedrich and Finer, we argue, did not succeed in elaborating any real alternatives. Have theorists, or practitioners, devised any believable structural alternatives that depart systematically from the classical model?

We argue both that theorists have devised alternative models of bureaucratic organization, and that empirical researchers have demonstrated the viability of these alternatives. These theorists include Martin Landau, who argues that organizational structures should be redundant and overlapping rather than neatly specialized as in the classical model;[14] they include Jonathan Bender, who argues for competition built into bureaucratic organization;[15] and they include Vincent Ostrom, who specifically eschews Woodrow Wilson's "scientific administration" for the checks and balances of a Madisonian administrative system.[16] All of these theorists quite consciously state the existence of a viable, even preferable, model to classical bureaucratic structure.

Each of these theorists has a particular perspective on what is wrong with the classical model of bureaucracy. However, we find it interesting that, in criticizing the classical model of bureaucracy, each seems to be driven toward a similar alternative conception of organization. Most importantly, we find it significant that these alternative theorists describe a kind of organization that is an *empirical reality*, in some places. That is, despite the predominance of classically organized bureaucracies, it is possible to point to particular bureaucrats who have deliberately violated the classical model of organization. Furthermore, in doing so, their performance has not been systematically worse than that of those bureaucrats who have followed the classical model. In fact, Thomas Peters and Robert Waterman argue that organizations which depart from the classical model of organization do systematically better, pointing as evidence to a sample of private firms.[17]

We propose to describe certain theoretical elements of the anti-bureaucracy, with empirical examples of organizations exhibiting these anti-bureaucratic characteristics. After having done so, we will point out that the existence of organizations that do *not* follow the classical model of structural organization emphasizes the main point of this book: that institutions can be chosen. For if it were impossible to imagine alternatives to classically organized bureaucracies like the State Department or modern police departments, then the "choice" of that institutional form is a trivial one. If viable institutional alternatives do exist, then once again the important question is political: Why do individuals choose the institutional alternatives they do?

On Specialization vs. Redundancy

The most striking departure of the alternative theorists is on the question of specialization and division of labor. While the classical model is insistent that specialized offices should not overlap in function, the alternative theorists see specific advantages to overlapping and duplication. The foremost example of this in modern public administration was Franklin Roosevelt, who (as we mentioned in Chapter 5) was not personally a believer in the classical model which he found it politically advantageous to support. Arthur Schlesinger, his biographer, reports that Roosevelt's "favorite technique was to keep grants of authority incomplete, jurisdictions uncertain, charters overlapping."[18] Roosevelt himself said,

> There is something to be said . . . for having a little conflict between agencies. A little
> rivalry is stimulating, you know. It keeps everybody going to prove that he is a better
> fellow than the next man. It keeps them honest too. An awful lot of money is being
> handled. The fact that there is somebody else in the field who knows what you are
> doing is a strong incentive to strict honesty.[19]

Thus, he had the liberal Harry Hopkins administer the Works Progress Administration as a public-spending mechanism to get people back to work, and he had the relatively conservative Harold Ickes administer the virtually identical Public Works Administration developing major capital expenditures. The demarcation between the two agencies was never clear, and the two leaders of these agencies hated each other. Each was continually fighting to expand his own program at the expense of the other. Needless to say, this was a gross violation of the orthodox prescription for specialized, non-overlapping offices.

Another redundant administrative practice that characterized the Roosevelt regime was the creation of numerous new agencies—often referred to as the "alphabet agencies" because of the confusing array of acronyms they generated—to carry out tasks normally assigned to established agencies. This strategy represented a form of passive redundancy:

> If the obvious channel of action was blocked and it was not worth the political trouble
> of dynamiting it open, then the emergency agency supplied the means of getting the
> job done nevertheless. And the new agencies simplified the problem of reversing
> direction and correcting error.[20]

While classical organization theory would say that similar functions should be placed in the same department so that they can be effectively coordinated from above, Roosevelt specifically created the kind of bureaucratic conflict that the classical theorists abhorred. He also consciously fanned the hatred of Hopkins for Ickes, and vice versa, by tantalizing each with the posibility of future budget expansions. Harry Hopkins observed, mildly, that FDR was "a bit puckish";[21] he seemed to enjoy the rivalry that his administrative structure generated, and, according to his biographer, he certainly benefited.

One way he benefited was by the increased flow of information to the top. With each bureaucrat willing, even eager, to "tattle" on his competitors, the chief executive managed to escape the situation of some later presidents—having a distorted, overly optimistic picture coming up the hierarchy from submissive bureaucrats. Unlike Johnson, who seemed to have been fed a particular view of the Vietnam War by the Defense Department, Roosevelt was able to get conflicting views of the world from enemies in the same policy arena.

The latter theorists of redundancy and competition, in contrast to the classical organization theorists, applaud Roosevelt's administrative style. Landau maintains that redundancy actually can increase the reliability of organizational performance beyond the reliability of any component of the organization. He points out that two braking systems in an auto don't just make the car twice as reliable, but many times as reliable as an auto with just one braking system.[22]

For redundancy to have beneficial effects on organizational performance, the parts of the organization must be functionally equivalent. Thus, specialization as practiced in the classical model does not count as redundancy, because specialization has come to mean different organizational components doing completely *separate* things. A brake and an engine in the same car are specialization, not redundancy.

Furthermore, the organizational units must be independent in the sense that they will not fail at the same time. A car with two braking systems that operate with the same machinery and which could fail at the same time would not improve the overall reliability of the auto. Similarly, if the people in two separate components of an organization operate according to the same rules and procedures, they are likely to perform equally well (or poorly) under a given set of circumstances. Thus, to improve organizational performance, it is better to have organizations actually *not* cooperating, but working at cross-purposes.

The building of an intercontinental ballistic missile system that can be launched from a submarine is considered one of the most successful projects ever undertaken by the military. The project, known as the Polaris, was finished ahead of schedule for less cost than projected. In addition, the performance characteristics of the missile exceeded the original specifications.

It is interesting to note that redundancy was a prime strategy employed by the Special Projects Office of the Navy in building the Polaris submarine. Although different subsystems of the Polaris were assigned to different Naval organizations, Harvey Sapolsky reports that, "Responsibilities were defined, but not fixed. Jurisdictions, at least in the initial years of the program, were uncertain."[23] Sapolsky also emphasizes that backup or parallel projects were widely used "where major uncertainties exist." In addition, "Independent technical evaluations occurred at a number of points. The design of the system itself included redundancy in the navigation, fire control, launch, and ship systems components."[24]

The same redundancy is illustrated in the better private firms. Peters and Waterman quote an IBM manager who claims that the IBM performance in development of computers is due to competition between redundant teams, which they call "parallelism." "Parallel projects are crucial. No doubt of it. When I look back over the last dozen projects we've introduced, . . . there were two or three (about five once) other small projects, you know, four- to six-person groups, two people in one instance, who had been working on parallel technology or parallel development efforts."[25] The probability of any one group failing is large; the probability that all will fail is small.

Vincent Ostrom ties these ideas on redundancy to the traditions of political democracy associated with the founders of the U.S. He argues that the "designers of the American constitution knew what they were doing and deliberately sought to base their political experiment upon an alternative design." The form of government that the early Americans sought to avoid was the French and English "unitary" form of government. These countries relied on centralized power and bureaucratic control, whereas Ostrom maintains that the Founders wanted the "federal structure of the American political system to be necessarily characterized by overlapping jurisdictions." He also states that the founders preferred, "A federal political system with substantial fragmentation of authority at each of the levels of government. . . ."[26]

Ostrom believes that in the years following the American revolution this "democratic" conception of administration succumbed to the more classic French/British model of bureaucracy. He cites the writings of Woodrow Wilson as indicative of the monocratic type of administrative philosophy that has unfortunately come to dominate public administration. He then refers to a more recent study by the Committee for Economic Development (CED) on proposals for modernizing metropolitan areas in the United States: "While focusing on the costs of overlap and complexity, the CED report completely discounts *any* costs associated with institutional weakness and institutional failure in large-scale public bureaucracies."[27] His resounding conclusion is that the founders of the U.S. Constitution intended to create a system of government based on fragmentation and overlapping jurisdictions and that this decentralized, pluralist system offers a viable alternative to the bureaucratic model.

Of course, this all makes sense if the chief executive *assumes* that his subordinates are going to be playing the kinds of political games with biased information discussed in Chapter 9. When subordinates have it in their power to bias information to enhance the political prospects of their own pet projects, then chief executives had better try to rely on multiple, competing sources of information. Roosevelt relied on his wife, guests, experts, amateurs, and the mail for informal sources of information. "Roosevelt's persistent effort . . . was to check and balance information acquired through official channels by information acquired through a myriad of private, informal, and unorthodox channels and espionage networks. At times, he seemed almost to pit his personal sources against his public sources. From the viewpoint of his subordinates, this method was distracting when not positively demoralizing."[28] This leads us to the question of hierarchy.

On Hierarchy vs. Autonomy

Because the alternative view of organizational redundancy is so contrary to the classical view of specialization, it is not surprising that the role of hierarchy is viewed quite differently as well. The alternative theorists specifically challenge the classical view of hierarchy in at least three ways.

First and foremost, the alternative theorists emphasize the role of delegation, which necessarily involves loosening of the tight "lines of authority" upward from every subordinate to the common, concentrated tip of the hierarchy. Once again, the theorists follow the practical example of Franklin Roosevelt. FDR's labor secretary, Frances Perkins, wrote, "He didn't like concentrated authority."[29] She also wrote that, "He had an instinct for loose, self-directed activity on the part of many groups."[30] This delegation to self-directed groups was not the same as giving up all authority, for the competition *between* the groups was sufficient to force the central decision making up to him. It did mean, however, that FDR didn't have to rely on the normal tight leash that seemed to be implied by the writings of the classical organization theorists, and this allowed for a much more energetic ferment of activity and innovation during the New Deal than otherwise would have been possible.

In the Polaris project, the special projects office followed a similar strategy of loose coupling and decentralization. Sapolsky states that, at the outset, the physical constraints constituted the only firmly fixed performance standards—the missile had to fit into a submarine. Beyond that, however, the director of the program concentrated his efforts "on the system interfaces rather than on the details of particular subsystems."[31] In business language, they did not "micro-manage" the projects, but allowed for considerable discretion within the subsystems.

In addition to this basic management policy of loose coupling, Sapolsky says that the Polaris project followed two other strategies: decentralization and competition. One example he cites is that "the burden of approving contractor design changes within a subsystem was placed on the field offices, the staff units closest to the actual development."[32] Sapolsky sums up the strategy of decentralized competition by stating:

> Everyone had an actual or potential rival and no one was assured of a monopoly. Thus, within the program everyone had a strong incentive to watch for problems in the designs offered by others while working diligently to avoid any of their own. Decentralization assured a manageable division of labor and competition assured the honesty of the laborers.[33]

It is interesting to note that some of the better private firms have learned the same pattern of management. Peters and Waterman point to such firms as Texas Instruments, 3M (Minnesota Mining and Manufacturing), Johnson and Johnson, and others. These firms, they argue, had consciously weakened their hierarchies by building the same kind of "loose, self-directed activity on the part of many groups" that FDR had allowed.

> It eventually became clear that all of these companies were making a purposeful trade-off. They were creating almost radical decentralization and autonomy, with its attendant overlap, messiness around the edges, lack of coordination, internal competition, and somewhat chaotic conditions, in order to breed the entrepreneurial spirit. They had forsworn a measure of tidiness in order to achieve regular innovation.[34]

The writings of Herbert Hoover and the other classical organization theorists make it clear that they did not want to give up any measure of tidiness in organizational structure.

Along with delegation, this alternative perspective on organizations attacks hierarchy by increasing the span of control, or the number of people reporting to a given supervisor. Increasing the span of control allows middle-level managers more autonomy and more room for flexibility and innovation; but it also is a direct attack on hierarchy in that it is impossible for a given supervisor to closely monitor a large number of subordinates, and reduces the number of layers of hierarchy in an organization of a given size. As Peters and Waterman note, "Decades ago Americans got hooked on the notion of optimal spans of control. We conventionally believe that no one can control more than five to seven people. The Japanese think that is nonsense. At one bank, more than several hundred branch managers report to the same person. The flat organization *is* possible."[35]

Finally, hierarchy is attacked in the alternative organization by emphasizing informality. Roosevelt encouraged informality to the point of encouraging criticism from his private brain-trusters, and accepting a "lack of deference" in his private discussions.[36]

In this way too, Roosevelt's administrative style bears a striking resemblance to that found in the nonbureaucratic firms identified by Peters and Waterman. They emphasize that in the best firms, communications are intense and informal. When a presentation is made at a meeting, "the screaming and shouting begin. The questions are unabashed; the flow is free; everyone is involved. Nobody hesitates to cut off the chairman, the president, a board member."[37] In the nonbureaucratic organizations, being a "yes man" is not encouraged. The authoritative basis for hierarchy is diminished.

On Rules vs. Flexibility

Just as central to classical bureaucracies as hierarchy are rules; and in the normal bureaucracy, rules are not meant to be broken. In the alternative bureaucracies, rules may well be broken, as decentralized and motivated subordinates attempt to get things done. Roosevelt "oriented the administrative machinery away from routine and toward innovation."[38]

The successful firms identified by Peters and Waterman were similarly biased against rigid rule-following behavior. The small groups that IBM set to work on project development habitually broke the rules, even to the point of misusing materials and funds, but the IBM managers expected and even encouraged it. "That's a time-honored thing. We wink at it. It pays off."[39]

In effect, while formal rules create incentives for rigid rule-following in most formal bureaucracies, informal rules encourage flexibility in the alternative bureaucracies. In the Peters and Waterman firms, personnel policies helped "assure security and make people in the company less dependent on the particular organization box they live in."[40] This is the opposite of the personnel rules in the State Department, where the selection-out system assured insecurity and required people to be rigid followers of the particular set of hierarchical orders and rules in their particular organizational boxes.

The same thing was true of another extraordinary public manager, Admiral Hyman Rickover, the developer of the nuclear Navy. While most of the Navy operated according to the time-honored principle of "go along to get along," Rickover created one unit of the Navy in which such principles were upset.

> His organization "was organization as it had not been before. It was unroutinized; formal roles meant little, existing structure altered as fast as the task environment did. . . . Instead of attempting to reduce uncertainty through standardization of people and procedures in order to produce a classical bureaucracy, Rickover found the multi-headed task environment confronting him ideal because he could manipulate it in toollike political fashion.[41]

Rickover, like the private entrepreneurs at IBM, created multiple, temporary task-oriented groups, and encouraged them to break whatever rules were necessary to get the job done.

This laxness about rules does not mean that individuals were allowed to do anything that suited them. On the contrary, the laxness about rules in these unorthodox organizations is only possible because the organization is so careful about making sure that *its members are absolutely clear about what the organizational goal is.* In other words, the unorthodox organizations go to great pains to avoid what was called in Chapter 6 the "displacement of goals." Indeed, the time that managers do *not* spend in enforcing rules, they *do* spend in clarifying organizational goals, and "cheerleading" for those goals. That is, the unorthodox manager wants subordinates to decide for themselves when it is appropriate to bend the rules for the greater organizational good.

Gordon Chase, the former administrator of New York City's Health Services Administration, had the habit of calling in his senior managers and asking them what they had been doing for the past weeks or months.

> Some of these senior officials would start by telling me how many meetings they had attended, how many memos they'd written, how many staff they'd hired, and similar benchmarks of bureaucratic activity. I'd look at them and say: "But whom did you make healthier today (or last week, or last year)? Did you make anybody in New York healthier—and how do you know?"
>
> In short order people came to realize where I wanted my emphasis—not on the mechanics of running public agencies but on the outcome of the services we were there to deliver.[42]

This preoccupation with outcomes is perhaps the most striking common trait of the successful, unorthodox manager. Note again Admiral Rickover:

> In further contrast to classical bureaucracy, there existed within his immediate task environment a sense of urgency and a set of phenomena explicitly time-related to the easily described central goal: the design, development and production of a nuclear submarine by the mid-1950s. This goal was neither subordinated nor temporarily ignored for an instant, especially not in Rickover's hearing. He was the cheerleader and the devoted servant of his mission who would work harder and longer than anyone, who would know more about things than anyone, and who would kindle in others for varying periods his own burning determination and self-discipline.[43]

Admiral Elmo Zumwalt, while commanding a Navy destroyer, had a smaller, more routine job to get done, but he used similar tactics to get it done.

> What I tried hardest to do was ensure that every officer and man on the ship not only knew what we were about, not only why we were doing each tactical evolution, however onerous, but also managed to understand enough about how it all fitted together that he could begin to experience some of the fun and challenge that those of us in the top slots were having. Our techniques were not unusual. We made frequent announcements over the loudspeaker about the specific event that was going on. At the beginning and the end of the day, I discussed with the officers, who, in turn, discussed with their men what was about to happen and what had just happened, what the competition [other U.S. destroyers!] was doing and what we should do to meet it. We published written notes in the plan of the day that would give the crew some of the color or human interest of what the ship was doing. I had bull sessions in the chief petty officers' quarters, where I often stopped for a cup of coffee. More important than any of these details, of course, was the basic effort to communicate a sense of excitement, fun and zest in all that we were doing.[44]

Zumwalt claims that these techniques were responsible for getting his ship raised from last to first in squadron efficiency ratings.

In the development of the Polaris missile, Vice-Admiral William F. Raborn insisted on the maxim "which stated that the program's objective was the construction of a deployable system and not the advancement of technology."[45] A corollary Raborn maxim stated that "all technological tasks other than those contributing directly to the deployment of a submarine-launched ballistic missile should be avoided."[46] In other words, Raborn, like the other administrative leaders discussed here, actively focused the organization's attention on the accomplishment of its immediate mission and constantly tried to prevent diversions into other fields of endeavor.

The unorthodox private managers, too, seem to define their own jobs as "cheerleading," creating in their firms a sense of the organization as a "family" rather than as a bureaucracy. Sam Walton of Walmart literally leads cheers at management meetings, and takes donuts to workers at distribution centers in the middle of the night. The founder of McDonald's restaurants, Ray Kroc, uses "hoopla and razzle-dazzle" to motivate his employees. Rene McPherson at Dana Corporation did away with time clocks and ordered his accountants to create a false set of records showing that every one of his subordinates came and left on time. McPherson instituted such slogans at Dana as "Ask Dumb Questions" and "Talk Back to the Boss."[47] These slogans would not be tolerated in the orthodox professionalized hierarchy.

On Experts vs. Champions

Franklin Roosevelt attracted many kinds of experts to the federal government during his administration, but those closest to him were not the kinds of experts who were happy in a narrow definition of their authority or role. "The men around Roosevelt were not easily contented or contained. They were always fanning out, in ideas and in power. A government well organized in the conventional sense would have given them claustrophobia."[48] This picture is a striking contrast to the picture of the professional bureaucrats in Chapter 6, whose professional outlooks seemed to provide them with a set of blinders to ensure a narrow outlook on the world. Roosevelt encouraged people to develop new ideas and be committed to them. He even told a group of reporters, "You sometimes find something pretty good in the lunatic fringe."[49]

He further encouraged his subordinates to break out of narrow professional areas of expertise. One subordinate, an expert on gold, said, "I would get to see the President about something and the fellow who was there before me talking about cotton would be told by the President, 'Well, why don't you stay.' Before we were through the guy who was there talking about cotton was telling him what to do about gold."[50] This was irritating to FDR's experts because it clearly sent the message that he did not regard professional expertise as the final word on a subject, that he wanted to hear professional authority challenged by smart people who were altogether outside of their field. In a way, Roosevelt was daring amateurs to challenge professional orthodoxy and challenging professionals to defend their orthodoxy against amateurs. This was precisely the kind of threat to professional standing that the classic model of bureaucratic administration was designed to eliminate.

Once again, there is striking similarity between Roosevelt's unorthodox style of administration and that of the unorthodox but successful firms. The head of the New Business Ventures Division at 3M claimed that their success was based on hiring and developing staff people who were not professional experts in the normal sense, but "champions" of a certain new idea; furthermore, he claimed, "We expect our champions to be irrational."[51] Like Roosevelt, who sought new ideas on the lunatic fringe instead of in the heart of established professional doctrine, the unorthodox administrators seem to adopt a style of personnel administration that calls into question the basic premise of rationality in scientific management.

The Status of Unorthodox Institutional Alternatives

We believe that the theories and evidence listed here indicate the viability of an alternative institutional design emphasizing redundancy rather than specialization, delegation rather than hierarchy, flexibility rather than rules, and champions rather than trained experts. The viability of this alternative structure is a logical necessity for the viewpoint of this book—that institutions of public administration are the result of meaningful choices by political actors.

We specifically do *not*, however, believe that this alternative institutional design is in any sense a final solution to the problems of public administration. To make such a claim would be to repeat the fundamental error of the Progressives, which was to believe that there is such a thing as a final institutional solution to political problems.

The danger in all of this, of course, is that the theories of redundancy and pluralist decentralization become the new dogmas of how to make institutional choices. That is, members of these schools of thought at times seem to be claiming that they have discovered a different recipe for the ideal government structure. Once again, they are in danger of claiming that *their* structure can legitimize policy decisions. In effect, they run the risk of saying: People who are dissatisfied with policy decisions made under a system of pluralist decentralization have no basis for complaint because they had their chance to articulate their demands in the great pluralist game.

But what if someone objects to the outcome of pluralist decentralization by claiming that *the institution of pluralist decentralization created an unfair bias against his or her own policy preferences?* Could that person legitimately challenge pluralist decentralization and demand a return to a more Progressive administrative model? We claim that there is nothing sacrosanct about any particular institution. *If an institution is to be judged by the policy decisions it renders, then a person who objects to the policy decisions made under a Madisonian system of checks and balances has a right to seek a change in the institution.*

While no system can avoid redundancy, redundancy can be built into a system in different ways.[52] Some ways favor some groups, while other ways favor other groups. The United States court system, for example, contains numerous checks and balances to prevent the innocent from suffering a wrong conviction. That is why, contrary to other countries, U.S. defendants are considered innocent until proven guilty. On the other hand, these kinds of redundancies have led to cases in which obvious murderers and other criminals have gone free because of some technicality in due-process law that was intended to protect the innocent. These redundancies have also led to long waiting periods between arrest, trial dates, and final court decisions.

The point of this is that pushing for one kind of redundancy maximizes one set of values only at the cost of another set of values. Similarly, having numerous checks in a policy system works to prevent the too-hasty passage of harmful laws. However, as Ostrom notes, even Hamilton was aware that "preventing bad laws inherent in the exercise of veto capabilities also involves the power of preventing good ones."[53] Different types of redundancies lead to different policy outcomes.

Second, although Ostrom and others correctly argue that centralization is not appropriate for everything, they too easily fall into the trap of believing that decentralization is universally preferable. Ostrom writes that the central problem of designing administration is "how to restrict the power of command to a minimum. . . ."[54] The judgment on what constitutes a public good also varies from one person to another. Ostrom seems to see very few public goods outside of national defense. Hence, he advocates that centralization is inappropriate for "community assistance programs, rural development, poverty, or the public security of neighborhood streets."[55] While we might agree with him about the security of neighborhood streets, issues of poverty and rural development clearly entail important collective-good properties. Indeed, Paul Peterson's thesis on the limits of city policy singles out explicitly redistributive policies.[56] He maintains that local governments are too small and too vulnerable to private companies to pursue redistributive policies successfully. An institutional system that uniformly promotes decentralization, therefore, will undoubtedly discount the interests and values of large numbers of people.

We believe, then, that institutions are chosen by political actors with differing sets of policy preferences, and that they must be judged by whose preferences they meet. There is no objective standard for the "right" amount of hierarchy versus delegation in a bureaucracy; nor is there a "science" of redundancy that tells us how much overlap is right for public agencies. Despite the fond wishes of the New York Bureau of Municipal Research, there is not even a science of personnel management that tells us how many "neutral experts" versus "partisan champions" should be hired for a given agency.

In other words, we believe that policies are not justified because they were derived from an objectively "fair" institution. Rather, if we seek particular policies, then we should be willing to consider whatever unorthodox institutions seem to produce those policies. This position might even drive us full circle; back to the political parties that have been the special nemesis of the nonpartisan, bureaucratic reformers over the decades.

A POLITICAL ALTERNATIVE: STRENGTHENING MAJORITARIAN PARTISAN INSTITUTIONS

We believe, along with Schattschneider,[57] that the most important factor in politics and administration is the ability to organize to promote a preferred course of public policy. The old political machines constituted a kind of organizational bias that included certain people but excluded large segments of the professional middle class. The movement the middle class sponsored—Progressivism—sought to gain for professionals, administrators, and small businessmen a better institutional arrangement that would give them more access to key decisions. They did not explicitly advocate a set of policies (although implicitly they often embraced racism and elitism), but rather a set of institutional choices that worked to their advantage.

If we are to be consistent with the approach of this book, then our criticism of the classical reform model must be that we don't like the policy decisions that come from this framework. That is, an analysis of "who gets what" under the classical reform institutions would reveal certain serious deficiencies. Much like Frank Levy,

Arnold Meltsner, and Aaron Wildavsky claim in their book on policy outcomes, we believe that a fundamental question of institutional choice is what outcomes these choices produce; and, also consistent with these authors' thinking, when we enter the realm of outcomes, we engage in normative judgments about "human preferences—likes and dislikes, pain and pleasure."[58] In other words, if institutions contain normative biases, judging them requires an assessment of their normative orientation to the distribution of policy benefits and costs.

When we ask "who gets what" from the imposition of the classical model of administrative institutions, we get several clear answers: The big gainers have been professionals, administrators, Congressmen, and resource-rich interest groups; the losers are the diffuse public interest groups and the groups poor in political resources. As David Stockman admitted in the famous *Atlantic* article that resulted in his being "taken to the woodshed" by President Reagan: "The trouble is that unorganized groups can't play in this game."[59] Senator Robert Dole, the majority leader in the Senate, also confided in explaining the configuration of budget cuts: "There are no Food Stamp PACS (Political Action Committees)."

Public Interest Groups

To some extent, majoritarian groups of all political stripes have made progress since the 1960s. Lee Fritschler claimed at that time that, "One-party jurisdictions, the seniority system, and concentration of power in congressional committees make it difficult, if not impossible, for the majority to work its will inside or outside Congress."[60] This description no longer holds true. Public interest groups proliferated; new legislation addressed issues of civil rights, the environment, consumers, women's rights, and so forth; and the Congress abandoned the old seniority and hierarchical committee system. Despite these changes, however, the basic subgovernment system remains intact. Policy in such diverse areas as military procurement, the channeling of rivers, and first-class postage still revolves around subgovernment priorities, not national policy interests. The question is: Why haven't the public-interest movements of the 1960s and 1970s made more of an enduring impact?

We believe that one deficiency of the public-interest movement has been its nonpartisan, neutral-competency orientation. In our analysis of the presidency, for example, we discovered that the very reforms designed to strengthen the president actually worked in the opposite direction: They created semi-independent, professional institutions that demonstrated high competency but low responsiveness to his programs. Similarly, reforms that advocate sunshine laws or sunset procedures, while admirable in their intentions, end up hampering effective majoritarian decision making rather than facilitating it. Behn's analysis of sunset laws, for example, convincingly shows that these laws run the danger of promoting more, not less, incrementalism and more, not fewer, opportunities for special-interest group interference in policy implementation.[61]

A similar criticism might be put forward for the congressional Budget and Impoundment Control Act of 1974. The Act created committees charged with the responsibility of macrobudgets, yet the committees that came into existence had neither the power nor the will to carry out that mission. The Act ignored the budget policy implications of the new institutions—a critical flaw. Rational budget theory said that congressmen should act responsibly to control budget totals for the good of the economy, but individual political relationships of congressmen worked in the exact opposite direction. While Congress was supposedly centralizing budget decision making, it was busy decentralizing political relations through the committee system.

Majoritarian Political Strategies

We share the goal of strengthening national, public-interest institutions; we do not share the preference for nonpartisan, neutral competency as a means for achieving this goal. Of course, at this point it would be irresponsible of us to recommend instituting a parliamentary two-party system or making cabinet officers stronger. As Terry Moe has pointed out, the parties cannot be blamed for weak governing; they act in an institutional and societal milieu that prevents any other course.[62] On the other hand, without trying to be comprehensive in any sense, it is possible to point to certain political changes that would move the institutional system more toward satisfying majoritarian preferences.

Throughout this book, we have depended upon examples from the Defense Department to illustrate inefficiency and ineffectiveness in large-scale bureaucracy. Although the Reagan administration has made some innovations in executive management toward the cabinet departments and the Congress, it seems to have done little to alter the processes of decision making in the military. The old saw that the government's favorite way to solve problems is to "throw more money at them" appears exactly descriptive of the Reagan approach to defense spending. The kinds of abuses of bureaucratic politics described in this book continue under the Reagan administration.

Unlike their dealings with domestic agencies, the Reagan people seem to let the military professionals' decisions on priorities and spending needs stand without the political imposition of any change. Building a stronger defense is being carried out with the blueprints of the military professionals, ignoring the criticisms of the way the military bureaucracy has operated over the years. In other words, the Reagan administration, in its relations with the military, has followed the Finer/Friedrich approaches of professional and bureaucratic decision making. Since the military, however, is the largest and fastest growing organizational component of the federal government, taking the classical reform approach here seriously undermines the administration's overall attempt to make fundamental changes in the way the federal bureaucracy does business.

Another reform option concerns the state of affairs in the Congress. Since the early 1970s, the committee structure in the Congress has devolved into numerous subcommittees with very little hierarchy. In the place of the old seniority and committee system of authority, we now see weakly emerging a more party-centered leadership that revolves around the party caucuses and the House and Senate party leadership. With the extreme decentralization of the committee structure, coalition building becomes more amorphous, freewheeling, and susceptible to central leadership.

President Reagan demonstrated the potential for leading Congress in this manner during his first year in office. He allied closely with the Republican leadership in both Houses to put through significant budget, tax, and economic legislation. Our preference would be to strengthen this trend, both through legislation that ties election closer to party affiliation and support, and through giving the party leadership and caucuses power over appointments to committees. Contrary to Ken Schepsle, we would oppose any return to the hierarchical committee structure of the 1950s and 1960s.[63] Such a move would merely re-create the conditions deplored by Fritschler, Schattschneider, and others.

On the other hand, we do not want to do away with committees and other forms of congressional specialization altogether. Without specialization, Congress would become little more than its European counterparts, with very little collective institutional power. Our aim here is to redress the balance away from the total dominance of special-interest committees toward more representation of majoritarian interests in the authority structure.

Reagan's Administrative Strategy

Second, we would like to see a more politicized presidency of the kind that the Reagan administration has adopted. In saying this, we are not lending support to the administration's substantive policies or political ideologies. We share with Terry Moe the belief that the president "is a politician fundamentally concerned with the dynamics of political leadership and thus with political support and opposition, political strategy, and political trade-offs."[64] He needs "responsive competency," not just neutral competency. Despite the basic political leadership role of the president, however, administrative reform consistently followed "traditional public administrationist notions: policymaking was political and belonged in the Domestic Council, management was nonpolitical and belonged in the OMB. . . . Again, the separation of politics and administration was formalized in the structure of government."[65] It is this fruitless sort of effort to strengthen the presidency that we would like to avoid.

President Reagan faced the same kinds of pressures toward fragmentation and insulation of the president from the rest of the executive branch that other postwar presidents have struggled with. On the one hand, he confronts expectations that he exert strong executive leadership of the government; on the other hand, he must work with an institutional structure that is fundamentally not responsive to the president's program. Reagan's approach to this enduring problem of presidential control both incorporates some of the strategies pursued by earlier presidents and sets out new strategies which, according to Terry Moe, ". . . places Reagan in a pivotal historical position, and could well establish him as the most administratively influential president of the modern period."[66]

The first common strategy that Reagan shares with other presidents is his administration's use of task forces and other ad hoc groups in the initial stages of his presidency to circumvent the permanent bureaucracy. In contrast to Kennedy/Johnson, however, he placed much more emphasis on partisan loyalty and ideological compatibility in selection of personnel. These task forces had open access to agency records, thanks to the reforms of the Carter era, and received close central coordination from the White House. In conjunction with the task-force strategy, the Reagan administration postponed appointing people to the top posts in several agencies, thus making it more difficult for these agencies to take actions contrary to presidential initiatives. In this manner, much of the initial tax and budget legislation of the administration developed outside the channels of the permanent bureaucracy.

The second strategy that the Reagan administration adopted from other presidents was the use of the president's appointment power to select people loyal to the White House. This political use of appointments originated with President Kennedy but became embroiled in controversy in Nixon's second term. Many people associated the appointments strategy with what they perceived as Nixon's megalomania and paranoia. They attacked his political appointments as violations of the norms of the neutrally competent bureaucracy. The Reagan administration, however, has gone much further than Nixon in its efforts to appoint politically loyal people to major posts in the executive branch.

In contrast to earlier administrations, the Reagan strategy sought to avoid the secrecy and insulation of the president from the cabinet, while at the same time it attempted not to succumb to the open bickering and conflict that dominated Carter's more open strategy. His strategy consisted of the Office of Policy Development (OPD), which parallels the domestic policy staffs of earlier administrations; the creation of six cabinet councils, which attempted to integrate White House staff with their counterparts in the cabinet; and the establishment of an Office of Planning and Evaluation (OPE).

The purpose of this policy network, according to Chester Newland, was not to develop detailed new proposals for presidential consideration, but rather to ensure that the executive agencies adhere to the president's general philosophy of governing.[67] Newland believes that this flexible policy network "helps to keep a government-wide focus on Reagan's agenda" and represents an administrative innovation over earlier efforts: "This policy network functions at a level which has been neglected in other recent administrations: coordination of vital secondary-level matters."[68]

The OPE divided into five functional areas that paralleled the initial five cabinet councils. A senior staff person headed each area, who also became an executive secretary to a cabinet council. The purpose of this arrangement was to avoid using White House staff to displace cabinet secretaries in actual decision-making roles, as had occurred under Nixon when Henry Kissinger functioned as the real Secretary of State, overshadowing William Rogers, who was the nominal head of the department. The policy staffs were supposed to provide technical staff support, coordination, and brokerage functions for the cabinet councils.

By mid July 1982, the full cabinet had met fifty times, an average of three meetings a month for the first eighteen months of the administration's term in office. The cabinet councils became the centers for detailed policy development, especially the Cabinet Council on Economic Affairs. Despite Newland's open dislike for Reagan's ideological and political approach to governing and Reagan's preference for reducing the size and scope of government activities, Newland still assesses the cabinet councils as a success. He states that the councils "pull together departmental and White House resources and policy processes"; minimize "we/they White House/agency divisions"; focus on the much neglected "second-level policy issues without compelling personal presidential attention to details"; and work "to keep the entire administration focused on the president's general agenda, resulting in unprecedented unity of direction."[69]

The OPE constitutes the other administrative innovation of the Reagan administration. The OPE produces strategic planning documents for the administration that focus on the next four to six months of policy issues. The documents analyze what tactics the administration should follow in carrying out its broader agenda. The OPE also completes assessments of current and past policy activities, such as its evaluation of the functioning of the cabinet councils. Finally, the OPE has introduced new information technology into the White House. This latter change was long overdue, since the filing system dated back to the Taft administration.

We would favor strengthening the active use of cabinet councils allied with members of the White House staff. We also support the wider use of political appointees in the Office of Management and Budget and elsewhere, and the strong political orientation of the Office of Policy Development. More broadly, we would like to see changes that somewhat moderate the independence of the regulatory commissions. One example would be to make the term in office of the chairman of the Federal Reserve Board coincide with the election of the president. Another would be to introduce legislation that would give the president the power to dismiss regulatory commission chairmen. The purpose of these recommendations is to strengthen the *political* leadership capacity of the president in ways that do not isolate him from the rest of the government, as occurred under the Nixon administration.

A caveat is needed here similar to that offered for congressional reform. Our intention is not to destroy or even weaken the "competency" component of executive branch management. Rather, our perspective is that the past emphasis on competency alone has gone so far that it works to paralyze rather than strengthen leadership. We want to tilt the balance back somewhat toward responsiveness to majoritarian interests. President Carter was undoubtedly a competent manager in the classical reform sense, and even tried to extend reform ideas; yet he had little success in the political dimension of leadership, in part because of his own capacities and inclination, but also because of the institutional setting in which he operated.

Local Political Leadership

Finally, we would favor a strengthening of partisan institutions on the local level through the mayor, the city council, and local party organizations. While garbage collection may not be a particularly political activity, transportation design, redistribution policies, crime, tax incentives, and urban development clearly do constitute inherently political decisions. We would abhor a return to the political machines of the late nineteenth century, but there is no reason to believe that modern local parties necessarily act that way. We would like to see in cities at least the presence of a majoritarian governing coalition that has some say in a wide range of government activities. We do not want to do away with legal protections or expertise in the management of local government; we do want to give majoritarian interests a channel for voicing their concerns and having them implemented.

Under present local systems, when citizens oppose some action of a city bureau, they often receive the right to attend a public hearing on the issue. These hearings, however, invariably weight the outcome in favor of the agency. The agency representative comes armed with jargon and statistics and professional expertise, while citizens often are learning about the matter for the first time. In addition, citizens face the free-rider problem in attending these hearings, a problem not faced by the agency representatives. Consequently, only with some kind of ongoing political organization can diffuse local publics have a say in city policies.

CONCLUSION

Because institutional structures are the result of political choices of politicized actors, it is pointless and perhaps harmful to maintain the myth of administrative neutrality. Rather, the issue is and must be "who gets what" from the political system. The classical reformers were seeking an ideal structure, one whose structural characteristics would legitimize its policy outcomes: "This distribution of the budget is right because it came out of this neutral, comprehensive budgeting process. This distribution of urban services is right because an expert city manager processed information according to professional standards and formulas known only to him and came up with this outcome. This regulatory decision is right because it was made by a neutral board of experts."

There is no ideal, neutral political structure; there is no structure whose neutrality, expertness, or other characteristics can automatically legitimize the policy choices it makes. Most fundamentally, we must recognize that an institution is justified by its outcomes, rather than the other way around. This is the most revolutionary critique to be made of the classical reformers. It means that institutional choice is inherently political; we must ask "who gets what?" from any institutional arrangement. This is just the kind of intrinsically political choice that the Progressives and millions of technical post-Progressives have been seeking to avoid. They see administration as a setting in which rational decision making can displace political conflict. If different institutions have biases toward different kinds of allocations of social values, however, then it seems to us to be inevitable that institutional choice will be the setting in which political conflicts over those allocations are settled.

Of course, prescribing controls, limits, and alterations on the administrative state must take into account the fact that such changes are unlikely to be readily adopted by people who benefit from the status quo. On the other hand, one of the main advantages that defenders of the status quo have is that people have trouble thinking of alternatives. The status quo, by simply being in place, legitimizes the classical, managerial orthodoxy. In debunking such orthodoxies as "bureaucratic neutrality," "rational comprehensive budgeting," or "single chain of command organizing," we make the explicitly political effort to train a generation to be skeptical of the application of classical reform ideas, goals, and procedures. If we begin to make headway in that effort, this book will have been a success.

NOTES

[1] PAUL STARR, *The Social Transformation of American Medicine: The Rise of a Sovereign Profession and the Making of a Vast Industry* (New York: Basic Books, 1982), p. 3. Copyright © 1981 by Paul Starr. Reprinted by permission of Basic Books, Inc., Publishers.

[2] JAMES MADISON, *The Federalist Papers* (New York: The New American Library of World Literature, Inc., 1961).

[3] THOMAS HAMMOND and PAUL THOMAS, "The Impossibility of a Neutral Hierarchy," unpublished manuscript, Michigan State University, 1982.

[4] EUGENE LEWIS, *Public Entrepreneurship: Toward a Thoery of Bureaucratic Power: The Organizational Lives of Hyman Rickover, J. Edgar Hoover, and Robert Moses* (Bloomington, Ind.: Indiana University Press, 1980).

[5]LEWIS, *Public Entrepreneurship*, p. 251.

[6]LEWIS, *Public Entrepreneurship*, p 251.

[7]ROBERT L. LINEBERRY and EDMUND P. FOWLER, "Reformism and Public Policy in American Cities," *American Political Science Review*, 61 (1967), pp. 701–716.

[8]DONALD WARWICK, *A Theory of Public Bureaucracy: Politics, Personality, and Organization in the State Department* (Cambridge: Harvard University Press, 1975).

[9]CARL JOACHIM FRIEDRICH, "Public Policy and the Nature of Administrative Responsibility," *Public Policy*, 1 (1940), p. 6.

[10]FRIEDRICH, "Administrative Responsibility," p. 12.

[11]FRIEDRICH, "Administrative Responsibility," p. 13.

[12]HERMAN FINER, "Administrative Responsibility in Democratic Government," *Public Administration Review*, 1 (1941), pp. 335–350.

[13]FINER, "Administrative Responsibility," p. 340.

[14]MARTIN LANDAU, "Redundancy, Rationality, and the Problem of Duplication and Overlap," *Public Administration Review*, 29 (1969), pp. 346–358.

[15]JONATHAN B. BENDER, *Parallel Systems: Redundancy in Government* (Berkeley: University of California Press, 1985).

[16]VINCENT OSTROM, *The Intellectual Crisis in Public Administration* (University, Ala.: The University of Alabama Press, 1973).

[17]THOMAS J. PETERS and ROBERT H. WATERMAN, JR., *In Search of Excellence: Lessons from America's Best-Run Companies* (New York: Harper & Row, 1982).

[18]ARTHUR M. SCHLESINGER, JR., *The Coming of the New Deal* (Boston: Houghton Mifflin, 1958), p. 528.

[19]SCHLESINGER, *New Deal*, p. 535.

[20]SCHLESINGER, *New Deal*, p. 534.

[21]SCHLESINGER, *New Deal*, p. 537.

[22]LANDAU, "Redundancy."

[23]HARVEY M. SAPOLSKY, *The Polaris System Development: Bureaucratic and Programmatic Success in Government* (Cambridge: Harvard University Press, 1972), p. 153.

[24]SAPOLSKY, *Polaris*, p. 147.

[25]PETERS and WATERMAN, *Excellence*, p. 205.

[26]OSTROM, *Intellectual Crisis*, p. 77.

[27]OSTROM, *Intellectual Crisis*, p. 116.

[28]SCHLESINGER, *New Deal*, p. 523.

[29]FRANCES PERKINS, *The Roosevelt I Knew* (New York: Harper & Row, 1946), p. 156.

[30]SCHLESINGER, *New Deal*, p. 534.

[31]SAPOLSKY, *Polaris*, p. 146.

[32]SAPOLSKY, *Polaris*, p. 250.

[33]SAPOLSKY, *Polaris*, p. 251.

[34]PETERS and WATERMAN, *Excellence*, p. 201.

[35]PETERS and WATERMAN, *Excellence*, p. 313.

[36]SCHLESINGER, *New Deal*, p. 525.

[37]PETERS and WATERMAN, *Excellence*, p. 219.

[38]SCHLESINGER, *New Deal*, p. 526.

[39]PETERS and WATERMAN, *Excellence*, p. 205.

[40]PETERS and WATERMAN, *Excellence*, p. 308.

[41]LEWIS, *Public Entrepreneurship*, pp. 60–62.

[42]GORDON CHASE and ELIZABETH C. REVEAL, *How to Manage in the Public Sector* (Reading, Mass.: Addison-Wesley Publishing Co., 1983), p. 177.

[43]LEWIS, *Public Entrepreneurship*, p. 62.

[44]ELMO R. ZUMWALT, JR., *On Watch: A Memoir* (New York: Times Books, 1976), p. 186.

[45]SAPOLSKY, *Polaris*, p. 141.

[46]SAPOLSKY, *Polaris*, p. 143.

[47]PETERS and WATERMAN, *Excellence*, pp. 242–258.

[48]SCHLESINGER, *New Deal*, p. 531.

[49]SCHLESINGER, *New Deal*, p. 526.

[50]SCHLESINGER, *New Deal*, pp. 524–525.

[51]PETERS and WATERMAN, *Excellence*, p. 202.

[52]LANDAU, "Redundancy," p. 356.

[53]OSTROM, *Intellectual Crisis*, p. 105.

[54]OSTROM, *Intellectual Crisis*, p. 129.

[55]OSTROM, *Intellectual Crisis*, p. 125.

[56]PAUL PETERSON, *City Limits* (Chicago: University of Chicago Press, 1981).

[57]E. E. SCHATTSCHNEIDER, *The Semi-Sovereign People: A Realist's View of Democracy in America* (Hinsdale, Ill.: The Dryden Press, 1960).

[58]FRANK S. LEVY, ARNOLD J. MELTSNER, and AARON WILDAVSKY, *Urban Outcomes: Schools, Streets and Libraries* (Berkeley: University of California Press, 1974), p. 2.

[59]DAVID GREIDER, "The Education of David Stockman," *The Atlantic Monthly*, 248 (December 1981), p. 52.

[60]LEE A. FRITSCHLER, *Smoking and Politics* (Englewood Cliffs: Prentice-Hall, 1975), p. 155.

[61]ROBERT BEHN, "The False Dawn of the Sunset Laws," *The Public Interest*, 49 (1979), pp. 103–113.

[62]TERRY MOE, "The Politicized Presidency," in *The New Direction in American Politics*, John Chubb and Paul Peterson, eds. (Washington D.C.: Brookings Institution, 1985).

[63]KENNETH SHEPSLE, "The Failure of Congressional Budgeting," *Society*, 20 (1983), pp. 4–10.

[64]MOE, "Presidency," p. 239.

[65]MOE, "Presidency," p. 256.

[66]MOE, "Presidency," p. 271.

[67]CHESTER A. NEWLAND, "A Mid-Term Appraisal—The Reagan Presidency: Limited Government and Political Administration," *Public Administration Review*, 43 (1983), pp. 1–22.

[68]NEWLAND, "Reagan," p. 5.

[69]NEWLAND, "Reagan," pp. 6–10.

Author Index

Abel, Elie, 112n
Abramson, Mark, 245n
Acheson, Dean, 194
Allen, Dr. William H., 38, 40
Allison, Graham, 111n, 112n
Almond, Gabriel A., 118n
Anderson, Admiral George, 112, 174, 175, 178
Appleby, Paul, 122, 123
Arnold, Peri E., 84n, 85n, 89n, 90n
Arrow, Kenneth, 11
Arthur, Chester A., 30, 44
Ash, Roy L., 160
Atkins, Rick, 4n

Bardach, Eugene, 142–143
Barnard, George, 29
Barry, Brian, 204n
Baxter, Sandra, 245n
Behn, Robert D., 142n, 269n
Bendor, Jonathon, 259
Berman, Larry, 85n, 210n
Blau, Peter M., 113n
Blumenthal, W. Michael, 157
Branch, Taylor, 183n
Brownlow, Louis, 86–90
Bruere, Henry, 40
Bryan, William Jennings, 34, 77
Burford, Anne, 137–142, 250

Burns, Euchre Katie, 19
Byrnes, Thomas, 28

Callahan, Raymond E., 60n, 61n, 62n
Callow, Alexander B., Jr., 18n, 19n, 20n, 22n, 28n, 31n
Calvert, Randall, 180
Campbell, Angus, 7n
Cancian, Mark F., 208n, 215, 216
Cannon, Joseph, 9, 26, 81
Carnegie, Andrew, 57
Caro, Robert, 148n, 192n, 193n, 234
Carter, Jimmy, 5, 97, 150, 155, 157, 166, 168, 203, 208, 210, 217, 226, 231, 271
    and civil service reform, 242–249
    reorganization strategy of, 162–163
Chase, Gordon, 157, 158, 238–240, 245n, 265
Childs, Richard S., 48
Clark, Marth A., 142n
Cleveland, Dr. Frederick, 40, 84–88, 209
Cleveland, Grover, 44
Conkling, Roscoe, 30, 37
Connable, Alfred, 22n
Cooley, Thomas, 34
Crenson, Matthew A., 15, 62n
Crockett, William, 176
Croker, Richard, 50

Culhane, Paul J., 97*n*, 98*n*
Curtis, George William, 34
Cusick, Maneater, 19

Dahlberg, Jane S., 35*n*, 38*n*, 40*n*, 58*n*, 88*n*
Devine, Donald, 248, 249
Dewey, Melville, 58
De Witt, Benjamin Park, 35*n*
Dexter, Lewis Anthony, 7*n*
Dole, Robert, 269
Downs, Anthony, 7*n*, 108
Dupuit, Jules, 211
Durham, Henry, 183

Easterbrook, Gregg, 200*n*
Ehrlichman, John, 158, 160
Eisenhower, Dwight D., 135, 247
Emerson, Harrington, 58

Fallows, James, 184*n*, 185*n*
Falwell, Jerry, 137
Farley, James, 91
Fenno, Richard F., Jr., 129–130, 132, 133, 136, 206*n*
Ferejohn, John, 211
Ferraro, Geraldine, 137
Finer, Herman, 258
Fiorina, Morris P., 8, 9, 82*n*, 189, 197, 199, 206, 225*n*
Fisher, Louis, 222*n*
Fitzgeral, A. Ernest, 182, 185, 186
Floyd, "Pretty Boy," 69
Fogelson, Robert M., 26*n*, 27*n*, 28*n*, 42*n*, 68*n*, 69
Ford, Gerald, 216, 248
Fountain, Lawrence, 197
Fowler, Edmund P., 8*n*, 257
Franklin, Grace A., 123*n*
Friedan, Betty, 137
Friedrich, Carl Joachim, 257, 258
Friedson, Eliott, 113–115
Fritschler, Lee A., 269*n*

Galloway, George, 81*n*
Gardner, Trever, 159
Garfield, James A., 30, 43, 44
Gaus, John, 257, 258
Gibb, Corinne Lathrop, 62*n*, 63*n*, 64*n*

Ginsburg, Sigmund G., 237–239
Goodnow, Frank J., 39, 40, 84, 209
Goodsell, Charles T., 118, 167
Gosnell, Harold F., 25*n*, 30*n*
Goulden, Joseph C., 126*n*, 127*n*
Gouldner, Alvin, 107, 108, 110
Grant, Ulysses S., 49, 70, 83, 233
Grassley, Charles, 186
Greider, David, 269*n*
Groo, Elmer, 220
Gulick, Luther, 6, 86–89

Haber, Samuel, 57*n*, 58*n*, 59*n*
Hague, Frank, 67
Haldeman, John, 241
Halperin, Morton, 159
Hamilton, Alexander, 16
Hammack, David, 146, 147
Hamman, Arthur, 213*n*
Hammond, Paul, 2*n*, 3*n*, 73*n*
Hammond, Thomas H., 215*n*, 218*n*, 226*n*, 255
Hardin, Russell, 204*n*, 205
Harding, Warren G., 153, 253
Harrison, Benjamin, 34
Harrison, William Henry, 16
Hart, Gary, 3*n*, 4
Hayes, Rutherford, 30
Hays, Samuel P., 93*n*
Heclo, Hugh, 242–244, 246, 248, 250*n*
Herring, Pendleton, 127–128
Hess, Jacob, 50
Hiatt, Fred, 1*n*
Hicks, Sir John, 211
Hirschleifer, Jack, 218
Hitch, Charles, 212, 214
Hofstadter, Richard, 35, 63*n*
Hoogenboom, Ari, 34*n*, 52*n*, 128*n*
Hoogenboom, Olive, 34*n*, 52*n*, 128*n*
Hoover, Herbert, 77, 84, 85, 89, 90, 153, 169, 210, 263
Hoover J. Edgar, 158, 169, 170, 190–195, 256, 257
Hopkins, Harry, 260
Horowitz, Donald, 138*n*
Humphrey, Hubert, 140
Humphrey, William E., 150
Hyde, Albert C., 233*n*, 235*n*

Ickes, Harold, 260

Jackson, Andrew, 15–18
Jacobson, Gary C., 225n
Johnson, Lyndon B., 124, 135, 142, 159, 248, 250, 251, 260
Jones, Charles O., 26n
Jones, General David, 1, 4
Judd, Dennis R., 16n

Kaldor, Nicholas, 211
Kaplan, H. Elliot, 234
Kaufman, Herbert, 5n, 39, 89n, 93, 94n, 95n, 96n, 147, 166n, 231, 236n, 237, 247
Kennedy, Edward, 197
Kennedy, John F., 3, 7, 111, 112, 123, 135, 141, 156, 168, 174, 176, 178, 184, 243, 248, 250, 251, 272
Kennedy, Robert, 160, 168
Khruschev, Nikita, 112
King, Martin Luther, 137, 192
Kissinger, Henry, 160, 168, 272
Knight, Frances, 133, 178
Knott, Jack, 151n, 162n, 215n, 218n, 222n, 226n
Kohlmeier, Louis M., Jr., 52n, 90n
Kolko, Gabriel, 82n
Kousser, Morgan, 48n
Krasnow, Erwin G., 198n
Kroc, Ray, 266

LaFaver, John D., 220n
LaFollette, Robert, 42, 44–47, 52
Landau, Martin, 259, 260n, 266n
Landon, Alf, 91
Layton, Edwin T., Jr., 62n
Lemay, Curtis, 111, 179
Levine, Adeline Gordon, 168n
Levy, Frank, 116n, 268, 269
Lewis, Eugene, 2n, 158n, 169n, 189–192, 256, 257, 264n, 265n
Lincoln , Abraham, 17
Lindbergh, Charles, 69
Lindblom, Charles, 10n
Lineberry, Robert L., 8n, 257
Lipsky, Michael, 109, 110
Lockard, Duane, 149

Long, Norton, 123–124
Long, William "Pudding," 19
Longley, Lawrence D., 198n
Low, Seth, 40
Lowi, Theodore J., 134, 145, 149, 196, 206
Lubove, Roy, 65, 66n
Lynch, Thomas D., 208n, 224n

Madison, James, 162, 254
March, James G., 108n, 171, 180, 228n
Marshall, William, 8
Maser, Steven, 9
Maslow, Abraham, 103, 104
Maxwell, Robert S., 42n, 44n, 45n
Mayhew, David, 7n
Mazmanian, Daniel, 137
McCarthy, Joe, 176
McConnell, Grant, 64n, 80n, 153n, 154n, 155n, 202, 206
McCormick, Richard L., 80n
McCraw, Thomas K., 125n
McCubbins, Mathew, 9, 82, 196
McGregor, Douglas, 104
McKean, Roland, 212, 214n
McKinley, William, 34, 49–51, 81
McNamara, Robert, 112, 216
McPherson, Rene, 266
Meltsner, Arnold, 116n, 117n, 269
Merriam, Charles, 86
Merton, Robert K., 23n, 111n
Miller, James Nathan, 154n
Mills, Wilbur, 221
Mitgang, Herbert, 68n
Moe, Ronald C., 163
Moe, Terry, 6, 156, 247, 250, 251, 270, 271
Mohr, Charles, 183n, 185n, 186n
Mondale, Walter, 137
Morgan, J.P., 57
Morris, Edmund, 28n, 37n
Moses, Robert, 111, 148, 192–195, 234, 256, 257
Mosher, Frederick C., 93n, 109, 114–116, 232, 241, 243
Mouzelis, Nicos P., 56n

Nader, Ralph, 137

Nagel, Charles, 79
Nathan, Richard P., 158n, 161n, 162n, 203, 226n, 241n
Navasky, Victor S., 169n, 191n
Nelson, "Baby Face," 69
Nelson, Gaylord, 197
Neustadt, Richard E., 152, 159, 161n
Newland, Chester, 249, 272
Nienaber, Jeanne, 137
Nixon, Richard M., 5, 10, 97, 166, 168, 204, 208, 216, 222, 224, 226, 248, 250, 251, 272
    and civil service, 240–242
    limits of executive control, 156–158
    and postal reorganization, 135–136
    reorganization strategy of, 160–163
Norris, George, 9, 81, 124, 128

Olson, Johann P., 228n
Olson, Mancur, Jr., 11n, 80n
Ostrom, Vincent, 259, 261, 262, 267, 268

Pareto, Vilfredo, 211
Parkhurst, Rev. Charles, 69
Patterson, John, 49
Perkins, Frances, 262
Perrow, Charles, 106, 113
Peter, Lawrence J., 10, 166, 179
Peters, Charles, 183n
Peters, Thomas J., 259–266
Peterson, Paul, 268
Pettit, James, 72
Phyrr, Peter A., 212
Pinchot, Gifford, 93
Platt, Thomas C., 50–51, 209
Plunkitt, George Washington, 19, 21–25, 44, 55
Polenberg, Richard, 86n, 87n, 88n, 89n
Pollack, Norman, 34n
Polsby, Nelson, 248
Pressman, Jeffrey L., 148, 149
Presthus, Robert, 7n
Price, Donald K., 90
Price, James L., 119n

Quirk, Paul J., 196n, 197n

Raborn, William F., 265

Ramspeck, Robert, 91–92
Rapoport, Anatol, 11n
Reagan, Ronald, 4, 135, 152, 155, 157, 159, 166, 169, 199, 204, 225
    administrative strategy of, 269–273
    and civil service reform, 247–251
Reeves, Richard, 183n
Resnick, Joseph, 130
Reveal, Elizabeth C., 157n, 158n, 238–240, 245n, 265n
Rice, Bradley Robert, 48n, 88n
Rickover, Adm. Hyman, 111, 256, 257, 264, 265
Riker, William, 7, 8n
Ripley, Randall B., 123n
Ritter, Lawrence S., 151
Rockefeller, John D., 57
Roethlisberger, F.J., 102n, 103
Rogers, Paul, 197
Rogers, William, 272
Rohde, David W., 81, 139
Rooney, John, 133, 178
Roosevelt, Franklin D., 74, 124, 135, 150, 210, 247, 250
    limits on executive influence, 154–157, 161, 175
    personal administrative style, 92–93, 259–268
    supports administrative reform, 85–92, 204, 235–237
Roosevelt, Theodore, 235
    and executive leadership, 49–51, 83
    supports civil service reform, 37, 91, 249
    supports customs reform, 30
    supports military reform, 72–73
    supports police reform, 28, 69
Root, Elihu, 72–73
Rosen, Bernard, 242, 243, 249, 250
Rosenbloom, David H., 233n, 235n
Rourke, Francis E., 151

Sapolsky, Harvey M., 261–266
Savas, E.S., 237, 239
Sayre, Wallace, 147
Schattschneider, E.E., 1, 134, 143, 201, 268
Schick, Allan, 209, 210, 212, 219, 222, 223

Schiesl, Martin J., 43n, 49n
Schlesinger, Arthur M., Jr., 168n, 201n, 259, 260n, 262n, 263n, 266n
Schmidt, Richard, 245n
Seabury, Judge Samuel, 68
Seashore, Charles, 105
Seidman, Harold, 6, 90n, 131n, 153n, 159n, 160n, 162, 163, 200n, 206
Selznick, Philip, 124, 125
Shabecoff, Philip, 155n
Shaefer, Elmer, 181
Shafritz, Jay M., 233n, 235n
Shepsle, Kenneth, 8n, 81, 139, 271
Sherman, John, 49
Silber, William L., 151n
Silverfarb, Edward, 22n
Simon, Herbert, 108, 171–173, 175, 180, 228
Skowronek, Stephen, 37n, 44, 47, 70n, 71n, 72n, 73n, 233n, 234, 235
Smith, Al, 192
Smith, Harold, D., 210
Smithies, Arthur, 221
Spaulding, Frank, 61
Starr, Paul, 55, 62–64, 254
Steffens, Lincoln, 24–25, 46
Stephenson, Isaac, 45
Stevens, Rosemary, 62n
Stockman, David, 142, 269
Sundquist, James L., 140n
Swenson, Peter, 81n

Taft, William Howard, 249
Taylor, Frederick W., 55–58, 102, 103, 105, 108, 211–212
Thayer, Frederick, 244, 246
Thomas, Paul, 255
Thompson, James D., 119
Thompson, Victor A., 112n
Truman, Harry S, 89, 194, 236, 247
Trumbull, Lyman, 233
Tweed, William Marcy, 18–26, 37, 233

Tyack, David B., 29n, 59n, 60n, 61n

Upton, Emery, 71
Urwick, Lyndall, 89

Vance, Cyrus, 184
Van Riper, Paul P., 17n, 91n, 92n
Verba, Sydney, 118n
Volcker, Paul, 150
Vroom, Victor, 106

Waite, Henry M., 49
Waldo, Dwight, 122n
Walker, Samuel, 27n, 28n, 29n, 66n, 67n, 68n, 98n
Walton, Sam, 264
Warwick, Donald, 6, 133, 175–178, 194, 196, 257, 258
Waterman, Robert H., Jr., 249–266
Watt, James, 250
Weber, Max, 12, 195
Weinberger, Caspar, 215
Weingast, Barry, 8, 9
White, Leonard D., 2, 30n, 49n, 83n, 84–85
Whyte, William Foote, 101
Wiebe, Robert, 33, 38n
Wildavsky, Aaron, 116n, 117n, 162n, 208, 212n, 213n, 221, 222, 269n
Williams, Winston, 186n
Willkie, Wendell, 124
Willoughby, W. Frank, 2, 84, 85, 209
Wilson, George C., 4n
Wilson, Woodrow, 36, 38–42, 52, 55, 58, 123, 155, 160, 235, 259, 261
Wirt, Frederick M., 149
Wood, Fernando, 20
Woolley, John, 151, 152
Wyszomirski, Margaret Jane, 250

Zeckhauser, Elmer, 181
Zumwalt, Elmo, 216, 265

Subject Index

Accountability, 2, 6, 88, 92–93, 118–119, 145–155, 164, 166, 176, 189, 206, 226, 254–257
and executive control, 156, 236–237
and local government, 146–150
and personnel, 238–242, 245
and the presidency, 161–163
as trade-off with efficiency, 256–257
Administrative agencies
and policy-making, 122–124
and political support, 124–125
Administrative orthodoxy, 6, 7, 12, 107–108, 156–157, 160, 163, 174–177, 189–195, 254–255, 258, 265
and budgeting, 209, 211, 226
challenge to, 170–187, 203–204, 211–212, 268–274
and the New Deal, 77–78, 92–93, 96–98, 101, 118–119, 122, 125, 145
and personnel, 231–233, 238, 241–242, 245–247
political advantages of, 189–204, 226–227
and the public interest, 204–206
compared to unorthodoxy, 258–268
Advisory Council on Executive Reorganization, 160–162
AFL-CIO, 201

Agriculture Committees. See Congress.
Agriculture Department, U.S., 82, 93, 97, 130–132, 141, 160–177, 202, 205, 211, 213–214
Amateurs in government, 15, 190
as challenge to professionals, 266
American Automobile Association, 79
American Bar Association, 63–64
American Civil Liberties Union, 139
American Dental Association, 63
American Farm Bureau Federation, 80, 130–132, 201
American Medical Association, 63, 87
American Society of Mechanical Engineers, 56
Appropriations Committees. See Congress.
Arms Control and Disarmament Agency, 156
Army, U.S.
Corps of Engineers, 80, 86
Ordinance Corps, 183–185, 187
War College, 3, 72
Associated Press, 176
At-large elections, 8, 9, 11

Bell Telephone, 126–127
Bendix Corporation, 157
Brookings Institution, 89

Brownlow Commission. *See* President's Commission on Administrative Management

Budget and Accounting Act of 1921, 77, 78, 209, 235

Budget and Accounting Act of 1950, 210

Budget and Impoundment Control Act of 1974, 208, 221–225, 269

Bureau of the Budget, 191, 209–211, 235, 247. *See also* Office of Management and Budget

Bureau of Efficiency, 235

Bureau of Reclamation, 152–155

Bureau of Standards, U.S., 111

Bureaucracy, 15, 123, 126, 145, 157–158, 160–164, 195, 198–201, 242, 258, 264, 268, 270–273
congressional support for, 128–130
discontent with, 5
dysfunctions, 107–118, 166, 171–187, 256–257
imperial, 169–170, 178
presidential control over, 134–138, 247–250, 270–273
as "red tape," 167–170
street-level, 109–110

Burroughs Corporation, 157

Business Week, 150

Cabinet Council on Economic Affairs, 272

California, 55

Carter Administration, 150, 162–164, 208, 231, 242–247, 248–250
and zero-based budgeting, 162, 217

Central Intelligence Agency, 156

Chamber of Commerce, U.S., 80

Chicago, 86, 102

Cicero, 102

Cincinnati, 43

Citizens Union, 50

City manager form of government, 7, 9, 11, 48–49

Civil rights movement, 164, 169–170, 191–192, 269

Civil service, 5, 11, 15, 91, 146, 158, 182, 190, 195, 201, 231–242, 248, 250, 254–255

Civil service *(Contd.)*
Congress and, 43–44, 77–82, 233–235
in New Deal, 91–93
reforms in, 239–240, 243–245
and seniority, 239, 244

Civil Service Commission, U.S., 37, 50, 83, 86, 87, 91, 92, 233–236, 242, 249
elimination of, 243

Civil Service Reform Act of 1978, 242, 249

Civil Service Reform League, National, 41, 91, 234

Civil War, U.S., 17, 49

Cognitive limitations, 169–181, 186, 187

Commerce Department, U.S., 80, 160

Commission on the Organization of the Executive Branch of Government (Hoover Commission), 89

Committee for Economic Development (CED), 262

Common Cause, 136, 139

Comptroller General, U.S., 86

Congress, U.S.
and agency support, 128–133, 153–155, 174, 178, 182, 194–195
and agency oversight, 96–98, 166, 176–177, 196–198, 205, 236–237, 256
and agency reorganization, 160, 200
agriculture committees of, 128, 130–132
appropriations committees of, 128, 133, 135, 177, 178, 191, 209, 221–223, 226
as beneficiary of administrative reform, 269
and budget reform, 221–226, 270
and civil service reform, 43, 44, 77–82, 233–235, 241–242, 245, 249
committee system, 8, 9, 200–201, 221–222, 224–226, 269–271
and delegation of authority, 197–198, 205
and executive management movement, 83–90
and the F.B.I., 190–192
and independent regulatory commissions, 82, 151, 196–197

Congress, U.S. (Contd.)
  and military reform, 70–73, 182–183,
    185–186
  and "reciprocity" norms, 132–133
  postal committees of, 129–130, 135–
    136
  and the presidency, 134–136, 152, 156,
    162, 200, 222, 225, 235, 247, 251,
    270
  and subgovernment alliances, 158,
    162–163, 185, 197–199, 236–237
  supports administrative orthodoxy,
    196–202
  See also House of Representatives, Se-
    nate
Congressional Budget Office, 223–224,
    226
Congressional Reform Act, 137
Constitution, U.S., 16, 156
  and redundancy, 261–262
Consumer Products Safety Commission,
    217
Corporate model of executive control,
    155–156
  and presidential organization strategies,
    159–164, 203–204
Corporations
  as allies of party machines, 47
  as models for administrative reform, 3,
    48–49, 60–62
  opponents of scientific management,
    57–58
  regulation of, 51
Corps of Engineers, 80, 86, 152–155,
    200–201
Corruption, 28–30
Cost–benefit analysis, 211–212
Council of Economic Advisors, 151–152,
    224
Court system, 138–139, 267. See also Su-
    preme Court, Judicial administration
Customs Office, U.S., 30

Dana Corporation, 266
Dayton, Ohio, 49
Defense Department, U.S., 1–5, 119,
    153, 162, 177, 185, 201, 208, 260,
    270

Defense Department, U.S. (Contd.)
  and PPBS, 214–216, 218, 228
  See also Weapons acquisition
Democratic Party, 7, 9, 16–18
Domestic Policy Council, 160
Dual systems of authority, 172, 174–175

Eastern rate case. See Interstate Commerce
    Commission
Economic Opportunity Act, 123
Education, 3, 7
  modern critics of, 98
  and party politics, 29
  and scientific management, 59–62
Education, Department of, 162–163, 202,
    205
Efficiency
  and cost–benefit analysis, 211–212
  in education, 59–62
  as an organizational ideal, 2, 3, 5, 6,
    39–40, 64, 147, 156, 162–164, 166,
    255, 258, 265
  in Passport Office, 178
  in personnel administration, 232–234,
    236–237, 239–240, 244–245
  in police administration, 66–70
  as trade-off to accountability, 256–257
  and weapons acquisition, 182–183
  and ZBB, 220, 227
Electoral college, 16
Elementary and Secondary Education Act,
    123
Energy, Department of, 163
Entitlements, 222, 226
Environmental movement, 97, 139, 140,
    142
Environmental Protection Act, 137
Environmental Protection Agency (EPA),
    137, 142, 168
Equal Employment Opportunity Commis-
    sion, 157, 236, 243
Executive management movement
  and budget reform, 208
  and efficiency, 155
  and independent regulatory commis-
    sions, 152
  in the New Deal, 85–90
  origins of, 83–84

Executive management movement *(Contd.)*
   and the presidency, 203
   in the twenties, 84–85
Executive Office of the President, 86, 88,
   210, 247, 249

Fair Employment Board, 236
Farm Bureau. *See* American Farm Bureau
   Federation.
Federal Bureau of Investigation, 158,
   169–171, 194, 201, 202
   and progressive reform, 170–171, 190–
   192
Federal Communications Commission,
   197–198
Federal Disaster Assistance Administra-
   tion, 168
Federal Emergency Management Agency,
   156
Federal Grants, 148–149
Federal Labor Relations Council, 243
Federal Reserve Board
   and independence from presidential
   control, 150–152, 273
   and interest group allies, 150–151
Federal Trade Commission, 141–142, 197
Flood Control Act of 1939, 211
Florida, 220
Food and Drug Administration, 196–197,
   231
Ford Motor Company, 106
Foreign Service, 157, 196, 239
Forest Service, U.S., 2, 86, 93–96, 196
Franchise Tax Bill, 50
Freedom of Information Act, 137
Free-rider problem, 273

Galveston, Texas, 48
General Accounting Office, 78, 183, 209,
   235
General Dynamics, 183–185
General Land Office, U.S., 118
General Motors Corporation, 137, 246
General Services Administration, 156
Gentlemen reformers. *See* Mugwumps
Geographic organization of government
   agencies, 15
Georgia, 219–220

Goal displacement, 172–174, 264
Grand Army of the Republic, 79

Harding Administration, 235
Hatch Act, 78, 91–92, 249
Hawthorne plant studies, 102–103, 106
Health, Education and Welfare, Department of, 160, 162, 168
Hepburn Act of 1906, 32
Hierarchy, 2, 6, 10, 15, 41, 148, 151, 163,
   174, 187, 189, 192, 194–195, 254,
   259
   in Army, 185
   vs. autonomy, 262–268
   and budgeting, 228
   and bureaucratic dysfunctions, 107–
   109, 114, 172–174, 251, 258
   and corporate model of executive control, 156–157, 160–161
   in FBI, 190–192
   in Forest Service, 94–95
   of human needs, 103–104
   promoting accountability, 240, 257–258
   in State Department, 175–178, 195–196
Hoover Commission, 162, 210
House of Representatives, U.S., 8, 9, 26,
   81, 130, 199–201
   Budget Committee, 223–225
   Foreign Affairs Committee, 132–133
   Interior Committee, 132, 152–153
   Interstate and Foreign Commerce
   Committee, 141
   Merchant Marine and Fisheries Com-
   mittee, 130–132
   Public Works Committee, 153
   Rules Committee, 81
   seniority system, 81, 225
   Ways and Means Committee, 128, 139,
   209, 221–222
Houston, 220
Human relations approach, 102–107

IBM, 261, 264–265
Incentives in organizations, 3, 102–103,
   106, 109, 115, 155, 170, 173, 174,
   177, 263
   biased, 174, 195
   and budget-making, 226, 228

Incentives in organizations *(Contd.)*
    and bureaucratic pathologies, 174–175,
        178–180, 182, 185–187, 255–257
    and imperial bureaucracy, 178
    and management of subordinates, 157–
        159
    and personnel management, 251
Independent regulatory commissions, 4, 7,
        8, 11, 125–128, 254–255
    and fragmentation, 150–152
    in New Deal, 90, 91
    and policy administration, 156
    in Progressive Era, 51–52
    See also particular commissions
Informal work groups, 102–105
Institutional change, 254–274
    as alternative to administrative or-
        thodoxy, 258
    and bureaucratic dysfunctions, 170–
        171, 254–258
    in cities, 48–49, 273
    electoral, 47–48
    as justified by eventual outcomes, 274
    and majoritarian concerns, 268–273
    supported by Congress, 77–82
    supported by interest groups, 78–81
    supported by professionals, 55, 73–74
    in Wisconsin, 46
Interest groups
    allies of bureaucracies, 87, 125–133,
        146–149, 153–155, 158, 178, 182
    and incentives to organize, 126, 134,
        137–139, 147
    organized by government agencies,
        79–80
    vs. political parties, 80–81, 134
    and prisoners' dilemma, 204–205
    professional, 56–70
    and subgovernment alliances, 158,
        162–163, 185–187, 197, 221
    support for administrative reform,
        78–79, 201–202, 205, 233, 269
    and weapons acquisition, 184–186
Interior Department, U.S., 34, 97, 152–
        153, 213–214, 250
Internal Revenue Service, 170
Interstate Commerce Commission, 8,
        51–52, 87, 127–128

Interstate Commerce Commission *(Contd.)*
    Eastern rate case, 52, 58, 59
    and scientific management, 58
Intimidators, in Wisconsin, 46

Jacksonian reforms, 15–17, 29–30, 62,
        195
Jersey City, 67
Johnson Administration, 212
Joint Chiefs of Staff, 1, 3, 4
Judicial administration, 29
Justice Department, 222

Keep Commission of 1905, 83
Kennedy Administration, 123
    Cuban missile crisis, 111–112, 174–
        175, 178–179
Kings and Kern River projects, 153–155

Labor Department, 160, 177
Labor unions
    opposed to scientific management,
        57–58
    in Wisconsins, 45
Lexow Commission, 26, 68
Lockheed, 182–183, 185–186
Long ballot, 16, 17
Los Angeles, California, 40, 41, 69
Love Canal, 167–170, 179, 181

Machine politics, 47–48, 69–70, 140,
        147, 149–150, 166, 250, 273
    and bureaucracy, 26–30
    and efficiency, 256
    in federal government, 25–26
    in state government, 24–25
    in Tammany Hall, 18–23, 233–234
    in Wisconsin, 45–47
    See also Political parties
Mafia, 189
Majority rule paradox, 8
Management by Objectives (MBO), 205,
        216
Managerial orthodoxy. *See* Administrative
        orthodoxy
McDonald's Restaurants, 266
McDonnell Douglas, 185

Merit principle, 9, 41, 103, 189, 190–192, 232–234, 237–239, 243–244, 259
Merit Systems Protection Board (MSPB), 243–244, 249
Middle-class, as supporters of Progressive reform, 35, 36
Military administration, 1, 5, 159
  and professionalism, 70–73
Milwaukee, Wisconsin, 47
Minnesota Mining and Manufacturing (3M), 263, 266
Model Cities Act, 123
Moral Majority, 137
Mugwumps, 34

National Academy of Public Administration, 161
National Aeronautics and Space Administration (NASA), 219–220
National Association for the Advancement of Colored People (NAACP), 139
National Association of Broadcasters, 141
National Association of Letter Carriers, 135
National Education Association, 162
National Organization of Women, 137
National Rivers and Harbors Congress, 153
National Security Act of 1947, 3
National Security Council, 160, 168–169
Navy, U.S.
  and Cuban missile crisis, 111–112
  Polaris project, 261–263, 265
  and unorthodox administration, 264–266
Nebraska, 55
Neo-institutionalism, 7, 8, 9
  See also Institutional change
Neutral competence, 231–233, 235–237, 240, 242, 247–249, 250–251, 255, 257, 268–273
New Deal, 6, 74, 77–83, 90, 124–125
  and administrative orthodoxy, 77–78, 92–93, 96–97, 101, 118, 122
  and independent regulatory commissions, 150
  and personnel reform, 235–236
New Jersey, 44
New Mexico, 220

New York Bureau of Municipal Research, 6, 39–43, 54, 67, 77, 83, 84, 86, 88, 89, 192, 226, 233, 268
New York, City of, 22, 27, 28, 50, 68, 146–148, 192–193, 234, 256
  Board of Estimate, 193
  Board of Supervisors, 18
  Civil Service Commission, 233, 234, 237–240
  Cross-Bronx Expressway, 148
  Health Services Administration, 157, 238, 265
  Park Department, 192–193
  Police Department, 26, 28
New York County Courthouse, 18, 26
New York State, 148, 168
  Department of Health, 167–168, 179
  government reorganization, 192
New York Times, 23, 142
Nixon administration, 160–162, 208, 216, 222, 224, 241, 248–249, 273
North Dakota, 164

Oakland, 116–117, 148–149
  Housing Authority of, 149
  Redevelopment Agency of, 149
Office of Management and Budget, 156, 160, 241, 243, 248–249, 255, 271, 273
Office of Personnel Management, 156, 243, 246, 249
Office of Planning and Evaluation (OPE), 272–273
Office of Policy Development (OPD), 272–273
Office of Special Investigations, 182
Ohio, 44
Olin-Mathieson, 184–185
Ombudsman, 198–199
Orthodox model of administrative reform. See Managerial orthodoxy, Reform model

Passport Office, 178, 183
Patronage, 15, 17, 91, 128, 209, 232–235, 250
  in the State Department, 175
  in Tammany Hall, 18–21, 193
  in Wisconsin, 45–47

Pendleton Act, 41, 42, 44, 233, 242
  See also Civil Service Commission
Pennsylvania, 44
Planning, Programming, Budgeting Systems (PPBS), 3, 208, 212–216, 232, 246
Police administration, 4, 5, 7, 10, 196, 259
  and bureaucratic dysfunctions, 108, 110
  modern critics of, 98
  and monitoring, 159
  and party politics, 26–29
  and professionalism, 66–70
Political neutrality, 3, 5, 12, 116–117, 143, 156, 163–164, 170, 187, 203, 232
  advantages of, 189–190, 194–195
  and personnel management, 241
  See also Neutral competence
Political parties
  in Congress, 128
  in Europe, 233
  exclusion from agency influence, 187, 203, 231
  and Jackson administration, 33
  and machine style of politics, 47–48, 69–70, 140, 147, 149–150, 166
  as majoritarian institution, 133–134, 139–140
  and reform, 201–202, 205, 233, 241
Populists, 34–35
Post office committees. *See* Congress
Postal Service, U.S., 37, 78, 201
  policy of, 133
  reform in, 10, 118, 135–137
President's Commission on Administrative Management (Brownlow Commission), 77, 86–88, 162, 210, 212, 235, 247
Presidency, 6, 10, 123, 201
  and administrative reform, 203–204, 226, 235
  and Congress, 134–136, 152, 156, 162, 200, 222, 225, 251, 270–271
  and direction of agency policy, 152–155, 259–262
  and independent regulatory commissions, 150–152, 235
  and limitations to administrative con-

Presidency *(Contd.)*
  trol, 155–164, 168–171, 236–237, 244, 247–250, 270–273
  and personnel management, 241–245, 247–251
  and representation of majority interests, 134–136
Primary elections, in Wisconsin, 45–47
Prisoners' dilemma, 11, 204–206, 225
Professionalism, 2, 3, 5, 10, 269
  and accountability, 257–258
  and bureaucracy, 62–73, 108, 112–113, 146–150, 155, 166, 170, 174, 193, 202
  and bureaucratic dysfunctions, 112–118, 172–173, 258
  and the "capture" hypothesis, 114–115
  in the Department of Justice, 115
  and "expertise," 266–267, 273
  in the FBI, 190–192
  and the Forest Service, 95–98
  in the military, 70–73, 186, 254, 270
  and the Open Market Committee, 151
  and personnel reform, 232–234, 250
  and police administration, 66–70
  and professional autonomy, 62–67, 146–150, 205–206, 236–237
  in the schools, 59–62
  in the State Department, 115, 175, 254
Progressives, 3, 5, 9, 10, 12, 150
  and budget reform, 208
  as formulators of administrative reform model, 30, 112, 113, 116–117, 123, 134, 136, 140, 170–171, 175, 187–189, 192–195, 201–202, 254–258, 267, 268, 274
  and fragmentation, 146–156
  and personnel reform, 231, 234–236, 239–240, 243–244, 249
  and Progressive Coalition, 10, 33–38
  and regulatory agencies, 51–52, 127–128
Public Health Service, U.S., 86, 141–142
Public interest groups, 269
  and the courts, 138–139
  as representatives of majoritarian interests, 136–137, 269–270
  and sunshine laws, 269
Public Works Administration, 260

Ramspeck Act, 92
Rational ignorance, 179–187
Rationality
  as an assumption about individual be-
    havior, 7–10, 157, 170, 173, 181,
    189, 195, 205
  and biased information, 180–182
  "bounded," 171–174, 178–180
  and budgeting, 213, 216–218, 221, 224,
    226–229
  and irrational structures, 173–178
  as an organizational ideal, 2, 6, 10, 125,
    157–158, 255, 267, 269, 274
  and prisoners' dilemma, 204–206
Reader's Digest, 154
Reagan Administration, 4, 135, 152, 169,
  199, 208, 224, 247–250, 270–273
Red tape, 4, 10, 108, 113, 176–178, 199,
  229, 236, 239. *See also* Bureaucracy
Redundancy vs. specialization, 259–262,
  267–268
Reform model of bureaucracy, 30
  challenged, 170–171
  compared with Carter reorganization
    strategy, 162–164
  congressional support for, 78–82
  congruence with professional goals,
    62–73, 116–117
  executive support for, 83–85
  extended, 257–258
  opposed to Theory Y, 104–105
Regulatory commissions. *See* Independent
  regulatory commissions
Reorganization Act of 1939, 88, 210
Republican Party, 9, 17, 26, 50, 52
Rigidity cycle, 108, 174, 179, 187, 256–
  258
Rivers and Harbors Congress, 80, 86
Rochester, 67
Rockwell International, 186
Rogers Act of 1924, 77–78
Roosevelt Administration, 153, 236, 266
Rules
  and bureaucratic dysfunctions, 107–
    110, 174–177
  as determinants of group choices, 7, 8,
    47–48
  in the FBI, 190–192
  vs. flexibility, 264–267

Rules (*Contd.*)
  in Forest Service, 94–95
  organizational, 3, 41–42, 101–105,
    189–192, 198–200, 238, 259
  in the State Department, 195–196

Safe Streets Act, 123
San Francisco, 28, 69
Satisficing, 172, 179–182
School boards. *See* Education
"Scientific" management, 55–59, 102,
  123, 190
  and budgeting, 211–212, 226
  in education, 59–62
  and personnel administration, 109,
    231–232, 234, 244–245, 267
  and Progressives, 58–62, 104, 107, 254
  and Theory X, 104–106, 245–246, 249
Selective attention, 172, 180
Selective Service Commission, 156
Senate, U.S., 141, 200–201, 225, 269
  Armed Services Committee, 1, 128, 132
  Budget Committee, 152–153
  Erwin Committee, 161
  Interior Committee, 152–153
  oversight of independent regulatory
    commissions, 150, 234
  party leadership, 270
Senior Executive Service, 243–245, 250
Sherman Act (1890), 52
Short ballot, 48
Sierra Club, 139
Small Business Administration, 160
Social reformers, 37, 38
Social Security Act, 92
Social Security Administration, 118, 170
Social work, 4, 65–66
  and bureaucratic dysfunction, 110
  under Nixon Administration, 161
  and party politics, 65
  and professionalism, 65–66
Soil Conservation Service, U.S., 213–214
Specialization in organizations, 15, 42,
  101, 111, 170, 228, 238
  and bureaucratic incentives, 174–177
  political advantages of, 189–193, 200–
    205
  and Theory X, 104–105
"Spoils" system. *See* Patronage

Standard operating procedures, 9, 107–
    108, 110, 161, 168–169, 171–172,
    174, 176–177, 179, 194–196, 198
State Department, U.S., 2, 10, 77, 98,
    106, 115, 133, 168–171, 222
    Area O, 176
    and bureaucratic dysfunctions, 175–
    178, 179
    and progressive reform, 170, 171, 254
    See also Passport Office
Strategic Missiles Evaluation Group, 159
Subcommittee Bill of Rights, 1971, 224
"Subgovernments," 130–133
    executive attack on, 156
    and fragmentation, 152–155
    and inefficiency, 154–155
    majoritarian politics as a challenge to,
    132–133
    and the presidency, 134–136
    tobacco, 140–142
Suffrage, 16
Supreme Court, U.S., 86, 90
    and class action, 138
    and independent regulatory commis-
    sions, 150
    and "private attorneys general," 138–
    139
Surgeon General, U.S., 141–142

Taft Administration, 273
Taft Commission of 1911, 209–210
Tammany Hall, 17–23, 170, 192–193
Taylorism. *See* Scientific management

Tennessee Valley Authority, 91, 124–125,
    128, 211
Texas, 48
Texas Instruments, 263
Trained incapacity, 172, 174, 187
    and "rational ignorance," 181
Transportation Department, 160, 256
Treasury Department, 151–152, 157–158,
    175, 209–210

Unions. *See* Labor unions
United Press International, 176
Urban merchants, 37–38

Veterans Bureau, 79, 87
Veterans Preference Act of 1944, 236
Vietnam, 4, 183–185, 260
Voter registration, 9

Walmart, 266
Washington Post, 167
Watergate, 161–162, 240–242, 248
Weapons acquisition, 1, 4, 182–187
    explaining failures in, 185–186
Whig Party, 16
Wilson Administration, 235
Wisconsin, 42, 44, 46, 52
World War I, 52, 77, 175
World War II, 3, 122, 128, 146, 148, 166,
    184, 197, 210, 251
Works Progress Administration, 260

Zero-based budgeting (ZBB), 162, 208,
    216–220, 227, 229